Werner Rüge

The Capital
of the 21st Ce

Werner Rügemer

The Capitalists
of the 21st Century

An Easy-to-Understand Outline
on the Rise of the New Financial Players

Translated by an English friend.

Slightly abridged and updated translation of the original
"Die Kapitalisten des 21. Jahrhunderts.
Gemeinverständlicher Abriss zum Aufstieg der neue Finanzakteure"
published by PapyRossa Verlag, Cologne, Germany in 2018

© 2019 by Werner Rügemer, Cologne (Germany)

Publishing House: tredition GmbH, Halenreie 40-44, 22359 Hamburg (Germany)

Cover image: pixabay.com

ISBN
Paperback   978-3-7497-1162-8
Hardcover   978-3-7497-1163-5
eBook   978-3-7497-1164-2

The German National Library lists this publication in
the German national bibliography; detailed bibliographic
Data is available on the Internet via http://dnb.d-nb.de

Die Deutsche Nationalbibliothek verzeichnet diese Publikation in
der Deutschen Nationalbibliografie; detaillierte bibliografische
Daten sind im Internet über http://dnb.d-nb.de abrufbar

Table of content

Introduction
History is open 7

I. The New Capitalist Players of the West 14
1. The big capital organizers: BlackRock&Co 14
2. Private equity investors: The exploiters 67
3. Hedge funds: The pillagers 101
4. Elite investment banks: The arrangers 111
5. Private banks: Discreet front for the big players 123
6. Venture Capitalists: The preparers 125
7. Traditional banks as service providers 130
8. The Internet capitalists 131
9. The civilian private army of transatlantic capital 194

II. The relationship USA – European Union 206
1. Reversal of the balance of power since the First World War 206
2. The Internet under US supervision 211
3. The capitalist-digital-military complex 216
4. Free trade: The EU in conflict with the USA 224

III. China – Communist-led capitalism 238
1. USA against Chinese self-liberation 238
2. The dialectic of the import of capitalism 240
3. State, Communist Party, Socialism 256
4. USA: Weaken China economically, threaten it militarily 261
5. China: Economic and peaceful globalization 269

IV. Present and Future of Earthly Society 293

List of Abbreviations 303
Bibliography 305

Portraits

The Norwegian Sovereign Wealth Fund Norges 38
The supreme populist: BlackRock boss "Larry" Fink 66
Stephen Schwarzman/Blackstone 72
Ray Dalio/Bridgewater 106
John Kornblum and Felix Rohatyn/Lazard 112
Wilbur Ross – From Rothschild-Banker to US Secretary of Commerce 118
Emmanuel Macron – From Rothschild banker to President of France 118
Peter Thiel / Founders Fund 128
Jeffrey Bezos/Amazon 148
Eric Schmidt – The Google-Instagram-LinkedIn-Pentagon-Complex 218
Jack Ma / Alibaba: "Inclusive globalization" 254

Tables and Lists

Top Twenty of the largest capital organizers 39
BlackRock&Co as co-owner of the 30 DAX companies 43
The 50 largest private equity investors 99
The largest dozen hedge funds 104
The centers of elitist digital populism 192
Electric vehicles, new registrations 2017 243
China's company purchases in Germany 272
China's company purchases in the EU 275
Four Chinese banks among the world's 10 largest banks 284
Silk Road projects 286

Introduction

History is open

World peace is maintained through collective measures.
Equal rights and the self-determination of
peoples govern international relations
Article 1, United Nations Charter,
after end of World War II, 1945

Si vis pacem cole justitia!
If you want peace, promote social justice!
Motto of the International Labor Organization (ILO) founded
after World War I, since 1945 sub-organization of the UNO

1,000 satellites orbit the earth and collect, it is said, "every piece of data" about our planet: Cities, villages, deserts, gorges, mountains, climate, winds, storms, volcanoes, traffic flows, ocean floors, schools of fish and birds, refugees, oil fields and metals deep in the ground, manned and unmanned aircraft, military bases, drones, terrorists – but who are the producers and operators of the satellites, who are the owners of the car factories, energy companies, apartments, skyscrapers, banks, electricity and transport networks, supermarkets, toll roads, hotel and restaurant chains, television stations? And who owns, for example, Coca Cola, Goldman Sachs, Exxon, Deutsche Bank, Ryan Air, Zalando and the New York Times? And who owns the world-famous digital giants Google, Amazon, Facebook, Microsoft, Apple, Uber and Airbnb?

Capitalism, financial capitalism, globalization, market economy: For decades, there has been a lot of general and, of course, always "critical" fabulation and claims about why they are bad or good after all or indeed should exist at all. The obvious question is: Who are the capitalists, the financial capitalists, the globalizers, the market economists? What are their names? How do they work (if it can be called that)? What do they do, in politics, in society, in nature, among themselves and above all in our working and social conditions? Another question: Are they involved in wars or do they promote peace? Or do they perhaps (seemingly) not care?

Western presidents and heads of government like the German chancellors of all populist parties and genders and the fake producers of the leading media talk about "the markets", mostly with a threatening undertone: If we do not obey "the markets", woe betide us! For example, the state must "save" and actually "save" even more. But who are "the markets"? Where do they reside?

Trade unions and leading media routinely fret about corporate boards and managers and their millions in income, but fail to ask about the owners and their hundredfold higher profits. Freedom of opinion does not apply here either. It is invoked as a high "Western value" – but it is devalued by the dismantling of freedom of information. And the dependent employees in the companies have no freedom of opinion, but a muzzle. Knowledge and freedom of expression for a small radical minority – ignorance and muzzle for the dependent majority.

When the big, powerful banks of the Western world between New York, London, Paris, Milan, Madrid and Frankfurt had speculated their way into joint bankruptcy up to 2007, they had to be rescued with state money, i.e. our tax money – to which they themselves had contributed little – at any rate, this was what the loud spokespersons of "the markets" claimed. The banks were rescued in breach of market rules because they were "systemically relevant". Aha – so there is a "system" enthroned above the sacred free market economy? A higher freedom, a higher system that can, so to speak, out of the blue or gloomy sky, override the iron market laws if necessary? Who is that? Are they human beings, or are they indeed extrahuman or superhuman beings?

After the bank bailout: The new capital powers
Following bankruptcy and bailout, these "systemically important" banks were stripped of their power. Capital organizers like BlackRock, who had also contributed to the financial crisis – they are now "the system", they are officially called "shadow banks", and they are now the owners of the big banks and the stock exchanges and, above all, the most important companies. Today, several dozen other top league financial players of the BlackRock ilk operate, largely unregulated and unknown; in addition, there are the new second and third

league financial players, who are also barely regulated, i.e. private equity funds, hedge funds, venture capitalists, elite investment banks and the Internet stars they promote and control, such as Apple and Microsoft, and the players in the platform economy, such as Google, Amazon, Facebook/Alphabet, Uber, Airbnb.

They practice a new, even more anti-social form of brutal accumulation of private capital. With the brutalization, however, the complexity of accumulation has also increased. However, the capital organizers mentioned and the company management boards are only the visible managing directors. The private owners, on the other hand, the ultimate beneficiaries of private profit – they are more invisible than ever before in the history of capitalism. The new capital powers domicile their property rights more resolutely than ever before in a global, occult parallel society of four dozen interwoven financial havens.

This transnational class of the anonymous super-rich, supported by a discreet, civilian private army of "renowned" enrichment professionals, assumes no liability, acts without responsibility for society and nature. It does not care about antitrust law, labor law, tax law or financial supervision.

It is by no means the case, as "globalization critics" denounce, that today's capital is funneled as digital fiction around the globe intangibly and weightlessly and has nothing (any more) to do with the "real economy" – on the contrary! BlackRock&Co have hundreds of thousands of the most important companies of the real economy in their grip, decide on jobs, work, living, nutrition and environmental conditions, on products, profit distribution, poverty, wealth, national debt. And the global corporations of the platform economy penetrate into the finest pores of the everyday life of billions of people, sound it out, turn it upside down – and cooperate with secret services.

These investors and their delegated directors and managers can break millions of laws with impunity, violate human rights, degrade and impoverish dependent workers, contaminate people and the environment, destroy the sense of justice, and plaster over reality – with the full tolerance of governments in Western capitals and in the European Union.

In this way, the invisible powers can accelerate their unproductive self-enrichment at the expense of the majority and democracy as never before. The public managers come along with soft, smarmy, also grassroots-democratic language, bloviate about transparency and responsibility and diversity and manage to death the potential for indignation about the "growing gap between rich and poor". In line with the venerated Silicon Valley pattern, the digital populists promise the happy life of the digitally standardized egoists and the improvement of all mankind.

This, our capitalism – or death for all

The wealth of the BlackRock milieu is increasing, but the national economies and the infrastructure important for the majority of the population – schools, apartments, hospitals, water pipes, sewage treatment plants – are decaying or being privatized and made more expensive by the capital organizers. Climate warming is being accelerated. Armament profits boom with the invention of new enemies. While the new capital masters have created diverse collective forms for themselves, they are destroying the remnants of previous collective forms of dependent employees and maneuvering them into professionally staged, ultimately joyless, sick loneliness.

With the inward war of the new, even more US-led capitalists against democracy, against the rule of law and the welfare state, they also became more outwardly aggressive. They wage declared and undeclared wars through their governments and military and intelligence services, expand their global military presence, secretly and openly arm their representatives. Even nuclear war on European soil becomes a calculated, incalculable possibility. Motto: This, our capitalism or death for all.

Populism and political corruption

Populism exists when entrepreneurs, investors, advisors, politicians, opinion leaders make promises to the people (Latin: populus) or the majority of the population (jobs, secure pensions, life security, peace, homeland, happiness, affordable housing), consciously or naively, in the interest of an unclear, minority interest and power group, that they are unable or unwilling to keep from the outset. On the heels of the primary populism of the previous "people's" parties of Christian, conservative, and socialist-social-democratic nature we are now seeing, because of their broken promises and the misery they helped to cause, secondary populism. Among the primary populists in Germany, as far as parties are concerned, are CDU, CSU, SPD, then the business associations, consultancy firms such as McKinsey, leading media such as FAZ, Zeit, Welt, Spiegel, Süddeutsche Zeitung, now also the public broadcasters such as ARD, ZDF and DLF as well as the major Christian churches.

Secondary populism is also promoted by the primary populists and the prevailing opinion makers by discrediting, obstructing and criminalizing the democratic, anti-capitalist opposition. Secondary populists like currently the US president Donald Trump, the French president Emmanuel Macron, in Great Britain the Brexit movement and in Germany the AfD represent "movements" that do not differ significantly from the discredited parties. Rather, values and practices stem from the same old "bourgeois" relics, including free private property, unproductive private gain, nationalism and racism.

Populism in US-led Western capitalism is organically linked to political corruption: The representatives of minority, sectional private ownership grant the ruling populists as well as those who are alternatively judged capable of government (reserve and secondary populists) secret as well as public and legalized advantages in the form of monetary donations, additional income in the private sector, and media support. This perverts or breaks the political will of the majority or initially of certain target groups (Latin: corrumpere, breaking the political will).

In US-led Western capitalist democracy, the large private owners have so far bred two main political parties through donations and media support. Occasionally, as in Germany, a third, smaller business party, the FDP, also comes into play, tipping the scales in the formation of governments. Because most populist promises prove to be essentially unfulfillable in the course of two parliamentary terms and one party will no longer win the elections, the main populist parties swap places in government after two terms at the latest. Left-wing alternatives that work for the common good are discredited, right-wing alternatives, lightly censured, are given preference. In the process, the democratic morale of the voters is further and further demoralized. The rhythm of the government changeover can be reduced to one parliamentary term. This pushes things towards an even more direct, authoritarian "solution" if the democratic self-organization is not strong enough. Dictators and oligarchs in states that belong to the Western sphere of domination and influence (ex-socialist Eastern Europe, the Gulf region, South America, Africa) are in any case staunch allies and pillars of the system parallel to the facade democracy in the metropolitan states.

Populism today juggles with various ideological clichés. They are combined and interpreted differently by the respective players, even if they contradict each other in terms of content (but not necessarily in practice): Nationalism (also Western or European nationalism) and global openness; open society and building walls against others (USA against Mexico, EU against refugees, Israel against Palestine, gated communities against the poor); conservatism and ultra-modernity à la Silicon Valley; liberalism and authoritarianism; digital improvement of humanity and digital surveillance; freedom and surveillance; democracy and superordinate "markets"; competition and monopoly formation; market economy and anti-market systemic relevance; corruption and anti-corruption; feminism of the upper class and exploitation of dependent women; secularization in connection with Catholicism and Evangelicalism; pro- and anti-Americanism, pro- and anti-Semitism, pro- and anti-Islamism. The incoherence of "values" is a sign of decay.

Human history is open

At the beginning of the 20th century, before and during the 1st World War, John Hobson, Rudolf Hilferding, Vladimir Iljitsch Lenin, Rosa Luxemburg, Nikolaj Bucharin and many others had established: The cartel and monopoly-forming banks from the then five most powerful imperialist states the UK, France, Russia, Germany and the USA assumed dominion in transatlantic capitalism – a thirty-year war with two world wars was the result. But a US-led empire has emerged from the rivalry of several imperialist states. The new financial players have further deepened US domination and the vassalage of the "allies", with the help of both an educated, smooth-talking US president like Barack Obama just as with the help of an uneducated, loudmouthed US president like Donald Trump.

The title of Lenin's world-famous analysis "Imperialism, the Highest Stage of Capitalism" was originally different. In 1916 Lenin spoke not of the "highest" but of the "latest" stage. The "highest" – also meaning "the last" – stage was then fantasized into it. One can understand the hope connected with it. But it was illusory when one considers the strength and merciless, treacherous and professionalized crimes and practices that the main players of capitalism at the time already displayed against democracy, international law, the labor movement, socialism and national liberation movements.[1]

The diagnosis "latest stage" was at the time and still is today closer to reality. But especially the rise of communist-led capitalism in the People's Repub-

---

1   After their Communist Manifesto of 1848, Marx and Engels had already erred in their hope for an early socialist revolution.

lic of China, which was unintentionally promoted by Western capitalism, and its globally developing New Silk Road network, demonstrate the fresh dawn of a new, different history. This turning point is also the most visible part of an international movement of newly unleashed decolonization, democratization and peace.

The post-history once proclaimed in the exuberance of defeated socialism in the 1990s, the end of history and the perpetuation of anti-Islamic, Christian-tinted "Western" capitalism are over. After decades of arrogant self-blindness, the neocolonial free trade globalization of the capitalist West is confronted not only with permanent internal opposition, but also with the completely different economic and globalization practices of the People's Republic of China. This book invites you to take a closer look at and compare the two great variants of recent capitalism, from within and from without, in terms of human rights and international law. History is open.

I.
The New Capitalist Players of the West

The new capitalism that has emerged since the 1980s and has dominated since the banking crisis of 2007 includes various classes and groups of globally active financial players. 1. The most powerful of these are the BlackRock-type capital organizers. 2. The second league so far consists of private equity investors ("locusts"), hedge funds and venture capitalists. 3. elite investment banks, private banks and the traditional big banks play various roles.

4. Promoted and shaped by these financial players, are the five "apocalyptic horsemen of the Internet": Google, Apple, Microsoft, Facebook Amazon (GAMFA), alongside the most important traditional corporations. 5. Finally, the youngest generation, the even more rapidly rising companies of the digital platform economy of the type Uber, Deliveroo, Netflix, Parship/ElitePartner, Upwork, Flixbus.

Smaller and diffuse financial players who flourish in the upheaval of Western capitalism (and can also perish) such as debt funds, organizers of crypto currencies and the diffuse army of financial advisors are not taken into account here, nor is the group of oligarchs, who indeed are more important for the primitive version of the capitalist transformation, who in part or for a short time also assume government or government-related functions such as Trump, Soros, Khodorkovsky, Timoshenko, Poroshenko, Djukanovic and Babishenko.

1.
The big capital organizers: BlackRock&Co

Not only since the "financial crisis" have the economies in the "Western community of values" stagnated, systemically and permanently. Not only the countries, but also the companies are investing less and less and at the same time are sinking ever deeper into debt, even more so than before the financial crisis. And this over-indebtedness is no longer recoverable with this type of economy. Likewise, private household debt has risen and continues to rise.[1]

Economic contraction, irrecoverable overindebtedness

The officially mostly higher growth in the USA stems from the more sophisticated statistical tricks and is overstated by up to two percent[2] – or is anyway based on nonsensical, military and environmentally harmful products. Unemployment and underemployment are permanently high and are also dressed up statistically. Under transatlantic capitalism, the share of income from dependent labor has been steadily declining since about 1990 and even faster since 2007.[3] Dependent employees are squeezed between either over- or underemployment and a state of working poor, poor in spite of work – or hassled with good pay.

In Western capitalism there is "secular stagnation", according to the former US finance minister Lawrence Summers,[4] who helped to spawn this development under President William Clinton. In practice, Western capitalism does not rely at all on "constant growth", as critics of globalization and growth point out disparagingly. In Western capitalism, private profit is growing, but the quality of work and life of dependent employees is declining. The infrastructure necessary for the majority of the population – affordable housing, schools, kindergartens, hospitals, nursing homes, local government, water and sewage systems, waters, long-distance and local transport – is neglected, shrunk, debased or is privatized and made more expensive.

There is an "investment strike in Europe", headlined the investor-friendly Handelsblatt (HB). But the authors, who are so well versed in "the economy", fall into a hazy psychology: "Apparently confidence in the future is simply not great enough."[5]

----

1   International Monetary Fund: Bringing Down High Debt, April 18, 2018

2   Norbert Haering: Ireland's absurdly high growth shows how dubious GDP statistics are. http://norberthaering.de/27-germannews, 23.8.2016; labor market statistics are also massively dressed up.

3   Jeronim Capaldo: The Trans-Atlantic Trade and Investment Partnership, Tufts University October 2014

4   https://www.businessinsider.com/larry-summers-imf-speech, 17.3.2013

5   Investitionsstreik in Europa, HB 15.8.2016

The BlackRock boss: "The chief of the leading capitalists"

Some can only laugh about this, initially furtively, now publicly. Certain investors do indeed have a great deal of faith in the future of over-indebted shrinking capitalism. Since the financial crisis, they have been investing even more, quietly and resolutely.

On the top floors of the Western world, BlackRock boss Lawrence Fink is idolized like no other. The leading media congenially call him "Larry". When he is flown into the annual World Economic Forum in Davos, Switzerland, the unelected and the elected elite click their heels. Because "they have all understood, the managers, entrepreneurs, bankers, big investors, politicians, economists, that the American is something like the undeclared president of the world financial community, the supreme of the leading capitalists, who determines the laws and fortunes of capitalism more than many others," says the Handelsblatt author, who was allowed to attend wide-eyed.[6]

Speculation with shares – fraud also possible

Let's take a look at some of the typical activities of the chief of the top capitalists in turn. Let's take an "investment" from 2016. BlackRock and other financial investors took out a billion euros in loans from other such investors and banks and bought on a loan basis a fifth of all Lufthansa shares ("loaned shares") from other Deutsche Lufthansa shareholders for a limited time. BlackRock&Co speculated that fears of terrorist attacks and Brexit would result in fewer flight bookings and send the shares southward. According to Western market laws, that is exactly what they did, sliding by 14 per cent. After a few weeks, the investors returned the loan shares to their rightful owners as agreed and bought up Lufthansa shares that had fallen in value – at a profit, as the value of the shares rose again afterwards.[7]

However, in this case BlackRock is not a speculator from outside, but one of Lufthansa's main shareholders. If you don't know anything about current capitalism, you might well ask: Why is a co-owner speculating on the decline in the value of his own company's shares?

---

6   Hans-Jürgen Jakobs: Wem gehört die Welt? Die Machtverhältnisse im globalen Kapitalismus. München 2016, p. 21

7   Hedgefonds greifen Lufthansa an. Leerverkäufer wetten auf einen Kursverfall der Fluggesellschaft. Der Spiegel 33/2016; Lufthansa-Aktie: Rückzug von Leerverkäufer Blackrock, http://aktiencheck.de 13.7.2016

In the capitalism of late, companies are the basis for speculation for owners like BlackRock. If they generate more than holding the shares and the annual wait for the dividend payout, then they invest in speculation – perverse to call something like this an "investment", isn't it?

BlackRock&Co constantly use parts of their shares in Lufthansa, Daimler, Siemens, Coca Cola, Goldman Sachs etc. for speculation. Let's take the random date of 18.8.2016: BlackRock reports to the German Financial Supervisory Authority – *Bundesamt für Finanzdienstleistungsaufsicht, Bafin* – short share sales at Kali&Salz AG, zooplus AG and ElringKlinger AG; the investor Marshall Wace reports short share sales at Deutsche Bank, Lufthansa and Grammer AG to Bafin; the investor AQR reports short share sales at the Bilfinger construction group to Bafin; the investor Lansdowne does the same at VW; Millenium does the same at Wacker Chemie AG etc etc.[8]

Scaremongering and fraud

These short sales on this single day are only a tiny fraction and are related only to Germany. Such short sales by BlackRock&Co take place simultaneously in many more companies in Germany and in many other companies and countries. BlackRock can "exacerbate price swings and thus cause panic", notes even the FAZ, otherwise an admirer of the speculator.[9]

Other speculations with shares enable fraud. BlackRock lends shares to other market participants for a fee. With the Cum-Ex – business BlackRock had lent its own shares for a certain time to rich individuals and banks. BlackRock gets a fee for this. The borrowers of the shares can declare themselves as owners to their tax office and be refunded unpaid capital gains tax. BlackRock&Co can play the innocent: We don't know what the borrowers do with them. Meanwhile public prosecutors in Germany have woken up and have carried out raids in the German branch of BlackRock.[10]

Violate laws, one-off fine from the petty cash

On such speculations, BlackRock has violated reporting obligations under Sections 21, 22 and 25 of the German Securities Trading Act. After random

---

8   Netto-Leerverkaufspositionen 2016-08-18, http://www.bundesanzeiger.de/ebanzwww/ wexsservlet?, downloaded 19.8.2016

9   Wie Blackrock&Co Unternehmen beeinflussen, FAZ 22.11.2016

10   Gerhard Schick: Cum-Ex: Die Umverteilung von unten nach oben muss enden. DGB: Gegenblende 5.12.2018

checks, the Bafin therefore imposed a fine of EUR 3.25 million on BlackRock in March 2015. This is by far the largest fine the Bafin has ever imposed. "BlackRock's disclosures about voting rights and financial instruments held were incorrect and/or came too late."[11]

As described above, BlackRock's business involves buying and selling blocks of shares in its companies on a daily basis, forming derivatives from them and exploiting price differentials between the world's stock exchanges. For this, tardy and false public announcements are profit-relevant. Bafin has to date not repeated the elaborate spot check from 2013.

BlackRock paid the 3.25 million without comment from the petty cash of the German branch. The Bafin is unable to cope with the comprehensive examination regarding BlackRock alone, not to mention regarding the other four dozen from the BlackRock club. This reduces the state financial supervisors of Western capitalism to ridiculous fools.

Mastermind of the Western economy

BlackRock speculates constantly with its own and third-party shares on all stock exchanges of the world. In the process, price differentials in the nano-second range between the stock exchanges in New York, Tokyo, Singapore, London, Zurich, Milan, Frankfurt, Paris, Luxembourg, Rio de Janeiro etc. are exploited. The same happens with securities of all kinds that build on the shares: Futures, derivatives, ETFs, iShares. For the most part, this happens automatically.

The programs belong to Aladdin, the robotized mastermind of BlackRock. This computer system of 5,000 mainframes is operated by 2,000 IT specialists, programmers and data analysts. The system requires so much power for cooling that most of the Western economy's largest financial data processing facility was set up 4,425 kilometers from Wall Street in the northwest of the US, near the town of Wenatchee with its population of 30,000. The hydroelectric power plants on the Columbia River there produce the cheapest electricity in the USA. It is also the home of the small, albeit soccer-field-sized data centers of Yahoo, Microsoft and Dell, for example.

Aladdin stands for Asset Liability and Debt Derivative Investment Network.

---

11   Bundesanstalt für Finanzdienstleistungen: Blackrock: Bafin verhängt Bußgeld in Höhe von 3,25 Mio Euro, Mitteilung 20.3.2015

Risk factors such as changes of government, wars and military actions, earthquakes, climate fluctuations, strikes and opposition movements, changes in consumer behavior, insolvencies and image campaigns are included. Surprising changes and the run-up to them are particularly interesting. The key is: How can one influence the performance of securities through prior knowledge – it can also be a matter of fractions of seconds – and exploit it to one's own advantage with purchases and sales? Strikes, government crises, actual and above all possible wars can by all means have a positive function.

BlackRock is, together with other capital organizers of this ilk – Vanguard, T Rowe Price, State Street, Fidelity, Wellington, Northern Trust, JPMorgan, Capital Group and others – simultaneously co-owner of the most important stock exchanges in the Western world, the NYSE in New York and the Nasdaq technology exchange as well as the London Stock Exchange and the German Stock Exchange – and co-owner of thousands of corporations such as Lufthansa and Coca Cola.

BlackRock thus combines the largest data processing capacity of the Western financial industry with the function of the largest financial and economic insider. Because BlackRock, for example, is also a major shareholder in Deutsche Bank, its asset management is controlled by Aladdin. Aladdin now also carries out risk analyses for over 150 smaller capital organizers, but also for foundations, sovereign wealth funds, insurance companies, pension funds and even for 50 Western central banks, including the US Federal Reserve and the European Central Bank ECB.[12]

In financial circles it is clear that these promoted speculations, also in favor of BlackRock&Co, "jeopardize financial market stability" and exacerbate the already systemic crisis-proneness of the current economic system.[13]

The transnational capitalist class

BlackRock has only 14,000 employees worldwide. The traditional big banks manage far less capital, but notwithstanding their rigorous policy of cutbacks they need considerably more staff: JPMorgan Chase has 230,000 employees, Deutsche Bank 100,000.

This has to do with the fact that BlackRock only has a comparatively small

---

12   Heike Buchter: Blackrock. Eine heimliche Weltmacht greift nach unserem Geld. Frankfurt/Main 2015, p. 220ff.

13   ETFs gefährden Finanzmarktstabilität, FAZ 8.4.2014

number of super-rich customers to serve. There are no walk-ins, no bank counters. All over the world, corporate heirs, corporate clans, entrepreneurs, corporate and banking board members and supervisory boards, managing directors, corporate foundations, billionaires and millionaires entrust BlackRock with their liquid capital. Such customers are called Ultra High Net Worth Individuals (UHNWI). From 50 million, better still from 100 million you are one of them. Traditional banks, insurance companies, central banks, corporate finance departments and pension funds also entrust BlackRock with their capital.

Those responsible and economically entitled in each case form the transnational capitalist class.[14] Only BlackRock&Co know the names of these, their customers. The public doesn't know the names, the tax offices usually don't know the names either. Even the companies in which BlackRock buys shares or other share certificates for these customers do not know the names of their "actual" owners. BlackRock&Co are an anonymization machine – this exclusive knowledge is also a source of their power.

BlackRock&Co thus form a global network of the super-rich, with millions of powerless and ignorant small investors still dangling from their coattails. The collected capital is invested by BlackRock&Co in the world's

---

14   Cf. Werner Rügemer: Die transnationale kapitalistische Klasse. Strukturen der globalen Machtelite, Hintergrund 1/2016, p. 72ff.; this class does not consist, as e.g. David Rothkopf portrays (Superclass. The Global Power Elite and the World They are Making, New York/London 2008), of 6,000 equally powerful individuals – heads of governments, banks and companies known to the general public – but from much larger and at the same time very heterogeneous, hierarchically structured groups and clans. It is not only "the rich" or "the billionaires and millionaires" that make up this class, but by all means diverse organizational forms with identical interests. These do not form a strictly uniform organization, no central committee, but are organized and informally networked publicly as well as non-publicly in many shapes and forms. Their differing influential power stems from various criteria: The number and extent of ownership of strategically important companies and their interdependence with one another (see the chapter "BlackRock&Co: The Super Cartel"), interweaving with important sections and members of the "civil private army of Western capitalism" as well as with leading members of state institutions – civil as well as military and secret service – both national and transnational. These include formal and informal parallel structures such as the systemic-professional use of financial havens and the public and surreptitious purchase and lobbying of politicians, journalists, academics, etc., as well as diverse cultural, academic, media, and social sponsoring. The mere existence of the "super-rich" alone does not mean participation in the transnational capitalist class. Thus, numerous "super-rich" emerge in China, but they do not have the instruments necessary for their existence as a ruling class, such as the constant financing of government parties, mass media, and the like.

most profitable companies, which in turn belong to the transnational capitalist network. We will come to the related government relations and the "civil private army" later.

Price cartels, takeovers, mergers

BlackRock and several dozen other such capital organizers are the biggest insiders of Western capitalism. They have close relationships with corporate boards, governments, rating agencies, international financial institutions such as the International Monetary Fund and the European Central Bank, and with top advisors such as PWC and Freshfields, who advise both corporations and governments. In this way, BlackRock&Co can not only anticipate longer-term developments more farsightedly than others, but also help shape and benefit from them.

Price cartels

Securities speculation is only one source of profit. To stay with Lufthansa: The company is to be made more profitable, costs lowered. Through outsourcing, the Group now consists of around 500 subsidiaries and associated companies (logistics, catering, engineering, IT services, various acquired and outsourced airlines...). Ground and cabin crews are paid less, pilots' pensions are cut, new pilots are hired via a low-cost subsidiary, and the company's own low-cost airlines are founded. The long-term vision: After a decade, about one tenth of the current 120,000 employees will remain.

Bank and airline cartels in the USA

Such ruthlessness would not be possible with the traditional means of a "German" company. That's where BlackRock&Co come in. BlackRock and Vanguard, currently the second largest capital organizer, are co-owners of Lufthansa, but also of the US airlines American Airlines and Delta Airlines. Mergers and takeovers drive profits. In BlackRock&Co's home country, the USA, BlackRock&Co have formed cartels with the banks in which they are also co-owners: Fees at these banks have been increased and at the same time the interest on credit balances has been reduced. At the same time, ticket prices were increased on US airlines.[15]

---

15   José Azar, Martin Schmalz, Isabel Tecu: Anti-Competitive Effects of Common Ownership, Ross School of Business Papers Nr. 1235, July 5, 2016

Bayer acquires Monsanto

The next step is mergers and acquisitions. Take the acquisition of the US bio-technology group Monsanto by the German chemicals group Bayer. This is not a "hostile takeover" of an "American" by a "German" corporation, as the leading and provincial media say.[16]

Rather, the takeover is being driven by the major shareholders – and these are the same in both groups. Bayer's largest shareholders are, in this order: BlackRock, Sun Life Financial, Capital World, Vanguard, Deutsche Bank. Monsanto's largest shareholders are, in slightly different order: Capital World, Vanguard, BlackRock, State Street, Fidelity and Sun Life Financial.[17] The consolidation of capital and power at BlackRock is even more intense: BlackRock is also a major shareholder of Bayer's co-owner Deutsche Bank. This is how the world's largest agrochemical group is created: it synergistically bundles the market leaders in seeds, pesticides, agricultural patents and global data on farmers, farms and agricultural markets.

Bristol-Myers Sqibb takes over Celgene

Of course, BlackRock, Vanguard, Capital, State Street, Fidelity, Wellington etc. are also major shareholders of other agricultural and chemical companies such as BASF, LG Chem (South Korea), Akzo Nobel (Netherlands) as well as Pfizer and DowDupont (USA). In 2019, the merger of the US pharmaceutical companies Bristol-Myers Sqibb and its former competitor Celgene began. They want to become the leading company for, among other things, cancer drugs.[18] The largest shareholders of Bristol-Myers Squibb are, in this order: BlackRock, Vanguard, State Street; the largest shareholders of Celgene are, in this order: Wellington, Vanguard, BlackRock, State Street.

Linde takes over Praxair

Linde, the European market leader in industrial gases, intends to acquire its US competitor Praxair. BlackRock&Co are at the same time the main sharehold-ers in both Linde and Praxair: The largest owners at Linde are the Norwegian sovereign wealth fund Norges, BlackRock and Sun Life, at Praxair they are Capi-tal World, Vanguard, State Street and BlackRock, followed inter alia by Norges

---

16   Monsanto bleibt stur, Der Spiegel 26/2016

17   Die Monsanto-Übernahme, HB 16.8.2016

18   74 Milliarden für Celgene, HB 4.1.2019

again.[19] The merger of Linde and Praxair would result in "the largest industrial gas producer in the world".[20] The aim is to cut jobs in both existing groups. The 8,000 Linde employees in Germany are to be protected from redundancies only until 2021. The legal domicile of the merged company is to be relocated to the financial haven of Ireland. Jobs and taxes will be lost in several countries.

Monopoly formation in the energy industry
In early 2018, the two largest energy groups in Germany, Eon and RWE, arranged a new division of labor. Eon bought the RWE subsidiary Innogy and took over the distribution of the energy and the infrastructure of the lines. Eon will thus get 75 percent of the German electricity market, 50 percent of the electricity grids and 40 percent of the electricity meters, which will soon be digitized and replaced and will offer new services. At the same time, RWE is monopolizing electricity production.[21] By the by, 5,000 jobs are to be cut.[22]

BlackRock is a major shareholder in both groups. At the same time, after RWE, BlackRock is also the largest owner of Innogy, followed by Templeton, Norges, Caffi Delen, Franklin and Vanguard. Innogy has 550 million shares in circulation.[23] To purchase Innogy, Eon paid shareholders EUR 40 per share.[24] BlackRock's 6.87 percent stake in Innogy adds up to 34.35 million shares. Multiplied by 40, this results in EUR 1.36 billion – profit for BlackRock. Templeton, Norges, Caffi Delen, Franklin and Vanguard together have 6.12 per cent of the shares, thus together rake in somewhat over EUR 1 billion.

Mergers of banks
BlackRock&Co are also driving the merger of banks on a national and international level. For the head of Deutsche Bank, there are "simply too many banks in Germany and the EU... We need more mergers – at national level – but also across national borders." Deutsche Bank could, for example, merge with Commerzbank.[25]

---

19   www.nasdaq.com/symbol/px/institutional-holdings, 19.8.2016
20   Linde confirms Merger Talks with Praxair, Wall Street Journal 16.8.2016
21   Ein neues Monopol, Der Spiegel 2.2.2019, p. 66f.
22   Innogy-Übernahme gefährdet 5.000 Arbeitsplätze, Zeit online 13.3.2018
23   https://www.finanzen.net/unternehmensprofil/innogy, abgerufen 13.3.2018
24   Zeit online 13.3.2018 l.c.
25   Deutsche Bank wirbt für Fusionen, Börsen-Zeitung 1.9.2016

In the USA, but also in France and Italy, similar things are on the agenda. BlackRock is the largest shareholder of four of the five largest American banks, and in Europe the largest shareholder, for example, of Deutsche Bank, the Dutch ING Bank, the British Hong Kong and Shanghai Banking Corporation (HSBC), the Spanish Banco Bilbao, and the second largest shareholder of BNP Paribas, Unicredit and Banco Sanpaolo.

Since the IPO in 2010, BlackRock's profit has risen steadily. In 2017, it was 16 percent higher than in the previous year. In the first quarter of 2018, net profit rose by a further 27 percent to USD 1.09 billion despite turbulence on the stock markets.[26]

Boosted by the financial crisis

We shall now look at the question: How and when did this new type of capital organizer emerge?

BlackRock was founded in 1988 by Lawrence Fink. He had worked on Wall Street for the investment bank First Boston. At that time, the major US banks began to free themselves from the previous regulations even before they were legally consecrated under William Clinton's government. Individual bank managers developed new financial products, experimented with them and sought investors.

At First Boston, Fink was regarded as the initiator of "securities" made up of securitized, i.e. those sold on by the banks, and then bundled real estate and other loans. For the development of such financial products and financial bets, he received loans from the private equity firm Blackstone. In 1994 he founded BlackRock out of Blackstone: the small "black stone" gradually became the much larger "black rock".

BlackRock made its first big leap forward thanks to the financial speculations co-developed by Fink. They led to the bankruptcy of traditional Western banks in 2007. In the 1980s, the head of BlackRock had "devised the mortgage securities at First Boston that contributed significantly to the crash in 2007/2008".[27] BlackRock's assets under management, for example, soared from around USD 300 billion in 2004 to USD 1.3 trillion in 2008.

The next major leap was made in the two years during which the financial

---

26   BlackRock steigert die Dividende das neunte Jahr in Folge, https://www.finanzen.net
      12.1.2018, Reuters 12.4.2018

27   Hans-Jürgen Jakobs: Wem gehört die Welt? ibid., p. 24

crisis unfolded. The US government under President Barack Obama commissioned Fink to manage the financial crisis. BlackRock coordinated the liquidation of the investment banks Bear Stearns and Lehman Brothers and the government rescue of the insurance group American International Group (AIG). This meant, for example, that Goldman Sachs and Deutsche Bank were paid the sums insured that AIG would have had to pay. The fee for BlackRock was USD 180 million.[28]

Far more important than the government fee was the fact that BlackRock was able to gain an even better market and power position via this insider position, e.g. by buying up smaller, even insolvent financial players, for which BlackRock received cheap loans. Rich investors fled from ailing Wall Street banks to government darling BlackRock: in the two years to 2009, assets under management skyrocketed to USD 3.3 trillion. By 2018 it was already over 6.4 trillion – about 20 times as much as the budget of the richest and most powerful EU state and twice as much as its annual gross domestic product.

Murky story: A government bank disappears
Having initially operated as an unregulated hedge fund, BlackRock became a stock corporation in 1999 with its IPO.

The largest owner is the provincial bank Pittsburgh National Corporation, PNC, with 25 percent of the shares. In 2017 it had been 34 percent – an unusually high share in this milieu. The next largest co-owners are Vanguard with 8.4 percent, Wellington with 7.2 percent, BlackRock itself with 6.9 percent, Capital World with 6.6 percent.[29]

Riggs: The Money Laundering Bank in Washington
The provincial bank PNC never belonged to the US financial center of Wall Street and has a much smaller business volume than the other BlackRock owners. What's the secret? It could have become public in 2005. Then PNC bought the Riggs National Bank in Washington. It was publicly unknown, but systemically relevant in the US capital: US presidents such as Abraham Lincoln and Jefferson Davis had their accounts here in the 19th century, a total of 23 US presidents, including Eisenhower and Nixon. Until 2005, it had been a secret accountant for a century and a half for 95 percent of foreign embas-

---

28   Geithner has phone friend at BlackRock, FT online 11. Oktober 2012, now deleted.

29   www.nasdaq.com/de/symbol(ownership-summary 8.2.2018

sies at the US seat of government and US embassies and consulates around the world. Dictator clans from Africa like Obiang/Equatorial Guinea received bribes from US oil companies like Exxon through dozens of Riggs accounts.

Of course, the bank had its legal head office in the financial haven of Delaware and branches in the City of London and on the Channel Island of Jersey, in the anti-communism headquarters in Berlin, in Miami and on the Bahamas. Legal advice came from Wall Street law firm Sullivan & Cromwell (Allen Dulles, John F. Dulles). Auditors and board members came from the "renowned" auditing firm Deloitte. Riggs linked up with the second, also publicly unknown, government-related bank in Washington, Alex. Brown, which worked closely with the CIA. It was to play a role in the rise of Jeffrey Bezos/Amazon. Riggs sat highly networked in the center of the "deep state".[30]

Obiang, Chodorkowski, Prinz Bandar, Pinochet...

In the plundering of post-socialist Russia under the corrupt Western darling Boris Yeltsin, Riggs helped Russian oligarchs such as Mikhail Khodorkovsky to transfer assets to the West by founding mailbox companies on the Cayman Islands for example.[31] All this actually fell under US money laundering laws. But it served good "Western" purposes.[32]

After the terrorist attack on the World Trade Center in New York in 2001, investigators hunting terrorist financing stumbled upon the Riggs accounts of the Saudi ambassador, Prince Bandar, who received bribes for mediating sales, for example of the British arms company BAE Systems. This "scandal" also had to be hushed up. But then prosecutors abroad, in Spain, France, Argentina, the UK and Chile found out – although the US judiciary refused legal assistance: The US-backed dictator Augusto Pinochet had placed his assets, corruptly filched with the help of the CIA, on ten Riggs accounts. To this end, Riggs had also set up mailbox companies for him in the Caribbean.

But this "scandal" was also quickly disposed of. The provincial bank PNC was ideal for this: In 1996 it had bought the still small but ambitious financial company BlackRock and financed its further rise. In 2005 PNC had earned a lot of money as BlackRock's main shareholder and as an unknown player

---

30   Peter Scott: The American Deep State, Lanham/Maryland 2015

31   William Engdahl: Manifest Destiny. Democracy as a Cognitive Dissonance, Wiesbaden 2018, p. 47f.

32   The Oligarch Who Came in from the Cold, https://www.forbes.com 18.3.2002, downloaded 19.4.2018

bought the scandal bank Riggs quickly and inconspicuously. The shareholders, among them boss Joseph Albritton, active in the Ronald Reagan Presidential Foundation, were allowed to keep the purchase price of USD 650 million unpunished. The 200-year-old traditional bank of the US capital has since been completely erased from public memory.[33]

In this way, BlackRock also assumed Riggs' customer base and government relations. The even swifter rise of BlackRock from 2006 onwards could begin.

The largest shadow bank in the world

The banking regulation of 2010 – Dodd Frank-Act (Wall Street Reform and Consumer Protection Act) – only regulated the traditional banks. But BlackRock&Co are not regarded as banks. BlackRock does a lot of bank-like business, but in legal terms is not a bank. This is also true for the other capital organizers, Vanguard, State Street, Fidelity, Capital Group, Wellington, Northern Trust, Amundi, Templeton, T Rowe Price and Franklin Resources.

As a result, they are referred to as shadow banks by experts and by international financial bodies such as the IMF and the Bank for International Settlements (BIS, the central bank of central banks).[34] Their lobby, with the help of ECB President Mario Draghi, has managed to ensure that they are still only monitored.[35] A regulation such as the one proposed by Jochen Sanio, then head of the German financial supervisory authority Bafin, came to nothing.[36]

And thus, they seized their new freedom. If they needed loans, they would get them from the regulated banks, which were delighted still to be allowed to play along. And BlackRock&Co bought shares in the banks and are now not only their key borrowers, but also their powerful co-owners. BlackRock is co-owner of over 17,000 companies worldwide.

---

33   US Senate Permanent Subcommittee on Investigations: Money Laundering and Foreign Corruption. Enforcement and Effectiveness of the Patriot Act. Case Study involving Riggs Bank, Washington July 15, 2004 (1,592 pages); Peter Scott: The American Deep State. Deep Events and Off-the-books Financing, The Asia-Pacific Journal 6.4.2014

34   Laura Kodres: What's Shadow Banking? Many financial institutions that act like banks are not supervised like banks, in: Finance and Development, June 2013, p. 42f. (IMF publication)

35   Global Shadow Banking Monitoring Report 2015, http://www.fsb.org/2015/global-shadow-banking-monitoring-report-2105

36   "Licht ins Dunkel des Paralleluniversums" – Bafin-Präsident Jochen Sanio im Gespräch über Schattenbanken, BaFinJournal 11-12/2011, p. 20 ff.

Largest organizer of mailbox companies

BlackRock&Co are building an occult parallel financial world. It pervades the entire Western economy, bypassing the national supervisory authorities.

Dark pools

Occult parallel finance includes dark pools. Although BlackRock&Co are co-owners of the stock exchanges in New York, London and Frankfurt, they also organize a non-public, non-regulated parallel system. These are off-exchange trading centers for shares and securities of all kinds. In these black holes in the financial system, BlackRock in particular mediates direct contact between buyers and sellers, i.e. above all between banks, companies and financial investors. All participants remain anonymous to the outside world. It is estimated that in 2014 40 percent of all stock transactions in the USA already took place outside the traditional, regulated stock exchanges.[37]

Systemic use of financial havens

The most important financial havens belong to the occult parallel world. Their use by BlackRock&Co goes far beyond what established "investigative media" such as Guardian, NYT and SZ reveal. The vast majority of BlackRock's individual funds, which legally act as shareholders of Bayer, Monsanto, Linde, Praxair, Deutsche Bank, Siemens, Deutsche Post DHL, Commerzbank, etc., have their legal domicile in one of the numerous financial havens.

BlackRock has distributed its 5 percent RWE shares over 154 (one hundred and fifty-four) fund companies and financial instruments, including Black-Rock Holdco 2 Inc., BlackRock Holdco 4 LLC, BlackRock Holdco 6 LLC, BlackRock Delaware Holdings, BlackRock Institutional Trust, BlackRock Netherlands B.V., BlackRock International Holdings Inc., BlackRock Group Ltd., BlackRock Asset Management Deutschland AG, etc. Most of them have their legal domicile in a financial haven, such as Delaware/USA, Jersey, Luxembourg, the Netherlands, Singapore and the Cayman Islands.[38]

As of March 1, 2018, BlackRock, as the largest owner of the energy group Eon, had distributed its total of 7.86 percent shares to itself as the controlling company and to 152 subsidiaries spread over Delaware (the most frequently mentioned location), Luxembourg, the Netherlands, Jersey, the UK, Singa-

---

37   Dark Pools: Finster und geheimnisvoll, Zeit online 3.7.2014

38   DGAP News Service: RWE AG, Mitteilung 6.2.2018

pore, Australia and Canada.[39] BlackRock has hidden its 10 percent shares in Germany's largest housing group, Vonovia, in 220 such mailbox companies. BlackRock follows this pattern with all companies in which the capital concealer invests its customers' capital. As do the other capital organizers like Vanguard, State Street, Wellington, Templeton, T Rowe Price etc.[40]

This is also the case for smaller companies: BlackRock holds 4.01 percent of the shares of the Austrian world market leader for special mechanical engineering, Andritz AG in Graz. These are distributed across several dozen individual funds, which are based in different countries: Germany, Australia, Japan, Canada, but also in the explicit financial havens of London, Jersey, the Netherlands, Cayman Islands and Delaware.[41]

To cite two other examples: The two largest cruise companies in human history to date, Carnival Corporation and Royal Caribbean, both have their operational headquarters in Miami/USA and their tax headquarters in Panama and Liberia respectively. The largest Carnival shareholders are Suntrust Banks, BlackRock, Vanguard, Northern Trust and Bank of America; the largest Royal Caribbean shareholders are Vanguard, BlackRock, Primecap, Baillie Gifford and State Street. The largest Carnival shareholder, Suntrust Bank, is owned by BlackRock, Vanguard, Capital World, Fidelity and State Street.[42] This means that the two cruise companies have their own tax domicile in financial havens and that at the same time their several thousand investors also have their tax domicile in financial havens.

BlackRock itself has its operational headquarters in New York, but its legal domicile is in Delaware, the largest corporate financial haven in the world. In addition, BlackRock has two offices in Wilmington, the capital of Delaware.[43]

Collusion with the rating agencies
BlackRock, Capital Group, Vanguard, State Street and T Rowe Price were the majority shareholders in the two dominant rating agencies S&P (formerly

39   https://eon.com/content/dam/on/eon-com/investors/voting-rights/180301_Stimmrechtsmitteilungen_eon.pdf, downloaded 13.3.2018

40   The data e.g. for Blackrock can be viewed at the New York Stick Exchange using its identification tag ISIN US09247X1019.

41   Stimmrechtsmitteilung der Andritz AG vom 9.3.2016, www.andritz.com/de/gr-notification-blackrock-10032016-de.pdf, downloaded 24.8.2016

42   https://www.nasdaq.com downloaded 11.5.2018

43   www.blackrock.com/locations, downloaded 5.2.2018

Standard&Poor's) and Moody's in the run-up to the last financial crisis and re-mained so even after the crisis.[44] For high fees, the rating agencies issued bogus assessments of the financial products of banks associated with BlackRock&Co, i.e. their owners.[45]

The rating agencies, which have a government mandate in the USA and the European Union to assess the creditworthiness of companies and countries, were major contributors to and profiteers of the financial crisis. However, they and their owners, such as BlackRock, were neither punished nor held liable for damages, nor were they subjected to new rules.

After the banks collapsed, the ownership of the agencies merely shifted within the family. S&P's three largest shareholders are now Fidelity, Vanguard and BlackRock. Moody's four largest shareholders are Berkshire Hathaway (Warren Buffett), Vanguard, Baillie Gifford and State Street (as of 2016, with BlackRock being a major shareholder of Berkshire Hathaway).

Thus BlackRock&Co also indirectly determine the credit conditions of countries, companies and banks. The boards of the 30 Dax companies in Germany, for example, commission the three US rating agencies to assess creditworthiness and credit conditions. BlackRock&Co are simultaneously co-owners of S&P and Moody's and co-owners of all 30 Dax companies. On the one hand, as agency co-owner BlackRock earns money from the high-priced assessments, on the other BlackRock has the possibility of privileged insight and, as co-owner of the assessed countries and companies, can be an information supplier of choice for the assigned agency.

The privatization of pensions and real estate

BlackRock&Co not only exploit the existing industrial and financial substance. They want to turn as many human needs as possible into monopolistic and privately tradable goods. For this purpose, forms of communal, collective organization are to be broken up.

BlackRock boss Fink, together with the bosses of JPMorgan Chase and General Electric, belongs to the hardline lobby of pension privatizers in the USA. Fink himself proposed as a particularly aggressive variant that the state force the population to save for their pensions: compulsory saving. The lobby

---

44   Werner Rügemer: Ratingagenturen. Einblicke in die Kapitalmacht der Gegenwart. Biele-feld 2012, p. 43ff., 61f.

45   United States of America: Financial Crisis Inquiry Commission: The Financial Crisis. Inquiry Report. New York 2011, p. 118f., 131f., 281f., 344ff.

was unable to push this through, but has learned to make do with a first step initially. More was politically unenforceable, but it was supposed to provide the opening gambit: The Obama administration introduced voluntary private savings (myRA = myRetirementAccount). It is intended for those for whom employers do not pay pension contributions. It is subsidized by the state, for example through tax breaks. Tradable funds are now being set up for this purpose.[46] "BlackRock owes its rise on the one hand to the privatization of retirement provision, with insurance companies and pension funds chasing high interest rates and carting their billions to BlackRock."[47]

Housing is also an object of desire. BlackRock bought the New York real estate complex Stuyvesant Town with 110 buildings and 10,000 apartments. It had been built by the municipal life insurance after World War II for war veterans, teachers, policemen, firefighters. BlackRock didn't want to know about the protection of the many long-term tenants. But here the plan did not work out. Tenants went to court and were proved right in 4,400 cases. BlackRock made losses.[48] In the USA there are not (any longer) many rented flats. But, as we will see: After the hop across the Atlantic, to Western Europe, BlackRock&Co will discover bigger spoils.

BlackRock's "People's Share"

In the meantime, BlackRock&Co have also developed something for the "people": robotized management of small amounts from EUR or USD 10,000, sometimes even from 1,000. The most widespread financial product of this kind is called ETF, Exchange Traded Fund. This speculative "security" was invented in 1993 on Wall Street during William Clinton's presidency by State Street, now the third-largest capital organizer. It was intended for large investors, but was made a mass product by BlackRock. This is not a stock, but a share certificate in a capital fund that invests in companies, real estate, commodities or anything else. The shares are traded on the stock exchange.

iShares as a control tool

iShares was developed as a particularly "popular" variant of ETF. This ETF subgroup is a bet on the performance of stock indices such as the German

---

46   BlackRock CEO: President Obama's new USD 12 trillion regulation is a great thing, www.businessinside.de/ 15.4.2016

47   BlackRock. Der Zauberer von OZ, WiWo 29.3.2018, p. 20

48   How Stuy town got a tourniquet while Blackstone gets Billions, http://gothamist. com/2016/03/31

DAX and the US index S&P500 and the New York MSCI index, in which 1,644 international corporations are listed. Such notes can be bought for a few thousand euros, the fees are very low. In 2000 BlackRock bought the department of the British bank Barclays that had developed this financial product. BlackRock&Co have started to sell iShares also as shares of individual DAX companies like Bayer, BASF, Siemens, but also of arms companies like Lockheed, Raytheon, Northrop Grumman, Safran. If the value of the iShares rises with the DAX value or the value of the Lockheed share, the value of the iShares automatically rises in train.

Apart from BlackRock, Vanguard and State Street also deal in ETF and iShares on a large scale. Together, these Big Three dominate three quarters of the world market with an estimated volume of USD 4 trillion (as of 2017).[49] They control the issuance, sale and repurchase of iShares by date, quantity, company and national and other entities based on unique insider knowledge. Increasingly, robots are using algorithms to control index funds and advise customers "personally".[50]

Via ETF and iShares, the Big Three are additional shareholders in the respective companies. In this way, the large capital organizers create a further source of income, operations and power for themselves. They let the little people participate in the big, economically nonsensical, even harmful business. The people fever along and then hope that "the stock markets" and the other "markets" will continue to rise.

In the financial sector, it is almost naturally assumed that the growing ETF trade will also contribute to the formation of a new bubble – and at some point a financial crisis will erupt again, on whose rotten financial products insiders will be able to place counter-bets, as was the case before the last financial crisis.[51]

Political influence networks

In order to safeguard these practices, BlackRock is expanding political influence networks in all important countries. The capital organizer brings renowned ex-politicians and ex-bankers into its committees.

---

49   The Three Largest Players have a 70 % Market Share in USD 4 Trillion Global ETF Industry, www.forbes.com 17.5.2017, downloaded 23.2.2018

50   Robo-Stox-ETF: Neue Revolution bringt Milliardengewinne, https://www.boerse-online.de 29.4.2016

51   Börsengehandelte Fonds werden immer beliebter, Süddeutsche Zeitung 5.3.2018

USA: Democrats are good, Republicans are also good

As is customary in US companies, Fink set up a Political Action Committee (PAC), to which senior executives in particular donate more or less voluntarily. The donations are judiciously distributed to both established US parties, Republicans and Democrats.

BlackRock had grown large with the deregulation seen under Presidents Clinton and Obama, Democratic Party. In 2013, Cheryl Mills, the chief of staff of then Secretary of State Hillary Clinton, became a member of the BlackRock Supervisory Board. Fink was considered a possible Treasury Secretary. Some members of the Obama administration switched to BlackRock.[52]

At first Fink could not approve the harsh criticism by the subsequently elected candidate Donald Trump of the greed of Wall Street and the corrupt swamp of politics in Washington. But after a year of Trump's government, Fink said, "Trump was good for the US economy and therefore good for the global economy." He praised Trump's corporate tax cuts and the termination of "asymmetric" free trade agreements, which were unfavorable for the US. Fink forthrightly praised Trump's mission "to make America great again".[53]

Switzerland, France

In Europe, Fink brought Philipp Hildebrand, former president of the Swiss Central Bank, to the global supervisory board as an influential agent.

In France, Jean-Francois Cirelli was appointed President of BlackRock France, also responsible for Luxembourg and Belgium. The top manager of the energy group Gaz de France has been active since President Jacques Chirac as a privatizer of the French energy industry and is still a member of the supervisory boards of French energy groups.[54]

UK

In the UK, Fink immediately brought the former finance minister of the Tories, George Osborne, into the BlackRock Research Institute as a supplement to Hildebrand. During his tenure, the minister had met with BlackRock representatives at least five times. He also earned money on the side for speeches

52   Larry Fink and His BlackRock Team Poised to Take Over Hillary Clintons Treasury Department, The Intercept March 2, 2016

53   Blackrock chief executive says Donald Trump has been good for the global economy, www.cityam.com 26.1.2018

54   Jean-Francois Cirelli est nommé président de Blackrock France, L'Agefi.fr 30.11.2015

to various US investors: GBP 85,000 from Citibank, GBP 68,000 from PE-Investor Centerbridge and GDP 40,000 from BlackRock.[55]

Osborne now remains a Member of Parliament and receives EUR 750,000 a year from BlackRock for four working days a month. His task: to push forward pension reform, which he had already promoted in the UK, at the European Commission in Brussels as well. Following the reform in April 2015, Osborne's Chief of Staff, Robert Harrison, was given the post of Strategy Manager at the British BlackRock subsidiary.[56]

Germany

In Germany, too, BlackRock draws on leading personnel of government-near enterprises and of government parties. Christian Staub of Allianz/PIMCO became Germany CEO of BlackRock, simultaneously responsible for Switzerland, Austria and Eastern Europe. He was succeeded in 2018 by Dirk Schmitz of Deutsche Bank. Former Deutsche Bank CEO Jürgen Fitschen became Chairman of the Supervisory Board of the Vonovia housing group, which is controlled by BlackRock&Co, in 2018.

In 2016, Friedrich Merz, the former head of the CDU parliamentary group in the Bundestag, was appointed chairman of the supervisory board of BlackRock Germany – to the delight of the business press. As a politician, Merz had already promoted the fully-funded private pension, then advised PE investors as a partner in the US law firm Mayer Brown and cultivated close relations with the elected and unelected US elite as chairman of the Atlantikbrücke (Atlantic Bridge).[57]

BlackRock provides advice not only on financial, but also on foreign policy. Since 2015 not only the German finance ministers Schäuble (CDU) and Scholz (SPD) met with Lawrence Fink, but also the German foreign minister Gabriel (SPD). The head of the Federal Chancellery, Braun, as well as Finance State Secretary Kukies, who had previously worked for Goldman Sachs, also held talks with BlackRock representatives. Merz was also involved in several meetings since 2017.[58]

---

55   Buy, George? World's largest fund manager hires Osborne as advisor, The Guardian 20.1.2017

56   George Osborne to be paid 650.000 pounds for working one day a week, The Guardian 8.3.2017

57   Das Comeback des Friedrich Merz, HB 2.11.2018

58   Antwort der Bundesregierung auf die Kleine Anfrage des Abgeordneten Fabio de Masi/

European Commission and ECB

From 2011 to 2018, the BlackRock representative office in Brussels increased its lobbying outlays tenfold from EUR 150,000 a year to EUR 1.5 million. The anti-corruption organization Transparency International calculates that EU Finance Commissioner Jonathan Hill did not meet with financial company lobbyists as often as with BlackRock in 2015/2016. Finance Watch notes that capital organizers like BlackRock invest millions to flood decision-makers with long statements and invite them to events "to play down the risks of their business".[59]

And, indeed, the BlackRock lobbyists in the EU capital, led by George Osborne, also succeeded in getting the European Commission to present a regulation on private pensions in 2017.

So much influence with so few shares?

Many citizens can't imagine why BlackRock&Co, with their three or ten percent stake in a company, can have such a big influence.

What is more, BlackRock stresses that they are merely trustees and only *manage* the capital for their clients. But that is not true from a legal point of view. Because for the 10 or 50 million US dollars or euros of a customer and investor, BlackRock founds a company shell, i.e. a letterbox company, which does not bear the name of the customer but that of BlackRock, e.g. BlackRock Holdco 4 LLC, BlackRock Netherlands B.V. And BlackRock exercises the voting rights in the shareholders' meetings, not the clients.

BlackRock&Co are by far the largest shareholder block in the most important companies with their 30 to 40 percent stakes and have far more influence instruments than the other shareholders.

The Influence Toolbox

BlackRock&Co have the board members of the corporations regularly come to the "roadshow" in New York, San Francisco or Houston and put pressure on them: "We have to use the power of our voices, we have to talk to the board and supervisory board and sometimes push for fundamental changes. And

---

Die Linke, Bundestagsdrucksache 19/6652 vom 5.12.2018

59   Ein Gesicht für den Riesen. Ex-Politiker Friedrich Merz soll für die Investmentfirma Blackrock Lobbyarbeit machen und neue Kunden finden, Süddeutsche Zeitung 18.3.2018

that's what we do. That's our job," says BlackRock boss Fink.[60] Johannes Teyssen, head of the Eon power group, reports: "They have us show up."[61]

In the EU, BlackRock&Co do not comply with national stock corporation laws, which lay down the supervisory duty of the members of the supervisory boards. Fink maintains a personal relationship with the chairmen of the supervisory boards of Siemens, Lufthansa, Eon and Deutsche Bank.[62] BlackRock&Co do not delegate members to the supervisory boards, but rather withhold information from the supervisory boards and establish their own decision-making procedure beyond the law. In Germany, they are thus also violating the Codetermination Act.[63]

There are also other instruments:
First, BlackRock&Co know about all important companies, including the competition in the same industry.

Second, BlackRock&Co are co-owners of the major companies and banks in the major Western economies: the US, Germany, the UK, France, Italy, Spain, and influence governments and financial institutions.

Third, BlackRock&Co are co-owners of the rating agencies that set the credit terms for companies and sovereigns. BlackRock&Co are also co-owners of the largest consultancies, such as Accenture and Capgemini.

Fourth, companies are also dependent on services provided by BlackRock&Co (risk analysis, financial management).

Fifth, BlackRock&Co influence the performance of the company's shares and thus also exert pressure on the members of the Management Board and Supervisory Board, whose performance is measured by the share value. In addition, the value of the personal share depots of the Management Board members depends on this.

Sixth, the largest capital organizers – BlackRock, Vanguard, State Street, Capital World, Wellington, Fidelity, Norges – coordinate their voting behavior at shareholder meetings. This is all the easier because Vanguard, State Street, Capital World, Wellington, Fidelity, Norges&Co are also shareholders of BlackRock.

---

60   "Die Deutschen haben zu viel Angst", Spiegel-Gespräch mit Larry Fink, Chef des weltgrößten Vermögensverwalters Blackrock, Der Spiegel 12/2015, p. 77

61   Blackrock. Der Zauberer von OZ, WiWo 29.3.2018, p. 20

62   Wie BlackRock die Konzerne kontrolliert, WiWo 2.4.2018

63   Alexander Sekanina: Finanzinvestoren und Mitbestimmung, Mitbestimmungsreport 42, Düsseldorf 4/2018

Seventh, BlackRock&Co coordinate their votes through the voting consultants they pay, such as ISS Corporate Solutions and Glass Lewis.[64]

The other winners

BlackRock&Co have "renowned" helpers who also earn very nicely. On the one hand there are the lenders used by BlackRock, who, for example, raise the double-digit billion euro Monsanto purchase price for Bayer, in this case the banks Credit Suisse, Morgan Stanley, Goldman Sachs – and BlackRock&Co are again involved as major shareholders in all of them.

In the case of mergers and acquisitions, many advisers earn on transaction costs: the sale of patents, land and parts of companies has to be arranged, politicians, trade unionists, the media and anti-trust authorities must be brought onside.

The fees for law firms such as Freshfields, auditors such as PWC and PR agencies such as Finsbury for a merger such as Bayer-Monsanto add up to around USD 2 billion. In the case of the Linde-Praxair merger, which has not yet been completed, this amounts to an estimated EUR 940 million.[65] The auditors also earn money by relocating the legal headquarters of the merged group to a financial haven.[66]

Sovereign wealth funds

States have also adopted the BlackRock pattern and set up sovereign wealth funds. Some Gulf states such as Kuwait, Qatar, the United Arab Emirates and Saudi Arabia do this with their income from oil and gas sales. China lets two sovereign wealth funds CIC and SAFE manage its large foreign exchange holdings and buy shares abroad. In Germany, Gulf State funds have major stakes: Qatar at VW, Siemens and Deutsche Bank, Kuwait at Infineon. But none of them have a presence remotely like that of BlackRock&Co – with one exception, the Norwegian sovereign wealth fund Norges.

64   Michelle Celarier: The Mysterious Private Company Controlling Corporate America, https://www.institutionalinvestor.com, January 29, 2018

65   Wer an der Fusion von Linde und Praxair verdient, FAZ 29.9.2017

66   Neue Heimat Irland, HB 8.3.2017; Boerse online 24.11.2017; HB 7.2.2018

Portrait:
The Norwegian Sovereign Wealth Fund Norges

The Norwegian sovereign wealth fund Norges is by far the most frequent co-owner in Western capitalist companies, in Germany it is all 30 DAX companies. It is the largest sovereign wealth fund of all.

Norges is co-owner of 9,000 companies in 72 countries worldwide. The focus is on the USA, Europe and Asia/Pacific. In Germany, in addition to the 30 DAX companies, the fund has holdings in a further 167 companies, 79 financing instruments and 16 properties such as the Kranzlereck in Berlin and the SZ Tower in Munich. The total volume of all capital investments worldwide amounts to more than USD 1 trillion, i.e. no less than one sixth of BlackRock. The return for the year 2017 is given as 13.7 percent.[67]

The fund was established in 1990 and built up using state revenues from the sale of oil. It is managed by the Norwegian Central Bank. "One day the oil will be depleted, but the income of the fund will benefit the people of Norway." The money is, according to the fund itself, invested long-term, responsibly and ethically. That sounds good, but it is untrue. First of all, the term pension fund is only partly correct. In addition to pension payments to former state employees, income can also flow into the state budget. As co-owner of Black-Rock and additionally as co-owner of its main shareholder PNC, Norges is jointly responsible for the practices of BlackRock. For example, for its shares in Allianz, VW, Vonovia, Deutsche Post DHL, Fresenius und Siemens Norges uses letterbox companies in the Netherlands. Norges also organizes tax flight for its customers worldwide.

Norges has invested capital in leading environmental polluter groups such as Monsanto and RWE, the agricultural and mining group Glencore, and the major oil companies Exxon, Chevron, Royal Dutch Shell, Total and BP. When arms companies were criticized for producing nuclear bombs, Norges left Boeing, Lockheed and others, but remained co-owners of Rheinmetall, Dassault, Raytheon, Daimler and Leonardo (Italy's largest arms company), for example, which are participating in the EU's rearmament program against Russia, PESCO.[68] Norges is a co-owner of Amazon and McDonald's and has never criticized their employment conditions, which breach human rights.

---

67   https://www.nbim.no, downloaded 1.3.2018; other figures also from this website.

68   "Wir verlieren Zeit", Interview mit Alessandro Profumo, HB 15.5.2018

Norges is co-owner of Deutsche Post DHL. The company employs post-men and pseudo self-employed forwarders in precarious jobs. In 2015, it suddenly hived off 10,000 employees into 47 subsidiaries (DHL Delivery) founded against the agreement with the trade union verdi, with lower wages and inferior working conditions. This is the Norges ethic: employees in an-other country are deprived of wages and pension shares, and the profits are used generously to finance the pensions of pensioners in Norway.[69]

Top Twenty of the largest capital organizers

Name	Operative base	Tax base	Deployed capital (USD trn)
BlackRock	New York/US	Delaware	6.30
Vanguard	Valley Forge/US	Delaware	5.10
State Street	Boston/US	Massachusetts	2.80
Fidelity (FMR)	Boston/US	Bermuda	2.50
Bank of NY	New York/US	Delaware	1.90
PIMCO/Allianz	New York/US	Delaware	1.75
Capital Group	Los Angeles/US		1.70
Goldman Sachs	New York/US	Delaware	1.50
PrudentialFinancial	Newark/US	New Jersey	1.40
Amundi	Paris/F		1.20
Northern Trust	Chicago/US	Delaware	1.20
Legal & General	London/New York		1.00
Wellington	Boston/US		1.00
Wells Fargo	San Francisco/US	Delaware	1,00
Natixis Global	Paris/F		0.99
T. Rowe Price	Baltimore/US	Maryland	0.99
Nuveen	Chicago/US	Delaware	0.97
Invesco	Atlanta/US	Bermuda	0.93
AXA	Paris/F		0.75
FranklinTempleton	San Mateo/US	Delaware	0.75

---

69   Post AG: Lohndumping, Streikbruch, Profitgier, https://arbeitsunrecht.de 15.6.2015, downloaded 3.4.2018

The major financial players are co-owners of several thousand to 17,000 (BlackRock) companies, banks and other financial players around the world and, with 20 to 40 branches in other countries, each looks after tens to hundreds of thousands of investors. The ranking changes from year to year, especially in the lower ranks from 5th place downwards and especially from 10th place. The table shows the status (according to published knowledge, which is by no means reliable) from March 2018.[70] The US dominance can also be seen in small details: BlackRock boss Fink receives a basic salary of USD 25 million, the boss of the largest European financial actor Amundi, Yves Perrier, a tenth of it: USD 2.5 million.[71]

The end of Germany plc

Germany plc – until the end of the old Federal Republic that meant: The three major German banks Deutsche, Dresdner and Commerzbank together with Allianz Insurance and Münchner Reinsurance (which in turn were interlinked with the three banks) are the main owners of the large industrial companies such as Bayer, BASF, Daimler, Hochtief, Holzmann, RWE, Siemens, Mannesmann, etc.

The banks held large ownership stakes – up to 40 per cent – in the companies, earned on the loans and controlled the German economy. To this end, about four dozen members of the bank boards and supervisory boards each held dozens of supervisory board mandates in the companies. The undisputed kings of this incestuous empire were the heads of Deutsche Bank from Hermann Josef Abs to Hilmar Kopper.[72] This was actually reinforced by the "reunification" of the two German states, i.e. by the expansion of Deutschland AG to the former GDR, with the help of the Treuhand-Anstalt.[73]

---

70 https://google.de/search, downloaded 3.5.2018. The tax domicile of US companies can be seen from the Form 10-K mandatory notifications to the US Securities and Exchange Commission (SEC); the tax domicile of some US companies could not be determined. In the case of European companies, the main tax domicile is likely to be the same as the operational headquarters, but does not exclude the other use of financial havens; Amundi also has domiciles in Delaware, Dublin, Luxemburg.

71 "Europa muss sich mehr als Macht begreifen", Interview mit Yves Perrier, HB 4.5.2018

72 Cf. the standard work by Rüdiger Liedtke published from 1990 to 2005: "Wem gehört die Republik? Die Konzerne und ihre Verflechtungen. Namen-Zahlen-Fakten". In the final edition 2005 BlackRock still does not feature.

73 Werner Rügemer: Privatisierung in Deutschland. Von der Treuhand zu Public Private Partnership. Münster 2008, p. 38ff.

Government program "Unbundling of Germany plc"
Then in the early 2000s, the SPD/Green government under Chancellor Gerhard Schröder laid the expanded business location of Germany at the feet of the new investors. The CDU/CSU/FDP government under Chancellor Helmut Kohl had already done some preparatory work. The most important step towards US-led globalization was the dominant role of US consultants in the privatization of the former GDR companies by the Treuhand-Anstalt 1990 – 1994.

After the 1998 Bundestag elections, the Anglo-American business press polemicized: "Germany – the sick man of Europe". The leading Wall Street bank Goldman Sachs criticized the all too generous welfare state and called for radical reform of the welfare systems, decentralized wage formation, pension cuts and further privatization. It was also emphasized that the economically pivotal but weakly growing Federal Republic of Germany would endanger the euro if it continued without "reforms". The EU would then no longer be so attractive for US investments and as a sales market for US products.[74] The US Chamber of Commerce in Germany and the US rating agencies followed suit and called for further deregulation of the labor market.[75]

Between 1999 and 2003, Schröder was in close contact with Wall Street – unnoticed by both state and private mass media. This was organized by his personal friend Sanford ("Sandy") Weill, founder and chairman of Citigroup, then the largest financial services provider in the Western world. The German Social Democrat and "the grey eminence of the banking world" had enjoyed "a close friendship between men" for years.[76]

Schröder was invited to give the eulogy to his friend Sandy at the Johns Hopkins University when he received the Global Leadership Award. The next day, Wall Street's second most powerful banker, Hank Paulson, head of Goldman Sachs, invited him to a meeting with 17 handpicked US bank and corporate executives. Result: "US business leaders consider it extremely important that Germany tackles the planned reforms".[77]

---

74   The sick man of the euro, The Economist 3.6.1999

75   Werner Rügemer: Ratingagenturen. Einblicke in die Kapitalmacht der Gegenwart. Bielefeld 2. Auflage 2012, p. 93f.

76   HB 25.11.2003

77   A Transatlantic Business Giant: Fred Irwin, The Atlantic Times August 2007; Werner Rügemer: Warum Bundeskanzler Schröder an der Wall Street für die Agenda 2010 warb, junge Welt 9.1.2004

The unbundling of Germany plc

Schröder pushed the critical finance minister Oskar Lafontaine out of the government, took advice from McKinsey, Roland Berger Consultants and the Bertelsmann Foundation. Then the Agenda 2010 brought tax cuts for companies, the labor market "reform" through the four Hartz laws, and increased personal contributions for the insured in the social systems. The consulting firms Accenture, Ernst&Young (now: EY) and Bearing Point were called in to redesign the employment offices. The overarching motto was "Unbundling Germany plc".[78]

From 1999 onwards, there was a deluge of investor incentive laws: Tax Relief Act (1999, reduction of corporation tax on retained profits); Tax Adjustment Act (1999, reduction of taxes on foreign income); above all, the Tax Reduction Act (2000, tax exemption on the sale of shares in companies; reduction of corporation tax to 25 per cent); Investment Modernization Act (2003, approval of hedge funds and short sales of shares). The four Hartz laws made it possible to reduce the cost of and disenfranchise dependent labor – part-time work, temporary work, fixed-term employment, reduction of unemployment benefits and disciplining the unemployed.

In 2004, the Federal Government had multi-page advertisements published: "Germany is on the move. Germany is the European champion as the most attractive investment location".[79] The Federal Government appointed Hilmar Kopper, former head of Deutsche Bank, as Federal Commissioner for Foreign Investments, providing him with a multi-member staff and an annual budget of EUR 5.5 million. "Delicate" large-scale sales of German companies were clarified beforehand in the Chancellery. Schröder's successor Angela Merkel (CDU) also adopted this clandestine policy: the economic transformation of Germany was and is (co)decided in the Chancellery, not in the Bundestag.

BlackRock boss sets the guidelines

In the mid-1990s, only 20 percent of all shares of the 30 DAX companies belonged to foreign investors. The proportion rose steadily: to 33 percent in 2001, to 44 percent in 2005, to 53 percent in 2007 and to 58 percent in 2012.

---

78   Werner Rügemer / Elmar Wigand: Die Fertigmacher. Arbeitsunrecht und professionelle Gewerkschaftsbekämpfung. Köln 3. Erweiterte Auflage 2017, p. 181

79   e.g. in FAZ 30.12.2004

Eight percent of the shares could not be designated nationally (financial havens), meaning that only 34 percent could definitely be ascribed to German owners.[80] This pattern has continued since then.

BlackRock boss Fink is the undisputed spokesman of the new capital organizers. "Germany's top managers have received mail from the most powerful man in the financial markets this week," reports HB. "BlackRock boss Larry Fink calls on top managers to think more about the long term." Part of this thinking is that employees are not given longer-term job guarantees, stresses Fink.[81]

BlackRock&Co as co-owner of the 30 DAX companies[82]

Since 2016, business media in Germany such as SZ, HB and WiWo have occasionally reported BlackRock's shares in the 30 DAX groups. However, there is no indication of the stakes held by other major capital organizers. The often hundreds of thousands of small and employee shareholders usually own between 1 and 5 percent of the shares. The companies themselves do not name any shareholders publicly, but refer to "free float". In addition to the major shareholders listed in the table, usually between one and four dozen more "institutional investors" are co-owners; they remain below the 3 percent reporting threshold applicable in Germany. In particular, the shares of BlackRock and the other large capital organizers fluctuate sharply due to their business model of stock speculation. For example, the BlackRock stake in Adidas fluctuated between 3, 15, 25 from 2009 to 2015 and now stands at 5.65 percent. Percentages of "other owners" in the list are only shown if they are larger than BlackRock's. The figures reflect the subscribed capital, not the voting ordinary shares – BlackRock&Co place store on the number of shares whose continuous trading is the basis of their business model and because the board members are influenced in other ways.

---

80   Focus Money online and Die Welt 10.5.2013 with reference to a study by EY

81   Weckruf an die Dax-Chefs, HB 16.1.2018

82   Shares in percent, as of end-March 2018. The figures come from various sources and date back to the first half of 2017.

Company	BlackR.	Other Stakeholders
Vonovia	8,30	Massachusetts Financial (9,3), Norges, Deutsche Bank, AXA, BNP Paribas
Fresenius Medical	7,37	Fresenius SE (30), Norges, Allianz Global
Merck	7,20	Vanguard, College Amercia, Wellington, Fidelity, Norges
Deutsche Post DHL	7,11	German state/KfW (20), Norges, Deutsche Bank, Vanguard, Invesco, Deka, Fidelity
Münchener Rück	7,11	SEB, Credit Suisse, Peoples Bank of China, Allianz, Berkshire Hathaway/Warren Buffett, Norges
Allianz	7,05	Harris Associates, Morgan Stanley, Deutsche Bank, Vanguard, Norges, State Street
Bayer	7,00	Temasek (Staatsfonds Singapur), Sun Life, Capital World, Vanguard, Norges, Deutsche Bank
E.ON	6,75	Norges, Credit Suisse, Morgan Stanley, Société Générale
BASF	6,61	Norges, Vanguard, Amundi, Deutsche Asset, Franklin, State Street, Deka
Deutsche Bank	6,51	C-Quadrat/HNA (China, 7,9), Paramount+Supreme Universal/ Katar, Norges, Cerberus
Deutsche Börse	6,45	Invesco, Capital Group, Dodge&Cox, Franklin Mutual, Royal Bank of Scotland, Norges, Baillie Gifford
Commerzbank	6,01	deutscher Staat/KfW (15), Cerberus, Norges, Capital Group
SAP	5,93	Gründer Hopp/Plattner/Tschira (23), Vanguard, Norges, Allianz, Deutsche Bank
Siemens	5,84	Siemens family (6), Katar, Vanguard, Norges, Deutsche Bank, State Street, Deka
adidas	5,65	Groupe Bruxelles Lambert (Albert Frère), Elian, Fidelity, Norges, Capital Group

Company	BlackR.	Other Stakeholders
Linde	5,60	Norges, Sun Life, Massachusetts Financial, Dodge&Cox, Artisan Partners
Infineon	5,23	Allianz (5,7), Norges, Capital Group, Sun Life, Kuwait State fond
RWE	5,02	KEB+RW Holding (this includes the original various holdings of cities in North-Rhine Westphalia), Vanguard, Norges, Dimensional Fund, JPMorgan, State Street
Fresenius	4,94	Family-Foundation (26), Allianz Global, Norges
Deutsche Telekom	4,92	German state/KfW (32), Deutsche Bank, Norges, Vanguard, State Street, Deka, Lyxor
Covestro	4,81	Bayer AG (14), Bayer Pensionsfond (9), Goldman Sachs, Norges, Standard Life
Lufthansa	4,50	Société Générale (5,1), Lansdowne, Norges, Deutsche Bank, Templeton
Heidelberg Cement	4,49	Morgan Stanley, EuroPacific, Capital Group, Norges, Artisan Partners, First Eagle, Efiparind
Daimler	4,16	Geely (9,7), Kuwait (6,8), Renault-Nissan, Norges, Harris, Vanguard, Deutsche Bank
Volkswagen	3,58	Porsche SE (30), Katar Staatsfonds (14), Land Niedersachsen (12), Norges, Vanguard
Continental	3,22	Schaeffler family (46), Harris, Vanguard, Norges, Deutsche Bank, Henderson Global, Oppenheimer, Allianz
BMW	3,10	Famalies Quandt/Klatten (46), Capital Group, Norges, Crédt Suisse
Henkel	3,08	MFS Inernational (3,9), Vanguard, Henkel AG, Swedbank, Allianz Global, Artisan Partners, Norges
ThyssenKrupp	2,82	Krupp-Foundation (21), Cevian (18), Elliott (3), Franklin Mutual, Norges
Beiersdorf	1,49	maxingvest/family Herz (51), Beiersdorf AG (10), Norges

The German state is (still) the largest shareholder in Deutsche Telekom, Deutsche Post/DHL and Commerzbank. At VW, the state of Lower Saxony is now (still) the third largest shareholder. The cities in NRW are (still) RWE's second largest shareholder. In all cases, however, the public sector has refrained from helping to shape the companies since the investors' entry, leaving the initiative to BlackRock&Co.

"German" capital is only of strategic significance in the two car companies VW and BMW: these are the Porsche and Piech family clans, who have preserved and expanded their power and property from the Nazi dictatorship.

BlackRock&Co's influence is reinforced by the fact that BlackRock, JP Morgan, State Street, Fidelity, Capital Group, etc. are also co-owners of other shareholders included in the list, e.g. Deutsche Bank, AXA, Allianz, Crédit Suisse, etc., and that the Norwegian SWF Norges, Wellington, Vanguard, State Street, Fidelity, JP Morgan, Morgan Stanley, Capital World and Masschusetts Financial are co-owners of BlackRock.

Furthermore, BlackRock&Co are co-owners of hundreds of other companies in Germany: BlackRock e.g. Rheinmetall, Fraport, freenet, Hochtief, Rhön-Kliniken, Heidelberg Cement, Heidelberg Druck, Jenoptik, Dürr, Hugo Boss, Symrise, Delivery Hero, Kion, Morphosys, Lanxess, Scout24, Ceconomy (the Real supermarkets spun off by Metro), Zalando, Scalable Capital, Wirecard, Kali&Salz, zooplus, Wacker Chemie and ElringKlinger and in any case in thousands of US corporations that are also involved in shaping the industries and policies in Germany and the EU, such as Apple, Google, Microsoft, Coca Cola, Amazon, Facebook, Hewlett Packard, IBM.

In 2018, the BlackRock branch in Frankfurt was expanded to 150 employees. A top manager of Deutsche Bank was installed as head. In recent years, we have already invested heavily in Germany, he explained, and this should continue: "The expansion of our business in Germany is one of our strategic priorities".[83] Austria and Eastern Europe are also "served" from Germany.

The largest owners of rental apartments
The end of Germany plc can also be illustrated by an area that has so far received little attention: BlackRock&Co are by far the largest private owners of rental apartments.

---

83   Früherer Deutsche Bank-Manager wird Deutschland-Chef von BlackRock, https://www.
      boerse-online.de 17.1.2018

Vonovia

The largest rental housing group in Germany is Vonovia. It owns 355,000 apartments in all major cities. In addition, it manages 65,000 apartments of other owners. Its expansion is by no means over.

The group was formed in the early 2000s by the preparatory work of Anglo-American PE investors: 1. Terra Firma from London had initially purchased apartments from the British military leaving Germany, railway worker apartments of the privatized railway company Deutsche Bahn AG and company apartments of RWE and merged them under Deutsche Annington AG. 2. Fortress had bought the 145,000 flats of the Federal Insurance Institution and 48,000 flats of the city of Dresden. Cerberus had bought up the municipal Berlin housing company GSW (65,000 apartments).[84] All these apartments now belong to Vonovia.

After the IPO in 2015, BlackRock became Vonovia's largest shareholder with currently 8.3 percent, followed by Norges with 7.3 percent, Lansdowne Partners with 5.1 percent and Massachusetts Financial Services with 3 percent. The new owners transformed Vonovia from a German stock corporation into a European SE (Societas Europaea). The financial operations were outsourced to the subsidiary Vonovia Finance B.V. based in the financial haven of Amsterdam/Netherlands. The Group is increasingly employing high-ranking personnel from Germany to provide security. The former CEO of Deutsche Bank, Jürgen Fitschen, was appointed Chairman of the Vonovia Supervisory Board because he had "a first-class political network".[85]

Deutsche Wohnen and LEG

In addition, there are the housing groups LEG Immobilien AG and Deutsche Wohnen SE. Deutsche Wohnen was initially a subsidiary of Deutsche Bank, founded in 1998, which had purchased company apartments of the pharmaceutical group Hoechst. Following various acquisitions, Deutsche Wohnen went public. The company with 160,700 apartments, more than 100,000 of which are in Berlin, is today owned by Massachusetts Financial Services with 9.94 percent of the shares, BlackRock has 9.52 percent and Norges 6.93. BlackRock also held an indirect stake until the beginning of 2019, Vonovia held 4.99

---

84   Rainer Neef: Privatisierung großer Wohnungsbestände, https://www.gemeingut.org 3.4.2014, downloaded 24.2.2018, Berliner Mieterverein: Schwarzbuch Privatisierung, Berlin 2006

85   Fitschens Neuanfang, HB 11.5.2018

percent – this stake was sold after Vonovia had failed in a hostile takeover of Deutsche Wohnen.[86]

The Landesentwicklungs-Gesellschaft (LEG) of North Rhine-Westphalia with 130,000 apartments was initially sold by the CDU-FDP state government to two US hedge funds in 2008. Then followed the arrival of BlackRock&Co. Since then, the new owners have been BlackRock (11.6 percent), Massachusetts Financial (9.3 percent), Deutsche Bank (4.5 percent), AXA Versicherungen and BNP Paribas (3 percent each).[87]

Ancillary costs as a separate business segment
In 2018, the Bremen Regional Court ruled in favor of a tenant in the second instance: Vonovia wanted to increase the rent by almost 40 percent due to renovation and energetic improvement. The tenant's lawyer, Valentin Weiß, puts the number of similarly affected tenants at 1,500 in Bremen alone. Vonovia is also trying to use the back door of refurbishment to circumvent the statutory rent brake.[88]

Investors have cut jobs rigorously. Contracts with the previous service providers for house maintenance, garden maintenance, heating and hot water measurement, repairs, winter services and TV/Internet were terminated. Vonovia has founded its own subsidiaries with low wage earners for this purpose. From numerous cities such as Berlin, Hamburg, Dresden, Hanover, Potsdam, Cologne and Magdeburg tenant associations and controllers report: via the "insourcing" Vonovia sets excessive costs, sends wrong and undocumented ancillary bills. According to the 2017 annual report, the profits of the subsidiaries rose by 80 percent.[89]

"Swarm towns". Targeting housing shortages
Vonovia & Co bet on "swarm towns": They buy, operate, modernize and convert flats into condominiums where the influx and housing shortages are greatest. In the outskirts, apartments are allowed to go to rack – in the "swarm cities" with large inflows, such as Berlin, where the housing shortage is high, investments are made in luxury renovations, driving up rents and old tenants

---

86   Vonovia steigt bei Deutsche Wohnen aus, FAZ 2.2.2019

87   https://www.leg-wohnen.de/aktionaersstruktur/, downloaded 8.2.2018

88   Vonovia scheitert in zweiter Instanz vor Bremer Gericht, Weserkurier 22.3.2018

89   Vonovias Profit mit Nebenkosten. Die Miet-Gewinnmaschine, Der Spiegel 19.11.2018

out. Energy-efficient modernization projects, the costs of which are passed on to tenants, are also popular, even though proof of the savings on heating costs does not have to be provided.

Vonovia's rent increases in 2016 averaged 9 percent. For the first nine months of 2017, Vonovia reported an increase of 4.6 percent – this average could include rent increases of up to 40 percent.[90]

BlackRock thus promotes the rent explosion in Germany and the impoverishment and expulsion of previous tenants and families. Vonovia increased its earnings for its shareholders for 2017 by 15 percent over the previous year. For 2019, a further 15 percent is envisaged, even though Vonovia intends to curb modernization projects in the face of numerous protests by tenants. At the same time, Vonovia is calling on the legislator to deregulate building law.[91]

Housing purchases in the EU
From Germany BlackRock is also expanding to Austria, Northern and Eastern Europe. At the end of 2017 Vonovia acquired the Austrian company BUWOG with 51,000 apartments. In Sweden, Vonovia snapped up 15,000 apartments from Victoria Park in the same year because "the housing market tends to be even tighter than in Germany," says CEO Rolf Buch.[92]

Via Victoria, Sweden is to be penetrated according to the German pattern. And to get started in France, Vonovia boss Buch is waiting "for President Macron to further liberalize the housing market".[93]

With the transformation of Vonovia und Deutsche Wohnen into a Societas Europaea (SE), the German Works Constitution Act is being undercut: In an SE, there is no legal provision for a works council like under german law.[94]

A little populism...
Hildegard Müller was elected to the supervisory board for populist political reasons – the CDU politician is a member of the Central Committee of German Catholics and president of the German-Israeli Economic Association.

---

90 Erkaltete Liebe, HB 19.2.2018
91 Vonovia will Mietsteierungen kappen, HB 7.12.2018
92 Vonovia steigt in Schweden ein, HB 4.5.2018
93 Expansion im Ausland, HB 9.5.2018
94 Michael Stollt / Erwin Wolters: Arbeitnehmerbeteiligung in der Europäischen Aktiengesellschaft (SE), Düsseldorf 2012, p. 22

Christianity and Zionism are also considered as reference values for Black-Rock.

Vonovia is headquartered in Bochum, Germany. Mass entertainment is intended to counter the displeasure among tenants: The "Vonovia Ruhrsta-dion" is now being sponsored for the traditional Ruhr Area football club VfL Bochum.

The state hands over the reins to BlackRock

Even where the state is the main shareholder of a company, as in the Deutsche Post DHL group, the federal government leaves all entrepreneurial decisions to the other shareholders, namely BlackRock, Capital Group, Norges, Lyxor, Vanguard, as with Telekom, Commerzbank, VW and RWE. This was the case, for example, with the raid-like spin-off of postal services and former employ-ees into 49 subsidiaries: These companies pay lower wages. The spin-off also violated the agreement with the verdi union.[95]

In response to the Left Party's interpellation about employment conditions in the Post Group, the Ministry of Finance answered: "The position as the main shareholder does not give rise to any rights or obligations to investigate the facts in question".[96]

The German government behaves in a similar way with Deutsche Telekom AG and Commerzbank AG. Here, too, the state is the main shareholder, but all decisions are left to the co-owners BlackRock, Capital Group&Co, including excessive bonuses for senior management and commissioning of always the same rating agencies and "auditors".[97]

Of course, federal governments do not address the issue of BlackRock&Co's nationwide organized financial and tax evasion. Here, too, the financial super-visory body Bafin is complicitly out of its depth.

Germany as bridgehead for the EU

US companies, banks, consultants and the military already expanded in con-tinental Europe after the First and Second World Wars and then after the col-lapse of socialism. Germany was always the most important investment lo-

---

95   Werner Rügemer: Der deutsche Staat als Privatunternehmer, Hintergrund 3/2015, p. 68

96   Kenntnis der Bundesregierung über die Arbeitsbedingungen bei der Deutsche Post AG, Bundestagsdrucksache 18/3796, 21.1.2015

97   Rügemer: Der deutsche Staat als Privatunternehmer l.c., p. 69ff.

cation in continental Europe, as well as the most important buyer of goods, supported by the Dawes Plan (1924), Young Plan (1930) and Marshall Plan (1947). A key objective was to prevent the combined potential of Germany and the Soviet Union.[98]

With its Agenda 2010 at the beginning of the 21st century, the SPD government paved the way for even more massive, legally promoted access. In the 1990s, the IMF and the US-led military had smashed up the state of Yugoslavia,[99] US PR agencies had made nationalist and racist sentiments socially acceptable,[100] and the German federal government played a pioneering role in the EU in the diplomatic recognition of right-wing secessionist states such as Croatia.

With the help of US consultants and Wall Street banks, West German corporations had incorporated the companies of the former GDR. Germany as a business location thus formed the bridgehead for the new financial players in the EU as well. We will discuss later the pioneering role played by PE investors in Germany since the mid-1990s – even before BlackRock&Co.

In the 1990s BlackRock&Co were not yet active in continental Europe. But VW, BASF, Bayer, Siemens set up new production plants in East Germany, then in the other ex-socialist states such as Poland, Hungary, Romania and Ukraine, mainly in order to take advantage of the low wage levels possible here. Poland alone has established 300 special economic zones for this purpose, with special advantages for foreign investors. General Motors, UPS, Microsoft, Monsanto and Amazon then also settled here.

With them, BlackRock&Co are now also present here. Here the logic becomes even more drastic: the existing substance created by others is emaciated, be it the well-trained and extortable labor force, be it the modernizable industrial rest, be it the consumer market that can still be developed despite poverty. But the status of the outsourced workbench remains intact with the help of nationalist, populist and right-wing governments. The EU regularly proclaims the fight against corruption there, without success.[101]

The economies are shrinking, oligarchs get rich, millions of impoverished

---

98 Werner Rügemer: Europa im Visier der Supermacht USA, https://www.nachdenkseiten. de/?p=25959

99 Cf. Hannes Hofbauer: Experiment Kosovo. Die Rückkehr des Kolonialismus. Wien 2008

100 Jörg Becker / Mira Beham: Operation Balkan – Werbung für Krieg und Tod. Baden-Baden 2008

101 EUGH: Hohe Kriminalität, Korruption, ineffiziente Justiz, FAZ 31.10.2012

Holcim (building materials), Adecco (worldwide agency work), SwissLife (life insurance), Swiss Re (reinsurer), GAM (global asset manager), Rieter (textile machinery), Barry Callebaut (chocolate), VAT (valves), Georg Fischer (precision technology), Temenos (banking software), Forbo (floor coverings), Galenica (IT healthcare) as well as, apart from the major banks UBS and CS, in the leading private bank Julius Baer.[112]

In 2015 the leading Swiss daily newspaper established with astonishment: 82.2 percent of the shares of the 30 largest companies and banks in Switzerland belong to foreign owners; among them the "US investment companies Black-Rock, Vanguard, Templeton, Schroders and Invesco" dominate.[113]

BlackRock&Co got the management of the assets of the Swiss Old Age and Disability Insurance AHV/AVS (*Schweizer Alters- und Invalidenversicherung*) under control. It is regarded worldwide as a role model. Because the returns at BlackRock&Co are higher or expected to be higher, BlackRock has overtaken the two major Swiss banks UBS and CS and is now the largest AHV asset manager. After UBS and CS, which were demoted to second and third place, come solely members of the BlackRock family: Schroders, Western Asset Management, Pramerica, Guggenheim Partners, State Street.[114]

BlackRock also dominates the iShares/ETF market in Switzerland. In addition, BlackRock sells a fund in Switzerland to investors that combines the shares of leading Swiss companies such as Lonza, Partners Group, Schindler, Tecan, Sika and Straumann.

BlackRock expanded its Swiss branch in Geneva in 2016. After the President of the Swiss National Bank Hildebrand had to leave because of "irregularities", he immediately received his upgrade as Europe representative of BlackRock.

BlackRock&Co in Italy

BlackRock&Co's presence in Italy is comparatively thin: there are still some remnants of the old sleaze with the state and rich families. In three of the 10 largest companies, the state is still represented with in some cases large stakes, in the largest arms company Leonardo (30 percent) and in the energy

---

112   La montée en force de BlackRock en Suisse, Le Temps 22.8.2016

113   Neue Zürcher Zeitung 21.8.2015

114   Le fonds de l'AVS confie davantage à BlackRock qu' aux grandes banques, Le Temps 16.6.2016

companies Enel (23 percent) and Eni (4 percent). Likewise, family clans still have large stakes, such as Del Vecchio in the Luxottica luxury group (60 percent) and Benetton in the Atlantia construction and toll road group (30 percent).

The big capital organizers are often represented in several companies at the same time, but not as intensively and nationwide as in Germany and France. They focus on very few companies that play a leading technological role, on the leading insurance company Assecurazioni Generali and on the two large internationally active banks Unicredit and Intesa Sanpaolo. The large remainder of the economy is not being developed further on a turbo-capitalist basis. Small and medium-sized enterprises and the South are being left further behind. Telecom Italia plays a middling role. The defining owner is the French media group Vivendi, in which BlackRock, Lansdowne, Vanguard, Fidelity and Lazard have stakes; the US hedge fund Elliott holds nine percent. A Chinese company also holds a stake in Telecom Italia.

Since the financial crisis, which clobbered Italy particularly hard, Chinese companies in particular have been taking care of the important parts of the rest. Leading the way is ChinaChem as the main owner of the tire and chemical group Pirelli with 26 percent. With smaller stakes, Chinese companies are participating in the strategic opportunities of Enel, Eni, Assecurazioni Generali and FiatChrysler and, as already mentioned, Telecom Italia. The Chinese central bank People's Bank of China (PBOC) bought into the three weakened banks Unicredit, Monte dei Paschi di Siena and Intesa San Paolo.[115]

The government formed in 2018 wants to overcome relative underdevelopment and free itself from EU restrictions. Economics Minister Giovanni Tria is full of praise for the Chinese New Silk Road project. Italy is the first state in the EU and the G7 to formally support it. Since 2000, Chinese investors have invested in 600 Italian companies, very few compared with Germany and France. For this reason, Chinese investments in Italy are to be intensified, both in mechanical engineering and fashion, but also in the ports of Genova, Trieste and Monfalcone and their infrastructure, which are to be connected to the New Silk Road. Italian investments in China are also to be encouraged, as are joint projects in Africa.[116]

---

115   Auf Shoppingtour, Süddeutsche Zeitung 8.7.2015

116   Rome's ruling elite pivots towards Beijing, Financial Times 9.3.2019

BlackRock&Co in the USA and worldwide

In terms of volume, BlackRock&Co's holdings in companies and banks in the USA are naturally on a far larger scale than in Europe. Among the two dozen or so capital organizers there is a marked concentration. BlackRock, Vanguard and State Street dominate the scene as the Big Three.

Among the 500 largest US companies that belong to the S&P 500 list, BlackRock&Co are the largest single shareholders in over 450 of them, including Tesla, Apple, Coca Cola, Exxon Mobil, Ford, General Electric, General Motors, Google, Goldman Sachs, Amazon, Facebook and Microsoft. On top of this, as giant peanuts, come the 1,200 of the other 1,700 largest US companies, in which BlackRock, Vanguard and State Street together hold 40 percent of the shares (as of 2012). The next larger stakes in the S&P 500 are in the hands of the somewhat smaller capital organizers Capital Group, Wellington, Fidelity, Invesco, T Rowe Price and others.[117]

Buffet's holding Berkshire Hathaway

Even celebrated individual investors who have been successful to date cannot escape this development. While the populist leading media on both sides of the Atlantic still celebrate the "investor legend" Warren Buffet, Vanguard and BlackRock are the largest stakeholders in the holding Berkshire Hathaway, followed by the Gates Foundation, Northern Trust, Fidelity, Norges and Capital World.[118]

BlackRock&Co:
The super cartel of Western world capital

BlackRock has 70 offices in 30 countries.[119] The focus is on the USA, followed by the EU and then, some way behind, Asia. In 2012 BlackRock was already a major shareholder in 282 of the 300 largest Western corporations (mostly US groups), closely followed by Vanguard (267), State Street (247), Fidelity (239), JP Morgan Chase (219) and Capital Group (172).[120]

BlackRock thus became co-owner in 17,309 companies, banks and other

---

117   These 3 firms own corporate America, http://theconversation.com 10.5.2017

118   Berkshire Hathaway Inc.: http://money.cnn.com, downloaded 12.7.2018

119   For all figures see www.blackrock.com

120   Georgina Murray / John Scott: Financial Elites and Transnational Business, Cheltenham / Northampton 2012, p. 32.

capital organizers worldwide at the end of 2017.[121] At Vanguard et al, the number of ownerships is correspondingly lower.

As shown, Vanguard, Wellington, Fidelity, Capital World, Norges and JPMorgan also have stakes in BlackRock. The German Monopolies Commission also noted that BlackRock is in turn a co-owner of State Street and Vanguard.[122] This super-cartel is not designated as a cartel by any Western cartel authority. Here, too, the nostalgic concepts and regulations of the old capitalism fail to bite, but sugarcoat the situation.

Part of the cartel is that BlackRock advises the US government, the IMF, the Federal Reserve, the European Commission, the ECB on the bailout of banks and countries, i.e. assumes government responsibilities. The representatives of BlackRock "go in and out of finance ministries, they advise the leading central banks of the Western world. Fink knows every president of the supervisory boards and every CEO personally".[123]

In other important regions of Western capitalism, comparable financial players have not emerged, not even in the most important countries, Germany and Japan. "We do not have any significant institutional investors in Germany," complains the Deutsches Aktieninstitut.[124] Comparable capital players have only formed in France in the shape of Amundi, Natixis and AXA, and in Norway with the Norges sovereign wealth fund.

Only the large number of BlackRock-type investors, their mutual interlacing, their backing in the global US-led economic system, the number of their ownerships, and then the combination with their insider position, government relations and functions and services for other financial actors – and this in conjunction with relationships with the already rich and influential capital-giving clients, the transnational capitalist class – plus the anonymity of clients protected by BlackRock&Co: this spawns the power of the new super-cartel of BlackRock&Co.

Shareholder theatre

The annual shareholders' meetings of the large Western corporations have thus become even more of a ridiculous spectacle than they were already. Well-

---

121   Barbara Novick: Remarks at OECD Discussion on Common Ownership by Institutional Investors, Paris 6.12.2017, http://www.oecd.org/daf/competition/common-ownership-and-its-impact-on-competition.htm

122   www.monopolkommission.de/images/HG21/HGXXI_Gesamt.pdf, p. 228

123   BlackRock. Der Zauberer von OZ, WiWo 29.3.2018, p. 20

124   Das Ausland setzt auf den DAX, HB 26.4.2018

known traditional companies in Germany such as Siemens and Deutsche Bank have several hundred thousand small German shareholders. They are fobbed off with sausages and glossy brochures. They listen to the words of the CEO with expectation and outrage as to how high the small, but perhaps increased dividend will be this time. Some of the larger of the small shareholders or representatives of critical shareholders sometimes express fierce criticism. But their tiny percentage of votes are powerless. The representatives of BlackRock&Co say nothing at all, give the nod without comment to the Board's proposals – they have long negotiated the decisions behind the scenes. "Shareholder" capitalism – that was once upon a time, long, long ago.

With high ethos completely free of morals

Of course, BlackRock has an elaborate moral code: Code of Business Conduct and Ethics. "Social responsibility" and "high standards" are written large. Even detractors with a critical reputation shower their buddy Lawrence Fink with praise; Joseph Stiglitz, the critical Nobel Prize winner: "Larry is convinced that capitalism must reinvent itself... he is fighting for the right cause."[125]

But in the third paragraph of the moral code the bottom line becomes clear: the ultimate goal is to "exceed the expectations of our clients". Employees are treated as "human capital", trimmed by specialized programs to "high performance" and "performance attitude". The aim is to train "great managers and leaders".[126] So the whole ethic is to generate the highest possible profit for the rich, anonymous clients. Universal human rights and the social and labor rights they contain, as well as international law, do not appear anywhere in the Code of Ethics.

Performance-free manager income

Just as BlackRock grants its own executives a share in the profits – strictly differentiated according to the hierarchical level – it also promotes this in the companies in which BlackRock&Co are co-owners.

Deutsche Bank, for example, may have been charged and convicted hundreds of times worldwide for fraud for years, face billions in fines, be over-indebted and on the verge of bankruptcy – since the financial crisis, the incomes of its top managers have risen ever faster. In 2017, 705 managers were income

---

125   BlackRock. Der Zauberer von Oz, WiWo 29.3.2018, p. 24

126   www.blackrock.com.corporate/responsability/human-capital, downloaded 19.3.2018

millionaires: one year earlier, at 316, it was less than half. 50 Deutsche Bank executives earned between EUR 3.5 and 8 million in 2017, more than the CEO.[127]

Environment polluters

BlackRock&Co do not "want" to pollute the environment. But they have and let it happen, as major shareholders in the largest companies in coal mining and lignite combustion, pesticide use, falsified car exhaust emissions, water privatization in India and Brazil (Nestlé...). The fact that the UN has declared free access to clean drinking water a human right[128] – BlackRock&Co promote the opposite. BlackRock, Vanguard, BPCE, Capital Group and the oh so highly ethical sovereign wealth fund Norges are involved in the destruction of the rainforest in Brazil through the Swiss agricultural and mining group Glencore.[129]

Degradation of dependent employees

In the moral code, "human rights" are in any case selectively boiled down into the values "inclusion" and "diversity" in the manner of the human resources concept.[130] National labor rights or the ILO conventions are not mentioned anywhere. Outsourcing as at Deutsche Post, the use of temporary workers on call, the dismissal of works council members – the law of silence about labor injustice is part of the business model.

BlackRock&Co are major shareholders in Amazon, Facebook, Microsoft, Apple, Google, which enforce extremely low wages at both the national level and in international supply chains. The German construction company Hochtief and the French construction company Vinci: they are building the facilities for the 2022 Football World Cup in Qatar. For years, they have been exploiting the state-disciplined ultra-low-cost workers under inhumane working and living conditions. None of the ILO conventions, such as free trade union activity, protection at the workplace, protection against dismissal, right to social insurance, right to paid holidays, are observed. The big ethicists of BlackRock as major shareholders cash in and remain silent.[131] Mergers lead

---

127   Mehr verdienen als der Chef, HB 19.3.2018

128   Wem gehört das Wasser? ARD die story 25.3.2015

129   Amazon Watch: Complicity in Destruction. Washington D.C. September 2018, p. 21

130   Rügemer / Wigand: Die Fertigmacher l.c. p. 65ff.

131   Amnesty International: The Dark Side of Migration. Spotlight on Qatar's Construction

to job losses: At Bayer-Monsanto alone, the number is expected to be 12,000, initially.

Corruptive health hazards

BlackRock, Vanguard, State Street, Price T Rowe, Lazard, Wellington, Massachusetts Financial have long been major shareholders in Medtronic, the world's largest manufacturer of medical devices, i.e. implants such as pacemakers and hip joints. For decades, the company has bribed doctors, paid hush money to injured patients, and delivered inadequately tested devices.[132]

Armament and War: Conscious Sleepwalking

BlackRock, Capital Group, Vanguard and State Street are the largest owners in the arms companies involved in the production of nuclear bombs, each with over USD 30 billion: Lockheed, Boeing, Honeywell, Northrop, General Dynamics, Airbus. BlackRock focuses in this order on Boeing, Honeywell, Lockheed, Northrop (all USA), Airbus (European Union), General Dynamics (USA), Safran (France) and BAE Systems (UK).[133]

In Germany, BlackRock is Rheinmetall's largest stockholder. The company circumvents export restrictions imposed by German law by outsourcing production facilities, for example to South Africa and Sardinia. Tanks are delivered to war zones and to warring parties in breach of international law such as Saudi Arabia (war against Yemen). Rheinmetall CEO Armin Pappberger is in favor of rearming the EU and NATO against Russia: "We must not just rely on America or wait for Asian forces to grow – Europe must be independent and show strength."[134] Rheinmetall is cooperating with the US armaments group Raytheon, where BlackRock is also the largest owner and also manages the pension fund.[135]

After a massacre in the USA it was publicly denounced that the assault

Sector Ahead of the World Cup. London 2013; 1,8 Millionen "moderne Sklaven" bauen die WM-Stadien in Katar, IGB und DGB: Pressemitteilung 18.12.2018; Glenn Jäger: In den Sand gesetzt. Katar, die Fifa und die Fußball-WM 2022, Köln 2018, p. 100ff.

132   Implant Files: Schweigsamer Riese, Süddeutsche Zeitung 26.11.2018; Faulty pacemaker raises concerns over medical device testing, The Guardian 25.11.2018

133   International Campaign to Abolish Nuclear Weapons (ICAN) und PAX: Don't Bank the Bomb. A Global Report on the Financing of Nuclear Weapons. 2018, p. 66f.

134   Rheinmetall träumt vom militärischen "Super-Zyklus", Die Welt 29.11.2018

135   ARD/die story 15.1.2018

rifle M&P15 produced by Smith & Wesson was the most common weapon in recent shooting-spree massacres: As a result, under BlackRock in 2016, Smith & Wesson was innocuously renamed American Outdoor Brand.[136]

BlackRock&Co don't say that they "want" to wage war and kill – that's not how their capitalism works. They professionally pursue their own profit and self-enrichment goals for themselves and their clientele. They do nothing against the internal and external conflicts, but simply give them more nourishment, more assault rifles and more tanks. Conscious sleepwalking.

Investing in themselves

BlackRock&Co exploit the existing substance of the companies in which they take up a stake. They use the profits not to create new substance, but to further increase their own value and that of their investors.

The companies in which BlackRock&Co have a stake buy back as many shares as possible from small shareholders and remove them from the market. "The motives: Fewer shares reduce supply, driving the price up. On top of that, earnings per share increase down the line because they are distributed among fewer share certificates... The dividend payout is also distributed among fewer shares, with the result that the remaining shareholders receive a higher dividend per share." And thus, the higher the BlackRock&Co stake, the more intensively companies act, as with Vonovia, Fresenius, SAP, Adidas, Allianz and Siemens.[137] This boosts the share value of the companies and at the same time the cartel-like, price-driving market power of BlackRock&Co. At the same time the economy shrinks according to the motto "reduction of excess capacity".

Undermining the foundations of the market economy

BlackRock&Co are shareholders in many large companies in the same industry at the same time. Mergers and acquisitions such as Bayer-Monsanto, Linde-Praxair and Eon-RWE are being driven forward, including the US chemical groups Dow and Dupont, Nestlé and Pfizer, Nestlé and Starbucks, the US telecom groups T-Mobile and Sprint.[138]

---

136 Where Do All The Assault Rifles Come From?, https://priceonomics.com, downloaded 10.5.2018
137 Programme ohne Fantasie, HB 28.5.2018
138 Höttges' größter Coup, HB 30.4.2018

Mergers and acquisitions lead to oligopolies and monopolies. This anti-market power of BlackRock&Co is occasionally criticized in the US-friendly FAZ: "The restrictions on competition associated with the growth of the fund companies lead to higher corporate profits. These benefit mainly American investors, who can thus continue to grow." And: these "big investors … undermine the foundations of the market economy".[139] But to what end does one have the role of leading medium of the educated academic classes and the politicians fit for government if one allows the "values" propagated by oneself to be destroyed – after all, it serves the good cause and the powerful master. Invoke "values", ineffectively grumble a little – that is the prevailing freedom of opinion.

European Union on BlackRock's coattails

BlackRock regularly makes demands on the European Union. European BlackRock Vice-President Hildebrand affirms: "Europe also has a structural problem. Labor and product markets are overregulated. Investments are not sufficiently rewarding... Politicians need to be prepared to break down existing structures." Germany was exemplary with the Hartz laws, but has since slackened in the strict eyes of BlackRock: "Germany must lead the way in Europe. In recent years, Germany has been less and less a leader when it comes to structural reforms. ... In some areas, indeed, it has even gone backwards, for example with retirement at 63."[140]

Hildebrand also calls for the cross-border merger of European banks, the disempowerment of national financial supervisors and central EU banking supervision under the auspices of the ECB[141] – which is already advised by BlackRock. Hildebrand sings from the same hymn sheet as the Rothschild banker and now French President, Emmanuel Macron.

The influence is invisible to the public, but it is swift and clear: in 2017 the German Monopolies Commission, the OECD and the EU Antitrust Authority criticized the dangerous concentration of power of BlackRock. Christian Staub, then head of BlackRock Germany, lodged a complaint with the Ger-

---

139   Die neue Macht der Fondsgesellschaften, FAZ 30.7.2016

140   Schwaches Wachstum, lasche Behörden: Finanzriese BlackRock warnt vor Risiken in Europa, Interview mit BlackRock-Vizechef Philipp Hildebrand, Spiegel online 23.11.2015

141   BlackRock-Vize Hildebrand attackiert Europas Bankenlobby und nationale Aufsichtsbehörden, Der Spiegel 25/2018, p. 56

man government. The Ministry of Economics then described the criticism as purely "theoretical conjecture" – discussion over.[142]

BlackRock advises the European Commission and the Central Bank
None of the major governments in the EU is more compliant than the German government, regardless of its party-political composition. In 2012 Finance Minister Schäuble had to take a holiday on Sylt at the request of Obama's Finance Minister Timothy Geithner in order to be "processed" away from Berlin. After the financial crisis, Geithner commissioned BlackRock to rescue banks and insurance companies. In the "selfish interest" of the USA – as Spiegel wrote – the ECB should flood the EU financial markets with cheap money, following the US model. Schäuble nodded. BlackRock became an ECB advisor. Shortly afterwards, ECB boss Mario Draghi promised "to do everything it takes".[143]

BlackRock advised and advises the ECB on its corporate and government bond buyout program. On behalf of the European Commission, BlackRock organized the stress test for the 39 largest banks in the EU, in many of which it is co-owner. BlackRock prepared the risk analyses for the bank bailouts in Ireland, Greece, the UK and Cyprus. ECB boss Draghi, ex-Goldman Sachs banker, "americanized" the European Central Bank according to the model of the US central bank Fed and also bolstered the access of US banks and investors.[144]

At the same time as the Troika, BlackRock agents were in Athens camouflaged as "Project Solar" and under the pseudonym "Claire" in Cyprus. In all these missions, the aim of the bank co-owner was directly and indirectly to rescue its own commitments.[145] In addition, advising the ECB on how to deal with endangered loans provided BlackRock with "exclusive access to European company data".[146]

"European savers lack reliable data and guidance on how to invest and plan for the future," Fink announced. That's why he paid former British Finance

142   Moritz Honert: Warum der Einfluss der globalen Geldverwalter gefährlich ist, Der Tagesspiegel 5.5.2018

143   US-Finanzminister Geithner bei Schäuble. Heimgesucht auf Sylt, SPON 30.7.2012

144   Adam Tooze: Crashed. Wie zehn Jahre Finanzkrise die Welt verändert haben. München 2018, p. 514ff., 619

145   Buchter l.c. p. 72ff.

146   Draghi holt den "König der Wall Street" als Berater zur EZB, Deutsche Wirtschaftsnachrichten 27.8.2014

Minister Osborne, who had pushed through the "pension revolution" in Britain for BlackRock. (Capital can carry out revolutions, dependent employees cannot). The lobbyist pushed through the PEPP Plan at the European Commission: *Pan European Personal Pension*. With the quality seal of BlackRock, but without a payout guarantee, employees in the other EU member states were also supposed to buy the BlackRock financial products ETF/iShares for private retirement provision.[147]

Portrait: The supreme populist: BlackRock boss "Larry" Fink

Lawrence Fink, the chairman of BlackRock's board of directors, is keen to be chummily called "Larry", and the mainstream media obediently tag along. He, who allows himself to be celebrated as the "supreme capitalist" when the unelected and the in some form elected elite are among themselves at the World Economic Forum in Davos, likes to present himself as advocate of the "little man" when criticized publicly. In populist manner, he even slips into the role of labor leader. When criticism arose in Germany in 2018 because Friedrich Merz, chairman of the board of BlackRock Deutschland AG, put his name forward for chairmanship of the Christian-lacquered CDU business party, Larry appealed from Wall Street in German for understanding among the Germans. He now wanted to introduce his company "personally". He had founded BlackRock "30 years ago with seven colleagues in a small office." The firm managed the assets of "many millions of people worldwide" – no, he did not say "assets", this time he said: "savings". Although Fink usually calls BlackRock an "asset manager" and solicits the investments of multibillionaires and multimillionaires, he now slinks into the souls of ordinary people and speaks of "savings". And among the many millions worldwide whose "savings" he manages are "workers and employees". The benefactor BlackRock, he said, provided them with "easy access to the investment markets from an investment amount of EUR 25. Your Larry Fink."[148] But to this end he does not have any mailbox companies to hand as he does for the super-rich. A populist needs only a few particles of truth to lie.

---

147   Paulo Pena / Harald Schumann: Achtung, Rentenfresser, der Freitag 26/2018

148   BlackRock – wer wir sind und was wir tun, https://www.blackrock.com/de/privatanleger/ueber-blackrock/letter, abgerufen 27.11.2018

2.
Private equity investors: The exploiters

PE investors act according to a similar pattern as BlackRock&Co, but one dimension smaller. They, too, are organizing the end of Germany plc, France plc, etc. They, too, are hastening the extremely unequal distribution of the wealth generated.

They, too, collect capital from already very wealthy clients, corporate foundations, top managers and multimillionaires. However, most of these clients belong to a lower class: they are less Ultra High Net Worth Clients and more High Net Worth Clients, i.e. without the Ultra. On average, they don't raise 50 to 100 million dollars or euros with one deposit, but maybe 5 to 50 million. Clients expect high profits and pay the PE managers annual fees of between 1.25 and 2 percent of the invested capital.

The business model
Blackstone is the biggest PE investor. The individual funds it creates with the client capital are called – according to the BlackRock pattern – Blackstone Real Estate Partners I, Blackstone Real Estate Partners II, III and IV and Blackstone Real Estate Partners Europe I – III, for example. At the third largest PE investor Carlyle, they are similarly called Carlyle Europe Real Estate Partners I, II, III and so on. The vast majority of them are domiciled in a financial haven.

With this hidden capital the PE managers buy stakes in companies. The PE investors manage their clients' capital and the company shares purchased with it on a "fiduciary" basis. But, as with BlackRock&Co, they are legally the representatives of the capital themselves, take out loans with banks in their own name with this collateral, buy the company shares and exercise the voting rights. Here, too, the actual investors remain unknown to the public, even to the companies themselves.

It is not the large public companies that are bought, but lucrative medium-sized and family businesses. Most of them are not joint-stock companies and are not listed on the stock exchange. "We are interested in mature, internationally active companies with sales of EUR one to two billion and stable cash flow," said Thomas Middelhoff, then head of the London-based PE investor Investcorp, in 2004.[149] Or one participates in the restructuring of large corpo-

---

149   Wer kauft den deutschen Mittelstand? Impulse 3/2004, p. 14f.

rations: "Selling the peripheral activities of large corporations", it's called in the consulting milieu.[150]

These investors are not interested in gutting or restructuring ailing companies, but rather they are on the lookout for gems in order to turn silver into gold, so to speak. PE investors do not buy into as many companies as possible like BlackRock&Co, but focus on a few in the short term. Over a period of two to seven years, these are restructured, exploited – and then resold or floated on the stock exchange – this exit is prepared from day one.

In terms of volume, everything is one size smaller than with BlackRock&Co. The largest PE investor Blackstone – from which BlackRock was founded – currently has USD 333 billion in capital employed, a twentieth of BlackRock's total. Blackstone has 2,200 employees, only about one-sixth of BlackRock's workforce. But you need comparatively more personnel, because clients who, although super-rich, are less rich create more work.

Return between 15 and 40 percent

These investors want to achieve a return far above the traditional forms of capital realization, also above BlackRock&Co. As a rule of thumb, Middelhoff spoke of an "average return of 25 percent".[151] Industry leader Blackstone announced a "30 percent return".[152] The British investor Candover reported a "33 percent annual return".[153] Individual investor funds, e.g. from Permira, even yielded returns of 85 percent.[154] The heyday with such returns lasted until 2007. In the meantime, the figure oscillates around 15 percent.

The high return is to be achieved with a combination of various instruments. The purchase price should be as low as possible. This is facilitated by the fact that only companies are bought that are not listed on the stock exchange and are therefore not subject to the standardized valuation of stock corporations. During price negotiations, the future privileges of the previous owners (additional lifelong pension, consultancy contracts) and the top executives (they receive shares and extra bonuses) are already included. This makes

---

150   Stefan Jugel (Hg.): Private Equity Investments. Praxis des Beteiligungsmanagements. Wiesbaden 2003, p. 263

151   Die Welt 30.11.2004

152   Finanzinvestoren nehmen das Schicksal der Deutschland AG in die Hand, FAZ 31.3.2005

153   Interview mit Candover-Manager Marek Gumienny, FAZ 7.6.2005

154   Finanzinvestoren nehmen das Schicksal der Deutschland AG in die Hand, Die Zeit 31.3.2005

it easier for them to agree to a lower selling price. Auditors such as PWC, EY and KPMG as well as commercial law firms such as Freshfields, Allen & Overy and White & Case, the investors' eternal advisors, establish low purchase prices for a high fee in their reports.

The investor then forces the company in its sights to take out loans so that the investor can procure the purchase price: The company slides into debt and is put under pressure to reduce costs.

Most important operation: The exit
After the purchase, the "exploitation cycle" begins. It is meant to last a maximum of seven years: The profits are generated firstly through redundancies of employees, wage cuts, reductions in benefits above the collectively agreed pay scale, through overtime with equal pay, through increased use of temporary workers and though outsourcing. Secondly, parts of the company, including land and real estate, can be sold. Thirdly, "tax optimization" is also being worked on, for example by setting up a holding company in a financial haven to which the legal and tax domicile is relocated. Fourthly, the investor extracts profits at an early stage, which are also financed with loans: The industry speaks of "recap".

The main profit, however, is to be generated in the third phase, through the exit: the streamlined, restructured company is sold on to the next investor or floated on the stock exchange. This exit is the most important event to which all measures during the exploitation cycle are geared.[155]

Wall Street and City of London: The new investor type
In the 1970s, criticism of the banking regulation of the reform era (New Deal, President Franklin Roosevelt, 1930s) gained momentum in Wall Street banks. Individual bankers set up PE departments inside or outside their banks or independent PE firms, much like Lawrence Fink had done in the run-up to founding BlackRock.

Goldman Sachs managers founded the PE subsidiary Whitehall. Citibank Venture Capital emerged from the investment bank Citicorp, later trading as CVC. KKR, still the second largest player in this league, was founded in 1976 by the three managers Kohlberg, Kravis and Roberts from the investment bank Bear Stearns.

---

155 Wolfgang Lenoir: Gestaltung des Exits als begleitender Prozess, in: Stefan Jugel ibid., p. 237ff.

Barings Capital was founded from the Barings Bank in London, later trading as BC Partners. The Bank of England, together with the largest British banks, founded the PE subsidiary 3i in 1986. The London investment bank Schroders founded Schroder Ventures in 1985 and renamed it Permira in 2001. Such abstract pseudonyms, which do not (and should not) mean anything to the public, are typical.

With bribery of officials and campaign financing for Republican politicians, KKR succeeded in getting state pension funds of individual US states, starting in Oregon, to have their capital managed. Capitalist newcomers such as the New York real estate speculator Donald Trump belonged to the scene. In Washington, elaborate lobbying was mounted. Deloitte's auditors issued courtesy opinions.[156]

In 1997, US Professor Myron Scholes was awarded the Nobel Prize for Economics for this shortly before his hedge fund Long Term Capital Management (LTCM) went bust and its creator was convicted of tax evasion. But he is still the undisputed director of PE investor Janus Capital,[157] and the Nobel Prize Committee has never criticized him, and this Nobel Prize will continue to be awarded predominantly to academically varnished propagandists of crisis-fueling and self-enriching financial operations.

Blackstone shaped the business model

In 1985 Peter Peterson and Stephen Schwarzmann founded the PE company Blackstone. Peterson was head of the New York investment bank Lehman Brothers from 1973 to 1984, where Schwarzman headed the mergers and acquisitions department. They combined the name Blackstone from their name components Schwarz (German=black) and Peter (Latin petra=stone). As a former trade minister under US President Richard Nixon, Peterson had already tried in vain to relax the banking laws. After a short spell he returned to Lehman in frustration and took deregulation into his own hands with Blackstone.

With the help of client capital and bank loans, Blackstone has since bought and sold around 600 companies, initially in the USA. The client assets under management of currently USD 333 billion are invested in 90 companies, in the

---

156   Sarah Bartlett: The Money Machine. How KKR manufactured Power and Profits. New York 1991, p. 144ff., 231f., 258ff.

157   HB 15.7.2014

USA, early on in the UK and since the end of the 1990s also in Germany, the EU and worldwide.[158] Blackstone's 2,200 employees work in nine US offices as well as in London, Paris, Düsseldorf, Madrid, Tokyo, Hong Kong, Singapore, Beijing and the Gulf States.

Blackstone is also the owner of Intertrust, the largest mailbox broker in the Netherlands,[159] with the Dutch state itself being the EU financial haven most frequently chosen by US groups, alongside Ireland and Luxembourg.

Like the vast majority of PE companies, Blackstone was initially a limited partnership. As a leading investor of this type, Blackstone was able to go public itself in 2008.

Networked with Democrats and Republicans
The rise of Blackstone, but also of the business model in general, was made possible by political relations at the highest level. Under the "democratic" President William Clinton, legal restrictions were formally lifted in the early 1990s. One of the Blackstone employees, Roger Altman, who had also come from Lehman Brothers, became deputy finance minister in the Clinton administration in 1993. He played a leading role in NAFTA (1994, US with Canada and Mexico), the new aggressive type of free trade agreement.[160]

Peterson expanded the political network in a different direction after the founding of Blackstone. In 1985, he succeeded David Rockefeller as President of the Council on Foreign Relations (CFR), in which bankers, entrepreneurs, business lawyers and PR agencies are involved in US foreign policy. From 2000 to 2004, Peterson also served as head of the Federal Reserve Bank of New York, which oversees Wall Street. Since 2007, he has devoted himself to the Peterson Institute for International Economics. In 2012, he sponsored the Republicans' "Fix the Debt" campaign: the government should cut social spending in order to take on new debts. He was described as "the most influential billionaire in the US"[161] – he is unknown to the public in the US and Europe.

---

158 Jakobs: Wem gehört die Welt? ibid., p. 104ff.

159 Wikipedia: Waterland B.V., downloaded 13.1.2017

160 Lori Wallach: Zwanzig Jahre Freihandel in Amerika, Le Monde Diplomatique 11.6.2015

161 Los Angeles Times 2.10.2012

Portrait: Stephen Schwarzman/Blackstone

Schwarzman graduated from the elite universities of Yale and Harvard Business School and became a director at Lehman Brothers. He co-founded Blackstone in 1985. Before going public, Schwarzman was required by US law to publish his salary for the first time: USD 398 million in 2006. That was four times as much as the incomes of all the CEOs of all 30 German DAX companies combined.[162] At the time of the IPO he remained the largest owner with 45 percent, the next two co-owners Jonathan Gray and Hamilton Kames have only 8 and 6.3 percent respectively. As leading executives at the same time, they reward themselves with a 20 percent dividend on their company's profits; for Schwarzman, that was about USD 640 million dollars in 2015, plus bonuses of USD 160 million dollars for him.[163]

His private wealth is estimated at USD 10 billion. His main residence is a 34-room apartment on New York's Park Avenue, once owned by John D. Rockefeller. He maintains villa-like estates on Long Island, in St. Tropez (France), Jamaica and Palm Beach/Florida. Politically he is extremely right-wing, on the right wing of the Republican Party, but also donates to the Democratic Party. The "King of Wall Street" celebrated his 60th birthday – he had not yet been replaced in this function by the BlackRock boss – with the State Department boss Condoleezza Rice, her predecessor Colin Powell, with Finance Minister Henry Paulson (previously Goldman Sachs), New York Mayor Michael Bloomberg and – Christianity belongs to this kind of private capital – Archbishop Edward Egan. For their entertainment, Schwarzman engaged the pop singers Rod Stewart and Patti LaBelle.[164] When US President Barack Obama proposed that the income of PE managers should no longer be taxed with the lower capital gains tax (as is the case for companies), but with the higher income tax, the professing Jew Schwarzman went berserk: "This is like Hitler's attack on Poland."[165] In 2017 he chaired the Strategic and Policy Forum of US President Trump. At the 2018 World Economic Forum, he defended Trump because

---

162   Blackstone-Chef streicht 400 Millionen Dollar ein, Der Spiegel 11.6.2007

163   Hans-Jürgen Jakobs: Wem gehört die Welt? Die Machtverhältnisse im globalen Kapitalismus. München 2016, p. 108

164   Der König der Wall Street feiert Party, www.faz.net 11.2.2007

165   Jewish Billionaire on Trump's Business Council Says People Called him 'Nazi' After Charlottesville, Haaretz 14.9.2017; "Wie Hitlers Angriff auf Polen", Süddeutsche Zeitung 18.8.2010

he was making the USA "the exemplary place of the developed world", also in distinction to communist China.[166] The Blackstone boss organizes a three-digit million scholarship program with other companies so that thousands of US citizens can study in Beijing – China is to be conquered from within, while Trump is also preparing the military conquest.

UK as bridge

These investors began in the USA with the purchase and short-term exploitation of medium-sized companies there that were not listed on the stock exchange. At the same time, these new investors also became active in the UK, traditionally the preferred investment location for US capital in Europe. During the decade until around 1990, Blackstone, KKR and CVC practically confined their shopping spree to the UK alone. They set up branches in the City of London. CVC alone bought 54 companies in the UK from 1981 to 1989.[167]

CVC made its first purchases in continental Europe in Germany from 1984 (HDI-Versicherung, Eisenwerke Kaiserslautern, Elogica), in France from 1986, in Italy from 1988, in Spain from 1989, in the Netherlands from 1991 and in Belgium from 1996. The number of purchases remained small. Of course, CVC was also on the lookout in Asia, especially in the particularly US-friendly states of Japan, South Korea and Indonesia. Other investors such as Blackstone, Bain Capital, Cinven, 3i and KKR acted similarly.

In Germany, the new investors bought only four companies in 1984, six in 1985, only three in 1986, 14 in 1987, 23 in 1988 and 25 in 1989. Germany thus lagged far behind the UK, but well ahead of other Western European countries.[168]

Germany: Upswing after the Treuhand-Anstalt

The CDU/CSU/FDP government under Chancellor Helmut Kohl brought US advisors into the Treuhand-Anstalt. Starting in 1990, they were to help privatize the approximately 8,500 former GDR companies as quickly as possible: McKinsey, PWC, KPMG, Goldman Sachs, JPMorgan. Roland Berger Consulting was added as a German US imitation.

---

166 Davos: Blackstone-Chef Schwarzman verteidigt die US-Strafzölle, https://www.finanzen.
    net 23.01.2018

167 http://cvc.com/Our-Portfolio/Historical-Portfolio.htmx?ordertype=5,   downloaded
    2.3.2018

168 Paul Jowett / Francoise Jowett: Private Equity. The German Experience. New York / London 2011, with tables on the individual years.

The US consultants used their know-how to carry out the ruthless valuation: In most cases an ex-GDR company was worth just DM 1, and only if it received an initial government subsidy of DM 30 million. But: Those who weren't members of the CDU Economic Council had little chance as buyers. The US players were allowed to give advice, but they should not and did not want to buy; former GDR companies were neither interesting nor accessible.[169]

From 1990 to 1998, mainly PE companies from the USA, some from the UK and only a few from Germany and Sweden bought companies in Germany. The number of purchases rose steadily from 1990 (29 companies) to 1998 (67 companies). Overall, 299 companies were purchased.[170]

Occasionally, German PE companies were also set up. A former manager of Morgan Stanley, who had represented the bank in Germany, founded Equity Capital Partners (ECM) in 1995. Jens Odewald of the CDU Economic Council, who as head of Kaufhof AG had been appointed chairman of the Treuhand Board of Directors by Kohl, founded his PE company Odewald & Compagnie after the end of the Treuhand in 1996.[171]

Copycats in Western Europe and elsewhere

For example, Allianz-Versicherung founded its subsidiary Allianz Capital Partners. The French insurance company AXA founded AXA Private Equity. Indeed, from Enskilda-Bank, which belongs to Sweden's richest corporate clan, Wallenberg, three PE companies were founded: EQT, SAC (Scandinavian Acquisition Capital) and IK (Industri Kapital). However, to date only a few of these European companies have climbed into the still US-dominated league; EQT is one of these few. In the meantime, PE companies have also been founded by sovereign wealth funds in the Arab Gulf states, such as Dubai International Capital (DIC).

There was a similar pattern in other EU countries. Governments and the European Commission welcomed this, but nowhere took stock of the consequences for jobs and working conditions, debt, the environment and the economy. These investors gradually broke up the German and Western European

---

169   Werner Rügemer: Privatisierung in Deutschland. Eine Bilanz, Münster 2008, p. 38ff.

170   Paul Jowett / Francoise Jowett: Private Equity. The German Experience. New York/London 2011, see the tables on the individual years 1990 to 1998.

171   Werner Rügemer: Bis diese Freiheit die Welt erleuchtet ibid., p. 163ff.

economic culture and also the legal situation and prepared the ground for the much bigger and more powerful ones, BlackRock&Co, who were to come after the financial crisis of 2007.

In the meantime, about 6,000 PE investors are on the romp in Western capitalism. Most of them, and the largest, are located in New York. In Europe, the City of London is by far the most coveted location.

The fresh impetus with the SPD/Green government

The SPD/Green government under Chancellor Schröder thus by no means invented the "decartelization of Deutschland AG" it propagated, but accelerated and deepened it.

The West German investments in the former GDR during the reign of Kohl (CDU) brought unemployment, lower wages and a dependent location in East Germany. The primarily US-American investments in the ex-FRG, beginning in the reign of Schröder (SPD), then also brought higher unemployment, lower wages and a dependent location in the west of the united Germany.

The SPD-Green government's "Agenda 2010" in 2002 included – with the agreement of the "opposition" parties CDU, CSU and FDP – that also the sales proceeds as well as the distributed profits of the PE investors were made tax-free (Corporation Tax Law § 8b)[172] – besides the other laws already described in the chapter on BlackRock.

Because investors could now afford more in several respects and snapped up firms much more frequently and ruthlessly, public attention also increased. Trade unions woke up, and the leading media also reported what was going on – at least in the early years.

The Bosch-Telenorma and Celanese cases

The second largest PE investor, KKR, was particularly active in Germany from 1999 onwards. KKR is the abbreviation for the three founders and owners Kohlberg, Kravis and Roberts. KKR acquired inter alia the Siemens subsidiary Nixdorf, the turbine manufacturer MTU, the Duale System Deutschland (DSD, waste recycling) and, in 2000, the Bosch subsidiary Telenorma, specialized in the construction and rental of telephone systems.

---

172 Stefan Jugel (Hg.): Private Equity Investments l.c., p. 224f.

The Bosch-Telenorma/Tenovis case

Let's stick with Telenorma. KKR gave the acquired company the artificial name Tenovis. Flags with the motto "We create a common future" were hung up in the company. Everybody had to use the familiar 'Du' form of address and first name: US capital populism took charge.

After the purchase, KKR founded Tenovis Finance Limited for Tenovis on the Channel Island of Jersey. The operating company, Tenovis GmbH & Co KG, based in Frankfurt/Main, took out a loan of EUR 300 million from this letterbox company to repay the purchase price to KKR. Tenovis GmbH in Frankfurt pledged its most lucrative 50,000 rental and maintenance contracts for the loan. In turn, Tenovis GmbH lent the loan to its legal owner, Tenovis Germany GmbH, which belonged to KKR. Thus, the KKR bank debts were redeemed, KKR was debt-free, the debts now lay with the purchased company.[173]

Like other PE investors, KKR generated a further profit with the following operation: The investor sold the hereditary building rights to the company's property in Frankfurt to its own subsidiary Tenovis Germany GmbH for EUR 50 million, which ended up with KKR. Tenovis GmbH & Co KG had to pay EUR 6 million annual rent to KKR for this. For the financial operations with the letterbox company in Jersey, KKR charged EUR 11 million. Furthermore, KKR sent its own consultants to carry out all these operations. Together, they received a double-digit million euro fee out of the Tenovis cash register.

In order to break the possible resistance against the restructuring, the investor made 70 managers co-owners with together 5 percent, also a common procedure.[174] If the managers did not have enough money to buy the shares, they got cheap loans from the investor, became (small) co-entrepreneurs, but also dependent and amenable. In 2002, they wrested a 12.5 percent wage sacrifice from the employees with the promise of preserving their jobs. But of the 9,000 employees, 3,600 were made redundant. In 2004, KKR sold the skeletonized and over-indebted company to the US corporation Avaya for USD 635 million. The total profit for KKR was about half a billion dollars.[175]

---

173 Nils Klawitter: Brutale Investoren – Wie KKR ein Unternehmen skelettiert, SPON 14.4.2004

174 Peter Zaboji: Change. München 2002, p. 205

175 cf. Werner Rügemer: Investitionen ohne Arbeitsplätze, WSI-Mitteilungen 1/2015, p. 49-54I

From mid-2003 to the end of 2004, KKR distributed USD 9 billion in profits to its clients from about a dozen acquired companies.[176]

Germany as a banana republic: The Celanese Case
The case of the chemical company Celanese is particularly well documented. Thanks to a lawsuit pursued by a hedge fund manager against Blackstone many details were revealed for once. Celanese "has become a synonym for the dubious methods used by financial investors in Germany to rake in money by buying and selling undervalued companies," was how manager magazin summarized the "raid".[177]

The magazine portrayed Germany as a "banana republic" in which US investors poached. The idea that was associated with the US economy, namely that the rights of workers are not protected there, but the rights of shareholders are protected (shareholder value), was also thrown overboard: German shareholders were mercilessly outmaneuvered by Blackstone.

How to generate a low purchase price
In 2002, the Celanese major shareholder Kuwait Petroleum Corp. announced its withdrawal from the company. Blackstone emerged as the savior: We join you and you have a strong partner again! For two years, the Celanese board of directors commuted time and again to Blackstone's New York office for negotiations.

In order to reduce the purchase price, the investor commissioned an army of expensive consultants. As usual in the top league of investors, these were the "auditors" EY and PWC, the leading German law firm Hengeler Müller (permanent client i.a.: Deutsche Bank) and Goldman Sachs. This private army is networked with and dependent on investors in many ways. EY, PWC and, alternately, KPMG and Deloitte are permanent consultants, permanent assessors and permanent auditors. Law firms such as Hengeler Müller, Freshfields and White&Case and PR consultants hope for further assignments. Goldman Sachs had given Blackstone loans for the Celanese purchase.

The very low purchase price achieved in this way, however, had a high additional price, but which was also mere peanuts: The more Celanese's Man-

---

176 "Wenig Wettbewerb ist immer gut". Interview mit dem KKR-Europachef Johannes Huth, Die Welt 31.1.2005

177 Der Raubzug. Manager magazin 5/2005, p. 58

agement Board and Supervisory Board agreed to a lower purchase price, the higher they were rewarded. "The managers were involved in the success of the deal. The less the financial investor Blackstone paid for the company, the more they earned."[178]

Extra reward for managers
Those who left after the takeover received up to four annual salaries. The departing CEO received USD 3.8 million, the new CEO USD 8 million. The newly appointed Blackstone board members, US managers David Weidman and Lyndon Cole, received between USD 10 and 5.6 million in the first year 2004 alone, made up of basic salary, bonuses and share allocations.

Celanese was listed as a stock corporation in New York and Frankfurt. Blackstone immediately delisted Celanese in the USA and set up a new supervisory board in Germany. It had nothing else to do but to simulate a supervisory board according to German law and to nod off all Blackstone decisions. One of the people called in to do this was Ron Sommer, former CEO of Deutsche Telekom. Sommer had been forced to resign in 2002 because of the privatized but then over-indebted company. But such people like to act in the play "supervisory body" for a few hundred thousand dollars.

The German small shareholders, many of them former employees of Celanese, were in a losing position. New York hedge fund manager John Paulson acted more effectively. On news of Blackstone's planned involvement, he had quickly snapped up 11.4 percent of Celanese shares. "The large and the small locust, as investor lobbyists baptized the two New York investors", according to manager magazin, met up again in court. Paulson lifted the lid on the manipulations of the share and company value and justified his counter-motion for higher shareholder compensation at the shareholders' general meeting on 19 May 2005 in Oberhausen.[179]

Paulson's motion was voted down because the majority of the shares were already owned by Blackstone. But the public dispute with the "small locust" was so unpleasant for the "large locust" that Blackstone paid Paulson USD 300 million in a court settlement in New York – the German shareholders saw nothing.

---

178   Der Raubzug l.c., p. 62

179   Gegenantrag zur ordentlichen Hauptversammlung der Celanese AG am 19. Mai 2005 in Oberhausen, Pressemappe von John Paulson & Co., Inc., http://www.presseportal.de/ story_rss.htx?nr=680819, downloaded 24.5.2005

The raid

Blackstone had paid USD 650 million to buy Celanese. Soon after the purchase, Blackstone had paid itself a "special dividend" of USD 500 million. Blackstone was paid USD 110 million for consulting services. The following year, Blackstone took Celanese back to the New York Stock Exchange and collected USD 800 million for a partial sale of the shares. By 2007, the investor had sold the remaining shares for USD 1.7 billion. After deducting the purchase price, the net profit within just over a year was USD 2.9 billion.[180]

Such a result is only possible if many play along. According to manager magazin, this is a "stitch-up by an alliance of investors, managers and consultants at the expense of shareholders".

The German stock exchange supervisory authority did not bother about the documents that speculator Paulson presented to the court with the accusation of fraud, thus winning the USD 300 million. The US Securities and Exchange Commission (SEC) began investigations, but let them fizzle out. Even the comparatively powerful US Securities and Exchange Commission was unable to cope with Blackstone's practices.

Ascent and successful disappearance

In the UK and Sweden, PE investors initially celebrated their greatest successes. Between 1999 and 2005, however, they bought around 2,000 large medium-sized companies and group subsidiaries in Germany. The US financial investors were the "New Masters" who buy "the fillets of the German economy".[181]

Blackstone, KKR&Co, which had initially operated from London and New York, now established branches in Germany. German top managers switched to the investors, for instance Heinz-Joachim Neubürger from the Siemens board of directors to KKR.[182] Blackstone appointed Roland Berger, the leading corporate and government consultant, to the Supervisory Board.[183]

It had symbolic significance: In 2004, Deutsche Bank sold 50 office buildings to Blackstone and rented them back. Deutsche Bank thus provided the foremost US investor with returns of between 15 and 25 percent – a return

---

180   David Carey / John Morris: King of Capital. New York 2010, p. 205

181   Neue Herren, WiWo 48/2004, p. 43

182   Die Helfer der Firmenfledderer, SZ 15.3.2007

183   HB 21.10.2004

that boss Ackermann announced as his bank's goal, but never achieved himself.[184]

In the early years from 1999, HB, FAZ and Die Welt reported in detail
on the acquisitions of well-known companies such as Telenorma, Celanese,
Demag (crane construction), ATU (auto parts Unger), Rodenstock, Ger-
resheimer Glas, MTU, Dynamit Nobel, Tank&Rast etc. In many cases even
these capital-friendly media scandalized the "plundering of German companies". Nevertheless, according to a study by EY, in Germany "things would only
really get going from 2005".[185]

The "locusts" criticism by SPD chairman Franz Müntefering

But then there was a censure break: In 2005, BILD published a statement
by SPD chairman Franz Müntefering, who was also Labor Minister in the
Grand Coalition: "Some financial investors do not give a thought to the people whose jobs they destroy – they remain anonymous, have no face, attack
companies like locusts, graze them off and move on. We will fight this form
of capitalism."[186] Müntefering was referring to the Old Testament, in which locusts are described as plagues of Egypt and devastators of the Garden of Eden.

Müntefering had not named any investors. But the cause was clear: In
Müntefering's Sauerland home, the world market leader in bathroom fittings,
Grohe, had been acquired by BC Partners in 1998 and sold on to Texas Pacific
Partners (TPG) in 2004. Both brutally gutted the company: "The new boss
David Haines appointed by TPG dismissed almost a quarter of the workforce,
slashed the number of products by two thirds, halved the number of suppli-
ers... (and) humped debts of EUR 1.1 billion on Grohe with an annual interest
burden of EUR 80 million."[187]

The magazine Stern published the cover story "Kapitalismus brutal – Das
große Fressen *(Brutal Capitalism – Blow-Out)*" and illustrated the front page
with an army of marching locusts in managerial suits. In the article "The Names
of the 'Locusts'" the following purchases were mentioned: Apax buys Kabel
Deutschland, BC Partners buys Telecolumbus, Blackstone buys Celanese and

---

184   Der Spiegel 7/2004, p. 75

185   Wer kauft den deutschen Mittelstand? Impulse 3/2004, p. 14ff.; Viele Okkasionen, Inter-
      view mit Investcorp-Partner Thomas Middelhoff, p. 24ff.

186   BILD am Sonntag 17.4.2005

187   Grohe: Viel Geld der Investoren versenkt, WiWo 8.3.2016

Sulo, CVC buys Vitera Energy, KKR buys Duales System Deutschland, MTU and Dynamit Nobel, Permira buys Debitel, Cognis and Rodenstock. Siemens Nixdorf and Tenovis were also named: "Like a lemon squeezed out by mailbox companies, loan procurement and repayments, rental payments and millions in fees for KKR consultants".[188] A critical summary before had appeared in the WSI newsletters of the Hans Böckler Foundation, which is close to the trade unions.[189]

The "Anti-Semitism" campaign
The historian Michael Wolffsohn accused Müntefering of using the rhetoric of the Nazis with the term "locusts": "60 years on, people are again being equated with animals which, resonating implicitly, must be 'exterminated'... The 'plague' today is called 'locusts', in those days 'rats' or 'Jewish pigs'".[190]

The chairman of the FDP, Guido Westerwelle, took up the polemics and at the FDP party conference in Cologne in May 2005 tore into the criticism of the investors as anti-Semitic and anti-American. For his part, he described the trade union functionaries who criticized the investors as "locusts" and "a plague" themselves – this animal name for trade unionists, however, did not prompt any criticism from Wolffsohn.

The SPD and Müntefering subsequently withdrew their public criticism and cancelled a planned conference on the subject. The accusation of anti-Semitism and anti-Americanism marked the end of public discussion of the topic. Müntefering and the SPD were not credible anyway: the SPD-led government had invited these investors in, and Müntefering as minister himself had sold the state-owned petrol station chain Tank&Rast to the investor Apax.

Bavarian civil servant as anti-Semitism plaintiff
However, the following fact is revealing: The Jewish historian Wolffsohn had previously kept completely silent about the genuinely Nazi-like outbursts of the Bavarian Prime Minister Franz-Josef Strauß.

Since 1968, Strauß had equated intellectuals who were then close to the SPD and Willy Brandt's reform and reconciliation policies with animals. In

---

188   Stern.de 28.4.2005

189   Werner Rügemer: Investitionen ohne Arbeitsplätze ibid.

190   Münteferings Heuschrecken. Streit um Wolffsohns Nazi-Vergleich, SPON 3.5.2005

the 1978 election campaign he insulted them as "red rats" and "red voles", also sometimes as "rats and blowflies". What was needed was the courageous citizen "who chases the red rats where they belong – into their holes". This was a tradition from the Adenauer Republic: Economics Minister Ludwig Erhard had called intellectuals "muckrakers and pipsqueaks".[191] The close friend of Strauß and CSU Secretary General, Edmund Stoiber, also insulted the PEN Chairman Walter Jens, the Chairman of the Writers' Association VS, Bernt Engelmann and the well known writer Martin Walser as "rats and blowflies".[192]

Strauß' and Stoiber's animal comparisons, however, had never been taken up by Wolffsohn. In 1981, the climax of the "rats" discussion was barely over, he had been appointed professor at the University of the Federal Armed Forces in Munich, which was sponsored by Strauß. In his family biography, Wolffsohn describes how he had always felt at home in the Adenauer Republic – the duplicitous accuser had never taken offence at its countless ex-Nazis and persecutors of Jews in government, administration, business and the media, not even at the numerous muckraker, rat and blowfly insults.[193]

Merkel and Blackstone change German capitalism
The anti-Semitism polemics abruptly ended the public criticism of the PE investors. That was when they really got going, at least up until the financial crisis and again afterwards.

Blackstone buys stake in Deutsche Telekom AG
At the beginning of 2006, Blackstone bought 4.5 percent of the shares of Deutsche Telekom AG. This small package of shares triggered another far-reaching change.

After one year, the English edition of the Financial Times took stock: The opposing "cultures" of the predatory US capitalism of a more recent coinage and the German social market economy had collided massively at Deutsche Telekom as nowhere before. The result of the conflict was that the German

---

191 Zusammenstellung unter: Franz Josef Strauß: "Ratten und Schmeißfliegen", Der Tagesspiegel 8.5.2015

192 Das deutsche Wort. Was veranlasst Strauß, Gegner als "Ratten" zu diffamieren? Der Spiegel 25.2.1980

193 Michael Wolffsohn: Deutschjüdische Glückskinder. Eine Weltgeschichte meiner Familie. München 2017

government, represented by Schröder's successor Angela Merkel, had, together with Blackstone, "changed German capitalism".[194]

To some, that sounded unlikely: to profoundly change the whole system of the most important capitalist state in Europe by acquiring a 4.5 percent stake in a single company?

Behind the scenes

Since the privatization of Deutsche Telekom in 1995, the state had gradually sold shares to foreign investors. This was called "free float". Names were never mentioned. The start had been made euphemistically with the promise of a people's share that was to be accessible to everyone and had also been bought eagerly and faithfully. This resulted in losses for the newly faithful people's shareholder in the era of Chancellor Kohl, but that was a long time ago.

In 2005, the grand coalition of CDU, CSU and SPD under Merkel was looking for a major shareholder who would finally turn Deutsche Telekom into a real global player. Three PE investors – Apollo (USA), BC Partners (GB) and General Capital (D) together made a non-public offer for a 30 percent package. That would have brought at least EUR 16 billion into the state coffers.

But Merkel did not want to startle the SPD and the unions. At the same time, the head of the most influential PE investor on the other side of the Atlantic had heard about the offer. Schwarzman called the Chancellor in Berlin, as is so easy in Western capital democracy, and a few days later appeared in her office with a colorful PowerPoint presentation.[195]

Just one week later, Finance Minister Peer Steinbrück was "summoned" to Wall Street in New York. Citigroup arranged a dinner with important bankers, just as Citigroup CEO Sandy Weil had done with Chancellor Schröder a few years earlier, before the adoption of Agenda 2010 in the German Bundestag. The Social Democrat Steinbrück and the Blackstone boss quickly agreed: out of consideration for the traditionally strong position of the trade union verdi in Telekom, which is also an original German jewel, the Blackstone share would have to remain low, inconspicuous so to speak. In return, however, the German state would remain by far the largest shareholder, retain the blocking minority of over 25 percent and thus be able to efficiently support Blackstone as the second most important shareholder. Blackstone would get a seat on the

---

194   Private Equity. How Merkel and Blackstone changed German capitalism. FT 2.7.2007

195   Unless indicated otherwise, the account follows the FT of 2.7.2007

supervisory board and the federal government would support Blackstone's reforms "quietly and behind the scenes". In addition, the German government
would help Blackstone with further investments in Germany and the EU –
Blackstone had previously tried unsuccessfully to gain a foothold in telecom
companies in Italy and Spain.

The latent "locust" question

This entry into Telekom was completely atypical for Blackstone: a comparatively tiny stake, unusual concern for trade unions and even the inner
workings of a government. But Schwarzman saw the advantages of the secret
alliance with the most important government in the EU. The state-run KfW,
which conducted the detailed negotiations, let Blackstone's competitors run
aground as agreed.

But the labeling of investors like KKR and Blackstone as "locusts" by Müntefering seemed to have deeply affected the hard-nosed Blackstone boss. At
one of her meetings with top international managers, Merkel praised Germany as an exemplary location. This met with general approval. But Schwarzman
stood up and asked: How could it be that a member of her government could
call him an insect? Merkel calmed him down.[196] Müntefering had not repeated
the criticism, and the left-wing of the SPD kept quiet for all time.

Disempower trade unions, cut wages, extend working hours

Blackstone bought the 4.5 percent of the shares for EUR 2.7 billion. Here, too,
the investor raised the largest part with the help of a loan. Deutsche Bank was
allowed to grant more than half of the loan, that was part of the deal. In order
not to unduly burden Blackstone with the 5 percent interest, the Merkel/Stein-
brück government had EUR 138 million transferred from the Telekom kitty
to Blackstone – for the interest payment to Deutsche Bank for the whole year.

Blackstone dispatched Lawrence Guffey to Deutsche Telekom's 20-mem-
ber Supervisory Board. Guffey managed the Blackstone Group's telecommunications shareholdings in Europe from London. He spoke as little as possible
on the Supervisory Board, but politely asked to be called Larry. Instead, he
coordinated with Steinbrück and the Chancellor's Office behind the scenes.
First, he demanded the dismissal of CEO Kai-Uwe Ricke, CFO Karl-Gerhard
Eick and Supervisory Board Chairman Klaus Zumwinkel. Above all, the trade
union members on the Supervisory Board were amazed: How could a mi-

---

196   Daniel Schäfer: Herrscher der Welt GmbH, FAZ 21.11.2006

nority representative be so brazen? When making these demands, Guffey suddenly spoke very quickly and sternly and the trade unionists nestled up to their headphones to catch the translation. The state secretaries representing the federal government smiled enigmatically. Ricke and Eick had to go. Zumwinkel was allowed to stay – as the simultaneous head of the privatized Deutsche Post, where the federal government was also the main shareholder, his dismissal would have been too vicious.

Guffey and Steinbrück swiftly conjured up a successor to Ricke, an ambitious young aspirant called René Obermann. He introduced himself with a restructuring plan that he could hardly have been able to come up with himself. The plan included a 12 percent wage cut for the core workforce of 50,000 employees. The trade union verdi organized a strike lasting weeks. The counterpart was personnel manager Thomas Sattelberger: the former co-founder of the Communist Workers' Federation of Germany (KABD) was a Blackstone fan.[197] Result of the strike: The 50,000 employees are outsourced to the service subsidiary T-Service, wages are reduced by "only" 6.5 percent, working hours are increased by four hours and made more flexible. There was "pure delight" on the stock exchange.[198]

This meant that the highly-organized trade union in the most important company was decisively weakened. It had been practically demonstrated more clearly than before: The state does not represent the interests of employees, and an SPD Labor Minister is not a friend of the trade unions. The so-called people's parties had shown themselves to be representatives of private minority interests.

Exit

Blackstone had undertaken to hold the equity stake for two years. That was enough. "Hardly any other German company mirrors the history of globalization as well as Deutsche Telekom. International investors have disempowered the CEO."[199]

After the "locusts" fuss and Blackstone's entry into Deutsche Telekom, in 2006 Steinbrück ordered the evaluation of experience with private equity to date. Professor Ann-Kristin Achleitner, wife of Paul Achleitner, was commis-

---

197   Rügemer/ Wigand. Die Fertigmacher ibid., p. 72f.

198   Telekom-Mitarbeiter fühlen sich von Gewerkschaft verraten, SPON 20.6.2007

199   Amerikanische Verhältnisse, HB 24.11.2006

sioned. He had advised the Treuhand-Anstalt for Goldman Sachs and since 1998 had been on the board of Allianz, which itself was active as an investor in this field with its subsidiary Allianz Private Equity Partners (APEP). Ms. Achleitner was director of the endowed chair for corporate finance at the Technical University of Munich, which was financed by the state-owned KfW Bank. She carried out the assignment together with the US law firm White & Case, which advised PE investors. The result of the study: Private equity is good for Germany, but the government should provide investors with further tax relief.[200]

The investors were now firmly in the saddle in Germany. And the criticism was over. Paul Achleitner later became head of the supervisory board of Deutsche Bank and smoothed the way for BlackRock to get involved.

Blackstone&Co set about expanding their political influence networks and brought "distinguished" right-wing politicians and entrepreneurs into their German advisory boards: Apellas got former CDU parliamentary party leader Merz, Blackstone got management consultant Roland Berger, Carlyle got BDI managing director Michael Rogowski, Cerberus got former defense ministers Volker Rühe (CDU) and Rudolf Scharping (SPD), Texas Pacific Group got former finance minister Theodor Waigel (CSU).

Renewed upswing after the "financial crisis"

Following Blackstone's breakthrough at Deutsche Telekom, investors in model location Germany clocked up their record years in 2007 and 2008 unnoticed. Every year, between 300 and 500 companies were bought and sold.

As up to 80 percent of the purchase price raised by investors consisted of bank loans – at Deutsche Bank, Lehman Brothers, Goldman Sachs, UBS – they contributed to the financial crisis. This led to a brief decline in business.

After the banks were rescued by the state in spite of their market and social maleficence and counter to the neoliberal creed, PE also quickly got back on its feet from around 2009. The ECB also promoted PE business with its low-interest loans.

Blackstone&Co received a further boost in the USA after the financial cri-

---

200 Christof Kaserer / Ann-Kristin Achleitner u.a.: Erwerb und Übernahme von Firmen durch Finanzinvestoren, insbesondere Private Equity-Investoren, 2007, hier zitiert nach Jowett, Private Equity ibid., p. 502 and 530

sis. In his second term in office, Obama appointed Jack Lew as Finance Minister. He had been responsible for Global Wealth Management at Citigroup and headed an internal hedge fund that bet on the bursting of the real estate bubble. After the government bail-out of the banks, Lew received a bonus of almost USD 1 billion.[201] After his term in office, Fed Chairman Benanke moved to the hedge fund Citadel, alongside his move to the large capital organizer PIMCO.[202]

Under President Trump, the US government is continuing to promote this aggressiveness. US hedge funds are stepping up their "investments" in the EU, in the rich countries where the economic substance can be exploited with the help of complicit governments, above all in France, Germany and Spain, as well as in the financial havens Ireland and Luxembourg.[203] KKR helped to make its banker friend Macron president of France. (see section on Bank Rothschild)

The international private equity lobby: Strengthened by Trump
The focus of the countries of origin of the investors who were active in Germany in 2014 and 2015 has shifted to the EU: 114 came from Germany itself, 40 from the USA, 23 from Austria and Switzerland, 22 from the UK, 17 from France and the Benelux countries, 4 from Scandinavia. However, in terms of the financial volume and the size of the companies acquired and exploited, the dominance of the investors domiciled in the USA and in second place in London remains unbroken.[204]

Blackstone, KKR and Carlyle remain the international kings of the industry. Their proximity to US President Trump gave them even more influence. Their aggressive investment practices and the extreme methods of self-enrichment of their bosses such as Schwarzman, Kravis and Rubenstein are closely related to those of the new US President, and French President Macron is also close to them.[205]

---

201   Citibanker wird Finanzminister, Wall Street Journal 27.1.2013

202   Bernanke, Trichet, Brown Join Pimco Advisory Board, Reuters 7.12.2013

203   KKR stärkt mit neuen Büro in Frankfurt seine Präsenz in Europa, deal advisors 23.1.2018

204   Unternehmen als Ware. Internationale Investoren dominieren, Böckler implus 6/2015, p. 7

205   The $132 Billion Dinner: Meet The Tycoons Who Ate With Trump Last Night, Forbes 25.4.2018

In the USA, there are ten lobby associations that specialize in different sectors and working methods. The most important association is the American Investment Council, in which Blackstone, KKR and the like set the tone.[206] In the UK, the British Private Equity & Venture Capital Association (BVCA) in existence since 1983 is the oldest association with 700 members.[207] In Germany, the Bundesverband deutscher Kapitalbeteiligungsgesellschaften (BVK) has several hundred members, including the German branches of KKR, Permira, Bain and Advent International from the USA and Ardian from France, as well as consultants such as Freshfields and PWC.

After the USA, the UK and Germany, investors from France are the most active. The Association Francaise des Investisseurs en Capital (AFIC) has 480 member firms, the largest being Ardian, founded by the AXA insurance group, with offices in Luxembourg, Jersey, Zurich, Frankfurt, London, New York and Beijing. EUR 60 billion is invested primarily in companies in Western Europe, partly in the USA and China. PE capital is currently invested in about 6,000 companies in France.[208]

Location Germany coveted

In 2001, PE investors in Germany already held stakes in 5,758 companies. In 2012, the figure was 6,622. As in the meantime several thousand companies have since been resold or the investors have left in some other way (management buy-in, IPO), the number is higher overall and is likely to total at least 10,000 from 1999 to 2018.[209] The Merkel governments were silent, as was the case with the rise of BlackRock.

2017 was a record year celebrated by the industry. Investors bought shares in 1,100 companies to the tune of EUR 11.3 billion, doubling their purchases compared with the previous year. This means that these investors are currently co-owners of "more than 5,000 companies". They have concentrated more and more on smaller companies: nine tenths have fewer than 500 employees. Small start-ups with new ideas are in great demand.[210]

---

206   www.investmentcouncil.org

207   https://www.bvca.co.uk/

208   www.franceinvest.eu/en/private-equity-in-france/key-figures.html

209   Howard Gospel u.a. (Hg.): Financialization, New Investment Funds and Labour, Oxford University Press 2014, p. 158

210   BVK: Beteiligungskapital auf Rekordniveau, Pressemitteilung 27.2.2018

Economic destructiveness

As with BlackRock, the business model follows the principle: the exploitation of the existing entrepreneurial substance takes precedence over the creation of new substance. The type of investment is not aimed at full employment. In addition, competition is also further reduced among medium-sized companies as well. "Little competition is always good," declared KKR's European head at an early stage.[211]

Between 40 and 70 percent of the capital required to purchase the companies stems from loans that are transferred to the purchased companies. This has contributed to the over-indebtedness of the acquired companies as well as the lending banks and thus to the financial crisis and is laying the ground for the next financial bubble.

Too much profit-seeking, inefficient capital

2,300 private equity professionals were perplexed at their annual investor fair, which also took place in 2017 under the motto "Super Return": "Financial investors are wrestling with a luxury problem: too much money. Far too much. In the past, they had to struggle to raise funds for the money pots they used to use to finance takeovers, today their new funds are often oversubscribed."[212]

The degradation of labor

As early as 2006, around one million employees in Germany had an employer that was dominated by a PE investor; these were particularly productive sectors that accounted for 7 percent of gross domestic product.[213] In the new upswing in the industry between 2011 and 2015, the owners of an average of 115,000 employees changed every year.[214]

Works council out! Cut wages!

The ruthless plundering practiced by Blackstone, KKR, TPG in the first decade was often mitigated initially. But unnoticed, unchallenged, investors can once again afford many brutalities and violations of labor and human rights. To this

---

211 "Wenig Wettbewerb ist immer gut", HB 31.1.2005

212 Klaus Max Smolka: Ringen um die Rendite, http://www.faz.net/aktuell/finanzen 31.3.2017

213 Finanzinvestoren sind überall, FAZ 8.12.2006

214 Christoph Scheuplein / Florian Teetz: Private-Equity-Aktivitäten in Deutschland 2014/15, Hans Böckler-Stiftung, Düsseldorf März 2017, p. 104f.

end, investors also benefit from the four Hartz laws that came into force in 2005 (temporary work, part-time and mini-jobs, disciplining and sanctioning the unemployed) and the widespread non-prosecution of violations of labor rights by entrepreneurs.[215]

The weakened unions have so far not addressed BlackRock's or Blackstone's practices in such a way that sustainable resistance has become possible. Resistance, when it emerges, is never well organized and fizzles out on site.

Workers in Germany particularly compliant
The head of KKR's European office said: "We have had good experiences with co-determination at company level". But he put that into perspective immediately. On the one hand, he lamented "the high ancillary wage costs" in Germany. And he sees co-determination as a disciplinary instrument, because: "In France or other countries the potential for conflict is much greater. In Germany, employees can be involved at an early stage".[216]

If the investor offers a company for sale after the exploitation cycle or wants to float it on the stock exchange, then the features "works council-free" and "reduced wages" boost profits. Having got a foothold, the investor gradually works towards such a result. Two recent cases will illustrate how this works.

DURA Automotive Systems
Even when it comes to thousands of jobs in a region – state governments and public broadcasters also keep their eyes, ears, noses, mouths, cameras and microphones shut. This will be illustrated by the example of a major automotive supplier.

Patriarch Partners: "America first"
The US investor Patriarch Partners owns 75 companies worldwide, broadly diversified: civil and military helicopters, fashion, cosmetics, automotive electronics. In the USA, Germany, France, the Czech Republic, Portugal, Romania, India, Japan, Korea and China, it acquired several automotive suppliers

215 Werner Rügemer: Arbeitsverhältnisse: Unternehmer als ungestrafte Rechtsbrecher, in: Klaus-Jürgen Bruder u.a. (Hg.): Gesellschaftliche Spaltungen, Göttingen 2018, p. 207-222

216 "Wenig Wettbewerb ist immer gut". Interview mit KKR-Europachef Johannes Huth, HB 31.1.2005

in 2010 and combined them under the holding company DURA Automotive Systems with 12,000 employees.

Patriarch's boss is billionaire Lynn Tilton. She raised her seed capital as a banker with Goldman Sachs and Merrill Lynch. She is part of the Made in America Movement. According to the US magazine Forbes, the female version of Trump snaps at her employees vulgarly, celebrates parties with Silvio Berlusconi and pats the backside of British ex-premier Tony Blair. She has homes on Lake Como, Italy, in Florida, Arizona, New Jersey and Hawaii.[217] She praised Trump for making "American workers" the top issue and for taking action against the "flooding of our market" by China.[218]

However, Patriarch Partners' website shows cute photos of US workers arm in arm with Ms. Tilton – their production facilities in India, China and the EU are kept secret.

Job cuts without a social plan
Most of DURA's locations are located in Germany with 4,000 jobs: Düsseldorf (head office), Daun/Eifel, Einbeck, Rotenburg, Selbecke and Plettenberg. The customers supplied include Ford, General Motors, Daimler, BMW, Volvo, VW and others. The largest site, Plettenberg (Sauerland), had 2,600 jobs at the time of purchase.

In the first two years, 570 jobs were cut, mainly in Plettenberg. After that another 900 employees were to be made redundant. As an alternative, Tilton offered that the works council could buy the company for EUR 1. Since the works council would of course not get loans from any bank for the continuation of the business and the purchase was not possible, Patriarch threatened with the announced dismissals, but did not enter into any negotiations about a social plan. At the same time, however, work was to be done at the weekend: The works council refused under these circumstances. The management initially wanted to hire temporary workers, but the labor court rejected this: the works council had a right of co-determination.[219]

---

217 Lynn Tilton: Is she really a Billionaire?, http://www.forbes.com/sites/jennago-udreau/2011/04/11, downloaded 30.10.2016

218 Right to Focus on American Manufacturing, https://www.patriarchpartners.com 22.3.2017

219 Cf. the ongoing reporting in the regional newspaper Süderländer Tageblatt, 23.1.016, 9.4.2016, 7.7.2016

Portuguese contractors flown in

Patriarch wanted to wear down the remaining 1,400 employees. On 7 October 2016, Patriarch had 280 workers flown in from its Portuguese branch Carregado to Plettenberg. The Portuguese took over the weekend shifts the following day.

Patriarch hired the law firm Kliemt & Vollstädt. The team of six lawyers under Dr. Markus Bohnau cobbled together a contract solution.[220] It was accepted by the Hamm Regional Labor Court: The deployment of the Portuguese contract workers at the weekend legally created a new company with different employees. The contract was part of entrepreneurial freedom. (LAG Hamm 13 TaBVGa 8/16). The contract was valid for almost three months until 31.12.2016.

The judgement of the LAG Hamm is a legal scandal for various reasons: A "new" company is constructed within the old company. The Portuguese workers have a double identity: they are employees of the company in Portugal, and at the same time they are contract workers for the same company in Germany. The legally quickly formed new contract company does not have its own equipment, but uses the same tools and machines as the regular employees.

PR agency: Disinformation

The investor by no means calculated from a business point of view, but instead fought an expensive power struggle without regard to the costs. The Portuguese workers were only allowed to work on Saturdays, Sunday work had been banned by the regional council (Regierungspräsident). The workers were accommodated in two far-flung hotels. They therefore had to be transported the 76 or 88 kilometers each time one and a half hours to work there and back. During the week and on Sunday the Portuguese could go for a walk, help themselves to the buffet and dream of the sun in their home country. They worked sloppily, customers sent parts back to Plettenberg.

Patriarch Partners hired the PR agency Brunswick. Its employee appeared as Dura Group spokesman from summer 2016. He supplied the local media with accusations against the union IG Metall.[221] The investor switches it

---

220   Arbeitsrechtlicher Streit: Dura setzt sich mit Kliemt Vollstädt gegen Betriebsrat durch, www.juve.de/nachrichten/verfahren/2016/10/, downloaded 31.10.2016

221   "IG Metall verspielt die Zukunft vieler Mitarbeiter und ihrer Familien", Süderländer Tageblatt 13.7.2016

managers on site every six months. In the meantime, it has sold patents and licenses to a company in the UK.[222] The exhausting and grueling dispute drags on.

In Plettenberg with its 26,000 inhabitants and in the region fear has reigned for years. We are talking about the biggest employer. In August 2016, 150 employees prevented a machine from being transported to Portugal in a nighttime blockade.

Cynicism and public silence

Of the initial 2,600 jobs in Plettenberg, only half remain eight years after Patriarch's entry: 1,300. That is still not the end. The company offers cynicism combined with inane chumminess: "There are currently no vacancies at DURA Systems. However, the company is looking forward to your unsolicited application".[223]

The IG Metall union turned to the state government of North Rhine-Westphalia, led at the time by the SPD and the Greens – no reaction. The Frankfurt headquarters of IG Metall also left their colleagues in the Sauerland province to their own devices.

Median rehabilitation clinics

McKinsey repeatedly praised the healthcare sector in Europe as a "golden opportunity for private equity". Active players include Advent, Bridgepoint, Cinven, CVC, EQT, Apax, Carlyle, BC Partners, IK Investment, Nordic Capital, Oaktree, Ardian, Orpea and others. They buy, exploit, sell thousands of nursing homes, hospitals, medical care centers, doctor's surgeries, rehabilitation clinics, medical test labs, outpatient care services and homecare companies across Europe and form chains. Bridgepoint (London), for example, has bundled 340 dialysis centers in 20 countries with 10,000 employees in the Luxembourg holding company Diaverum S.a.r.l.. These investors largely shape the quality of healthcare in the EU – apparently unnoticed by the public.

In the following we will look at PE-Investor Waterland B.V. in the Netherlands. The backers of this investor, founded in 1999, come mainly from the USA, Western Europe, Asia and the Gulf States. Clients also include two

---

222   Mitteilung des Betriebsrats in der Niederlassung Plettenberg vom 1.2.2017

223   https://karriere-suedwestfalen.de/dura, downloaded 19.2.2017

multi-billionaires from Belgium: Marc Coucke, founder of Omega-Pharma, and the carpet dealer Filip Balcaen.[224]

"Waterland supports entrepreneurs in growth markets who want to further expand their already advantageous market position through acquisitions and strong organic growth," the website says. Waterland prides itself on having generated more profits than comparable investors since its founding: "Above-average performance".[225] Since its foundation, Waterland has acquired and exploited 400 highly diverse companies. Waterland currently owns 35 companies, mainly in the Netherlands, Germany and Belgium, but also some in Poland and the UK.[226]

Dog food, casinos, poor and rich rehabilitation patients
For Waterland, all attainable human needs are the object of exploitation. Rehabilitation patients are just as much a part of the target group as gamblers and hungry dogs. The acquired companies are active in the following areas: waste and bottom ash recycling, sports food, dry food for dogs and cats, frozen bakery products, playgrounds, debt collection, insurance brokerage, holiday travel, golf.

The health sector also includes test laboratories for cancer detection, fertility, rehabilitation and acute clinics. Waterland is also expanding the luxury segment in the healthcare sector. Under the label "Median Premium", "high-quality medical care with the ambience of a first-class hotel" is advertised. The target group is private patients and self-paying patients "with individual aspirations" from home and abroad.

Transform the healthcare system with McKinsey
Since 2011, Waterland in Germany has been buying rehabilitation clinics of various sponsors and combining them into a chain under the name Median. It has 15,000 employees. Waterland prides itself on having created the largest rehabilitation group and one of the five largest hospital groups in Germany. The exit is planned for 2020.[227]

---

224   Fincieele Dagblad 28.8.2017; derijkstebelgen.be/de-lijst, downloaded 19.2.2018
225   Median: Übernahme der AHG. Median Geschäftsführung zu Vorständen der AHG AG bestellt, Pressemitteilung 21.11.2016
226   http://waterland.be/de/, downloaded 19.2.2018
227   http://waterland.be/de/, abgerufen 19.2.2018

Legal advice is provided by the large law firm Hengeler Müller. The London investment bank Rothschild advises on credit management. The world's largest real estate service provider CBRE from Los Angeles checks the technical and financial value of the buildings. KPMG advises on the search for the most favorable tax loopholes.[228] The most important consultant is McKinsey.

The German head of Waterland, Carsten Rahlfs, began his career at McKinsey. Rahlfs is not only manager but also co-owner of Waterland. The CEO of the Median chain, André Schmidt, also earned his spurs at McKinsey. At its McKinsey Hospital Institute, McKinsey is developing proposals for the privatization of the healthcare system. The USA is seen as a role model. Private hospital chains are to be formed. Outsourcing, for example, will apply not only to cleaning, laundry and catering, but also to clinical areas.[229]

Rahlfs and Schmidt are pursuing this concept at Median. They are also using an upshot of the hospital "reform". The flat rate per case for individual diseases and operations has boosted the commercialization of hospitals;[230] patients are discharged from inpatient hospitals as early as possible ("bloody discharge"): hence the increasing need for post-operative rehabilitation places.

Exploitation of hospital buildings
Waterland sold 40 Median hospital buildings for EUR 770 million to the US real estate fund Medical Properties Trust (MPT). Median therefore has to rent back MPT's buildings for 27 years. Median pays for the clinics an annual rent between 8 and 11 percent of the purchase price plus an annual inflation premium of one percent. In the final year 2043, the rent will therefore be between 35 and 38 percent of the purchase price. The owner and landlord MPT is not responsible for maintenance, this is the responsibility of the tenant.[231]

Median and MPT formed a joint subsidiary for the exploitation of real estate, in which MPT acquired 5.1 percent of the shares: MPT therefore does not

---

228 Deal in Focus: Waterland sticks to buy-and-build strategy with Median, 15.8.2016, http://unquote.com/uk/analysis/3001475/

229 McKinsey: Das Krankenhaus der Zukunft. Healthcare Systems and Services 2016, https://hospitalinstitut.mckinsey.de/files/publications

230 Verein demokratischer Ärztinnen und Ärzte (VdÄÄ): Was ist falsch am Fallpauschalensystem? https://krankenhaus-statt-fabrik.de/122, 16.2.2018

231 Charles Kingston: US REIT in $900 takeover of leading German healthcare provider, refire-online.com, November 10, 2014

have to pay real estate transfer tax according to a special tax regulation. The German state promotes such economically damaging transactions to its own detriment – in this case alone a two-digit million sum is lost.

In addition to the profit for Median and its investors, the excessive rents for MPT now have to be paid additionally by the Median clinics, i.e. above all by the salaried and outsourced employees and pension providers.

Trade union-free, politically right-wing

Nor is MPT, the owner of the 40 Median buildings, a social enterprise. It also uses financial havens and shuns trade unions. The group, which is currently expanding strongly in Europe, has had its operational headquarters in Alabama since 2003, but legally in the US financial haven of Delaware.[232] Its report for the Securities and Exchange Commission states: "None of our employees are members of a trade union".[233]

The founder, boss and main owner of Waterland, Rob Thielen, positions himself on the political right. In 2014 he sponsored the election campaign of VVD politician Hans van Baalen in the Netherlands. The VVD criticizes the overly extensive welfare state, wants to restrict immigration and emerged as the governing party with this program.[234] Thielen is also involved in politics in the UK: in 2016 he donated GBP 50,000 to the British "Conservatives". They introduced the zero hour contract: This is an employment contract under which employees must be available at all times on demand, but are not entitled to a certain number of working hours.

Works councils out!

The law firm Beiten Burkhardt (Düsseldorf), with three employment lawyers, has been commissioned to wear down works councils and recalcitrant employees as well as to act against the trade union verdi. On its arrival, the Waterland managing directors immediately terminated the collective agreement and refused to negotiate with verdi. With "flexible wage models", the wages of the dependent employees in each individual clinic are to be adapted to the respective market situation.

---

232   Annual Report 2014, SEC Form 10-K, p. 1

233   SEC Form 10-Q, Quarterly Report 9-Nov-2016, https://biz.yahoo.com/e/161109/mpw10-q.html

234   VVD in wikipedia

On 30 June 2016, the management closed an entire clinic without econom-ic necessity, the Weser Clinic in Bad Oeynhausen. The probable reason was the experienced and militant works council. Its chairman was also a member of the general works council of the acquired Quellenhof clinics in Bad Salzu-flen.[235]

The chairman of the works council appealed against his forced retirement before the labor court and was proved right. However, the court ruling is no reason for the investor to acknowledge it. When the 63-year-old wanted to turn up for work, the management had the keys taken from him and accused him of trespassing.[236]

Low-wage earners in!
Via the Expert Migration Healthcare mediation program run by DEKRA Management Consultants Median recruits low-wage earners from Albania, Montenegro, Bosnia-Herzegovina, Ukraine and Serbia. In a crash course the DEKRA Academy awards them the certificate "German B 2 + Care" with the most needed German phrases and a brief introduction to nursing care.[237]

Inferior medical quality
While the McKinsey acolytes are expanding premium offerings for the wealthy international clientele, they are cutting spending on standard services.[238]

Patients are grouped into large groups for physiotherapy. There are 20 year old and 60 year old patients, who have very different rehabilitation needs. Wounds that do not belong to the narrow treatment profile remain untreated.

The laboratory operations of several clinics, even those that are far apart, are centralized. As a result, some blood samples are left lying around for so long that the red blood cells decompose and the test results become unreliable. A laboratory assistant who did not agree with this lost his job.

---

235 Median – "Unwürdig, unanständig und empörend", Verdi Fachbereich 03: Infodienst Krankenhäuser 75/2016, p. 22ff.

236 Jörg Stuke: Median-Klinik setzt Betriebsrat vor die Tür, Neue Westfälische 24.10.2016

237 https://www.dekra-akademie.de/de/expert-migration-healthcare-kurz-kompakt/, downloaded 19.2.2018

238 The picture portrayed here is based on Joern Kersten: Finanzinvestoren bei Rehaklini-ken, ARD plusminus 28.3.2018. Objections from Waterland/Median were not notified.

Sick health care operation

The investor thus contributes to the formation of a monopoly in the hospital sector, to the flight from collective bargaining, to the reduction of labor income, to labor migration in the European Union, to the additional burden of overpriced sale and lease back transactions with real estate and not least to tax evasion. How the quality of medical and psychological treatment develops under these conditions of extreme capitalization has so far only been rudimentarily investigated publicly and academically.[239]

WMF and Gesellschaft für Konsumforschung (GfK)

It is striking how even ruthless measures by well-known investors silently pass off in Western democracy. This is briefly illustrated by the case of two large German companies. And the trade unions, even if they fleetingly fight desperately locally, also remain speechless overall.

The WMF case

In 2012, KKR bought the German market leader for cutlery and kitchen appliances, WMF AG: Württembergische Metallwarenfabrik was founded in 1853. In its main location in Geislingen and in the surrounding region, WMF was the principal employer with a good 6,000 employees. However, since the beginning of the "unbundling of Germany plc", the lucrative company with its rich tradition had already been in the sights of smaller PE investors, most recently Capvis from Switzerland.

KKR cut 400 jobs, stores in various cities were closed and the traditional brands Auerhahn and Alfi were sold. KKR logged the purchase price of EUR 600 million as WMF debt. In 2015, KKR took WMF off the stock exchange and transformed it into a limited liability company via a letterbox company.[240]

In 2016, KKR transformed the private company back into a public limited company and sold it via a letterbox company on the Cayman Islands to the French kitchen appliance manufacturer SEB: selling price EUR 1.6 billion. Profit for KKR: just under EUR 1 billion. The debts have not yet been repaid and are maintaining the pressure on the new owner to cut costs.[241]

---

239 Rainer Bobsin ibid.

240 Küchenspezialist verabschiedet sich von der Börse, HB 23.3.2015

241 Thomas Baumgartner: Hohe Rendite in kurzer Zeit, Frankfurter Neue Presse 19.3.2016

KKR thus also contributes to the further formation of monopolies in the EU. With the purchase of WMF, SEB was able to expand its collection, which already includes the well-known brands Rowenta, Krups and Moulinex from Germany. As with WMF, the names remain the same – and the public should be under the illusion that everything is as it has been for 150 years.

Gesellschaft für Konsumforschung (GfK)
One of the biggest deals in 2017 was the purchase of GfK by KKR. It was founded in 1935 by Ludwig Erhard, later German Minister of Economics, among others, and has retained its high ideological significance. The legal owner now is KKR-Fonds Acceleratio Capital N.V. in the financial oasis Netherlands.

The investor took the company off the stock exchange immediately, thereby limiting its information obligations. The previous management was almost completely dismissed. Peter Feld, who had just finished selling off WMF, is now in charge. GfK had 13,000 employees worldwide. Of the 13,000 employees, 7,000 are to be made redundant over the next two years.[242]

The 50 largest private equity investors (2017)[243]

The approximately 6,000 PE investors worldwide hide the capital of hundreds of thousands of wealthy clients in financial havens. Even in the companies bought by the investors, the investors are not known. Large investors such as Blackstone and KKR each have a three-digit billion sum at their disposal, which is topped up by bank loans when a company is purchased, have so far asset-stripped several hundred companies and are currently co-owners of around 100 companies. The largest players from Europe are on rungs 24 (Ardian, France), 31 (EQT, Sweden) and 33 (Partners Group, Switzerland).

---

242 KKR-Europachef verteidigt Umbau der GfK, Capital 22.3.2018

243 Private Equity International: List of the largest private equity investors for 2017 (PEI 300), https://www.privateequityinternational.com/database/#/pei-300, downloaded 24.2.2018.

Name	Location
Blackstone	New York
KKR	New York
The Carlyle Group	Washington D.C.
Texas Pacific Group (TPG)	Fort Worth, Texas/USA
Warburg Pincus	New York/London
Advent International	Boston/USA
Apollo Global	New York
EnCap Investments	Houston/USA
Neuberger Berman	New York
CVC Partners	London
Bain Capital	Boston/USA
Thoma Bravo	Chicago
Vista Equity Partners	San Francisco
Apax Partners	London
Clayton Dubilier & Rice	New York
Cinven	London
Leonard Green & Partners	Los Angeles
Ares Management	Los Angeles
BC Partners	London
Permira Advisers	London
Riverstone Holdings	New York
Goldman Sachs Principal	New York
Silver Lake	Menlo Park/USA
Ardian	Paris/France
Hellman & Friedman	San Francisco
MBK Partners	Seoul/South Korea
Stone Point Capital	Greenwich/USA
General Atlantic	New York
Platinum Equity	Beverly Hills/USA
NGP Energy Capital	Irving/USA
EQT	Stockholm/Sweden
L Catterton	Greenwich/USA
Partners Group	Baar-Zug/Switzerland
Bookfield Asset Management	Toronto/Canada
Energy & Minerals Group	Houston/USA
Inventis Investment	Shanghai/China

American Securities	New York
Russian Direct Investment	Moscow/Russia
RRJ Capital	Hongkong
Insight Venture Partners	New York
The Abraaj Group	Dubai/UAE
Cerberus Capital	New York
Bridgepoint	London
HgCapital	London
Alpinvest Partners	Amsterdam/Netherlands
Onex	Toronto/Canada
TA Associates	Boston/USA
Energy Capital Partners	Short Hills/USA
BDT Partners	Chicago/USA

3.
Hedge funds: The pillagers

Like BlackRock and Blackstone, hedge funds also work with the capital of wealthy clients and supplementary bank loans. However, they specialize in very specific interventions in individual companies and in speculative transactions in equities, corporate and government bonds, commodities and foreign exchange for narrowly limited periods of time. Hedge funds take particularly high risks and thus pervert the term hedge, which means the opposite, namely hedge against risks. The methods are also diffusely referred to as "alternative investments": This means that they deviate particularly strongly from traditional methods.

George Soros: Quantum Fund
The hedge fund of the oligarch George Soros is publicly known: he founded the pioneer Quantum Fund in 1973. With speculation on the devaluation of the British pound, the US citizen earned his first billion in 1992. He domiciles his Quantum Fund and other funds in financial havens such as Curacao and Virgin Islands.

Soros also speculated successfully in other countries, including in the financial crisis of 2007. He publicly opposes regulations that impede the freedom of financial players. Occasionally he is convicted for insider trading, for example.[244] He embellishes his approach ideologically with the "open society" concept of the philosopher Karl Popper. For this, he was awarded honorary doctorates by the elite universities of Oxford (UK) and Yale (USA). He founded the Open Society / Renaissance Foundation. With numerous national subsidiary foundations, the globalizing populist promotes "citizens' initiatives" and state institutions that give financial players free rein, for example in Ukraine.[245] As foundation backers, he also involves other financial players and, in the case of Ukraine, NATO's public relations department.[246]

Hedge funds as non-banks too

Hedge funds are also players and an upshot of the deregulation seen in the 1990s in the USA. In 2000, the business volume of hedge funds worldwide was about USD 500 million, but by 2014 it had already increased sixfold to USD 3 trillion.[247]

Like BlackRock and Blackstone, hedge funds have no defined legal status. The British Financial Supervisory Authority diffusely refers to them as "non-bank and non-insurance financial institutions with global systemic significance".[248]

Since 2006, hedge funds based in the USA have had to register with the SEC. However, this only applies to the larger funds. The requirements are minimal. Above all, it should be avoided, based on previous experience, that investors who make their capital available are cheated.[249] How hedge funds deploy the capital is not regulated. Harming dependent employees is permitted. The industry revels in its "fool's license".[250]

In Germany, hedge funds were approved by the SPD/Green government in 2004: The Investment Modernization Act refers to them fuzzily as "special funds with additional risks", allowing, for example, short sales of securities

---

244   Urteil gegen Soros bestätigt, manager magazin 6.10.2011

245   Matthias Holland-Letz: Die Macht des George Soros, SWR2 8.11.2017

246   Werner Rügemer: Jazeniuk made in USA, Ossietzky 9/2014, p. 293f.

247   Financial Conduct Authority (FCA): Hedge Fund Survey, London June 2015, p. 11

248   Financial Conduct Authority ibid., p. 3

249   Security Exchange Commission, Release No. I A-2333: Registration under the Advisers Act of Certain Hedgefonds Advisers (2005)

250   Die wahren Paten der Wall Street, Anlegertrends 11/2018, p. 12

and imposing some conditions for taking out loans. However, these already minimal restrictions do not apply to foreign hedge funds.

The Federal Ministry of Finance still sees the characteristics of hedge funds today in the fact that they are "fundamentally subject to no or only minimal investment guidelines and make use of all forms of capital investment. They also use short selling and/or leverage techniques. Both lead to the fact that these investment funds are regularly subject to a higher risk than normal investment funds, combined with the possibility of achieving a higher, 'absolute' return". Hence we see SPD and CDU finance ministers, Steinbrück and Schäuble, helpfully repeating the self-portrayal of hedge funds.[251] Bafin, the financial supervisory authority, is responsible, but, as with BlackRock and Blackstone, it cannot conduct supervision at all due to a lack of regulations, even if it wanted to.

The EU Directive 85/611/EEC of 1985 had legitimized *undertakings for collective investment in transferable securities* (UCITS) – this very abstract wording also authorized hedge funds. A year before the German law, Dresdner Bank, Deutsche Bank and the noble private bank Metzler, known as a patron of the arts, had already sold hedge fund certificates worth around EUR 10 billion.[252]

Small and large hedge funds
The several hundred hedge funds are mostly managed by individuals, who surround themselves with just a few dozen managers. But traditional banks such as Goldman Sachs, JPMorgan Chase and Deutsche Bank have also adopted the hedge fund methods and set up corresponding departments. During the financial crisis, for example, Deutsche Bank in New York had its hedge fund managers under Greg Lippman sell bets on the crashing mortgage bonds. After "earning billions of dollars" for Deutsche Bank, Lippman set up his own hedge fund Libre Max Capital in 2010.[253] And BlackRock&Co also make use of the practices with their own departments. Blackstone is also constantly setting up small hedge funds.[254]

The owners and the few executives take an even higher share of the profits for themselves personally than is the case with BlackRock and Blackstone. At two per cent, the management fees for investors are double in comparison to

251   https://www.bundesfinanzministerium.de/Hedgefonds, downloaded 27.2.2018
252   Hedgefonds werden zum Modeinstrument, FAZ 20.5.2003
253   Unaufhaltsamer Aufstieg, HB 29.2.2012
254   Alternative Anlagen. Risikokapital für junge Hedgefonds, HB 3.5.2018

BlackRock, on top of this come success fees in favor of the fund managers of up to 20 per cent – that is the price for the hoped for, far above-average profits. Transparency is even lower. This enables extreme insider trading and fleecing of clients – but this is permissible and known to those involved. In this way, individual founders and bosses quickly became multi-billionaires.[255]

Here, too, a few big-hitters dominate the scene. The 10 largest have 83 per cent of the market in their hands, the 20 largest control 92 percent.[256] In 2016, profits increased by 17 percent for the market leader Bridgewater, 28 percent for Two Sigma and as much as 42 percent for Renaissance Technologies. Since the risks are very high at the same time, losses are also sometimes very high. The invested capital can fluctuate wildly. Some funds go bankrupt. This is why some well-known and at times very successful hedge funds such as Paulson do not appear in the following ranking.

The largest dozen hedge funds (2016)[257]

Name	Boss/Founder	Operative HQ	Deployed capital
Bridgewater	Ray Dalio	Westport/USA	122 USD bn
AQR	Cliff Asness	Greenwich/USA	69
JPMorgan	Mary Erdoes	New York	45
Renaissance Tech	James Simons	East Setauket/USA	42
Two Sigma	David Siegel	New York	39
DE Shaw	David Shaw	New York	35
Millennium	Israel Englander	New York	34
Man Group	Luke Ellis	London	34
Och-Ziff	Daniel Och	New York	33
Winton Group	David Harding	London	32
Elliott	Paul Singer	New York	31
BlackRock	Lawrence Fink	New York	28

255 List of the 45 richest hedge fund billionaires: https://www.forbes.com/pictures/ghm45/mfmk, downloaded 14.3.2018

256 Financial Conduct Authority l.c. p. 13 (as of 2014)

257 Earnings figures are taken from the following sources: Business Insider.de 26.6.2017; Pensions & Investments http://www.pionline.com 19.9.2016; https://www.investopedia.com 5.7.2017, downloaded 10.3.2018. The figures can change quickly. The Forbes list puts deployed capital for Bridgewater in 2018 at USD 160 bn.

The Apple hedge fund

Companies also operate hedge funds. Apple founded the Braeburn hedge fund in 2005 (like the Group, it was named after an apple variety in an ecologically correct way). The fund is based not far from the company's headquarters in Cupertino, Silicon Valley, but in the neighboring US state of Nevada, one of the domestic financial paradises in the US. There, no tax is levied on corporate profits, unlike the state of California, which levies 8.84 percent.

In its global tax reduction strategy, Apple shifts profits that are not distributed to shareholders like BlackRock into the Braeburn apple. It "generates" profits with USD 268 billion in managed capital (as of 2017) according to hedge fund methods, above all it reduces the annual tax payments of the parent company by a two-digit billion sum. The tax losses are incurred in 20 US states and in most EU countries.[258]

Hedge funds in Germany and in the EU

In 2013, 36 small German hedge funds were permitted in Germany under the Act. But the Federal Association of Alternative Investments (BAI), founded in anticipation in 1997, has 178 members. Not only Commerzbank, Deutsche Bank, Hessische Landesbank and Evangelische Bank are represented, which sell hedge fund products. The insurance groups Allianz and Talanx are also members.

But major foreign banks with their hedge fund departments are also members, such as Goldman Sachs, JP Morgan, United Bank of Switzerland, BNP Paribas, Rothschild and Schroders (both London/New York). France's largest PE investor, Ardian, is also present with its hedge fund division. BlackRock, Wellington and Amundi from the top league also attach importance to membership.[259]

Financial haven focus: Cayman Islands

Like BlackRock and Blackstone, hedge funds also have their operational offices in the financial centers of New York, London, Paris, Frankfurt and Milan. But the individual subsidiary funds, which are endowed with customer capital, have their legal domicile in a financial haven.

---

258   How Apple Sidesteps Billions in Taxes, New York Times 28.4.2012

259   https://bvai.de/mitgliederverzeichnis, downloaded 28.2.2018

However, hedge funds have a preference for one particular financial paradise: 69 percent of all funds are domiciled in the Cayman Islands. The Cayman Islands, too, with tax sovereignty, feed themselves essentially on the hiding fees of part of the transnational capitalist class. As a British Overseas Territory, this fake state is headed by the Queen, who until 2018 was represented locally by a female governor, Helen Kilpatrick: Female advancement, tax evasion and monarchical subjugation go well together.

Portrait: Ray Dalio/Bridgewater

Ray Dalio, "the most successful hedge fund manager of the world",[260] founded the hedge fund Bridgewater Associates in 1975 after studying at Harvard Business School. He shaped this type of investor and found many imitators. For him, investments are far removed from what the man on the street understands by investment. With diverse financial instruments, bets are placed on every movement in the market of stocks, derivatives, commodities, precious metals, government bonds. These bets are sold as securities. These operations by no means take place in a "vacuum". Dalio explained it at one of his rare public appearances: he "cares about Europe", as the Handelsblatt also reported with concern. Because: "On average, labor in the EU is twice as expensive as in the United States... That is why Europe urgently needs to become more competitive and less bureaucratic."[261] The basis also for hedge fund betting is the exploitability of concrete human labor. Governments should ensure that this is the case. In 2017, for example, Dalio and his Pure Alpha Fund bet USD 22 billion on the drop in shares of companies in Europe that cut jobs particularly aggressively, such as Deutsche Bank, Siemens, Allianz and BASF. Bridgewater has earned USD 50 billion since its foundation, which makes its competitor Soros, who earned only 44 billion, look bad, as the FAZ reported.[262] After Trump's election, Dalio was ecstatic. The new president's administration could shape the world more profoundly than Reagan's, Thatcher's and Kohl's generation of politicians: they had meritoriously "dispelled socialist governments". But Trump could go further in "ig-

---

260   Dennis Kremer: Der rücksichtslose Mr. Dalio, FAZ 11.4.2016
261   Europa bleibt nur noch wenig Zeit, HB 16.2.2015
262   Dennis Kremer: Rücksichtslos, superschlau, superreich, FAZ 19.2.2018

niting animal spirits and attracting productive capital". This pro-business government would create "with political stability, the protection of property rights
and favorable corporate taxes uniquely attractive conditions for those who
make or have money".[263] In Westport, near New York, Dalio employs 1,500
people. Up until 2018 he led them like a sect sworn to his person. He had all
conversations in the company recorded and practiced "total surveillance of
employees".[264] With private assets worth USD 17.7 billion, he climbed to 67th
place on the Forbes list of the richest people on earth and 26th place among
the richest US individuals, far ahead of BlackRock boss Fink and Blackstone
boss Schwarzman, although they have much more capital under their command. But times have changed. With Bridgewater, Dalio now also wants to
expand in evil but heavily communist China. That is why he has now criticized Trump's withdrawal from the climate accord and his hyperbolic conflict
with China. Dalio recognizes that China's leaders think longer-term and more
strategically than the current US president.[265] That's why Bridgewater's leadership is being extended to include several co-owners: Not only Singapore's
sovereign wealth fund but also the IMF are joining in: in the struggle for, in
and against China, parts of the transnational capitalist class are pooling their
methods and potential here too.[266]

"Making money from the failure of states"

It is precisely the oscillation between possible failure and the possible rescue
of states and companies threatened with insolvency that is a lucrative field of
business: Prices fluctuate wildly, you can bet on that. The FAZ hedge fund wor-
shipper Dennis Kremer admiringly describes how hedge funds "earn money
from the failure of states".[267]

   And, in the example of Greece, that happened and is happening like this:
When the Greek government negotiates for months with the EU finance ministers and the Troika about bailout or no bailout, the hour has come for hedge

263   Ray Dalio on Trump, www.businessinsider.de/bridgewater 20.12.2016

264   Kremer: Rücksichtlos ibid.

265   Hedge Fund Billionaire RayDalio calls Trump's Trade War Talk "Political Show", www.
      forbes.com/sites 5.3.2018

266   Bridgewater plans to Become a Partnership as Ray Dalio Takes a Step Back, NYT
      28.6.2018

267   Staatsanleihen: Zocken mit den Griechen, FAZ 27.7.2015

funds. As long as the disbursement of the next loan tranche is still unclear, it remains unclear whether the previous loans can be serviced or will have to be (partially) written off. Hedge fund managers buy and sell the ailing government bonds and the threatened credit insurances. They are going cheap as long as Greece's insolvency is or seems possible. But then, after months of "tough negotiations", the state is (temporarily) saved, the government bonds and credit insurances are suddenly worth much more – and the hedge funds have "earned" billions of euros.[268]

And it was acted out in exactly this way before, during and after every nail-biter between the Troika and Greece – 2010, 2012, 2015 and so on. Some hedge funds do the same with bonds issued by vulnerable Greek companies and banks. In the meantime, hedge funds are threatening to take Greece to the European Court of Human Rights (ECHR) in order to at least force a compromise on the forced debt haircut[269] – what a mockery! Hedge funds and human rights! "Hedge funds have earned a great deal from Greece's decline," an expert from Baader Bank sums up.[270]

In 2016 the hedge funds Worldview, Jabre, PVE and VR also got involved in Greece.[271] Speculation can also backfire, as in the case of the son-in-law of former US President Clinton, Marc Mezvinsky, whose hedge fund Eaglevale Hellenic Opportunity went bankrupt in 2016.[272]

After Greece, Ukraine as well

Ukraine, the oligarch state pampered by the EU and NATO, is also being handed over to the speculators, although it is supposed to be being helped against the nasty Russians. But Ukraine opens up similar profit opportunities as Greece in the same game between possible insolvency and then, after all, (temporary) rescue.

Here the various classes of the new financial players are active on the same field, dividing the work between them. The big capital organizer Templeton gets a loan at zero interest from the ECB and uses it to buy Ukrainian government bonds, on which it receives 12 percent interest from the Ukrainian

---

268   Griechenland-Pleite. Hedgefonds werden für Ausfälle entschädigt, HB 9.3.2012

269   Hedgefonds drohen Athen mit einer Menschenrechtsklage, FAZ 20.1.2012

270   Profit mit Pleite. Spekulationen gegen Griechenland, ZDF frontal21 31.1.2012

271   Hedgefonds wetten auf Griechenland, HB 7.5.2016

272   https://www.boerse-online.de 30.5.2016

state, for example in 2014. However, it was uncertain whether the state, with its crashing economy and high military expenditure, could pay interest in the long term. Hedge funds such as Greylock and Golden Tree as well as PE investor Carlyle therefore bought such government bonds worth EUR 45 billion. "Opportunities for Ukraine" proclaims the business press.[273] More correct would be: opportunities for hedge funds.

Greylock prides itself on having conducted such business with several vulnerable countries since 2002, including Argentina, Ivory Coast and the Philippines. The author of the FAZ, which is highly committed to the rule of law, who traces this trail of success, melts into cool admiration: "One may find this reprehensible, but in the world of hedge funds by contrast it is an acknowledged investment category."[274]

Elliott: Heel snapper for the big boys

Stada AG is a successful pharmaceutical company with its operational headquarters in Bad Vilbel, Germany. Its 11,000 employees produce and sell branded and generic medicines in 30 countries. Top sellers for example are Grippostad and Ladival. The two established PE investors Bain and Cinven, advised by Bank Rothschild, bought 64 percent of the shares for EUR 5.4 billion. However, in order to implement the usual profit-increasing practices, other shareholders – 75 percent overall – had to approve a profit transfer and control agreement with the Stada parent company Nidda Healthcare GmbH.

Since most German shareholders were wary, the hedge fund Elliott, owned by multi-billionaire Paul Singer, tipped the scales: in the slipstream of Bain and Cinven, it had quickly bought up 15 percent of the shares. It was able to blackmail the two big names and extracted a payment in the double-digit millions: as a result, the required majority was achieved at the extraordinary shareholders' meeting on February 2, 2018. Unwilling small shareholders were simply squeezed out.[275]

Now Bain and Cinven can asset-strip Stada in peace according to their PE methods. Co-beneficiaries are members of the BlackRock family, Norges and

273   Die Hedgefonds kommen – Chancen für die Ukraine, WiWo 27.3.2014

274   Dennis Kremer: Staatsanleihen. Zocken mit den Griechen ibid.

275   Hauptversammlung stimmt Beherrschungs- und Gewinnabführungsvertrag mit der Nidda Healthcare GmbH zu, Pressemitteilung der Stada AG 2.2.2018

the Bank of America, who after Bain and Elliott are the third and fourth largest co-owners of Stada respectively. After this operation, Elliott will sell its shares at a profit and has already reconnoitered its next booty.

"Activist Shareholders"

Elliott plays the avant-garde of the "activist shareholders": that's how the heel snappers are called in the business press. They covertly snap up blocks of shares in companies on the verge of splitting up or merging, tip the scales and then allow themselves to be rewarded by the big players. This is what Elliott is currently doing at ThyssenKrupp, in cooperation with the Swedish PE investor Cevian.

The hedge funds Cerberus, Lone Star and Flowers, with the help of pressure from Brussels and state subsidies running into billions, are pushing ahead with the privatization of ailing state banks such as HSH Nordbank (Hamburg and Schleswig-Holstein). The hedge funds get the state banks "almost free of charge", can asset-strip the recoverable remainder and cut thousands of jobs.[276] The medium-term goal: privatization of the savings banks. The success is encouraging: "Aggressive hedge funds have discovered Germany for themselves".[277]

But also in Italy, the Netherlands and other EU countries such US hedge funds are turning the economy inside out.

"Future Fund" in BILD newspaper style

If, as editor-in-chief of gutter newspaper BILD, you've been the "little man's advocate" for years and at the same time promulgated the splendor of high society, then you can also found a "People's Fund". Former editor-in-chief of BILD, Kai Diekmann, who had raged against Hartz IV recipients, published a new "People's Bible" and presented it to the arch-reactionary Pope Benedict in Rome, got together with a has-been ex-banker. Extoled as a "dream team" in the business press, they founded a "Future Fund".[278]

A cent saved is a dollar earned: that is the experience of the populist-nationalist gutter newspaper. Along the lines of the concept of BlackRock and its

---

276 Ohne sie geht nichts mehr, SZ 28.11.2018; Die Investoren reich, die Länder arm, SZ 28.12.2018

277 Aktivisten schüren Fusionsfieber, HB 22.6.2018

278 Zwei Sonnyboys und ihr Milliardentraum, HB 15.3.2018

Germany lobbyist Friedrich Merz, the "Future Fund" now wants to collect the money of the little people who for years have been sitting frustrated on their zero-interest savings books. Diekmann and his banker friend plug their "fight against old-age poverty".

The banker's name is Leonhard Fischer, chummily called "Lenny" in the advertising for the fund. He attempted to earned his spurs at JP Morgan, then at Dresdner Bank, then at Crédit Suisse, always almost rising to the top. Now he is trying his hand with the people. Lenny & Kai, as clever kids at the Catholic Marienschule in Bielefeld, already produced Germany's most successful school newspaper together – stories like these are intended to help the little people's project worth billions get off the ground. Catholic – that's always good in dumb Western capitalism. With an annual fee of 1.4 percent, every fool should be able to participate in the Future Fund. As a consultant for the digital taxi service Uber, Silicon Valley fan Diekmann is already also ensuring poor working conditions worldwide and present and future poverty.

4.
Elite investment banks: The arrangers

The elite investment banks are a particularly light-shy and unknown industry. They are also pushing ahead with the neoliberal liberation of private capital and received further impetus after the last financial crisis. They concentrate on the restructuring of companies and states and in their own way increase the self-enrichment and power of the transnational capitalist class.

Lazard Ltd.

Lazard, with operational headquarters in New York, branches in 26 states and 2,500 employees, is considered the inventor of the most important investment speciality, Mergers & Acquisitions. After the statutory separation of the crisis-causing investment banking business from the small-client business in the USA – Roosevelt's New Deal in the 1930s, as a consequence of the bankruptcy of Wall Street banks – Lazard withdrew completely to this specialist area. While the state protected small customers and consumers, it gave and gives investment banks free rein.

Companies and ailing states

In recent years, Lazard has advised the French luxury group L'Oreal, the Japanese steel group Nippon Steel, the chemical group Sanofi and the largest construction group in the Western world, Vinci, on the acquisition of smaller companies worldwide.[279]

Lazard also advised PE investors such as Blackstone on the purchase of supermarkets in Italy and the over-indebted Italian bank Monte dei Paschi di Siena on the sale of departments. Lazard organized the IPO of the Vapiano restaurant chain. The Belgian, South Korean, Moroccan and Australian governments were also advised on purchases and sales.

A particularly lucrative business is advising over-indebted states, which are forced to implement rigorous cutbacks and privatization measures: Shielded from the public, in Greece, Croatia and Ukraine, Lazard and BlackRock on behalf of the Troika represent the interests of the lenders, who also prefer to remain in the background. The bank maintains close relations not only with investors but also with governments in order to get mandates.

The "normal" over-indebted Western states are also easily-exploitable business partners: Infrastructure financing with long-term government guarantees is the magic word. Wealthy clients are promised an annual return of between 3 and 12 percent if they participate in PPP contracts worth EUR 5 million or more, e.g. for motorways and telecommunications networks.[280]

Portraits: John Kornblum and Felix Rohatyn/Lazard

John Kornblum embodies the close links between elite investment banks and corporations, governments, the military and intelligence services. From 1997 to 2001, he was US Ambassador to Germany. Previously, he was US Ambassador to NATO. In the war against Yugoslavia, he was involved in NATO's eastern expansion. In 1985, he negotiated the exchange of GDR citizens, who had been recruited by the CIA and unmasked as informants, together with the then US Ambassador Richard Burt.

After his time as ambassador, he became president of Lazard Germany

---

279   See "Recent Transactions" at https://www.lazard.com, downloaded 9.4.2018; the information below is also available here.

280   Solide Rendite mit Autobahnen, FAZ 27.12.2018

– and a member of the supervisory boards of German companies that were being restructured, such as ThyssenKrupp, Bayer and Motorola Europe. With his connections, the former ambassador helped the bank "to become one of the leading investment banks in Europe".[281]

He advises the Center for Strategic and International Studies (CSIS, Washington) and serves on the boards of the US Chamber of Commerce in Germany, the Berlin American Academy and the American Council on Germany.[282] He advises the US corporations Boeing, Pfizer and Accenture.[283] Since 2015 he has been a member of the team of real estate developer BEWOCON, which manages "exclusive residential real estate in Berlin", such as Living Spree, the Stadtpalais Wilmersdorf, the Tizian Gardens ("A piece of heaven in the middle of lakes and inner cities"), the Blücherhöfe and the Diplomatenpark: Kornblum's role is to bring the rich clientele from the USA and Asia to Berlin with his contacts. He sees the transatlantic division of labor as follows: "The EU with its soft power is only successful in conjunction with US hard power".

To this day, Kornblum is cited by the leading German media and in TV talk shows as the most important expert on relations between the USA and Europe; however, they mention only that he was US ambassador to Germany – his more important functions remain unknown to the audience.

At the same time as Kornblum in Berlin, Lazard banker **Felix Rohatyn** was US ambassador in Paris for France and Monaco (1997-2000). As a banker, he advised on numerous mergers, including Daimler and Chrysler, and helped General Motors outsource suppliers abroad. He advised the City of New York on the restructuring of the New York City budget through wage freezes and layoffs.

He left Lazard in 2010, but is still a member of the Council on Foreign Relations and with Kornblum in the CSIS. Cooperation between the military and companies within the framework of NATO is part of his field of work.[284] As ambassador in Paris, Rohatyn organized the French American Business Council, in which he brought together the presidents of the USA and France (Clinton, Bush, Chirac, Sarkozy) with CEOs.

---

281   Wikipedia English: John Kornblum, downloaded 5.5.2018

282   https://www.csis.org, downloaded 9.4.2018

283   www.americanacademy.de/staff-memberr/john-c-kornblum, downloaded 9.4.2018

284   Cf. Jean-Paul Béchat / Felix Rohatyn: The Future of the Transatlantic Defense Community. Final Report of the CSIS Commission on Transatlantic Security and Industrial Cooperation in the Twenty-First Century, Washington D.C. 2003

Owned by BlackRock&Co

"Lazard prefers to recruit leading characters who bring a good network with them": Lazard appointed Rüdiger Grube, former CEO of the state-owned Deutsche Bahn, as Chairman of Lazard Deutschland in 2017. Grube had commissioned the bank to partially privatize the railway subsidiaries Schenker and Arriva.[285] In 2016, Lazard appointed Matthieu Pigasse, a former employee of the French Ministry of Finance, as Chairman in France. He is also a shareholder in Le Monde and Huffington Post. Lazard also appointed the German Jörg Asmussen, former State Secretary in the Ministry of Finance and later Director of the ECB, as Head of European Business.

Politically, the bank has traditionally been on the side of governments which wage war. The political direction played a subordinate role: in the 19th century, it lent money to the US northern states in the civil war; with ITT, it supported the putschist general Pinochet in Chile.[286] In the meantime, the connected private bank has fallen into the more sovereign hands of today's financial powers. Its main shareholders are Vanguard, BlackRock...[287] The legal domicile is in the financial haven of Bermuda: in its capital Hamilton, the representatives of Vanguard, BlackRock etc. meet every year in a relaxed atmosphere for the general meeting.[288]

Rothschild&Co

"We have the confidence of governments, major institutions, families and private clients who are among the most fortunate in the world."[289] The English word fortunate means "happy", but also "wealthy". Incidentally, this is in line with the constitution of the state in which the bank does most of its business: the US constitution guarantees the right to individual happiness, which consists above all in the individual enjoyment of the greatest possible wealth. Like Lazard, Rothschild can build on a centuries-old tradition of top political relations. Belmont Rothschild, for example, was chairman of the Democratic Party anchored in the southern US states and opponent of

---

285   Von der Bahn zur Bank, Süddeutsche Zeitung 13.7.2017

286   Richard Parker: Bankers Behaving Badly, New York Times 27.5.2017

287   https://www.nasdaq.com/laz/institutional-holdings, downloaded 9.4.2018

288   Lazard Ltd.: Annual Report on Form 10-K 2017, p. 1, investors.shareholder.com/lazard/SEC filings

289   https://www.rothschildandco.com, downloaded 9.4.2018

President Abraham Lincoln. Until well into World War I, the bankers were the advisors of kings and governments of all colonial powers and warring states and acted in the center of the then transnational "military-industrial complex".[290] With 3,400 employees in 63 branches in 44 countries, the bank today advises governments and companies on purchases, sales, mergers and loans. It can rely on the "fortunate ones" from the milieu of HNWI and UHNWI.

"Number 1 in the world"
The Rothschild Continuation Holding, headquartered in the tiny financial haven of Zug/Switzerland, legally combines the globally active Rothschild branches and numerous subsidiaries in Zurich, Paris, London, Amsterdam, New York, Bermuda, Frankfurt, Dubai, Bucharest, Tokyo, Singapore, Hong Kong, Australia and Beijing. The Jardine Matheson Holdings are the major shareholders alongside the family tribes – a global mixed group that emerged from the smuggling of opium in the 19th century,[291] with operational headquarters in Hong Kong and legal headquarters in Hamilton/Bermuda.

The bank presents itself as "number 1 in Europe and the world" for M&A, and that since 2006. 650 transactions with a total value of USD 560 billion were carried out in 2017. The annual report mentions a number of advisory mandates: Koch Equity Development, a subsidiary of Koch Industries, which belongs to one of the richest and politically most reactionary oligarch families in the USA; the French luxury groups Arnault/Christian Dior; Metro Group in the splitting up of the group (Germany); Vivendi on the acquisition of the media group Havas (France); Royal Dutch Shell (Netherlands / UK); US Steel and Avaya (USA); the pharmaceutical groups Boehringer Ingelheim and Sanofi (Germany / France); Intel on the acquisition of Mobileye (USA / Israel). The PE investors Bain Capital and Cinven were also advised on the purchase of the chemicals group Stada (Germany), Waterland on the purchase of clinics in Germany and the PE investors Cerberus and Golden Tree for the IPO of Bawag (Austria). The over-indebted government of Ukraine was advised on the issue of Eurobonds, the over-indebted government of Ireland on the

---

290   Niall Ferguson: The House of Rothschild. The World's Banker 1849-1999. London 2000, p. 412ff., 441ff.

291   Wolfgang Reinhard: Die Unterwerfung der Welt. München 2016, p. 826f.

privatization of the ailing Allied Irish Bank. Turnover was doubled compared to 2012, profits climbed to USD 1.18 billion in 2017.[292]

Master of privatizations throughout the western world

In 2007, Rothschild boasted that, since the 1980s, it had advised more than 60 governments on more privatizations in Europe and worldwide than any other investment bank. Rothschild began working for the British Tory governments under Edward Heath and especially Margret Thatcher in the 1970s, selling state-owned gas and electrical companies, oil production licenses, British Telecom, British Steel, British Coal, British Rail. Rothschild bankers became ministers, and ministers became Rothschild bankers. This continued in the late 1990s with the socialist-tinted New Labour under Anthony Blair and the new privatization blueprint Public Private Partnership (PPP).

Rothschild privatizations became a global export hit between Brazil, Australia and Zambia. Via Blair, Rothschild also came to Germany as a PPP advisor to the then German Chancellor Gerhard Schröder.[293] Privatizations here include Telekom and Fraport Airport, in Turkey the telephone network (sold to Vodafon), in Serbia the telephone network (sold to Telenor), the Portuguese airline TAP, in Denmark the electrical company DONG (sold to Vattenfall) and the ferry company Scandlines, in France the power company EdF and the telephone company France Telecom.[294]

"This immense transfer of public wealth into the private sector was one of the most important economic changes in the world economy of the late 20th century."[295]

Inbreeding with government personnel

Such privatizations work with the revolving door mechanism between the state and the private sector. They harm taxpayers and citizens, and they benefit consultants and their "fortunate" clients. To this end, Rothschild gathers and funds hundreds of high-ranking politicians and officials in its international, regional and national advisory councils. They usually get less than USD

---

292 Rothschild&Co: Rapport Annuel 2017, p. 12ff.

293 Brummer l.c., p. 23; Der Spiegel 12/2017, p. 17

294 N M Rothschild&Sons: Relevant Experience, 25.10.2007, Memorandum for the Swedish Government, www.regeringen.se/contentassets, downloaded 11.4.2018

295 Ferguson: House of Rothschild l.c., p. 494

100,000 for two to three meetings a year, but this "(a)social capital" is obviously worth more.

After his tenure in office, former Chancellor Schröder was appointed to the European Advisory Council for a decade to serve as a door opener, especially in Russia and Eastern Europe.[296] Further advisory board members at the time of Schröder's appointment were the former heads of Coca Cola, Volvo and the Bank of England as well as Klaus Mangold of DaimlerChrysler, who is still chairman of the advisory board of Rothschild Deutschland GmbH today and with which he also has an even better paid consultancy contract.

The government of Schröder's successor Merkel (CDU) did not lose the connection either. For the bank rescue fund SOFFIN, Finance Minister Schäuble fetched Rothschild as consultant, in the usual convoy with the US law firm Mayer Brown and its co-owner Friedrich Merz, then KPMG, PWC, Freshfields and Goldman Sachs.[297]

Rothschild marriage in the White House
Lady Lynn Forester de Rothschild, head of The Economist magazine (BlackRock is on the board), CFR member, was advisor to US President Clinton and co-funded all of the two Clinton election campaigns. Her marriage was celebrated with the Clintons at the White House. But when Obama prevailed against Hillary Clinton in the Democratic Party, the Rothschild lady coolly supported the right-wing republican McCain.[298]

The revolving door culture of the "fortunate ones" takes many forms. After his tenure as head of the US Federal Reserve, Paul Volcker immediately became head of Rothschild USA.[299] Lord Nathanael Rothschild is a member of Blackstone's International Advisory Board.[300] These people manage the assets of the most fortunate, but, like the colleagues from Lazard, alongside BlackRock&Co, they do not think themselves too good to also push as a shareholder for the highest possible profit at a company such as Ryan Air with its radical low-wage policy.

---

296   Schröder berät die Investmentbank Rothschild, FAZ online 24.3.2006

297   Wie sich PWC und KPMG die Bälle zuspielen, WiWo 11.6.2009

298   https://www.politico.eu 5.8.2015, abgerufen 11.4.2018

299   www.americanacademy.de/person/paul-volcker/

300   https://family.rothschildarchive.org/people, abgerufen 11.4.2018

Portrait: Wilbur Ross –
From Rothschild-Banker to US Secretary of Commerce

Wilbur Ross began his banking career in 1976 at Rothschild's New York office before founding his own investment firm in 2000. But the connections were not lost. When Rothschild advised the Irish state on its bank rescue in 2011, Ross bought a third of the Bank of Ireland's shares with a US group of investors after the Troika took over the guarantee. As a result, the value of the shares then tripled and Ross was able to collect his share of the USD 500 million profit. He proceeded similarly in the EU crisis states Greece, Portugal, Spain and Italy, advised by Rothschild, Lazard & Co.[301] With this damage to Irish taxpayers, Ross had qualified for the position of Commerce Secretary in the Trump administration.[302] Through a chain of mailbox companies, Ross has a stake in Navigation Holdings, a shipping company based in Panama: He bet on the slide in the share price because, as US Secretary of Commerce and thus as an insider, he knew or could assume that orders for transports from Russia would fall because of the embargo against Russia which he himself had agreed to.[303] As a member of the transnational capitalist class, Ross demonstrates how, with "America First", self-enrichment is organized globally.

Portrait: Emmanuel Macron –
From Rothschild banker to President of France

Probably the largest M&A deal by Bank Rothschild in recent years was the following: The co-owner Emmanuel Macron advised the food group Nestlé on the takeover of the baby food division of the US group Pfizer. Nestlé paid USD 11.8 billion dollars, the bonus for Macron was one million.[304]

The opportunist

At this time Macron was also the economic advisor to the radical right-wing president Nicolas Sarkozy. Because his re-election stood no chance, Macron

---

301 U.S. billionaire Wilbur Ross cashes out Bank of Ireland stake, Reuters 10.6.2014

302 Trump adviser more than tripled his money in Ireland, https://www.irishtimes.com 1.12.2016

303 Ganz schön abgezockt, Süddeutsche Zeitung 21.6.2018

304 Nestlé machte Macron reich, Blick (Switzerland) 30.9.2017

mercilessly and opportunistically joined the election campaign team of social-ist leader Francois Hollande. Macron embodies the political attitude of the new financial players: "conservative" or "socialist" or then "non-partisan" – no matter. Demagogy is part of the business model: while Hollande railed against "the financial world" and called for a top tax rate of 75 percent, advi-sor Macron prepared the opposite.

As Economics Minister, he privatized part of the transport system (long-distance bus transport), but quit when he could not make any progress with the "reform" of working conditions. Because the re-election prospects of the socialists were hopeless and the primary populist parties were corrupt and degenerate, his milieu promoted a form of secondary populism that superfi-cially distanced itself from the previous capital-friendly parties: With the "En Marche" movement, Macron became France's president.

The populist

The master of populist fake production maintains that he will finally over-come the old left-wing and right-wing antagonisms, but is pursuing an in-tensified ultra-right-wing policy. His most potent supporters come from the center of the new financial players. During the operation with Nestlé and Pfizer, he was in exchange with their major shareholders BlackRock&Co. Henri de Castries, former head of the insurance group AXA (owner: BlackRock&Co) and coordinator of the Bilderberg conference, as well as the head of the second largest PE investor KKR, Henry Kravis, contributed concept and money for the campaign of the transatlanticist – KKR owns 18 companies in France.[305]

Macron is not the first post-war French head of state from the House of Rothschild. Georges Pompidou moved from the Bank's Directorate General to the government as Prime Minister in 1962 to become President from 1969 to 1974. He promoted the automobile and nuclear industries, had railway lines shut down, committed the state in 1973 with the "Loi Rothschild" to borrow only from private banks, brought US Pop Art to France with the Museum Centre Pompidou and, as a transatlanticist also, warned US President Richard Nixon against withdrawing troops from Europe.

---

305 Thierry Meyssan: Envers qui Emmanuel Macron est-il débiteur?, Réseau Voltaire 11.12.2018

The militarist, the nationalist...

The USA admirer Macron also wants to arm the EU to become a parallel world power, designed to expand Western and especially french capitalism worldwide alongside NATO and the USA. In the failed state of Libya Macron supports the eastern warlord in Benghasi against the western warlord in Tripolis who is supported by the german government of Merkel and the NATO. Macron prepares to sell off state-owned companies, some of which have already been partially privatized, such as the SNCF railway and the capital's two airports.

The friend of the "fortunate ones"

Macron has drastically reduced the tax burden on the "fortunate ones": He abolished the wealth tax as well as the tax on dividends. He cut the housing allowance for the poorest by EUR 5 a month. He is disempowering the public administration and wants to privatize the social security system.

Wage formation is being taken away from the trade unions and shifted into the jungle of individual company agreements. Faced by widespread protest of the "yellow vests", he promised to increase the minimum wage by EUR 100. But this increase is not paid by the entrepreneurs, and the payment by the state is highly bureaucratic and uncertain.[306]

The propagandist of the Catholic Nation

For the self-enrichment of the "fortunate ones", co-organized by the state, the globalizing banker also wants to restore the counterrevolutionary unity of nation and Catholic Church. French Enlightenment, democracy – everything is over. Before the assembled bishops of France the Jesuit pupil evoked "the indestructible bonds between the French nation and Catholicism... the Catholic power must again and forever bring our nation to life".[307]

The prophets of morally and democratically run-down capitalism use every attainable and appropriate symbol, every attainable religion – Catholic Church, Evangelicals, Judaism, Islamism – every tradition, however saturnine, every shining palace of old oppressors.

---

306   Serge Halimi: Alles kommt an die Oberfläche, Le Monde Diplomatique Januar 2019

307   Emmanuel Macron tend la main aux catholiques, Le Figaro 10.4.2018

Schroders PLC

Like Lazard and Rothschild, Bank Schroders, long named Schröder because of its German founders, also has a tradition stretching back to the beginning of the 19th century. In 1863, together with the Parisian bank Erlanger, it financed the Confederates in the American Civil War against the northern states. Before World War I it financed German overseas trade, which collapsed during the war; after the war it advised the German government and, together with Barings and Rothschild, was one of the largest banks in London.[308]

Behind private equity

Like Lazard, Schroders withdrew into strategic consulting for companies and governments. In 2017 it managed GBP 447 billion of UHNWI capital. The PE subsidiaries Permira and Cazenove invest part of their capital in company acquisitions. With headquarters in London, branches in 29 states and 4,600 employees, the bank is mainly active in the USA, then in Germany, Switzerland, the Gulf States and China. The use of the British financial havens of Gibraltar, Jersey and Guernsey as well as the financial havens of Luxembourg, the Netherlands and Switzerland belongs to the obvious business tools. This traditional family bank has also recently become the property of the new financial players. PE investors dominate, but Vanguard and Fidelity are also co-owners.

Behind Rothschild, the bank had played a leading role in privatizations in Western Europe since the 1980s, for example with the investment bank SG Warburg in the privatization of water under the government of Margaret Thatcher. Major mandates included the privatizations of the French state bank Crédit Lyonnais and Deutsche Telekom.[309]

Founding the Group of Thirty

With Gordon Richardson, Schroders provided the Governor of the Bank of England, with James Wolfensohn the President of the World Bank from 1995 to 2005. Schroders CEO Geoffrey Bell founded the Group of Thirty in 1978 with the support of the Rockefeller Foundation. This exclusive capital lobby of only 30 members is currently led by the President of Wall Street Bank JPMorganChase. 13 members, including the former head of the US Federal Reserve,

---

308   Richard Roberts: Schroders. Merchants and Bankers, New York 1992
309   Corporate Profile Schroders, The Independent 10.11.1999

Ben Bernanke, come from the USA. Other members come from major central banks and the World Bank. Mario Draghi, President of the ECB, who came from Goldman Sachs, is also represented, as is recently Philipp Hildebrand, Vice-President of BlackRock.[310]

Macquarie Group LC

In Australia, too, bankers took deregulation into their own hands at an early stage, even before it was legally legitimized, following the models in New York and London. As early as 1969, the new investment bank Macquarie was founded in Sydney. Today, with offices in New York, London, Paris, Frankfurt, Abu Dhabi, Hong Kong, Beijing, etc. and 14,500 employees, it is the world's largest private financier of infrastructure.

Master of private infrastructure
Macquarie arranges M&A and invests its funds, in which capital from HNWI, insurance companies and companies is collected, in privatized or privately constructed new infrastructure: ports, airports, toll roads and bridges, tunnels, hospitals, drinking water and sewage plants, power stations: here, too, the state profit guarantee plays an important role – contrary to the neoliberal lie theory according to which state economy is of the devil. Macquarie also advises other investors such as Bain Capital, Bridgepoint, Odewald and Permira on buying and selling companies using the PE method.[311]

Initially in Australia, the Bank promoted privatizations for the state and regional authorities. With the tools acquired here, it also became active in Europe in the 1990s. In Germany, for example, it arranged the construction and operation of the Warnow Tunnel near Rostock with the French construction group Bouygues and the lenders Deutsche Bank and HSH Nordbank. It was launched in 2003 according to the PPP model, even before the German Bundestag had passed the PPP Act. The tunnel was to be refinanced over a period of 30 years through car, bus and truck tolls. However, the courtesy feasibility report procured by Macquarie did not prove to be true. The toll was tripled and the term extended to 50 years.[312]

---

310   http://group30.org, downloaded 9.4.2018

311   See https://macquarie.com/our deals

312   Werner Rügemer: "Heuschrecken" im öffentlichen Raum. Public Private Partnership. Bielefeld 2012, p. 135

During Tony Blair's tenure in the UK, Macquarie bought the water and sewage system of London, Thames Water. With the help of loans Thames Water had to take out, Macquarie generated an annual return of between 15.5 and 19 percent for its investors. In 2017 the bank sold its last shares and left behind a company sitting on a debt pile of GBP 2 billion.[313]

Perella Weinberg

The most recent start-ups of this type of bank are often casually referred to as investment "boutiques". One of these is Perella Weinberg, founded in 2006 and now employing 650 people, with headquarters in New York and London and branches in San Francisco, Denver, Abu Dhabi and Dubai. European boss Dietrich Becker, who learned at Merrill Lynch and Morgan Stanley, outlines the new tasks: We are now expanding in the EU, not only because of Brexit. He remains silent about the individual mandates. From other sources it became known that Perella Weinberg was advising E.ON on the takeover of RWE subsidiary Innogy.[314]

When advising the industrial gas manufacturer Linde it became known: Perella Weinberg receives a fee of EUR 36 million. During the preparation of the merger with its US competitor Praxair, Wolfgang Reitzle, Chairman of the Supervisory Board of Linde, was at the same time co-owner of Perella Weinberg and the most important driving force behind the merger. Only after the start of the official merger negotiations and after public criticism did Reitzle let his partnership "rest".[315] Here, too, "consultancy" is another term for coordinated, privileged self-service.

5.
Private banks: Discreet front for the big players

Almost invisible to the general public, the small, fine private banks are also active, with fresh momentum following the financial crisis. This "silent industry"

---

313   How Macquarie bank left Thames Water with extra GBP 2bn debt, BBC News 5.9.2017

314   "Es gibt auch gute Gründe für Frankfurt", HB 9.4.2018

315   Wer an der Fusion von Linde mit Praxair verdient, www.faz.net 29.9.2017

has "grown rapidly" in recent years, according to the Elite Report 2018.[316] We take a look at the situation in Germany.

The Elite Report presents 66 such banks. In 2017 they managed assets in excess of EUR 1 trillion – in the previous year it had been just under EUR 900 million. These banks receive their capital from medium-sized entrepreneur families, wealthy freelancers, senior citizens and heirs, as well as from Catholic dioceses and Protestant institutions.[317] "Our target group are the 10,000 richest Germans, who hold over 50 percent of the total assets of the German population," Matthias Graf von Krockow, head of Sal. Oppenheim, the largest of these banks at the time, announced at the beginning of the 21st century.[318]

These banks usually have a main regional catchment area, especially large cities such as Munich, Hamburg, Cologne, Frankfurt, Berlin, Leipzig and Stuttgart, but also regional centers such as Düsseldorf, Bielefeld, Nuremberg, Münster, Hanover, Dortmund, Bremen and Augsburg. The banks seek out their sub-groups from the target group spread across the country, which has probably quadrupled since the Oppenheim boss's statement. For example, at DZ Privatbank you can start with a deposit from as little as EUR 250,000, whereas at ODDO BHF you are particularly welcome with a deposit of EUR 25 million or more.

The better-known names are Merck Finck, Berenberg, HSBC Trinkaus & Burckhardt (with Friedrich Merz on the Supervisory Board), Fürst Fugger Privatbank, Weberbank, Bethmann, Metzler, Hauck & Aufhäuser. Foreign private banks also have branches in Germany, for instance Pictet and Julius Baer from Switzerland and Liechtenstein Global Trust LGT from the Principality of Liechtenstein. At the same time, the larger private banks also have branches abroad, in Chicago, New York, San Francisco, Luxembourg, Vienna, Geneva and Zurich.

This "silent industry", as a kind of upfront organization, gives part of its clientele's assets to the big players to grow them, sells BlackRock's financial

---

316 Elitereport extra: Ausgezeichnete Vermögensverwalter, www.elitereport.de, downloaded 27.4.2018, as supplement in the media of the target audience HB, WiWo und FAS, April and May 2018

317 Elitereport ibid., p. 3ff.

318 Werner Rügemer: Der Bankier. Ungebetener Nachruf auf Alfred von Oppenheim, Frankfurt/Main 2006, p. 92. The bank went bust in 2009, the Wealth Management Division was bought by the Deutsche Bank.

products and participates as capital provider and lender for PE investors. They are particularly discreet and soundless. The private banks, which employ a high proportion of aristocratic personnel, have been practicing this for centuries.

Switzerland is still the leading location in Western Europe. The two largest, Pictet and Julius Baer, alone, manage almost as much client assets as the German private banks combined: just under EUR 800 billion. For some years now, both have been expanding their branches within the EU, which is disintegrating into rich and poor. And they too are professionals in organized tax evasion: "After Switzerland, Guernsey, Hong Kong, Monaco, Singapore and the Bahamas, Germany is one of the seven accounting centers of the Julius Baer Group".[319]

6.
Venture Capitalists: The preparers

The risk or venture financiers are constantly on the lookout for small start-ups that still have few employees but promise a great future. Then the venture capitalists move in gradually. This can start with 100,000 dollars or euros and can rise up to a three-digit million sum. Often several venture companies join forces to jointly finance a start-up.

After two to four years, either the IPO, the takeover by a company or the resale to the next venture- or PE-investor is successful. In most cases, the start-up founders remain in the company as senior managers with a stake of between 5 and 10 percent, while the venture capitalists sell their stake at a profit after a few years; when things go really well, BlackRock&Co ultimately get involved, as we will see at Facebook&Co.

Origins in the technology-intensive industries
The method was developed in the 1960s in the USA. The focus was on data processing in the vicinity of Stanford University and the local armaments companies such as Lockheed. General Electric, IBM, the telephone company AT&T and the car manufacturers Ford and General Motors – large

---

319 https://www.juliusbaer.com/de, downloaded 10.5.2018

armament producers – were also constantly on the lookout for the latest technologies. Having long been limited to the arms industry and the traditional large corporations, it spread to independent start-ups.[320] In 1983 alone, Hambrecht&Quist from San Francisco financed 66 start-ups mainly in Silicon Valley. Hundreds of software and chip developers and data analysts were supported every year. From the beginning of the 1980s, global corporations such as Apple, Microsoft, Amazon, Google, Facebook, Uber and Spotify were able to emerge within a few decades and then more and more quickly.

Banks and corporations too

The venture capitalists are also mostly ex-bankers. Their companies remain small and usually have only a few employees, between five and 50. But banks also use this method and set up venture capital subsidiaries. This is what corporations like Google do anyway, which have themselves been formed in this way and then expand further by constantly buying up start-ups.

Other companies do the same, such as chip manufacturer Intel, Siemens, BASF, eyewear seller Fielmann, Bosch, Evonik and Deutsche Lufthansa. The Boston Consulting Group (BCG) founded BCG Digital Ventures. The digital venture subsidiary of Axel Springer-Verlag and the digital venture subsidiary of Porsche supported the joint start-up company Accelerator.

After all, the big capital organizers of the top league such as BlackRock, Fidelity and Wellington also create such specialized subsidiaries – in the case of private equity they do the same.

... and also intelligence services

Secret services, which are constantly in search of even better surveillance technologies, also maintain venture capital subsidiaries: the CIA's best-known company is called In-Q-Tel.[321] It invested in the rise of Palantir, for example. This company quickly expanded to now 2000 employees in 15 locations worldwide. CIA, NSA, US Department of the Interior and US military are the main clients.

---

320   Werner Rügemer: Neue Technik – Alte Gesellschaft. Silicon Valley, Köln 1985, p. 165ff.

321   Christian Bergmann / Christian Fuchs: SAP arbeitet für die NSA, Zeit online 10.3.2015

Biotechnology, climate, media, social media...

Among the financial stars of Silicon Valley, Brian Singerman is currently right at the top. He co-founded Founders Fund with Peter Thiel. He supported the start-up Stemcentrx, manufacturer of a drug to fight cancer. Founders Fund invested USD 300 million and two years later was able to sell the company to the pharmaceutical company AbbVie at a profit of USD 1.4 billion. Singerman had previously promoted the start-up Climate Corporation (weather and soil measurements) and sold it to the agricultural company Monsanto. Similarly, Deep Mind was promoted and sold to Google. Founders Fund also financed the rise of the broker of private and hotel rooms, Airbnb.

Sequoia Capital invested in the messenger WhatsApp and was able to sell it to Facebook for USD 3 billion. Baseline Ventures invested in the photo/video online service Instagram, founded in 2009, and sold it to Facebook three years later for USD 1 billion.[322]

The largest venture capital firms are based in the USA, in the Silicon Valley strongholds San Francisco, Palo Alto and Menlo Park, some in New York, Boston and Texas. The largest is the subsidiary of the chip manufacturer Intel with a capital volume of USD 9 billion, followed by Oak Investment, Insight, IDG, Accel, Draper Fisher, Intellectual, Vantage Point, the already mentioned Founders Fund (3 billion) and Sequoia, then Austin Ventures, Highland, General Catalyst down to Google Ventures with USD 1.6 billion.[323]

The method is also used in China, Asia, South America and Europe. There are several dozen venture capitalists active in Germany. However, Google Ventures, Intel Capital, Comcoast, Salesforce and Cisco Investments dominate the field. The first German companies are subsidiaries of corporations and are ranked 26th (retailer Tengelmann), 36th (Bertelsmann Digital Media) and 49th (pharmaceutical group Boehringer) in Germany.[324]

---

322 Midas 2017: Meet the 100 Best Venture Capitalists in the World, https://www.forbes.com 18.4.2017

323 https://en.wikipedia.org/wiki/list-of-venture-capital-firms, downloaded 20.3.2018

324 https://www.gruenderszene.de 12.1.2018 und 8.11.2016, downloaded 20.3.2018

Portrait: Peter Thiel / Founders Fund

Peter Thiel is the best-known venture capitalist in Silicon Valley. He studied at Stanford. He then worked at the Wall Street law firm Sullivan & Cromwell, which is known as the launchpad for Allen and John F. Dulles, who represented German and US corporations simultaneously since the 1920s; Allen Dulles became CIA Director after 1945, John F. Dulles became US Secretary of State. After a stopover at Credit Suisse, Thiel set up his own business as a venture capitalist and floated PayPal, YouTube and LinkedIn on the stock exchange. He was one of the first Facebook investors in 2004. He founded the venture capital firm Founders Fund, which promoted about 100 start-ups, including Spotify, Lyft, SpaceX and Palantir. Thiel also serves on the supervisory boards of Facebook and Palantir Technologies. Palantir (the seeing stone) is one of the major software suppliers to US intelligence, Department of Home Security, Air Force, Marines and the US Civil Protection Agency. Thiel invited former Secretary of State Condoleezza Rice and former CIA chief George Tenet to join the advisory group.[325] The government instructed Palantir to neutralize the publication of secret military and diplomatic data by Wikileaks. Palantir's Big Data systems are used in war zones such as Afghanistan to search for and kill "terrorists", as well as to check Muslims entering the US and for automated securities trading.[326]

Like Amazon boss Bezos, Thiel described himself as "libertarian": for "authentic human freedom as the highest good", mankind must create politics- and state-free zones, in cyberspace/internet, in space and with settlements on the sea. The freedom of the individual is not compatible with democracy, the welfare state and women's suffrage. "I do not believe that freedom and democracy are compatible."[327] He considers competition in capitalism to be alien to its nature, everyone must acquire as much as possible by all means: "Competition is something for losers."[328] He donated USD 1.25 million to the radical right-wing candidate Donald Trump.[329]

---

325 Der geheimnisvolle Aufseher, HB 19.4.2018

326 Sam Biddle: How Peter Thiel's Palantir helped the NSA spy on the whole world, Intercept 22.2.2017; Dieses Genie baut die "wichtigste Firma der Welt", Die Welt 3.5.2016

327 Peter Thiel: The Education of a Libertarian, https://www.cato-unbound.org 13.4.2009; Peter Thiel: Auf dem Sprung, HB 19.2.2018

328 "Competition is for Losers", Wall Street Journal 12.9.2014

329 Thiel spendet für Trump, FAZ 18.10.2016

As a delegate to the Republican National Convention in 2016, he promoted Trump, who would lead America back to "a bright future" and continue the Cold War that the United States had won. Thiel was rewarded with a standing ovation from the party conference, which had initially been somewhat perplexed: "I am proud to be gay." But then: "I am proud to be a Republican. Above all, I am proud to be an American."[330] He is also proud to be a Christian. After Trump's election, he worked with the heads of Blackstone, KKR, Amazon, Facebook, Google, Apple, Cisco, Tesla and Uber as economic advisor to the new US president and continues to advise and donate to him. The multi-billionaire founded SpaceX with Tesla CEO Elon Musk to bring US rocket technology to a new level and colonize first Mars and then other areas of space with a rich elite. He promotes seasteading, the building of settlements for rich individuals at sea outside the reach of existing states. In addition to US citizenship, he also secured German and New Zealand citizenship. As a transhumanist, he has researched how the biological aging of successful humans can be halted. He wants to live eternally with the blood of young people.[331]

Silicon Valley comes to Europe
According to Silicon Valley Bank (SVB), it has already financed 30,000 startups since 1983. It does this directly, but also through loans to PE investors, hedge funds and other venture capitalists. The SVB promises its investors double-digit returns.

Since 2004, the SVB has opened offices in the UK, Israel, Hong Kong and China, and now it's the turn of Germany and Canada. In May 2018 the branch office in Frankfurt/Main was opened. As with Amazon, Facebook and Microsoft&Co, the investments focus on artificial intelligence, life science and medical technology. The business press interprets the opening of the Frankfurt branch as the "accolade" from the much-admired Silicon Paradise for Germany as a business location.[332]

---

330 https://www.gruenderszene.de 22.7.2016; www.businessinsider.de 22.7.2016

331 Die Zeit 19.12.2018. The other well-known Silicon Valley venture capitalist Thomas Weisel sponsored many start-ups as well as the team of cyclist Lance Armstrong, who won the Tour de France seven times in 1999-2005 using state-of-the-art doping. In 2006, Weisel received the National Venture Capital Association award for his life's work. In 2013 Armstrong confessed to doping only after long denial.

332 Ritterschlag für deutsche start ups, HB 4.5.2018

7.
Traditional banks as service providers

Following the financial crisis of 2007, the traditional major banks were rescued by the state and lightly regulated. They have lost their previous position vis-à-vis the new financial players. On the one hand, BlackRock&Co are now the owners of these banks. Secondly, BlackRock, Blackstone, Bridgewater, Founders Fund and Rothschild are turning existing companies, banks and states inside out. Thirdly, the new financial players have more capital backing from their wealthy clients.

Service providers for the new financial players
The disempowered banks battle to grant loans to the new financial players for their operations. The banks ambivalently drag the millions of small customers around with them: Compared to the capital deposits of rich and institutional customers with the new financial players, the salary and savings accounts and small securities deposits of "normal earners" and recipients of state transfers and pensions are meager and horrendously expensive to manage. Belatedly, the banks are now busy rationalizing, automating, digitalizing, yet all this still does not generate much. Close branches or not?

With their lending to the new financial players, the traditional banks are once again contributing to the next possible financial crisis. Next time round, it is possible that they will no longer be rescued – BlackRock&Co will then be "systemically relevant".

Two-class system USA – Western Europe
The big banks continue to trade in securities of all kinds. A good business is the organization of IPOs, i.e. when a start-up company that has been featherbedded by the new financial players is ready to go public. The banks earn between 5 and 7 percent of the share volume.

However, here and more than in the past, US banks now also dominate the business in Europe. In Germany, the order in which IPOs are organized according to share volume today looks as follows: Goldman Sachs, JPMorgan, Crédit Suisse, Deutsche Bank, UBS, Citibank, BNP Paribas, Bank of America Merrill Lynch, Berenberg Bank, Morgan Stanley.[333]

333　HB 22.3.2018, as of Q1 2018

When it comes to M&A, "German" banks play no role at all. In this field, the investment bank Rothschild leads the pack.[334] Rothschild is followed by Citibank, BNP Paribas, Bank of America Merrill Lynch, Perella Weinberg, JPMorgan, D'Angelin, Catalist Partners, Goldman Sachs. Lazard leads in infrastructure securities.[335] Goldman Sachs & Co are also continuing to expand their branches in the EU countries and especially in Germany.

The former largest bank in Germany, Deutsche Bank, has slipped further down the international rankings. In addition, two remaining German members were removed from the Supervisory Board in 2018 and replaced by two Wall Street bankers.[336]

"Europe's banks are struggling to keep up with the US competition. The lead of Wall Street houses is getting bigger and bigger", the result is a "two-class society".[337] While BlackRock&Co grant the head of Deutsche Bank an annual salary of only three million, they grant the head of JPMorgan ten times as much, namely 30 million.[338]

8.
The Internet capitalists

The Internet was founded by the US military after the Sputnik shock in 1957. After the collapse of the socialist states in 1990, it was released for commercial use. At the latest due to the new financial players, it became an indispensable business medium. Apart from a few brave peace activists like Lockheed engineer Robert Aldridge, the military's leadership function was taken for granted.[339] Multifarious cooperation, including secret services, still exists today.

---

334   www.regeringen.se/contentassets, downloaded 11.4.2018

335   HB 22.3.2018, 23.3.2018 und 26.3.2018

336   Neue Kontrolleure, HB 9.4.2018

337   Zweiklassen-Gesellschaft, HB 23.3.2018

338   Jeden Tag 81.000 Dollar, HB 23.3.2018

339   Werner Rügemer: Neue Technik – alte Gesellschaft ibid., p. 105

Key questions
Public knowledge about the five "digital vampires" or "apocalyptic riders" of the Internet – Google, Amazon, Microsoft, Facebook, Apple (GAMFA)[340] – and about the platform economy is widespread, but fragmentary. The following analysis, using exemplary depictions, therefore focuses on the following questions: the role of the new financial players, labor relations, economic and environmental effects, relations with politics and the state, interdependence with secret services and the military, and finally resistance and alternatives.

Pioneers of digital everyday life: Apple and Microsoft
For today's digital technology, the new computer and software companies Microsoft and Apple (founded in 1975 and 1976) played a preparatory role together with the companies that had been militarily involved from the outset, such as Hewlett Packard, IBM, Texas Instruments, Motorola and Intel. Then the platform economy expanded with Amazon and Google (founded in 1994 and 1997), then Facebook (founded in 2004) and then with the even faster rise of Uber, Airbnb, Netflix, Parship&Co (founded in 2009) and the like.

Apple: Personal computers and much more
In the mid-1970s, the production of ever more powerful, ever smaller semiconductors had progressed so far that they became ever cheaper due to mass production. From 1972, Texas Instruments also produced chips for pocket calculators. Thousands of technicians, including former military engineers, built the first home computers.

Invention and vision
On 5 March 1975, 32 such nerds met in Menlo Park/Silicon Valley. They founded the Homebrew Computer Club. Homebrew – "we brew our computers ourselves", just like you can brew beer at home. Then they met twice a month in a lecture hall at Stanford University/Palo Alto. They introduced each other to the hardware and software they had put together. In 1976 a certain William Gates, who at the time worked in a small software supplier in the second most important high-tech armaments region – Seattle with the Boeing aircraft and armaments company – protested that the club had stolen his program.

Club member Steve Jobs had worked briefly at Atari, a company founded

---

340   Digitale Vampire, HB 23.3.2018

in 1972 that produced the first home computers, computer games and game consoles. In 1974 he toured India like many US hippies and quickly absorbed some elements of Hinduism and Buddhism. At the club, the 21-year-old and his friend Steve Wozniak presented the homemade Apple I – a small desktop computer in a wooden case. Jobs chose the name Apple because he was a convinced fruitarian (a kind of vegetarian). Several specimens were sold. Jobs and his friend founded the Apple Computer Company in 1976. At a computer fair in San Francisco in 1977 they presented the Apple II.

Communitarian techno-world

Until his death in 2011, the ingenious inventor Steve Jobs played the fruitarian visionary and pied piper. In 2001, he had further expanded his initial vision: The digital device – after the refined computer Macintosh now the latest version of the smartphone – is to become the center of life. Digital technology penetrates everyday life with music, images, speech and peripheral devices and makes life, indeed mankind, better. This was proclaimed by the sensitive visionary on large stages, dressed in washed-out jeans, sandals, baggy sweater and nickel glasses.

Jobs and thousands of his peers like William Gates were inspired by the New Communalists: The communitarians proclaimed an egalitarian, liberal, non-hierarchical counter-model to the "advanced industrial society", which the "critical theory" also called or hoped for as "late capitalism".[341] The new, clean technology enables access to all information regardless of gender, race, faith and purchasing power. This partly overlapped with "New Left" and was somewhat diffusely directed against church, tradition, big business and the government in Washington.[342]

In the early days Jobs even dreamed of a *corporate socialism*: A company like Apple provided its employees with all the amenities not even socialism promised: child care, fitness breaks, enthusiastic work at airy workplaces, culture, a vegetarian canteen, free travel to the workplace – all employees are equal, everyone uses first names.[343] As his success grew, he gradually dropped the suffix socialism, leaving *corporate* and support for General Electric press spokesman and US President Ronald Reagan.[344]

---

341   Herbert Marcuse: The Onedimensional Man, Boston 1964

342   Fred Turner: From Counterculture to Cyberculture, Chicago 2006, p. 33ff.

343   Werner Rügemer: Neue Technik – alte Gesellschaft ibid., p. 47f.

344   Declan McCullagh: Silicon Valley's Dangerous Political Blind Spots, reason.com 15.4.2018

Planned obsolescence with Microsoft

Once commercial success became apparent, the venture capital companies Davis&Rock, Venrock Associates, Sequoia and Singleton moved in one after the other in 1978. The next leap forward was made possible by the Xerox copy machine and office technology group. Xerox had set up a research center in the industrial park of Stanford University in 1970. It was here that the user interface was developed, initially for the military and later then also important for Apple, which allows users to click icons with a "mouse" and quickly and easily access games or other programs on the computer.

The Xerox Group made it a condition that it received Apple preference shares prior to the upcoming IPO. After the IPO in 1980, the marketing director of Pepsi Cola became Apple's boss. The alternative outfit gradually became a normal but more modern US corporation.

In 1997, Apple began working with William Gates, Microsoft, a software company that had been founded at the same time and had also risen rapidly. Cross-licenses were agreed and a cartel was set up. The obsolescence of the digital products was planned with military precision, each new version of a software, of a computer was equipped with some new features (storage space, installation of third-party software, GPS), but not with all that were possible – they came only in the next and next but one version. In order to stir up the public hype for the next version, users and fans were studiously spied on. Without revealing the depth of the spying, the snug motto was "We want to understand you better". In this way hysteria could be generated that one simply had to buy the newest version in order to "keep up". Apple and Microsoft became leaders in the planned psychological-technological obsolescence.[345]

Conventional US capitalism with Silicon Valley flair

The Apple leadership gradually did what US corporations do: The founders and top managers reaped the big advantages with preference shares, side businesses and bonuses – albeit with a sharp hierarchical structure.

In populist manner, Jobs had forgone a salary since 2001 and had a symbolic dollar paid out to him each year – and accumulated a billion-dollar fortune in the process. In 2006, Jobs collected USD 657 million from stock options at Apple alone. He was thus several times ahead of the highest paid

---

345   Geplante Obsoleszenz, https://www.focus.de, downloaded 6.4.2018

bosses of Wall Street banks and the largest oil companies.[346] But that was only part of his income: since 2006 he was also the largest shareholder of the Walt Disney Company.

Cartels, customer spying, violations of the law: Like any US company, Apple also organizes tax evasion with the help of a web of mailbox companies in Ireland and the Netherlands, for example.[347] Apple sold its mobile phones in the EU with a one-year warranty and additional insurance for a longer warranty even though a two-year guarantee is the norm in the EU.[348]

Depending on their level in the hierarchy, the Apple managers are rewarded with two-digit and single-digit millions, and sometimes they were allowed to fly in the private jet provided by Apple for Steve Jobs. Most employees grapple with overtime – some gladly, others less gladly. The spotlessness of the bungalows, swimming pools and front gardens of the high-tech middle class on the mountain heights of Silicon Valley is ensured by black and Mexican day laborers.

Low-wage armies between Asia and Ireland

Far away in Asia, in the murderous and suicidal treadmill of subcontractor Foxconn, Apple has the hard work done that you can't see in the Californian paradise.[349] The production of the luxury computers designed in Silicon Valley, later the MP3 players, peripherals, notebooks, smartphones, tablets, was and is outsourced to regions with dubious labor and environmental laws. In the meantime, about one million people work 12-hour shifts in low-wage countries around the globe.

A former employee at Apple's European headquarters in Cork, Ireland, has summarized her experiences: 5,000 low-paid telephone consultants, divided into large groups of 500 each, are constantly rated by superiors and have 8 minutes a day to go to the toilet, so they drink as little as possible. The suicide rate is six times higher than in the rest of the Irish population. Complaints up to boss Tim Cook changed nothing. The Hollyhill site is therefore called Hollyhell among the workforce.[350]

---

346   Steve Jobs: 1 Dollar Gehalt, 647 Millionen kassiert, Computerwoche 4.5.2007

347   Apple avoids taxes with 'complex web' of offshore entities, Senate inquiry finds, The Washington Post 20.5.2013

348   Apple droht Ärger wegen Produkthaftung, Frankfurter Allgmeine 1.12.2012

349   Apple-Zulieferer: Drei Foxconn-Mitarbeiter stürzen sich in den Tod, SPON 18.5.2013; Apple-Zulieferer knechtet bis zur Erschöpfung, Welt N24 19.12.2014

350   Wie ein "Traumjob" in der Apple-Zentrale wirklich aussieht, N24 18.3.2017

Employees in the German Apple stores are sometimes spied on to see how often they visit the toilets and what they do in the break rooms. A joint representation in the form of a works council is considered a disruption.[351] But every employee is expected to identify with the company by wearing an Apple shirt and in large meetings applaud the visions of the respective boss to rescue mankind.

In the lap of BlackRock&Co, NSA included

Apple's digital populism ultimately ended up in the lap of the new big capitalists. Apple's largest shareholders are Vanguard, BlackRock, State Street, Berkshire Hathaway, Fidelity, Price T Rowe, Northern Trust, Geode Capital, Bank of New York Mellon, Norges, Invesco, Morgan Stanley, Bank of America, Goldman Sachs.[352]

Between 2012 and 2017, they were able to redistribute Apple's annual net profits between USD 50 billion and USD 71 billion – equivalent to a profit rate between 20 and 30 percent – from Apple's worldwide mailboxes to their own worldwide mailboxes and then to their clients' mailboxes.

Hundreds of millions of Apple devices are protected against access by petty criminals, but not against access by US intelligence services. Apple devices – like the corresponding devices from comparable manufacturers – are the modern bugs in the private, social and entrepreneurial sphere of citizens. These bugs no longer have to be installed laboriously and secretively in apartments, under the bed and in the telephone receiver by secret service sleuths – Apple & Co deliver them as part of beautiful everyday life.[353] Since 2001, Apple has also been subject to the Patriot Act and the official government "fight against international terrorism".

Elitist Feminism

Since 2011, the Supervisory Board has been gradually filled with representatives of US top business, such as the former heads of the Northrop Grumman and Boeing armaments groups and of Walt Disney. However, the newer obligatory values are now also present: the company doesn't give a toss about the environmentally friendly procurement and disposal of the rare earths re-

---

351 https://bigbrotherawards.de/2013/arbeitswelt-apple, downloaded 6.4.2018

352 https://www.nasdaq.com/symbol/apple/institutional-holdings, downloaded 30.3.2018

353 Sicherheitslücken im iPhone. Wie Apple die NSA einlädt, FAZ 22.7.2014

quired for Apple devices – but to provide a soft environment image, former US Vice President Al Gore now collects his royalties on the Supervisory Board.

Young women in faraway poor countries were left to work without safeguards – but, in line with the times, the "successful women" department was expanded. BlackRock co-founder Susan Wagner joined the Apple Supervisory Board, as did the young Andrea Jung: she is the boss of Grameen America. Based on the innovation of Nobel Prize winner Mohammed Yunus, this "bank of the poor" grants micro-credits to poor women in the USA to set up businesses.[354] However, this bank is now linked to the two large PE investors Apax and Pomona Capital, with Morgan Stanley and the largest hedge fund Bridgewater.[355] And Andrea Jung also sits on the supervisory boards of General Electric and Daimler. The situation of the majority of women in precarious employment, on the other hand, is not an issue.[356]

Microsoft: The software monster

William Gates, of the same age as Apple founder Jobs, had also dropped out of his studies and founded Microsoft. Together with friends, Gates created the software for the many home and personal computers at the time. Soon Microsoft also produced software for companies and states, became the largest software producer and has remained so to this day with 120,000 employees worldwide, 74,000 of them in the USA, and numerous suppliers and subsidiaries. Here, too, the mission of world improvement is indispensable: "Our mission is that every individual and every organization on the planet can achieve more".

As with Apple, the breakthrough came with the help of a major corporation. IBM was also building personal computers and adopted the MS-DOS operating system from Microsoft in 1981. With Windows, initially the graphical extension of the operating system, the office software Windows Office and many other applications were developed. Microsoft thus became the market leader for the personal computers now installed in all offices. This enabled the company to go public as early as 1986.

Like Apple, Microsoft penetrated everyday work and life even further with programs for mobile telephony, spreadsheets, word processing, Power Point,

---

354   https://www.apple.com/leadership/, downloaded 6.4.2018

355   www.grameenamerica.org/about-us (Board of Directors)

356   Cf. Great Expectations: Exploring the Promises of Gender Equality, IPPR 13.3.2013

Internet access and Internet telephony, with hardware such as keyboards, game consoles, music devices.

Monopoly and cartel formation

Microsoft expanded its monopoly early on. Individual products such as Internet Explorer were combined with operating systems and programs to form product bundles. Competitors were bought up, their programs changed. Occasionally a hostile takeover did not work out, as in the case of Yahoo. The use of software from other manufacturers was made more difficult or impossible. Computer manufacturers were forced to pre-install Microsoft's programs and operating system. Users were spied on to monitor compliance with Microsoft rules.

In 1998, the US Department of Justice and 19 US states filed an anti-trust complaint. A year later, the verdict was: To break the monopoly, Microsoft must be split up. But here the government of US President George W. Bush came to the rescue. The company, which had worked with Bush's campaign agency Century Strategies, set up a lobby organization in Washington with Bush's campaign consultant and donated USD 4.6 million to a dozen Republican and Democratic MPs. Bush had the verdict overturned in 2001 by the newly appointed head of the Federal Cartel Office.[357]

European Union as Microsoft colony

Between Helsinki, Lisbon and Bucharest, state administrations, municipalities, police forces, companies, the military and organizations continue to pay for the expensive and exclusive Microsoft programs, even if they don't work so well at all. Only Microsoft experts know the source code.[358] This violates EU public procurement law, impedes technical progress and keeps prices high. Users let them spy on them and don't even know where the data ends up in the USA.[359] Although cities like Rome and Barcelona, the French National Gendarmerie and even the Italian military want to break the shackles – the European Commission, the governments of Macron and Merkel and also the CSU in Bavaria are cementing the Microsoft colony. Microsoft cooperates with the NSA secret service.

---

357 U.S. vs. Microsoft: The Lobbying; A Huge 4-Year Crusade Gets Credit for a Coup, NYT 7.9.2001

358 Elisa Simantke: Europe's dire dependency on Microsoft, Investigate Europe 21.6.2017

359 Harald Schumann / Arpad Bondy: Das Microsoft-Dilemma. ARD 19.2.2018

The much-vaunted transparency crumbles into dust when it comes to Microsoft First, linked to America First. Gates hates it when US war crimes come to the public eye. He considers whistleblower Edward Snowden a lawbreaker who deserves no support.[360]

Benefactor in the lap of BlackRock&Co

In other respects, too, for Microsoft laws are there to be circumvented, and loopholes and special regions are being used everywhere. Operations centers are outsourced: the cheap production of devices to the US colony of Puerto Rico and Asia; tax evasion to Delaware, Ireland, the Bahamas, etc.; in structurally weak regions such as Reno/Nevada state subsidies are being milked.

Operating in this way, Gates, God's gift to mankind, gifted himself first and foremost: From 1994 to 2014 he topped the Forbes list of mankind's richest individuals 15 times with private assets worth an estimated USD 90 billion.

In 1999 the Gates couple founded the Bill and Melinda Gates Foundation. "All lives have equal value" is the motto, "Empower the poorest, especially women and girls, to transform their lives" is the mission.[361] With a foundation capital of USD 43 billion, thousands of health and agricultural projects in 100 countries, especially the poorest in Africa and Asia, are supported.

The foundation with its 1,300 employees works in "philanthropic partnerships" with elite universities as well as with the Rockefeller Foundation and the OECD. The business club Rotary International received USD 255 million. The Foundation funds 11 percent of the UN's World Health Organization WHO budget and is represented on its Advisory Council.

After the initial distance to the new President Trump usual in the milieu, Gates quickly made friends with him after his election: Under Trump, the removal of regulatory barriers could unleash innovations and make the USA the world's leading nation again.[362] The world's largest private foundation wants to replace the state and the UN anyway and organize "development aid" and world health itself.

To finance this type of charity, the Foundation also invests its capital in those who cause the problems it seeks to combat, such as Monsanto, Bayer, BASF, Exxon, BP, Shell, Glencore, Rio Tinto, Coca Cola, Merck, Novartis,

---

360   Rolling Stone 13.3.2014

361   https://www.gatesfoundation.org/de, downloaded 12.4.2018

362   Wird Bill Gates zum Trump-Fan? FAZ 15.12.2016

SmithKline and Pfizer. And here they link up with BlackRock&Co. Following public criticism, the foundation sold some shares, although it is unclear whether it has kept share packages below the statutory reporting threshold.[363]

While the founder boss still holds 6 percent of Microsoft shares, Microsoft also belongs to the new capital organizers. They are almost the same as at Apple and in only a slightly different order: Vanguard, BlackRock, State Street, Capital World, Price T Rowe, Fidelity, Wellington, Bank of New York Mellon, Northern Trust, JPMorgan Chase, Geode Capital, Invesco, Bank of America and also Norges.[364]

The Platform Economy

The Internet became the basis for new business models. With populist accompaniment, the digital techniques are used to manipulate consumers on a massive scale and to degrade dependent employees. Military and secret services and digital corporations cooperate – here too.

Amazon: The trade monster

Over two decades, Amazon, with operational headquarters in Seattle, legal headquarters in Delaware and 575,000 employees worldwide, became the largest Western online mail order group. Its founder, Jeffrey Bezos, became the richest individual in the US and on Planet Earth in 2018 with private assets worth USD 147 billion.

Military Internet, venture capital

Having studied in Princeton, Bezos began on Wall Street and moved to the hedge fund D.E.Shaw in 1990. Its founder, Professor Shaw, had worked with ARPANET, the military prelude to the Internet, at Stanford University and then at Columbia University in New York. He transferred the forms of digital communication developed there, including e-mails, to the financial sector. Bezos worked in the online retail division, was promoted to vice president and turned self-employed with Amazon in 1994.[365]

---

363 Bill Gates und sein Image: "Die Stiftung hilft mit Blutgeld", Deutschlandfunk Kultur 28.2015

364 https://www.nasdaq.com/symbol/msft/institutional holdings, abgerufen 30.3.2018

365 Michelle Celarier: How a Misfit Group of Computer Geeks and English Majors Transformed Wall Street, New York Magazin 1/2018

The company started with selling books. The family foundation of his rich parents, Bezos himself, friends and the venture capitalist Kleiner Perkins invested.[366] This was so successful so quickly that Amazon was able to go public in 1997 with only 256 employees. However, this was only possible because the mainstream media celebrated Amazon as the world's next largest bookseller and because three experienced financial players organized the IPO: Deutsche Morgan Grenfell, Hambrecht&Quist and Alex. Brown & Sons.

Morgan Grenfell was the branch of Deutsche Bank in London. The venture capitalist Hambrecht&Quist from San Francisco had organized IPOs such as those of Apple, Genentech and Adobe since the 1980s. Alex. Brown & Sons was the oldest investment bank in the United States and, like the Riggs Bank was important to BlackRock, had a close relationship with the Washington establishment; bank president Alvin Krongard cooperated with the CIA at the time. He became its deputy director in 1998 and secured the private mercenary company Blackwater its first major government contract: "Moving from Alex. Brown to the CIA isn't such a long step," he explained.[367]

Deregulation, internal and external expansion

New founders such as Bezos were boosted by the deregulation of the financial system begun by President Clinton. In 1994, a new type of free trade agreement, NAFTA (US-Mexico-Canada), promoted an even more aggressive round of deregulation, including the outsourcing of labor to low-wage countries. In the same year, employers were allowed to replace strikers with temporary workers.[368]

With the help of the exploding stock market value and the gradual entry of capital organizers such as BlackRock, Amazon bought up competitors and suppliers – at least 128: First other online booksellers such as Telebook in Germany, digital antiquarian bookshops, on-demand publishers, digital address miners, chip, touchscreen and microphone manufacturers. The company also acquired companies for digital home and kitchen surveillance, garage door control, payment systems, translation machines, speech machines, data man-

---

366 Jeff Bezos told what may be the best startup investment story ever, http://www.businessinsider.de 21.10.2016

367 Baltimore Sun 1.2.1998, articles.baltimoresun.com/1998-02-01/news/1998032022_1_buzzy-krongard-tenet-alex, downloaded 10.4.2018

368 James Gross: Broken Promise. The Subversion of U.S. Labor Relations Policy 1947 – 1994, Philadelphia 2003, p. 277

agement (Amazon Web Services, AWS), children's clothing, electronic every-day surveillance, food delivery, streaming and production services for mu-sic, videos, games, audio books, films and TV. Most recently, the food chain Whole Foods was purchased. With its own airline and drones, and with maxi-mum discount contracts with major forwarding agents such as DHL, UPS and US Postal Service, it is now setting up its own delivery logistics.[369] Artificial intelligence (AI) is particularly important.[370]

With his venture capital company Bezos Expeditions, Bezos financed start-ups such as Lookout, Juno Therapeutics, Workday, Twitter and Rethink Ro-botics, which are intended to contribute to the expansion of Amazon.[371] Bezos Expeditions also financed the rocket company Blue Origin and the purchase of the Washington Post newspaper.

Top managers discipline the army of the precarious
Depending on the region, state and balance of power, the employees of the lower ranks are severely squeezed. Temporary contracts, part-time, temporary and seasonal work with the lowest possible pay prevail. Amazon rejects col-lective agreements with trade unions in all countries. The large warehouses are located in structurally weak regions with cheap and (supposedly) willing labor. The bosses encourage mutual denunciation among the employees, low performers and the sick are mobbed out, a reporter team found out in exten-sive research.[372] The sickness rate at Amazon is higher than the industry aver-age, which is why the management introduced a group bonus: If no one in a group calls in sick during the month, the gross salary can rise by 10 percent – but a single sick note obliterates the bonus.[373]

Violations of the law are in the first instance factored in, as long as em-ployees and authorities do not resist. In the low-wage region of Poland, for

369 Zoe Henry: Amazon Has Acquired or Invested in More Companies Than You Think – at Least 128 of Them, https://www.inc.com/magazin/201705/, downloaded 10.4.2018

370 AI includes the recognition and evaluation of intentions, feelings, moods, linguistic and non-linguistic expressions, texts, photos, faces, objects, movements of people (individu-als, groups, crowds; also movements of eyes and lips), voices, noises, music; translations, text creation.

371 Sally French: All the companies in Jeff Bezos's empire, https://www.marketwatch.com, 10.4.2018

372 Amazon's Bruising, Thrilling Workplace, NYT 16.8.2015

373 Petra Welzel: Amazon – Wer sich krank meldet, gefährdet die Anwesenheitsprämie aller, verdi publik 3/2017, p. 15

example, Amazon did not pay wages in the event of illness, overtime was not paid, wages were paid too late and accidents at work were not reported.[374]

Globally organized precariousness
Amazon uses digital means to take the business model of the largest traditional retailer to a new level: in just a few decades, WalMart expanded to become the largest supermarket group in the world with 1.5 million employees in the USA and 2.3 million worldwide.

The methods: Lowest possible pay for as many part-time, temporary and seasonal workers as possible, union busting, constant worldwide search for even cheaper suppliers, daily special and lowest offers, tapping state subsidies. The only reason many full-time employees do not starve is because they receive state meal vouchers from the Supplemental Nutrition Assistance Program (SNAP).[375] And Amazon even manages to turn this into another business: the company allows its employees to redeem the vouchers at Amazon's food delivery service.[376]

As early as the 1980s, WalMart bought cheap products on a massive scale in China and around the world and found a steadily growing group of buyers among the working poor in the USA. Because of its market power, WalMart exerted pressure on hundreds of thousands of suppliers in the USA and then worldwide to supply the consumer goods at even lower prices. The result was and still is widespread wage cuts: many millions of working poor far beyond WalMart.[377]

That's how Amazon operates, too: Anti-unionism, precarious working conditions, blackmailing suppliers for discounts, exploiting structurally weak regions worldwide, milking subsidies from the otherwise hated state.[378] Amazon employees in European countries are also fighting for collective agreements,

---

374 Die "Versklavung" der polnischen Amazon-Mitarbeiter, Die Welt 18.7.2015

375 United Nations, Human Rights Council: Report of the Special Rapporteur on extreme poverty and human rights on his mission to the United States of America, New York 4.5.2018, p. 9

376 Claire Brown: Amazon Gets Tax Breaks While its Employees Rely on Food Stamps, The Intercept 19.4.2018

377 Anthony Bianco: WalMart: The Bully of Bentonville. How the High Cost of Everyday Low Prices is Hurting America. New York 2007

378 How Amazon Undercuts Wages and Working People at Taxpayers Expense, www.jwj.org 7.2.2017

permanent jobs and compliance with labor rights.[379] Bezos himself invested in other digital platform companies such as Google, Airbnb and Uber, whose business model is also based on the exploitation of precarious servant armies.

Civilian and secret service surveillance of employees and consumers
With its down-to-the-second, disciplining monitoring of lower-rank employees, Amazon ratchets up WalMart practice with the help of the latest digital technology.

Amazon also uses the same technology to spy on its consumers. The voice assistant Alexa penetrates everyday life. The smarthome device Amazon Echo allows you to download music, TV, weather, traffic and sports news and home cinema in your home or at any other location, in response to commands such as "Turn on the light in the basement" to regulate light, heating temperature, external camera, refrigerator stock, telephone calls, medication dosage – without the involvement of those being spied on, Amazon evaluates their most intimate private life and devises its strategies for further penetration of everyday life, along the lines of the Apple Siri, Google Assistant and Microsoft Cortana programs.[380]

Alexa is cloud-based. AWS, Amazon's cloud, also serves the US Army and US intelligence services. No measures are known that prevent them accessing consumer data.

Anti-innovation monopoly
Amazon cooperates with WalMart, now also with wage-dumping market chains in Europe. With their combined market power, global wage dumping is being accelerated. Like Microsoft, Amazon is also striving for a monopoly. Competitors have to be snapped up or eliminated.

Amazon forces the two million external dealers whose products are sold not to offer them cheaper anywhere else (price parity clause). At the same time, traders must accept all monopolistic Amazon services (product description, advertising, storage, logistics, etc.).[381]

Amazon sweeps up all accessible data of employees, contractual partners, individual and corporate customers and their third-party contacts. The al-

379   Jörn Boewe/Johannes Schulten: Der lange Kampf der Amazon-Beschäftigten. Rosa-Luxemburg-Stiftung, Berlin 2015

380   https://bigbrotheraward.de/2018/verbraucherschutz-amazon-alexa, downloaded 22.4.2018

381   Heike Buchter: Amazon und Walmart – Pioniere der Ausbeutung, Die Zeit 6.4.2017

gorithms of the opaque data monster constantly optimize the data through interactive mechanisms (combination of different purchases and reactions, additional offers, requests for level of satisfaction). In this way the identities of the researched individuals, organizations, companies are dissected and re-assembled, made Amazon-compatible.

Thus, the creative potential of the new technologies is monopolized and perverted in huge secret silos: artificial intelligence silos.[382]

Genome revolution instead of curative medicine

In early 2018 Amazon, Berkshire Hathaway and the largest US bank JPMorgan announced: We're setting up a joint venture to break up the overpriced and ineffective healthcare system.[383]

The US healthcare system, the most expensive and unjust in the world, is a corrupt web of pharmaceutical industry, insurance companies, private hospitals and rich doctors. On the one hand, it excludes millions of uninsured citizens and, on the other, drives up insurance premiums much faster than incomes rise. There are good reasons to break up this web. However, President Obama's reform of the Affordable Health Care for America Act (2009) merely scratched the surface.

Bezos, Buffett and JPMorgan boss Dimon explained that the new system should initially be good for their own employees and their families, but then also for all citizens of the USA. But is Amazon, where employees are treated as too expensive and worn down and the sick are weeded out, the one to bring a better solution? The study "The Genome Revolution" by Bank Goldman Sachs stated: Curative medicine, i.e. the cure of chronic diseases, is "not a sustainable business model". Because when a disease is cured by an effective drug, for example, the number of patients falls – as do profits.[384]

Organized tax flight: International and national

Amazon also makes excessive use of the opportunities in the USA, in the EU and in all states to circumvent the taxation of its profits. As was the norm, Bezos moved its legal headquarters to Delaware shortly before the IPO. In

382   Die Jagd auf unser digitales Ich, FAZ 24.2.2018

383   Amazon, Berkshire Hathaway and JPMorgan Team Up to Try to Disrupt Health Care, NYT 30.1.2018

384   Goldman Sachs asks in biotech research report: 'Is curing patients a sustainable business model?', https://www.cnbc.com 11.4.2018

2004, the European headquarters was relocated to Luxembourg under the name Goldcrest: Here the bulk of the turnover and profits in the EU states are registered and taxed at a minimum. In 2016, for example, sales in Germany amounted to EUR 13 billion; however, only 1.5 billion were actually reported and taxed in Germany itself. Tax authorities in the USA, the UK, France and the EU investigated the case. Amazon commissioned the auditors Deloitte and PWC for favorable counter-assessments. The proceedings have dragged on for years and have not yet been finally decided.[385]

In structurally weak US regions and in other countries the company extorts public subsidies and tax exemptions with the promise of creating many permanent jobs in the huge fulfillment centers. However, the promises are often not kept. Bezos played off 238 US cities and states against each other: Who offers the most perks for the location of the second corporate headquarters? Detroit offered a 30-year tax exemption, New Jersey a total of USD 8.5 billion. Ultimately, New York won with even higher subsidies.[386] Finally a broad alliance of citizens' initiatives prevented the settlement.

Aiding and abetting tax flight for others
Amazon helps other companies to escape taxes. Via Marketplace Fulfillment by Amazon (FBA), 64,000 traders from all over the world conduct sales for which Amazon, for a fee, handles advertising, storage, delivery and payment transactions. No sales tax is due, FBA operates as an internal financial haven. This is another reason why Amazon is able to offer goods at lower prices. For a long time, Amazon refused to provide German tax investigators with any information with reference to the European parent company in Luxembourg, according to which all customer data had to be kept secret.

The Federal Fiscal Court ruled in 2016, after years of proceedings, that Amazon must release the data, but only for the originally requested years 2007-2009. The tax investigators now have to check the data, e.g. for completeness. And for subsequent years, new proceedings will drag on for years. Amazon is represented by the lobbying firm Hengeler Müller.[387]

---

385 Christoph Trautvetter u.a.: Unternehmenssteuern in Deutschland. Frankfurt/Main 2018, p. 51ff.

386 Teuer, unwürdig, sinnlos, SZ 16.11.2018

387 Tatort Amazon, HB 6.12.2016

Aiding and abetting consumer deception

Via the Marketplace, Amazon also facilitates the sale of products whose quality is not checked. According to Amazon itself, the wholesaler obliges suppliers to comply with local and national sales conditions. However, such formal assurances are part and parcel of the Western deceptive standard in transnational supply chains and sub-sub-contractor systems.

A check of the products sold via Marketplace revealed 93 violations of the EU Cosmetics Regulation. Only two of the 24 products were properly marketable. Honolulu Bronzing Powder, for example, contained preservatives that exceeded the maximum permitted concentration. The Argan oil shampoo against hair loss contained no Argan oil at all. Only if in individual cases consumers or authorities present sound laboratory analyses, does Amazon every now and then remove a product from its range. Amazon takes advantage of the well-known fact that everywhere in the EU the control authorities are far from equipped to monitor compliance with laws and regulations.[388]

For Democrats, for Republicans

Like the other Internet giants, Amazon falls into line with the corrupt political establishment. Only the two established parties receive donations. Amazon has its own lobby office in Washington. In 2015 Jay Carey was hired, who had been President Obama's spokesman from 2011 to 2014.[389]

For a long time, Bezos, like Gates and Jobs, also preferred the Clinton and Obama Democrats. But donations always go to Republicans as well, especially when it comes to pertinent decisions in Congress, such as the approval of drones for the delivery of goods. Managers of Amazon subsidiaries pay standardized, regular donations, about USD 5,000 each, into the company's own donation committee. Since Trump's election victory, donations have been divided roughly equally between the members of the two monopoly parties.[390]

Landed in the lap of BlackRock&Co

To squeeze employees, suppliers, municipalities and states, Amazon gets its executives – as McKinsey, BlackRock, Goldman Sachs, Google and Microsoft also do – from the most prestigious business schools: Harvard Business

---

388   Gefährliche Bestellung, Der Spiegel 23/23018, p. 62f.

389   Amazon holt früheren Obama-Sprecher, FAZ 28.2.2015

390   See the monthly reports to the Federal Election Commission: docquery.fec.gov

School, London Business School, INSEAD (Paris), IESE (Barcelona) and ESMT (Berlin). Amazon lures the best graduates in the first year with USD 173,000.[391]

Profits are distributed according to a strict hierarchy. Bezos holds 17 percent of the shares. His 16 top managers are kept on a tight leash – they have between 1,000 and 85,000 shares. Together, that's not even one percent.

The really big chunk is in other hands. The biggest shareholders, who financed the expansion and continue to co-organize it, are, totally clichéd and also boring again, almost exactly the same as those at Apple, Microsoft, Coca Cola, General Electric: starting with Vanguard, then BlackRock, Fidelity, T Rowe Price, State Street, Capital World, Capital Research, Baillie Gifford, Invesco, Northern Trust, Morgan Stanley, Geode Capital, Bank of New York Mellon, Norges, JPMorganChase ... with a total of 60.5 percent in all.[392]

Portrait: Jeffrey Bezos/Amazon

Amazon founder Jeffrey Bezos, born in 1964, became the richest individual in human history in 2017 with USD 130 billion in private assets. He sees himself as a "libertarian". This is a step up from "liberal" to even greater aggressiveness towards states, trade unions and any form of binding community. Like Peter Thiel, he wants to break the boundaries of humanity. In 2000 he founded the space company Blue Origin: Wealthy individuals are to fly in space with reusable missiles, which are better than those of NASA, initially in our solar system, and look out for new investments. In Seattle, the Amazon headquarters, Bezos donated to the initiative against a bill that sought to provide homeless people with housing through moderate taxation of local corporations; he donated to an initiative to recognize gay marriage; he donated to an initiative to promote charter schools; he also donated to the Clock of the Long Now, which indicates the time of the next 10,000 years. And for the current 575,000 employees, there is no past, only future. The office towers in Seattle are known as Day1 South, Day 1 North: each day is the first day in the further expansion in the service of the almighty boss, highly stylized as such by the leading media.

391   Führungskräftenachwuchs. Großer Staubsauger aus Seattle, HB 23.2.2018

392   https://www.nasdaq.com, downloaded 14.4.2018

The fast climber had got to know the world of big business thanks to his exiled Cuban stepfather Mike Bezos, manager at Exxon in Houston, Texas. After studying in Princeton, he became a banker in New York. In 1990, he moved to the recently established hedge fund D.E. Shaw, with its close links to the secret service. For the libertarian ideologist majority of employees are a disruptive cost factor. Even if they, modest as they have become in US-led capitalism, only demand a "living wage" in Germany (a wage that is just enough to survive), they are an eyesore to him. He therefore calls for further automation and robotization. Huge windowless halls, operated by robots, are Bezos' vision. With his company Nash Holdings, he bought the Washington Post daily newspaper for USD 250 million. He immediately converted it to digital services and cut company pensions and the research budget.

Alphabet/Google/XXVI: The civil-military search engine

"Our mission is that information serves everyone, not just a few... We want to make the world a better place." In this way, prophet Sundar Pichai repeats the populist digital message. On the wide stage in Pittsburgh in 2017, for example, he stands alone in the spotlight in front of a large darkened audience, dressed in the cliché of washed-out jeans ritualized since Steve Jobs and an open shirt without a tie. Part of the mythical narrative is that the visionary has risen from the poorest Indian background to head of Google, the world's largest search engine operator and advertising group.[393] Fast-movers who come from the bottom can become particularly unscrupulous and cynical executors.

Stanford and early IPO

Like Apple and Facebook, Google was hatched at Stanford. Students Larry Page and Sergey Brin initially worked on the Stanford Digital Library Project. The project, funded by the National Science Foundation, was to use digital technology to create an integrated universal library with complete archive, search and ordering capabilities. The first version ran on the university's website.

In 1998 Page and Brin quickly transferred their academic activities into company form. The first financial support for Google Inc. was provided by a co-founder of the computer manufacturer Sun Microsystems: this company

---

393 Googles Gehirn. Sundar Pichai hat sich aus ärmlichen Verhältnissen in Indien an die Spitze von Google hochgearbeitet, Die Zeit 4.3.2018

– Sun is short for Stanford University Network – also owes its origins to the academic preparatory work at the university. Just one year later, the venture capitalists Kleiner Perkins and Sequoia joined in. In 2003, Microsoft recognized the future potential and either wanted to buy Google or merge with it. But in 2004 Morgan Stanley and Goldman Sachs chose to pursue the IPO.

The IPO was conducted under the usual motto: "The company that does good things for the world." At first, Page and Brin only allowed clearly defined text advertising, but soon realized that the big money was to be made with colorful product advertising on behalf of large companies.

Partnerships with corporations, NASA, Vatican
Starting in 2005, Google entered into partnerships with companies in various industries and developed new programs with their help and for them: Video search and advertising placement with News Corporation/Fox, AOL/Time Warner and British Sky Broadcasting; Google Earth and YouTube with America Online; software with Sun Microsystems; Google Maps with KIA and Hyundai. In 2009, Google agreed with the Vatican to create a dedicated Youtube channel for Pope Benedict XVI, who was struggling for popularity, to boost his presence in the leading media.[394]

A particularly close cooperation was established with the space agency NASA. Google engineers maintain laboratories, offices and apartments in the NASA Ames Research Center. As with Bezos/Blue Origin, the focus is on the development of private spaceflight and space exploration. Related areas are climate developments on Earth and on the planets of the solar system. Together they have discovered an eighth planet orbiting the sun-like star Kepler-90. Since 2009, signals from 150,000 stars have been processed using neural data processing and a new, super-fast quantum computer.[395]

Transhumanism
Google is working with NASA, supported by other transhuman technology fans such as Peter Thiel and Elon Musk (Tesla), to push the research paradigm of Nano-Bio-Info-Cogno: linking microprocesses, changing living organisms, information technology and artificial intelligence.[396]

---

394   Papst bekommt eigenen YouTube-Kanal, https://www.heise.de 19.1.2009

395   Google, NASA Find 8th Planet in Distant Star System, www.forbes.com 14.12.2017

396   Nao-Bio-Info-Cogno: Paradigm for the Future, http://hplusmagazin.com 12.2.2010

At the Singularity University, co-founded by Google on the NASA campus, managers, investors, inventors and students can inform themselves about the new paradigm of "transhumanism" for USD 25,000 in 10-week courses with Google speakers and other specialists. How can the life of individuals be extended to hundreds of years or even death be overcome by combining the human body and brain with new technologies?[397]

Penetration of everyday life
Like Apple, Microsoft and Amazon, Google also penetrates everyday life. The instruments include the Android operating system, the browser Chrome, translation programs, the Google Home digital assistant, the maps service Maps, the Gmail e-mail service, and the youtube video platform. The higher up companies and individuals want to be placed in search results, the more they have to pay: For example, the room booking company Booking.com pays USD 2.3 billion annually to be placed at the top of Google search queries.[398]

The company no longer develops more and more areas itself. Its own venture capital companies GV and CapitalG have so far promoted at least 25 start-ups, including SpaceX, Magic Leap, Symphony Communication, DocuSign, Robinhood, Carbon3D, Slack Technologies, Nextdoor, Credit Karma, CrowdStrike, Glassdoor, Airbnb, Thumblack, Stripe, Gusto, Zscaler, CloudFlare (with Microsoft). Like Amazon, CapitalG is increasingly investing in the healthcare sector, for example in the companies Outcome Health (procurement of medical practices), Oscar Health, 23andMe, Flatiron Health and Clover Health.[399]

Holding Alphabet
In 2015, Alphabet Inc. was founded as a holding company for the sprawling group, and in 2017 it was merged into XXVI Holdings Inc. The Roman numeral XXVI symbolizes the 26 letters of the Roman alphabet. Google was split into individual, legally independent companies. The new holding company is the sole owner of Access & Energy (networks), Calico (bio- and genetic engineering), Chronicle (security), Deepmind (artificial intelligence), Jigsaw

397 Merely Human? That's So Yesterday, NYT 12.6.2010

398 Die Welt geht auf Reisen, FAZ 28.4.2018

399 https://www.cbinsights.com/research, downloaded 17.4.2018

(think tank for combating extremism and Internet censorship), Sidewalk (traffic management), Verily Life Science (life sciences), Waymo (self-propelled cars) and X (Google Glass, Project Loon).

Google remains the largest subsidiary in terms of turnover. But Google was taken off the stock exchange and, like the other subsidiaries, transformed into an LLC, similar to a German GmbH. Alphabet/XXVI claim greater transparency, but the opposite is true. Because all subsidiaries now have a limited reporting obligation.[400] In addition, the state of Delaware is also the legal and tax domicile for Alphabet and XXVI, with their operational headquarters in Mountain View/Silicon Valley.

XXVI/Alphabet encompasses 85,000 employees, operates in 173 languages, generates a turnover of USD 120 billion, a net profit of USD 23 billion and, with 92 percent, dominates the EU market with 3 billion search queries a day (as of 2017).[401]

Patient data now protected?

The reorganization with Alphabet was in part triggered by the anti-cartel investigations of the EU. Google had paid a fine of EUR 2.7 billion. However, the investigations are continuing.

Another trigger was the British data protection authority. The Google department DeepMind, responsible for AI, had a contract with the British National Health Service. DeepMind had secretly disclosed data from millions of personally identifiable patients to Google's advertising department and had violated the UK Data Protection Act.

Whether patient data is now better protected is questionable. The violation of the law was also possible because those responsible in the British healthcare system did not exercise sufficient control. And whether no data is passed on between the legally separate Alphabet/XXVI companies in the USA – who controls this?[402] Google's business model is based on spying on its users and customers and it is a leading player in surveillance capitalism.[403]

---

400   Google parent Alphabet forms holding company XXVI to complete 2015 corporate reorganization, Bloomberg 4.9.2017

401   https://www.luna-park.de 28.12.2017

402   Bloomberg 4.9.2017 ibid.

403   John Foster / Robert McChesney: Surveillance Capitalism, Monthly Review 3/2014

Digital benefactor

Google has realized that the previous digital world happiness message is no longer so easily believed. That's why Google offers free digital education in key locations. To this end, the company cooperates with chambers of industry and commerce (IHK) in Germany. By 2020, two million young Germans are to acquire digital skills in "future workshops", often supported by scholarships.[404]

Together with the Bertelsmann group, Google founded the digital learning platform Udacity in 2016. It awards 75,000 scholarships for training in Google's Android product, data analysis and web development. 20,000 scholarships are reserved for experienced programmers. The program covers the whole of Europe and was extended to Israel, Egypt, Romania and Turkey in 2017.[405]

Media promotion

Google also wants to sweeten up the media in Europe. That's why the company set up the USD 150 million Digital News Initiative (DNI) in 2015. Selected media in Europe are to develop innovative, digital media projects with the help of Google.

USD 27 million was distributed in the first year. In 2016, 124 media outlets received a total of USD 24 million. The main focus was on Germany, followed by France, the UK, Norway, Portugal, Greece and Italy, as well as the Eastern European countries of Romania, Poland and Hungary. Five media outlets in Germany received over USD 300,000 dollars: Correctiv, Rheinische Post, SPON, Schwäbischer Verlag, Der Tagesspiegel. Other recipients included WiWo, Deutsche Welle (state-run), taz and Mittelbayerischer Verlag. Using algorithms, Google presents selected articles from the FAZ under "Facts check" as background material.[406] This is by no means neutral in content, but rather promotes media that criticize Russia and China and praise the governments of Israel.

How Google deceives and gets others to deceive

The Google deception is not necessarily that fake news is spread subjectively and deliberately. The deception lies, for instance, in getting paid publications to lend an academic aura to its own particular company interests. For this, no instructions are needed.

---

404 Google setzt in Hamburg auf Angebote für die digitale Bildung, Welt kompakt 21.3.2018

405 https://www.berrtelsmann.de/verantwortung/projekte-weltweit, downloaded 19.4.2018

406 https://netzpolitik.org 17.11.2016

Google finances think tanks, professorships and studies depending on the importance of the market and where criticism bubbles up. The critical Google Transparency Project in Washington records unchallenged: Between 2005 and 2017, 330 "academic" publications were financed. In the EU, Google latches on to renowned universities – e.g. the Technical University of Munich, HEC Business School (Paris) – and establishes institutes along the lines of the Internet & Society Institute financed at Stanford. Its goals include "Internet Freedom" and "Open platform for debate". That sounds harmless, but in practice "Internet" and "society" are identical with Google. The Humboldt-Institut in Berlin will receive EUR 11.25 million up to 2019, that is 65 percent of the budget, the rest comes from Cisco, Deutsche Bank and others in which BlackRock is also a co-owner. Important heads of government such as Merkel and Macron are courted, "digital women" and more jobs promoted.[407]

The lobby office in Brussels presents the European Commission with studies against planned regulations – the studies are financed by Google, but this is often not noted on them. After EU Competition Commissioner Joaquim Almunia tried to impose some restrictions on the company, he ended up in the Brussels Center for European Policy Studies (CEPS), co-financed by Google.[408]

Revolving door in Washington

Until the IPO in 2004, the creed of the Google founders was the same as Trump's: Stay away from the political establishment in Washington!

After the IPO, Google set up a lobby office in that very Washington. With NetPAC, the usual PAC for corporations was set up, into which employees pay in under unspoken pressure. By 2013, the office had grown to over 100 employees. In 2012, long-time Congresswoman Susan Molinari was appointed Chief Lobbyist. In her first year, she distributed USD 18.2 million to lawmakers, for example to the chairman of the Committee on Communications and Technology, which is of such importance to Google.[409]

While the then boss Eric Schmidt publicly promoted Obama's Democrats, with Molinari he opted for a Republican. Although her fundamentalist rejection

---

407 Google's Academic Influence in Europe, Washington D.C., March 2018, p. 8ff., https://googletransparencyproject.org

408 Google's Academic Influence ibid., p. 23ff.

409 Google's Washington Insider, NYT 2.6.2013

of abortion violated the liberal principles of the Silicon Valley milieu, her influence in the Republican Party was more important. The Washington office was
also augmented with ex-employees of the Republican hardliner John McCain.

Google became part of the previously criticized political establishment. In
2013, 14 of the more than 100 employees in the Washington office were officially registered as lobbyists – 11 of them came from the Republican and Democrat government apparatus. Google overtook traditional major donors such
as the arms company Lockheed and its competitor Microsoft. In 2017, Google
topped the list of those seeking to influence political decisions in Washington
with money.[410]

Social media in US foreign policy

In 2010 Schmidt hired Jared Cohen from the State Department. After his stud-
ies in Stanford, he was in the planning staff of the State Department of Condoleezza Rice and Hillary Clinton responsible for integrating social media into
US foreign policy, for example in the organization of opposition movements in
US target states, e.g. in Eastern Europe and North Africa. Cohen was already a
member of the CFR at a young age. In 2010, he used this experience to found
Google Ideas, the company's own think tank, which was later renamed Jigsaw.
Together with Google boss Schmidt, he wrote the book "The Networking of
the World", in which they advocate the networking of digital corporations and
swarm intelligence with the military.[411]

In 2012, Schmidt brought in director Regina Duncan from the Pentagon's
technology research center DARPA. She continued her work as head of the
Advanced Technology and Projects Group (ATAP) in Google before moving
to Facebook in 2016 for the same role.

In the lap of Vanguard, BlackRock&Co

The two founders Page and Brin and the long-time boss Schmidt, with their
low percentage of shares and their side businesses, have generated a double-
digit billion fortune, while the new boss Pichai still sits on a single-digit billion
fortune.

Alongside 2,000 other small shareholders, the large capital organizers

---

410   Google for the first time outspent every other company to influence Washington in 2017,
      The Washington Post 23.1.2018
411   Eric Schmidt / Jared Cohen: Die Vernetzung der Welt. Reinbek 2013

dominate the company with a total of 70 percent. Vanguard leads the pack, closely followed by BlackRock, Fidelity, State Street, Price T Rowe, Capital World, JPMorganChase, Northern Trust, Bank of New York Mellon, Invesco.[412]

Facebook: The data thieves

The Internet companies described above promise the improvement of human life and humanity. To this end, they scoop up the data of their customers in an authorized and unauthorized way. Facebook is the special variant as a "social network". Founder Mark Zuckerberg plays a populist role as a social love and community apostle: Facebook is "a powerful new tool for staying connected to the people you love, for making their voices heard and for building communities and businesses," he said at a hearing in the US Congress.[413]

Cozying up to "the people".
After every major data scandal that unmasks these promises, the Facebook boss flatters the tracked customers chummily with full-page ads in the leading media of the western world: "People use Facebook to stay in touch with friends and family. But maybe you don't want everyone on Facebook to see everything about you. That's why we've worked with privacy experts to develop privacy settings based on your feedback. That's how you choose what's right for you. For more information, see fb.me/myprivacy."[414]

Actually, Zuckerberg admitted that Facebook "sees everything about you" so far. And oh, how nice, Facebook is now hiring "data protection experts" – didn't one of the world's largest data companies have them before? And isn't the declaration of intent that he now wants to protect privacy the admission that he didn't have that intention before?

A few weeks later, the Facebook boss followed up with a personal signature in another large ad: "You may have heard about a quiz app built by a university researcher that leaked Facebook data of millions of people in 2014. This was a breach of trust, and I'm sorry we didn't do more at the time. We're now taking steps to ensure this doesn't happen again. Mark Zuckerberg."[415]

---

412   https://www.nasdaq.com, downloaded 18.4.2018

413   Transcript of Mark Zuckerberg's Senate hearing, The Washington Post 10.4.2018

414   Du hast die Kontrolle über deine Daten auf Facebook, HB 23.2.2018

415   HB 27.3.2018

Gigantic manipulation machine

The young multi-billionaire's apology is demagogic, his promise misleading. Because the business model is: Get as many users and data on the digital Facebook infrastructure as possible, scoop them up, exploit them as quickly and deeply as possible. If an abuse becomes known later, then we have already done the most important thing and can make a few deletions – and create new tools to involve other users. Facebook calculates coolly that the majority of users are not aware of the theoretically possible rejection of certain uses – for example through a new EU regulation – do not seek or find the tools necessary for this.

Even US-friendly capitalist media admit: Facebook is a "gigantic manipulation machine".[416] Facebook is "the commercialization of the human private sphere organized with military precision".[417]

In 2007, the Facebook platform was expanded in such a way that not only individual people can present themselves. Companies can now also present themselves, develop and operate apps for social networks, e.g. photo programs, games and calendars with friends' birthday dates. Companies can access data from third parties. The companies must pledge not to misuse the data, but as with Apple, Microsoft, Google, this is a mere formality, and "misuse" is not precisely defined. There is no government control anyway.[418]

From individual users to companies

Today, Facebook has over two billion individual subscribers with a personal profile in over 80 languages and one billion users a day on the platform. Not only their data and contacts, but also their purchases and behavior, their changing locations are recorded, evaluated and sold on to tens of thousands of companies and advertising agencies.

Like Amazon, Microsoft and Apple, Facebook has snapped up dozens of other companies (WhatsApp, Instagram...), provides services for (video) telephony, video conferencing, job search, disaster victim search, music and TV uses. Celebrities and artists can entertain fan communities. Companies can advertise and offer discounts and vouchers. Advertising is the main source of income.

---

416   Im perfekten Sturm. Facebook hat sich zu einer Manipulationsmaschine gewandelt, HB 23.3.2018

417   Zum Wohle ihrer selbst, WiWo 13.4.2018, p. 39

418   Datenskandal bei Facebook, HB 27.3.2018

The infrastructure for data management is complex, possibly even larger than for BlackRock's Aladdin. Facebook maintains tens of thousands of servers in server "farms" across US territory. For Europe, the first server farm was set up in 2013 in icy northern Sweden, where millions of dollars can be saved on the costly cooling of hot devices. With Microsoft, Facebook is laying the most powerful transatlantic submarine cable.

The foundation

Mark Zuckerberg attended an elite boarding school and befittingly studied at Harvard. It was there that the fashion had just emerged for students to publish yearbooks with their photos (=facebook). Some students who were friends with Zuckerberg had the idea: We could also present Facebook HarvardConnection on the Internet and turn it into a business! Zuckerberg, who could program, took over the idea and registered the company thefacebook.com in 2004.

Later Zuckerberg denied the plagiarism accusations, but paid the originators of the idea USD 65 million. His former companions characterized him as "completely unscrupulous"; Zuckerberg called people who voluntarily disclose their lives on Facebook "dumb fucks".[419] That's his business model: to ruthlessly exploit the gullibility of "dumb fucks", to tickle out their secret desires, confirm, strengthen, bundle, and turn them into the basis of a completely different business.

Ascent with government personnel

"Google organizes the world's information, but Facebook organizes the world's people." The venture financier Thiel recognized the potential of the social network at an early stage and initially moved in with USD 500,000, brought Zuckerberg to Silicon Valley and is still a member of the Facebook supervisory board. Among the first financiers were the venture capitalists Accel, Greylock, the German Samwer brothers, General Atlantic and Li Kashing from Hong Kong. Interpublic (IPG), one of the largest holding companies of advertising agencies (McCann Erickson et al.), joined in 2006.

Shortly before the IPO in 2012, the major capital organizers also began to participate: Initially Fidelity, T Rowe Price and Goldman Sachs. The IPO was a great success. Facebook was able to get top managers from other companies.

---

419 "Außer Kontrolle", Der Spiegel 13/2018, p. 15f.

Harvard graduate Sheryl Sandberg, initially office manager for US Treasury Secretary Lawrence Summers, then vice president at Google, became Facebook's chief operating officer in 2008. Theodore Ullyot came from George W. Bush's government, where he was the office manager of the Department of Justice, and became head of the legal department.

There was also movement in the other direction: with My.BarackObama.com, Facebook co-founder Chris Hughes took over the cuddly online election campaign management for the US presidential candidate in 2007. Obama was ultimately elected with the help of this instrument. The "yes we can" slogan was an ingenious catch-all for people according to the Facebook method: Speak to the deep desires of the large crowd – simply, but also highly ambiguously and non-committally, and then make something completely different out of it! (even more low wages, even more state bank rescues, even more drone murders).

Facebook as NATO instrument

Within a few years Facebook had arrived at the very top, not only on Wall Street, but also in Washington. Politicians who needed good advertising were publicly seen with Zuckerberg, not just US President Obama. The German Chancellor Merkel and the French President Macron and their ministers vied to be visited by Zuckerberg at their seat of government and photographed with him. When criticism of Facebook came up, Merkel merely said that one had to "have a look" at Facebook's practices.[420]

Although the daily skimming and exploitation of billions of customer data and the transfer to "many thousands of companies" was generally known,[421] it was not until 2018 that the transfer of the data of several million customers to the agency Cambridge Analytica (CA) became a (short-lived) scandal. The agency creates psychometric profiles of individuals as well as of small and large groups of people. As far as is known to date, the tool has been used since 2014 for election campaigns, for example in the USA (President Trump) and India (President Modi).[422] The transfer had already taken place in 2015, Facebook had said nothing about it publicly.

"We are open to all people." This populist lie can be seen in the agree-

---

420 Regierungserklärung 23.11.2016, www.bundesregierung.de/content
421 Cambridge Analytica ist kein Einzelfall, HB 27.3.2018
422 Awanish Kumar: Facebook-Skandal in Indien, junge Welt 4.4.2018

ment with the Digital Forensic Research Lab. It belongs to the Atlantic Council of NATO and observes electoral behavior worldwide. NATO has agreed a
"partnership" with Facebook for this purpose: A worldwide "digital solidarity
movement for democracy and truth" is to be established.[423] Since 1961, the Atlantic Council has had the task of disseminating the fake justifications for US
and NATO military strategy and operations for the leading media – Facebook
as a NATO instrument.

Complicit Governments

Facebook has learned that even with the most powerful governments you can
get away with almost anything. EU leaders can "largely be kept quiet with mi-
nor tweaks". Facebook can also "simply ignore" EU regulations.[424] Facebook's
core business remains intact, as does access by the US secret services.

In 2012, Facebook had switched off facial recognition of its users at the in-
stigation of the European Commission. In 2018, Facebook switched it back on
again. This allows users to be recognized when photos or other images appear
somewhere in the data jungle.

Other states have at least temporarily blocked Facebook, such as Saudi
Arabia and Brazil. But only China has stuck to the ban since 2009, as long as
Facebook – along with Alphabet/Google and Twitter – do not comply with the
laws of the People's Republic.[425]

Precarious slaving for simulated freedom of expression

Facebook allows all incoming entries onto its platform: The more data, the
bigger the business. When it was increasingly criticized that this also included
war massacres, torture videos of "rebel" groups, depictions of accidents, hu-
miliations, personal insults, outbursts of hatred, exhibitionism, pornography,
cruelty to animals, sexual harassment and fake news, and that their dissemi-
nation was not part of freedom of expression, Zuckerberg played the issue
down: Facebook was not a newspaper and not a TV station, but only a neutral
mediator, a technically neutral platform. But because the criticism did not die
down, Facebook set up a complicated procedure: Users can file a complaint

---

423   Atlantic Council's Digital Forensic Research Lab Partners with Facebook to Combat Dis-
      information in Democratic Elections, www.atlanticcouncil.org 17.5.2018

424   Facebooks Datenleck offenbart einen großen Kontrollverlust, Die Welt kompakt
      21.3.2018

425   WhatsApp in China blockiert, https://www.t-online.de 19.7.2017

about individual Facebook entries. Facebook set up control teams to investigate complaints and decide whether to delete them.

As with other services, Facebook also commissions subcontractors for this, in Germany the Bertelsmann subsidiary Arvato and Competence Call Center (CCC). They have so far hired 20,000 content moderators with 40 different languages in various countries, split them into teams of 500 to 1,000 employees, and have them based in open-plan offices in Berlin, Essen or Casablanca/Morocco. The employment is mostly temporary, the income in Germany is just above the minimum wage.[426]

The moderators are supposed to check between 1,300 and 2,000 data packets per day – texts, photos and photo series, videos with texts and music – for violations of freedom of expression and decide whether to delete them. The deletion criteria are superficial and based on the Silicon Valley world view: No child porn! No hate sermons! No beheadings! On the other hand, labor rights and international law are just as little a part of the criteria as are the respective national criminal and media rights, at most an unclear selection from them.

The superficiality was shown for example here: The world-famous photograph of the 9-year-old girl Kim Phuc, who fled the US napalm bombing during the Vietnam War, was deleted because it was forbidden for children to be naked. The profile of the Norwegian photographer who took the photo was also deleted. The Norwegian newspaper Aftonbladet, which reported on the deletion, was also deleted. The Swedish Prime Minister's comment on the matter was also deleted.[427]

On Facebook's Whats App, on the other hand, child porn marketers can spread freely for months, only slightly encrypted. They are only hesitantly restricted after many complaints – until Facebook has saved the data elsewhere. The situation is similar with iMessage, Telegram and Signal from Microsoft.[428]

Facebook thrives on emotionally charged, indeed emotionally overloaded outbursts, often sexualized rule violations and atrocities that violate hitherto held "Western values". For it is precisely this that helps to prolong stays on the platform, boosts customer loyalty and advertising value. The expensive deletion activities are a populist diversionary maneuver.

---

426   Facebook. Zu Besuch bei der Internet-Feuerwehr, HB 14.5.2018

427   Facebook zensiert norwegische Ministerpräsidentin, www.faz.net 9.9.2016

428   WhatsApp child-abuse groups flourish as encryption thwarts easy monitoring, FT 21.12.2018

Slaving in the digital deletion proletariat

Many moderators quit after a while, frustrated and worn out. They have reported from the review and deletion work of their "digital proletariat": The few seconds of review time are usually not enough for a well-founded decision. Facebook also constantly changes the deletion criteria. Shift work is strictly reglemented with breaks of a few minutes. Many sequences are disgusting and shocking, the moderators have to deaden their feelings in order to survive mentally and to meet the numerical deletion targets.

Facebook covered up the windows of the open-plan offices of the deletion teams so that nobody could look inside. Government commissioners were also denied access. Employees were not allowed to talk to journalists. The company, which wants to publish as much as possible about people and promote transparency, presents itself as "one of the most secretive companies in the world".[429] Subcontractors like Arvato defend this practice.

Like Amazon, Facebook also wants to overcome the bothersome engagement of living, independently thinking people. Zuckerberg expects that in 10 years at the latest robots will take over the deletion work.[430]

Asociality oblivious to history

Facebook promotes human behavior that is characterized by individualistic instant reactions to extremely abridged emotional impulses. This is combined with automated, robotized affirmation and control of such behavior. Both the individual and the collective history are extinguished. Long-time Facebook top manager Chamath Palihapitiya confirmed this in front of a large auditorium at Stanford University: Such social networks "destroy cooperation and civil discussion, promote disinformation and lies".[431]

Sean Parker, who helped build the company, explains the deliberate construction of the concept: We wanted to "exploit a weakness in human psychology. We were aware of that. And we did it anyway. God knows what it is doing to our children's brains".

Andreas Weigend, former Chief Scientist at Amazon, confirms that many employees have seen through the Facebook boss: "Like many colleagues in Silicon Valley, I don't believe a word Mark Zuckerberg says about his 'We at

---

429   Facebook setzt auf Floskeln, Süddeutsche Zeitung 27.12.2016

430   Künstliche Intelligenz löscht Youtube-Videos, SZ 25.4.2018

431   Außer Kontrolle, Der Spiegel 13/2018, p. 23

Facebook care...'. He doesn't care about the individual at all... That's an intolerable arrogance towards people and a disregard for social structures."[432]

Facebook also disbands the achievement of civilization that media have a legal and thus sanctionable obligation to truthfulness. The technological unleashing that "every human being" can bring everything into the public sphere without being checked first is proving to be the death of every democratic public sphere under the leadership of Facebook&Co.

Domination in space and the Atlantic
Unimpressed by "scandals", Facebook can continue to expand the group. Like Google, Thiel and Tesla/Musk, it is preparing Internet stations (satellites) in space and the further exploration and colonization of space.

Together with Microsoft, from 2016 to 2018 Facebook built the world's most powerful submarine cable to date between the USA and Europe: Marea runs 6,400 kilometers between Virginia Beach and Bilbao in Spain. From Spain, fast connections are also to be established to Africa, Asia and the Middle East. The entire database of the US Library of Congress can be whooshed through in a single second, it is vaunted: 160 terabytes per second. We are talking about the daily data of billions of individual users, but above all about the databases of globally active companies ("Internet of Things").[433]

This is the beginning of the further privatization of the transatlantic cable system, which is currently 1.3 million kilometers long and access to which is still marketed by the telecom groups. Facebook&Co want to directly control access for the fastest and most important Internet traffic.[434]

Arrived in Washington
Facebook's presence in Washington is constantly being expanded. The company's own PAC not only distributes millions of dollars in donations during election campaign years, but also buys individual members of parliament on an ongoing basis when it comes to pertinent decisions in Congress. In the 2016 election year, 55 percent of the money went to the Republicans, 44 per-

---

432 "Unerträgliche Arroganz", HB 4.6.2018

433 A Cable stretching 4.000 miles between the US and Spain is the key to a high speed future, https://news.microsoft.com/europe, downloaded 20.4.2018

434 Seekabel – Der unsichtbare Krieg, arte-TV 14.4.2018

cent to the Democrats. In 2018, Facebook upgraded the Democrats a little: 52 percent to Republican lawmakers, 47 percent to Democrats.[435]

As criticism of data misuse increased, Facebook hired Covington&Burling's lawyer Erin Egan as head of the office at the seat of government.[436] This law firm is the largest in Washington and closely intertwined with the government and financial apparatus. She has represented (and still does represent) Apple, Microsoft and General Electric, for example, as well as corporations facing particularly serious charges, such as Xe Services (successor to the private mercenary Blackwater), Chiquita (deployment of paramilitaries in Colombia), Southern Copper (environmental and health damage in Peru).[437] Obama's Attorney General, Eric Holder, who legitimized torture and the non-prosecution of corporate crime if it was in the national interest,[438] was and is co-owner of the firm. Facebook also brought in Louisa Terrell, ex-Special Assistant to the US President in the White House, to reinforce the Washington representation.

Like Amazon, Facebook can also tap juicy government subsidies thanks to its proximity to politics: The state of Texas, for example, subsidizes a data center in Fort Worth with USD 150 million.[439]

As chief lobbyist in the EU, Facebook hired the former British Deputy Prime Minister Nick Clegg. Sir Nick, who was elevated to the nobility by the monarchical puppet state in 2017, now acts as Facebook's Head of Global Affairs and Communications. In San Francisco, he was given a five-bedroom villa. He is supposed to mitigate the EU's regulatory efforts. In the financial haven of Dublin he heads a war room which is supposed to fight fake news from China against Facebook.[440]

Arrived at BlackRock & Co

Like Apple, Microsoft, Amazon and Google, Facebook has ended up in the hands of the big capital organizers. In addition to multi-billionaires such as Zuckerberg (private wealth about USD 60 billion), over 70 percent of the shares are owned by the capital organizers (in this boring order) Vanguard,

---

435 https://www.opensecrets.org, downloaded 27.4.2018

436 Facebook Will Now Have A "Director of Privacy", https://www.forbes.com 13.9.2011

437 Wikipedia: Covington & Burling, downloaded 26.4.2018

438 Jürgen Heiser: Der Doppelagent, junge Welt 28.10.2015

439 Shining a Light on Corporate Handouts, jobs with justice 27.2.2017, www.jwj.org

440 Facebook to create 'war room' to fight fake news, Nick Clegg says, The Guardian 28.1.2019

BlackRock, Fidelity, State Street, T Rowe Price, Capital World, Northern Trust, Invesco, Geode Capital, Morgan Stanley, Bank of New York Mellon, JPMorganChase, Norges, Goldman Sachs, Baillie Gifford...

The advertising monopoly of Facebook and Google

Advertising in print media, TV, radio, posters and telephone directories has been declining steadily since around 2010. Digital advertising via desktop / personal computer is stagnating. Only advertising on the Internet via mobile phones is growing, and faster and faster.

rom 2015 to 2017, Facebook's annual advertising revenue per user increased on average worldwide from USD 21 to USD 36, in Europe from USD 24 to USD 46 and in the USA from USD 67 to USD 136. Most of the growth ends up with Facebook – advertising accounts for 98 percent of revenue, at Google 86 percent.[441]

The two advertising giants are therefore driving up the number of users by offering more and more additional services, initially free of charge, thereby further blurring the traditionally increasingly blurred distinction between advertising and information beyond recognition.

Israel: Skimming off the occupation technology

"The young soldiers, 18 or 19 years old, are given every freedom in the huge development departments the military has created to be at the forefront of the digital world." This is how Israeli author Ronen Bergman reports on his years of research into Israel's digital industry.[442]

Israel is the most sophisticated digital laboratory in the Western world for combating riots and killing people who are labeled terrorists by intelligence agencies without a court order. Amazon, Facebook, Microsoft, Google, Apple are constantly buying start-ups in Israel, e.g. Anobit, LinX, PrimeSense, Slick-Login, Waze, Annapurna. With 5,000 start-ups to date, the majority of which were bought by US and other Western companies, Israel has the highest start-up density per inhabitant.

Most of the companies are launched by ex-officers of the Israeli army, they often start while still in the army. Here they use their experience in the remote

---

441   Das allmächtige Werbe-Monopol, HB 17.4.2018

442   Ronen Bergman. Der Geheimdienst-Experte über Israels Spione, ihre gezielten Tötungen und den gescheiterten Atomdeal mit dem Iran, HB 11.5.2018

and close detection, combating and killing of Palestinians in "civil" entrepreneurial form. The Israeli soldiers are pampered as heroes and national elites. The military is the "innovation driver". "Those who serve in one of the well-known elite units bring valuable knowledge with them and often set up their own business a few years later."[443]

The practice of the decades-long occupation regime, in breach of international law and human rights, is a training campus of moral-free disruption. "You break things", "You are software Ninjaneers", the praise rings out. Since the deployment of remote-controlled killing drones in the first Intifada, Israel's military-industrial digital complex has continuously developed new and better technologies to capture all kinds of data associated with people – acoustic, optical, linguistic, non-linguistic, color, haptic, gestural and motional, interactive, environmental, electronic, digital – and to evaluate them in an integrated manner and at the highest speed according to target input.[444] No other economy and media industry in the world is as militarized as that in Israel. A-levels, university exams – in Israel, officer rank is what counts most for jobs in business.[445]

Four decades ago, the chip manufacturer Intel was the first company to come from Silicon Valley – when production there was still primarily for the US military. Today, Intel employs 11,000 people in Israel, including many ex-militaries. For some years now, the five GAMFA giants have been expanding the purchased start-ups to up to 1,000 employees and award contracts.

Google maintains its own start-up area on the Stanford University campus in Tel Aviv. No other state subsidizes digital research and development as much as Israel. The products and services are mainly exported, to the USA and the EU. Even before Trump had the wall to Mexico extended, the Obama administration had already brought Israeli detection and defense technology for thousands of kilometers of the high-tech fence to Mexico, which had already been started under President Clinton.

The cyber war software Stuxnet was developed jointly by US and Israeli bodies under the Microsoft Windows operating system after Obama approved it. Stuxnet was placed as a destruction worm in the control system of the Iranian nuclear center Natanz and led to the "self"-destruction of the centrifuges.[446]

---

443   Gründergeist aus der Wüste, HB 11.5.2018

444   Cf. David Rosenberg: Israel's Technology Economy, London 2018

445   Interview mit dem start up-Mobileye-Gründer Ziv Avram, SZ 9.7.2018

446   Schmidt / Cohen: Die Vernetzung der Welt ibid, p. 157f.

Digital Knowledge Populism: Wikipedia

"The biggest encyclopedia of mankind", "the biggest collaborative project of mankind": this is how Wikipedia praises itself. Founded in 2001, Wikipedia currently contains 39 million articles in 300 languages. After Google, Youtube (belongs to Google), Facebook and Baidu (China), Wikipedia follows as the most frequently used Internet portal according to its own figures. The encyclopedia is linked to GAMFA: They finance and promote each other.

With the agency of "free knowledge" everyone can contribute their knowledge and write articles. Tens of thousands of students, academics and others work for the grassroots swarm intelligence – voluntarily, joyfully and free of charge, it is said. The demise of the Brockhaus lexicon, for example, really does not need to be regretted. But is Wikipedia the free, academic alternative?

The penultimate level of domination knowledge

Wikipedia is a private US company. It organizes the domination knowledge of the new capitalists. "Wiki" means ""fast". Wikipedia organizes and represents the quickie knowledge prevailing today for the more or less bourgeois educated or miseducated strata of the population.

95 percent of all Western high school graduates and students use Wikipedia, among journalists it is likely to be at least five percent more. "Normal citizens" also enjoy the easily consultable, free encyclopedia. The "normal citizen" can have the feeling – the hope and the claim on it are justified! – to participate in the hitherto exclusive university knowledge. Many articles and article subsections on the level of factual enumeration (historical data, biographies of personalities, population figures, personnel composition of governments and organizations, chemical and physical formulas, literature references, etc.) are correct and useful for initial swift orientation.

However, the decisive knowledge in Western capitalism is developed internally, e.g. at the BlackRock Research Institute and for Aladdin, in think tanks, in PR agencies such as Cambridge Analytica, in university institutes financed by companies, in state administrations and by government consultants, by rating agencies, business law firms, management consultants, business "auditors" and, last but not least, in secret services and NATO – the internal, economic and military-strategic decisive knowledge accumulated here is not accessible for the mass of Wikipedia authors. Also the internal knowledge, which Google, Facebook, Microsoft, Apple and Amazon siphon off from their customers – all this remains closed to both the normal citizen and the normal Wikipedia author: "Freedom of opinion" yes, but not free-dom of information.

The hard facts of modern-day capitalism are not accessible to normal Wikipedia employees nor to journalists and academic scientists – unless they are intentionally and selectively fingered by responsible agencies and PR smoothies and, as is often the case, are bound to secrecy. How much university research, especially that financed by companies, the state and the military, is subject to secrecy or is deformed by it, but intrudes covertly in everyday life!

The self-deception of the precarious Wikipedia knowledge workers is promoted by the fact that, in some formal respects and in many texts, Wiki-pedia satisfies conventional academic methodology and also contains the knowledge, which is not directly relevant to domination, completely. This self-deception is also encouraged by the fact that the most used and the most respected sources of quotations in Wikipedia are the leading media of the aca-demic public – in Germany Spiegel, FAZ, Zeit, Welt, Süddeutsche Zeitung, ARD, ZDF, tagesschau.de as well as the books of "renowned" publishers. The fact that the credibility of these leading media has long since been shattered has not yet reached Wikipedia.

It is not original documents – contracts, court rulings, parliamentary deci-sions – that appear topmost in the search engines. The leading media closely linked to the new financial players – smoothly adapted to every situation in the respective language region, in the respective state – are the most important sources of quotations for Wikipedia articles. Because these media and publish-ing houses are at the same time the important customers and big funders of the Internet companies like GAMFA, which also finance Wikipedia. Media and (specialist) publishers that are not market-powerful customers or are re-garded as "left-wing", "anti-Semitic" or "anti-American" are frowned upon as quotation sources.

The concept of truth is being destroyed

In different ways the concept, hence also the possibility of truth is being de-stroyed. Truth is not something absolutely fixed, but a process of debate. But it depends on how it is organized and how it can unfold.

First: The authors work under a pseudonym. All editors also work under a pseudonym. Personal responsibility for the development of knowledge is eliminated. Wikipedia knowledge is without responsibility.

Second: US foreign policy in the guise of "neutrality." The concept of truth itself is discredited as inadmissible, as unscientific. For Wikipedia there are only "opinions." The substitute for truth is "neutrality" (Neutral Point of View, NPOV) and the prohibition of theorizing (No original research). These criteria for the writing of Wiki texts are intended to find a capital-compatible, rather than just any, middle ground between different selected opinions. The most important exclusion criteria so far are Scientology and nudity of the human body; the accusation of anti-Semitism is extremely over-represented – but not anti-Islamism. The authors and editors in the case of the much-quoted anti-Semitism watchdog Psiram, for instance, enjoy the privilege of remaining completely anonymous at Wikipedia. Universal human rights, the labor rights of the ILO and international law are not criteria. Statements by authorities are generally considered neutral – but only if they are "Western" authorities. In today's explosive foreign policy conflicts, such as those involving Russia, China, Iran, Israel, Syria, Cuba and Egypt, Wikipedia generally operates within the spectrum of US foreign policy, albeit including its liberal variants à la NYT. The foreign policy relevant articles in the leading US Wiki are produced by a tiny group of homogeneous, missionary, anonymous authors, as a long-term study at Purdue University has shown.[447]

As a rule, the articles first reproduce the official self-portrayal of states, companies and shadow banks, authorities, parties, celebrities, organizations and the official version of financial products, medicines, etc. When it comes to Russia, China, Cuba, Venezuela, etc., on the other hand – in accordance with US foreign policy – the criticism is already contained in the introduction. For the other articles, the separate section "Criticism" follows only at the end. This is limited to what has been published in leading Western media that are high in the ranking of Wikipedia sponsor Google and pay for it, e.g. SPON, Zeit online, NYT.

Third: Opaque and anonymous editorial system: Wikipedia maintains an opaque editorial system. It consists of a six-level hierarchy: Marvin Oppong found out for the German version that 24,411 passive viewers form the lowest level, 14,232 active viewers stand above them, 260 administrators above them, these in turn are subordinate to 6 bureaucrats (that's what they're really called), 5 oversighters rank further up on the penultimate floor, then right at

---

447 Sorin Adam Matei / Brian Britt: Structural Differentiation in Social Media. New York 2017

the top the 5 final decision-makers, called checkusers (as of 2014). They are all anonymous. This system applies to Wikipedia in all issues. In this nameless jungle, the decisions are taken as to which article version is approved and which is not.

Fourth: The PR industry's playing field: Because the image of companies and shadow banks, states, cities, regions, holiday resorts, political parties, politicians, church leaders, celebrities, authors now also hinges on what is written about them in Wikipedia, they often commission PR agencies to permanently monitor the entries and neutralize unwelcome insertions. The author or PR agency with the most time and money is the one who gets his way after months, often years, of to-ing and fro-ing with changes and deletions.

Both CDU and SPD embellished their entries, FDP blabbermouth Christian Lindner had his entry changed 40 times via an IP address in the Düsseldorf state parliament. BMW, Ebay, Dell, the CIA and the Vatican manipulated entries. Specialized PR agencies monitor Wikipedia articles on a standing order for a fee, insert something, change, delete – and also under harmless pseudonyms.[448]

76.9 percent of the 20,000 authors of the German Wikipedia have inserted something into an article at most nine times since their registration. They stand for voluntary, committed and unpaid swarm intelligence. By contrast, Achim Raschka, co-founder of the Wikimedia Foundation, which finances the German Wikipedia, has so far carried out 78,000 edits using a pseudonym. This was not swarm intelligence, but paid commissioned work: The Ministry of Consumer Protection supported the Wiki project "Renewable Resources" (318 entries) with EUR 234,000. The pseudonymous author 7Pinguine, who works from an IP address of the Leibinger group and has obviously been released from work for this, has managed 15,000 edits since 2007, with manipulations in favor of Nestlé and the FDP. Wikimedia does not answer questions about the manipulations: no transparency, no grassroots democracy, no responsibility, no controversy.

"The free encyclopedia Wikipedia is written by volunteer authors", Wikimedia proclaims.[449] This is untrue: when it comes to important things, paid professionals do the writing. The employment agency of Amazon, Mechanical

---

448 Marvin Oppong: Verdeckte PR in Wikipedia. Das Weltwissen im Visier von Unternehmen. Frankfurt/Main 2014, p. 39ff.

449 https://wikimedia.de, downloaded 11.5.2018

Turk (MT), offers the writing of Wikipedia articles, among other things.[450] This is how digital grassroots democracy became a plaything of the PR industry. "Public relations and manipulation are ubiquitous in Wikipedia."[451]

Fifth: Digital annihilation: Andreas Weigend, the aforementioned former chief scientist at Amazon, had the opportunity to gain deep insights into the digital economy, which directly supports Wikipedia financially. "Google and Facebook can destroy people's identities. If you write and publish something that doesn't suit the company or a country, the company tweaks the algorithm in such a way that you no longer appear in the search results. And then you're dead meat."[452]

"America First"

The non-profit association Wikimedia Deutschland, operator of the German Wikipedia, was headed by Christian Rickerts until 2016: He formed the executive board, which consisted only of himself. He was the boss of the then 60 full-time employees. The highly paid manager (salary and performance-related bonuses) came from the management consulting company Capgemini. In addition to his function at Wikimedia, Rickerts also served as Vice President for Corporate Communication at the private Bertelsmann Foundation. At the same time, he was the sole representative managing director of the Wikimedia association, which collects the donations; in 2015 they amounted to EUR 11 million. The association stresses that 422,000 people donated an average of EU 25. Names of larger donors are not mentioned.

Wikimedia Germany, the second largest branch after the US one and the first foreign branch approved by the parent Wikimedia Foundation Inc. in San Francisco, has to have its donations administered and distributed by the capitalist Central Committee in California. This is how all national Wikipedia associations are treated: "America First".

Big sponsors Apple, Google, Microsoft...

The Wikimedia Foundation Inc. currently employs over 300 people and has annual revenue totaling USD 91 million (2016/17). The major benefactors

---

450 Die Crowdworking-Plattformen Amazon Mechanical Turk und Upwork, https://www.bisbrotherawards.de/2015

451 Oppong: Verdeckte PR in Wikipedia, p. 93

452 "Unerträgliche Arroganz", HB 4.6.2018

are corporate foundations and entrepreneurs: Apple, Google and Microsoft; Google founders Sergey Brin and Anne Wojcicki; Alfred Sloan Foundation (Sloan, former head of General Motors); Lisbet Rausing, Vice President of Asset Management at Harvard University and heir to the TetraPak Group; Teterev Foundation (car wholesaler and film producer from Latvia); Cards Against Humanity ("party games for horrible people"); Craig Newmark (Craiglist advertising agency); David Siegel Foundation (hedge fund Two Sigma); Charina Endowment (Goldman Sachs partner Richard Menschel); Humble Bumble (video games); Mathworks (software); Richard Seidel (music producer).

The birds of paradise among the regular main financiers are Antoine Bello, Ayn Rand fan and supporter of the French politician Nicolas Sarkozy; the Princess of Asturias and wife of the Spanish heir to the throne, as well as the Erasmus Foundation, which promotes spiritual healing and reincarnation.[453] These sponsors – Wikimedia does not mention the amount of the donation – pay, as far as is known from other sources, between USD 500,000 (Brin/Wojcicki) and USD 1 million (Sloan Foundation, Craig) annually. The next category of patrons, who pay up to USD 49,000 annually, include William and Melinda Gates, Boeing, Goldman Sachs, Intel and others. To be found in the next category (leading donors), who pay up to USD 14,999 dollars, are among others the Bank of America, Adobe and Chevron.

Main sponsor: General Motors Foundation
The Alfred Sloan Foundation is particularly revealing. It is the largest and perpetual sponsor. In 2008, it donated USD 3 million for the rapid expansion.[454] Sloan was the leading figure at General Motors from 1923 to 1956. He is regarded as the inventor of planned obsolescence, i.e. the built-in, premature deterioration of technical products and the technically unnecessary, rapid renewal of models.[455] Sloan increased the group's profits and his personal fortune by producing armaments first for Hitler's army (not only via the German GM subsidiary Opel), then simultaneously for the US military, and this also during the Second World War.[456]

---

453   https://wikimediafoundation.org/wiki/benefactors, downloaded 11.5.2018

454   Sloan Foundation donates $3M to Wikipedia, USA Today 26.3.2008

455   Die Geschichte der geplanten Obsoleszenz, https://obsoleszenzblog.wordpress.com 10.11.2015

456   Jacques Pauwels: Big Business avec Hitler. Bruxelles 2013, p. 204f.

Sloan set up his foundation in 1934. It was directed against Franklin Roosevelt's reform policy and financed educational projects for the masses with school programs, cheap exercise books and animated films. To provide academic justification, it published the journal Popular Economics. Goal: To bring the principles of free American business to the people in an easily understandable, fast, free form[457] – namely, what Wikipedia does with today's technological and ideological means.

Wikipedia: The anti-science
Wikipedia – that is not a science if you understand it as being based on hard facts, characterized by the unconditional, incorruptible interest in truth, borne by personal responsibility, and geared to the long-term survival interests of the majority.

Summary GAMFA
The prophecy of the digital liberation of individuals and the technological improvement of the world is being perverted into the merciless in-depth spying on and automated control of the everyday lives of the masses. People are being acclaimed as customers and consumers – but degraded, exploited and impoverished as workers and citizens. At the same time, the major shareholders are accumulating hitherto unknown private wealth and determining politics. "We connect all people with each other" – but connected according to the principle "America first". If a European visiting Cuba orders a book for delivery to Germany via the Internet from Amazon Germany, the order will not be executed. Reason: Location Cuba.[458]

The digital populists, who present themselves as innovative, young and modern and as anti-establishment, buy their influence on the oldest and most corrupt parties of Western capitalism in the traditional way and are in on the Washington establishment act. The anti-state activists skim off state subsidies and cooperate openly and secretly with the US intelligence services and the military. The state supervisory authorities in the US and the EU end up acting as accomplices, because anti-democratic politicians in particular – even if they call themselves "liberal" – see GAMFA as useful.

---

457 See the 75th anniversary publication of the Sloan Foundation "A Grantmaking History 1934-2009"

458 Volker Hermsdorf: Der lange Arm der USA, junge Welt 7.5.2018

GAMFA has driven the privatization and capitalization of the Internet and thus the spying and disinformation so high, to the detriment of freedom of opinion, ideas and speech, "that even the NSA would blush with shame," says Bob Goodlatte, chairman of the Justice Committee in the US House of Representatives.[459] At the same time, this makes GAMFA indispensable for the US secret services, which are not ashamed at all, but happily join in.

The simulators of grassroots democracy aim to eliminate competition and create monopolies. Via the major shareholders BlackRock&Co, they are also part of the largest capitalist cartel ever established and are building exclusive infrastructures. They start with anti-competitive dumping prices in order to replace them at the first opportunity with maximum prices in contravention of market rules.

With the help of bought politics, the humanity reformers organize tax and tariff flight, disempower and impoverish countries.

Imperialism of language, thought and emotions
The digital populists organize themselves collectively, while mercilessly destroying old and new forms of collectivity of the pried-on users. People can be manipulated millions, even billions, of times all the more easily and lucratively the more isolated the individuals sit around digitally networked in their bodies and rooms.

With the robotized text assistant Inbox/Smart Reply, Google captures search queries, evaluates them according to keywords and offers target group-specific response modules. The default answers, inserted at the push of a button, are conflict-avoiding ("I'm very sorry") and euphemistic ("We all miss you") like the prevailing soft language that is spread across the suffocated injustice. Conflict whitewashing also means: the past is repressed, forgotten. History is killed, thus also alternatives, resistance.[460]

The AI assistant Duplex from Google, part of the robotized global language economy, conducts telephone calls independently with a "human" voice. It creeps into the thoughts, language and feelings of the telephone partners, simulates thoughtful pauses, adds abashed sounds like "err" and "hmm", whispers, changes the pitch of the voice, is supposed to lead to a predetermined goal.

---

459 "Die NSA würde rot werden vor Schaum", SZ 22.12.2018

460 Cf. Frederic Kaplan: Linguistic Capitalism and Algorithmic Mediation, in: Representations 1/2014, p. 57-63

In the lap of BlackRock&Co

The selfish wealth accumulators practice technological colonialism internally and externally. Human labor as well as raw materials and natural resources are mercilessly exploited without regard for the consequences for third parties. Wars in breach of international law and their facilitation are natural implications of GAMFA rule.

The founding bosses, such as Zuckerberg, are celebrated as a media figure-head. But without hedge funds and venture capitalists, the corporations would not have risen to the top, are in the hands of BlackRock&Co, and finance politicians.

Trade unions and other emancipatory associations are organizing themselves nationally and now worldwide against this. But they are (still) weak.[461]

Share Economy: Global corporations with day laborer army

Even more aggressively than the "five apocalyptic horsemen" of the Internet, Uber&Co want to break existing laws and rules. *Disruptive innovation* is the motto: Existing laws, rules, procedures, products, services are to be interrupted, disrupted, suppressed: "We don't just want technical innovations. We want the break. We want to overthrow the old order. We want to change humanity's path."[462]

At the same time, the platform capitalists play the populist with the share economy. The grassroots democratic promise "We share everything" is to apply to all situations in life, and this ever cheaper, faster, more enjoyable, without bureaucracy.

Uberization

In the English and French-speaking world, the term uberization has established itself. It refers to companies that use the Internet, smartphones and tablets to mediate contact between consumers and providers of products and services. The best-known are the eponymous Uber, provider of taxi services, Airbnb, the private housing and hotel room agent, the food deliverers Deliveroo, Takeaway and Delivery Hero, the streaming services Spotify and Netflix, the employment agencies Upwork, Wework and Amazon Mechanical Turk,

461 Big Tech: We must change the rules of the monopolies' game, www.uniglobalunion.de, downloaded 10.5.2018

462 Ray Zinn: Tech, Disruption And Policy, https://forbes.com 12.7.2017

the travel agent Booking, the dating service Parship/Elite Partners and the bus network service Flixbus.

Like Apple&Co, such companies are usually created as start-ups and mostly by young graduates from the elite universities, especially Stanford, meanwhile also from related milieus in London, Berlin, Tel Aviv and Paris. As soon as they reach a certain market size, these companies also receive loans from venture capitalists, later from major banks and other digital corporations such as Facebook, Google and industrial corporations such as Toyota, Daimler and General Electric. Several years of high indebtedness are accepted in order to eliminate competitors and expand worldwide.[463]

The largest taxi service on earth: Uber

Founded in New York in 2009, Uber provides driving services to private car owners and professional rental car and taxi drivers. Uber sets the fares and collects the fees. Passengers pay to Uber via payment services such as PayPal.

The taxi services are set up in the metropolitan conurbations. After New York and US major cities, Uber expanded in Paris, then London, Sydney, Singapore, Cape Town, Seoul, New Delhi and Beijing, then major cities in Eastern Europe (Warsaw, Kiev, Moscow) and Africa (Lagos/Nigeria). Later, in Western Europe, Zurich, Vienna, Berlin and Munich for example were developed in. In 2017 Uber was present in 70 countries, also with the food delivery service UberEATS, which was launched in 2014.

Wild West capitalism

For Uber, the laws and regulations of the USA and other countries initially count for nothing. Like other founding stars and like Peter Thiel, Uber founder Travis Kalanick invoked the Tea Party saint Ayn Rand. She had fled from the Soviet Union to the USA as a young woman in 1926. In her major work *The Fountainhead* released in 1943 and other books, she propagated the "rational egoism" of individuals who have to defend themselves against all communitizations and the state in order to achieve happiness. For this the many individuals must be led by particularly strong "leaders" with a "leader mentality". In the 1930s, Rand, along with much of the US business community, fought Roosevelt's reformist New Deal and its promotion of trade unions as "communism".

---

463 Marktwert von Uber bereits auf über 60 Milliarden Dollar taxiert, http://ictk.ch/content/marktwert-von-uber, 4.12.2015

Kalanick encouraged the personality cult surrounding himself – the leading media assisted him, as they had with the other digital gurus. With multiple voting rights for his shares and an extreme hierarchy, he secured a position as sole ruler[464] – a missionary leadership role that the founding bosses of Silicon Valley companies also celebrate.

Global tax flight

Uber also adopted the practices of extreme tax flight. The holding company Uber Technologies Inc. has its headquarters in Delaware, 60 subsidiaries in the USA and 75 in other countries, in Europe mainly in the Netherlands.

When, having ordered by iPhone, a passenger in Kuala Lumpur/Malaysia has taken the Uber taxi and paid by credit card, the Uber company Raiser Operations B.V. in Amsterdam transfers the amount to an account of Uber B.V., also in Amsterdam, and then transfers 80 percent of the amount to the driver's account in Kuala Lumpur and the 20 percent for Uber to a complicated mailbox company network. Uber B.V. is a subsidiary of Uber subsidiary Uber International C.V., based in Bermuda.

Uber operates 10 companies in the second largest financial haven of the EU, the Netherlands, whereby only one, Uber B.V., has some employees, the other 9 companies are mailbox companies co-administered by Uber B.V., i.e. they are present on a computer of the Amsterdam commercial register in digital form, and smuggle millions of dollars through from about 70 countries. The complicit state of the Netherlands has legalized this arrangement in the Intangible Property License Agreement. It earns money because it collects about one percent in taxes.[465]

Conspiracy against states

National rules are deliberately violated worldwide: transport regulations, competition laws, labor and social rights. One can speak of conspiracy in the sense of the US criminal offence of conspiracy: Secret agreements between more than two parties using illegal means for the purpose of private gain.[466]

Uber began the installation of its taxi services without informing the

---

464 Crisis inside the 'cult of Travis', FT 10.3.2017

465 Sathyvelu Kunashegraran: How Uber, Google, Facebook and Other Tech Giants Avoid Paying Billions in Tax, https://medium.com 30.4.2017

466 Criminal Law Act 1977 Section 5,2 und 5,3; U.S. Code § 371

city authorities or even applying for a permit. Uber had 16 self-propelled cars circulating in San Francisco[467] – until one of them ran a red light. In March 2017, a self-propelled Uber car hit another car in Arizona. After that, the prematurely started tests were suspended.[468] But then the tests resumed and were only stopped when an automatic Uber car killed a pedestrian in Tempe/Arizona.[469]

Already in the early years, the authorities of several cities, in the USA as in other countries, tried to regulate the taxi service. It came to notice that Uber made false statements in the permit applications. To get to know the real practices, government officials ordered Uber-Taxis. On the other hand, Uber management had the VTOS (Violation of Terms of Service) program developed. According to the official description, this was intended to identify people who conduct sharp practice and want to harm Uber. These persons were to be excluded from use.

In reality, the VTOS Greyball software was directed against government employees. The programmers obtained their private data via credit cards and social media as well as the addresses of the authorities. When the employees ordered a taxi, they were shown ghost cars that didn't come, or the information was: No taxi available! The program was known to 50 people in the company and approved by the Ethics Council under Vice President Ryan Graves. The fake program was initially used in several US cities.[470]

When criticism and resistance become too great, Uber makes some concessions – sometimes reluctantly, sometimes with exaggerated self-criticism. After Uber had to erase Greyball in the USA, it continued to be used in other countries.

Jobs: As few as possible, preferably none at all

The world's largest taxi company does not own a single taxi, but passes on the costs of the vehicles to the drivers and owners. Millions of recreational and professional taxi drivers from New York to Sydney are for Uber pseudo self-employed, at least that was the initial concept. Not a single one has an employment relationship with the company. Uber does not register the drivers with

---

467   Mitfahrdienst widersetzt sich Verbot für Roboterwagen, FAZ 19.12.2016

468   Uber gerät in Schieflage, HB 28.3.2017

469   Self-Driving Uber Car Kills Pedestrian, Where Robots Roam, NYT 19.3.2018

470   Mike Isaac: How Uber Deceives the Authorities Worldwide, NYT 3.3.2017

any tax or social security office. They have to provide the car themselves and assume all risks.[471] The cars of the private drivers do not have to have a calibrated odometer. Sometimes these drivers get USD 5, sometimes USD 10 an hour, the average gross revenue per hour in the USA is currently USD 8.[472] As far as it is concerned, Uber has nothing to do with the precarious status of the drivers – one only mediates. In New York, some drivers stick a begging letter on the back seat: Please tip![473]

For the automated monitoring of drivers and passengers, Microsoft supplied the program *Cognitive Services*. The program captures acoustic, visual and physical information and evaluates it according to wishes, habits and emotions.[474] The drivers were also monitored during the time when they were not on duty: Uber checked to see if they were working for other tax services or whether they were joining demonstrations.[475]

Kalanick fought all attempts by drivers and employees to organize themselves. Uber spent millions of dollars working with law firms to destroy any such attempts.[476] Employees, who often depart swiftly, described labor relations as a chaotic jungle struggle of all against all. The global corporation gets by with just under 7,000 of its own employees. Like other companies in the platform economy, it conducts research on how best to maintain the company without human resources. "Robotaxi" is the name of the vision.[477] With the subsidiary Uber Freight, self-propelled trucks are to be developed.[478]

Subsidized predatory pricing and monopoly formation
Uber has climbed to the top global financial league in just a few years. In 2017, the group had a market value of USD 70 billion, more than double that of Deutsche Bank and ten times that of Deutsche Lufthansa.

---

471 Valentin Bontemps/AFP: "Uberisation" of economics pinching state tax revenues, http://businessinsider.com/afp-uberisation, downloaded 20.8.2016

472 Steven Hill: Krieg gegen Bus und Bahn, HB 23.3.2018

473 Süddeutsche Zeitung 2.2.2017

474 Microsoft Cognitive Services provides 25 tools that can detect emotions, recognize vision and more, https://blogs.microsoft.com/firehose 27.2.2017

475 Nick Srnicek: Plattform-Kapitalismus. Hamburg 2018, p. 86

476 Shannon gegen Goliath, HB 1.11.2015

477 Crisis inside the 'cult of Travis', FT 10.3.2017

478 Revolution im Transportgewerbe, HB 3.1.2017

For this expansion, Uber initially received capital injections from Silicon Valley venture capitalists such as Menlo Venture and Lowercase Capital, from PE investors such as General Atlantic, but also from major capital organizers such as Fidelity, Wellington and BlackRock. In a second phase came Goldman Sachs, Morgan Stanley and Saudi Public Investment. In 2017, the German media group Springer also acquired a stake in the company.[479]

When the scandal-ridden boss Kalanick had to be replaced in the same year, Google and other Silicon Valley investors withdrew, fearing for their reputation. The Japanese electronics manufacturer Softbank is now the largest shareholder, followed by Dragoneer Investment, Tencent (China), Texas Pacific Group and venture capitalist Sequoia. The retired founder Kalanick retains 10 percent.[480]

"Most of Uber's enthusiastic customers don't know that the company subsidizes every single trip. Those who get into a Uber car only pay half of the cost. The other half is borne by Uber's rich venture capitalists. As a result of these subsidies, all transport brokers are deep in the red." Uber's loss for 2017 rose to USD 4.5 billion, up from USD 3 billion in 2016.[481] Investors are relying on the ultimately secured monopoly, which will then rake in enduring profits.

And in the short term, too, every situation is used to create a monopoly, for instance when strikes and catastrophes lead to bottlenecks. For example, Uber took advantage of the emergency situation of a hostage-taking in Australia, when citizens had to be evacuated, in order to triple fares.[482]

Environmental pollution: Uber congestion
The new taxi services advertise with "Smart City". US researchers have investigated the effects of Uber's and its competitor Lyft's taxi services. In the major cities of Boston, New York, San Francisco and London, there are now two to three times as many "free" drivers as there are professional taxis.

The convenient pick-up from home saves traipsing to the bus, metro and tram stops and then from the exit stop to the final destination. This promises comfort and time savings. Combined with the subsidized fares, this creates

---

479   Axel-Springer-Verlag beteiligt sich an Uber, SPON 19.4.2017

480   Diese Investoren setzen auf Uber – und diese könnten aussteigen, WiWo 29.12.2018

481   Steven Hill: Krieg gegen Bus und Bahn, HB 23.3.2018

482   Uber provoziert nach Geiselnahme in Sydney, FAZ 15.12.2014

new demand. The use of public transport in the Uber cities has been declining since 2010. Since then, inner city traffic has slowed by 15 to 23 percent: "Uber congestion", even more pollutants in the air.[483]

Uber&Co concentrate on the largest cities. But the growing need for mobility, especially in the world's growing cities, cannot be meaningfully met by expanding space-devouring individual car traffic. The use of Uber Air planned for 2023 would also clog up urban airspace: the five-seater drone taxis for passenger air transport, with an envisaged airspeed of 240 to 320 kilometers per hour, are to take off from inner-city platforms and house roofs.[484]

The hyped *disruptive innovation* is turning out to be an obstacle to innovation. The innovation needed calls for new forms of collective and public transport. Here, too, the Silicon Valley "culture" follows the model of the pampered, well-paying individual.

Help from Obama's campaign leader and EU Commissioner
Despite all the (apparently) righteous anti-state ideology and contempt for "politics", Uber also gets help from politicians and media strategists. Shortly after its launch, Uber spent more money on lobbying than the established major corporations. Uber hired Barack Obama's campaign manager, David Plouffe, directly from the White House and recruited city officials.[485]

"Prestigious" politicians were happy to be consultants, such as Neelie Kroes, former EU Competition Commissioner, former US Transport Minister Ray LaHood and former Peruvian Prime Minister Roberto Donino. They were given shares in the company and are supposed to improve the public and state legitimacy of the group.[486] Kroes also advises the investment bank Merrill Lynch; before taking office in the European Commission, she had lobbied for Lockheed Martin and McDonald's. The new up-and-coming companies, too, who are supposedly enacting the major break with the old economy, are seeking a close relationship with it – and vice versa, the representatives of the old economy are seeking a close relationship with the new winners.

This is why Princess Reema bint Bandar Al Saud also became an Uber ad-

---

483   Steven Hill: Krieg gegen Bus und Bahn, HB 23.3.2018

484   Uber kämpft um Vertrauen, HB 14.5.2018

485   Dorothea Hahn: Uber überleben, verdi publik 2/2018

486   Frühere EU-Kommissarin Neelie Kroes heuert bei Uber an, www.faz.net 5.5.2016

visor after the Saudi sovereign wealth fund Saudi Public Investment Fund had
bought into the global corporation with USD 3.5 billion.[487]

BILD Editor-in-Chief, Daimler, NASA

After the German media group Springer acquired a stake in Uber, Kai Diekmann, long-time editor-in-chief of the Springer lead medium BILD, was appointed to the advisory board.[488]

The car manufacturer Daimler concluded a cooperation agreement with
Uber to develop driverless cars. The US space agency NASA wants to develop
flying taxis with Uber. Uber does not fail to point out that this is more environmentally friendly than urban taxi transport.[489]

Following the removal of Kalanick, the new boss, Dara Khosrowshahi, explained that the expansion is also to be intensified in this direction, especially
throughout Asia – still with competitive prices subsidized by the new investors.[490]

Worldwide protest

In most countries, including the USA, both private and professional drivers
have protested against the Uber practices. Authorities and courts have imposed conditions. The company has adapted. In some countries, such as Germany, the UberPop service with private drivers has been completely terminated. Only the services UberX (car rental with licensed drivers), Uber Black
and Uber SUV are still operating.

In late 2017 the European Court of Justice (ECJ) ruled: The Uber taxi services do not constitute intermediation, but fall under transport services. The
drivers are therefore not self-employed, but must be paid, insured and taxed
as dependent employees. However, for the EU this is only a preliminary ruling. "It follows that it is for the Member States to regulate the conditions under
which such services are to be provided."[491]

The Swiss State Secretariat for Economic Affairs (SECO) also decided that

---

487   Now that's surge pricing: Saudi Arabia invests USD 3.5bn in Uber, Independent 2.6.2016

488   Kai Diekmann wird Uber-Setzer, www.faz.net 14.4.2017

489   https://autorevue.at/maennersache/uber-nasa-fliegendes-taxi 10.11.2017, downloaded
       20.3.2018

490   Uber will in Asien weiter expandieren, HB 23.2.2018

491   Gerichtshof der Europäischen Union: Pressemitteilung 136/17, 20.12.2017

Uber was to be treated as an employer. The company has to hire the drivers and pay social security contributions. The British trade union GMB also successfully contended that Uber bicycle couriers were to be treated as regular employees.[492] In Egypt, a court has ruled on a complaint by professional taxi drivers that Uber as well as Careem, the comparable local taxi agent, must cease activities. Bangladesh banned Uber only a few days after its launch.

After a number of lower court proceedings, the Supreme Court of California ruled in 2018: Bicycle couriers may only be treated as self-employed if the company can attest three things: It does not exercise any control, the service is outside the core business, the courier also works for other clients. However, the platform lobby is appealing against this ruling, and 40 US states have allowed exceptions for the platform industry with regard to minimum wages and social security.[493]

Food delivery: Deliveroo and Delivery Hero
Even if Uber is being tamed to some degree by fierce resistance and subsequently also state measures, the disputes in other areas of platform capitalism rumble on or are only just beginning. A look at food delivery services will exemplify this.

In 2013 the US banker Will Shu founded the food delivery service Deliveroo in London. Shu had worked for the New York hedge fund SAC, which was closed by the US Securities and Exchange Commission for insider trading. Shu then moved to the London branch of Morgan Stanley. Deliveroo now has a global presence in 150 major cities in the UK, the Netherlands, France, Germany, Belgium, Ireland, Australia, Singapore, the Middle East, Dubai and Hong Kong: 1,500 employees, orders from 23,000 restaurants, food transports by tens of thousands of bicycle couriers, many millions of customers.

Big Investors
In Germany, couriers get EUR 5.50 per delivery. Customers are charged a delivery fee of between EUR 2.50 and 4.90 each. Deliveroo collects 25 percent of the meal price from the restaurants.

---

492 Claudia Wrobel: Lohn pro Auftrag, junge Welt 8.11.2016

493 California ruling puts pressure on Uber, Lyft and other gig economy employers, http://money.com 1.5.2018

With these low revenues, Deliveroo has to maintain cost- and personnel-intensive logistics. Customer orders have to be flexibly combined in a matter of seconds with restaurant orders and with the respective position of the couriers currently available, so that the ordered food is prepared quickly, picked up promptly in the urban jungle in any weather and at any time of day or night, and reaches the customer's home as early as 30 minutes after the order has been placed. Germany boss Felix Chrobog wants to shorten the average 32 minutes to date to 10 to 12 minutes.[494]

Deliveroo has been making losses so far. But for the salaried staff, the offices, the software, the advertising, the lobbyists, the drivers and for the national and international expansion, constant investments have to be made. Popular restaurants have to be rebuilt according to delivery requirements. How is this financed? The New York investment bank Morgan Stanley stepped up to the plate in the search for investors. In 2016, venture investors Bridgepoint, DTS Global, Greenoaks and General Catalyst contributed USD 275 million.[495]

In the following year, the really big boys joined in: Fidelity and T Rowe Price, which, in each of the third rounds, had already been involved in the rise of other global digital services such as Facebook, Airbnb and the electric car manufacturer Tesla. With a total of GBP 600 million of venture capital, Deliveroo was able to ratchet up its workforce from 230 to 1,050 jobs and boost sales by 60 percent.[496]

The Anti-Slavery Declaration

The key to low costs is the lowest-possible payment for the many thousands of couriers who zip around by bicycle in the middle of city traffic – nimbly, swiftly and often dangerously. Deliveroo initially paid the couriers in the UK an hourly rate of GBP 7 (about EUR 8) and a premium of GBP 1 (EUR 1.14) per delivery.

In 2016, the system was also reorganized in other countries as well: Since then, riders have been paid GBP 3.75 per delivery in the UK. Waiting times are not paid. The bicycle, repairs, smartphone, mobile charges, occupational insurance have to be paid for by the riders themselves. Those without a bicycle can rent one from Deliveroo for GBP 5 a day.

---

494   Tagesspiegel 30.7.2017

495   https://www.gruenderszene.de 5.8.2016, downloaded 19.3.2018

496   Deliveroo raises USD 385m in new funding, now values over USD 2bn, https://techcrunch.com 17.11.2017

The management of Deliveroo in the UK reacted to growing protests and strikes by riders with the "Declaration on the Modern Slavery Act". The "conservative" dominated parliament had passed the law in 2015 because in recent years many other pseudo self-employed of platform capitalism had protested against their working conditions even before the Deliveroo drivers.

The anti-slavery declaration begins like this: "Our purpose is to be the definitive food company, bringing people the world's best food whenever and wherever they want it. We do this by embedding our values in everything we do and we oppose all forms of slavery, servitude, compulsory or forced labor and human trafficking."[497] Are we still in the slavery age that we need to make such declarations of intent? Why position oneself against the lowest possible working conditions? More appropriate would be the commitment to ILO labor rights, which were ratified to a large extent by the UK Parliament and are established law, even if that was several decades ago and has been repressed.[498]

Precarious pseudo self-employed
The rudimentary specification of working conditions in the Declaration shows, in slippery share-economy language, the way to labor injustice: "We provide well-paid flexible work to thousands of riders across the UK who take pride in getting customers' deliveries to them as quickly as possible."

Intensified efforts by riders to get hourly wages and to establish a works council are fought tooth and nail by Deliveroo: Elected works councils in Germany are stripped of their role by not renewing their temporary contracts. After the entry of T Rowe Price and Fidelity, the management in Germany converted the fixed-term employee contracts based on the midi-job model (low income between EUR 450.01 and 850 per month) into pseudo self-employment – and such "self-employed persons" are not allowed by law to elect a works council, argues the large law firm Gleiss Lutz commissioned by Deliveroo.[499]

First successes of the resistance
In the UK the riders went on strike, some took court action against their employment contracts. The British Labor Inspectorate established: The riders

---

497 https://deliveroo.de/de/modern-slavery-act-statement, downloaded 19.3.2018

498 See www.ilo.org/conventions/UK

499 Betriebsratsbehinderung, Scheinselbständigkeit, Lohndumping. Aktionstag Freitag der 13. April gegen Deliveroo, www.arbeitsunrecht.de 16.3.2018

are not self-employed.[500] Riders also went on strike in other countries such as Belgium, Germany and the Netherlands. Here, too, labor inspectorates and courts ruled: riders do not have the characteristics of self-employment, but are dependent employees: a single employer, uniforms, advance notification of shifts.[501]

In France, the labor and social security inspectorates have analyzed financial and employment relationships in detailed dossiers. With the help of the pseudo self-employment of 2,286 riders in the greater Paris area alone, Deliveroo evaded social security contributions amounting to EUR 6.4 million in 2016. This is punishable by up to five years in prison.[502]

While Deliveroo claims not to have anything to do with the employment relationships of the drivers, but only to perform an intermediary function, the labor inspectorate states: The riders are dependent employees. They receive instructions, given working clothes and transport containers with uniform Deliveroo logos and colors. Riders are prescribed the formulas to use when picking up from restaurants and delivering to customers. The Deliveroo Staffomatic scheduling system has to be installed on riders' smartphones and tablets. They are continuously monitored by GPS during work and their data is evaluated.

The labor inspectorate quotes from internal guidance from the Deliveroo management to its employees: "Terms such as work, order, employment, remuneration may not be used! Instead, it should read: activity instead of work, invitation instead of order, income instead of remuneration." Of course, Deliveroo, like the other platform services, is now trying to invoke France's "reformed" labor law of 2016, in which the admissibility of "independent workers on digital platforms" has been introduced. The interpretation is left to the courts.

Customer data and cooking robots
In the mostly unread terms and conditions, customers agree that Deliveroo can pass on the customers' data "to carefully selected marketing companies". The aim is to explore, market and shape rewarding target groups, preferred

---

500   Deliveroo workers strike again over new pay structure, The Guardian 15.8.2016

501   Gerrit Hoekman: "Selbständige" ausgebeutet, junge Welt 28.3.2018

502   Michel Déléan / Dan Israel: Ubérisation – une enquete judiciaire ouverte sur Deliveroo, www.mediapart.fr 7.6.2018

dishes, affluent milieus and their other needs. It is also not meant to stop at the delivery of food.[503]

In order to reduce costs, Deliveroo is initially setting up a pilot project in London with mobile, decentralized kitchens. The kitchens are equipped with cooking zones for the most popular restaurants in each district. The aim is to shorten delivery times and make them cheaper. The remuneration of the cooks has not yet been fully clarified, but Deliveroo anyway wants to have the cooking done by robots as soon as possible.[504]

Self-service for owners and top managers

As a company, Deliveroo makes losses. But the top managers reward themselves generously. During the rider strikes and the judicial review of pseudo self-employment, CEO Will Shu awarded himself a 22.5 percent salary increase in 2016. With his 12 percent stake, he is also a multimillionaire and benefits from the increase in the stock price. In 2016, the investors approved a pay rise of almost 500 percent for the top management in the UK under head Dan Warne, namely from GBP 212,000 to GBP 1 million (EUR 1.14 million), plus GBP 4.5 million in the form of shares.[505]

Delivery Hero

Let's take a look at the world leader in digital food services: Delivery Hero S.E., "the world's leading online marketplace for food ordering and delivery". Founded in Berlin in 2011, the company has 6,000 employees worldwide and 1,000 at its Berlin headquarters. In 40 countries on all five continents, tens of thousands of cyclists pedal away to deliver millions of meals to customers as quickly as possible. "We are the United Nations of food delivery".

In order to expand, more than a dozen competitors were acquired in several countries within a few years, including in Germany Lieferheld, Pizza. de and Foodora, Talabat (Middle East), Foodfly (South Korea), Yemeksepeti (Turkey), Foodarena (Switzerland), Rappi (South America) and Deliveras (Greece). In 2018, the German subsidiaries were already sold on in total to

503 Deliveroo: Where's the money? https://corporatewatch.org 24.10.2017

504 Deliveroo: Where's the money? ibid.

505 Deliveroo boss gives himself 22.5 % rise amid battle over riders' pay, The Guardian 21.9.2017; Deliveroo: Where's the money? ibid.

the Dutch supplier Takeaway: Delivery Hero becomes a major shareholder there and expands in Asia and South America, where Takeway is not yet represented. The motto is to eliminate competition.[506]

Major investors
This is only possible with the help of big investors. This enabled the well-supported company to go public – it was the largest IPO of 2017 in Germany. After Rocket International (the Samwer brothers), who have only a minority stake, the main owners are now the largest African media group Naspers, then Insight Ventures, Gavril Abramovich Yushvaev, Luxor Capital, Team Europe, Schroder Investment, Putnam, Artemis and Baillie Gifford.[507]

For the representatives of these major investors, namely the major banks Goldman Sachs and Citibank, Delivery Hero managers in New York, Zurich, San Francisco, Geneva and Paris have to be on call for road shows.[508] As with BlackRock, these take place outside the regular meetings of supervisory boards and shareholders. The managers have to justify the measures taken to date and disclose the new measures for the current year: How are turnover, share value and profit to be increased? The managers' remuneration – basic salary, performance bonuses, preferred stock awards, special benefits – also hinges on this.

A relic from the past: "The Honorable Merchant"
In the share economy, high ethical standards and modern slavery form an organic unit. In the Corporate Governance Code, Delivery Hero's Board of Management and Supervisory Board commit themselves to the "Responsibility and Transparency of Management", based on the principle of the "Honorable Merchant". This "honorable merchant" is a relic of 19th century Western European capitalism. It still does the rounds in the nostalgic statutes of German Chambers of Commerce, which, by the way, also used it to deny their activities in the aryanization of Jewish companies during the Nazi era.

Platform companies penetrating everyday life
Other financial investors follow this pattern with the Uber competitors Grab-Car and Lyft (Asia), with AirBnB (rooms) and Booking (travel), Netflix (TV,

---

506   Duell mit zwei Siegern, HB 27.12.2018

507   www.4-traders.com, downloaded 19.3.2018

508   See Investor Relations press releases on the website: https:// ir.deliveryhero.com

film), Gett (inner-city letter delivery), Spotify (music streaming).[509] New areas such as the granting of direct loans, the placement of domestic help and repairs, the supply of groceries are being developed. Within the space of a few years, some of these companies became global corporations with high market values. The young founders can become multi-billionaires in just a few years.

Brokers of binge watching

In 2009, the founders of the streaming service Netflix published the manifesto "Freedom and Responsibility". This was also one of the share economy visions: You can watch the movies and TV shows you want, whenever and wherever you want – that was the promise. To this end, Netflix delves deep into the souls of its users. "Netflix reads user behavior. The rest is asked: What kind of topics would be exciting, how many series, who could play that part?"[510]

With 100 million subscribers in 190 countries, Netflix reaches more households than traditional TV stations. The company acquired all Disney licenses and uses the best-paid directors and actors to produce successful films that cover all clichéd entertainment formats: Horror thrillers, black comedy, mystery, music and history dramas, science fiction. The humanity-enhancing vision aims to keep subscribers as couch potatoes in their homes and to make them addicted to ordering the next DVD package and exposing themselves to new thrills: Binge watching it's called in the advertising scene.

Matchmaking

Media groups are also on the lookout for new business areas and target groups. The partner agency Parship, to which GayParship for homosexual target groups belongs, founded in Hamburg in 2000, was quickly snapped up by the Holtzbrinck publishing group (HB, Die Zeit, Scientific American).

When Parship expanded into the rest of Europe, it was acquired by PE investors Oakley and Permira in 2015.[511] They also bought the love broker ElitePartner. In September 2016, the newly formed Parship Elite Group already changed ownership again: The TV company ProSiebenSat.1 wants to expand its digital and advertising business with the several million single subscribers.

---

509   Angriff aus dem Dunkeln, HB 15.8.2016

510   Großartig – Der Streamingdienst Netflix hat sich etabliert, HB 16.12.2016

511   Angriff aus dem Dunkeln, HB 15.8.2016

Private and hotel room reservation

Airbnb is the abbreviation for Air bed and breakfast. The company acts like Uber as an online platform and arranges accommodation with private landlords and in hotels. Founded in San Francisco in 2009, it now operates in virtually every country on the planet. The airbed image has long since been discarded: In the meantime, luxury suites are also available in the most expensive hotels.[512]

Airbnb gained a foothold in Germany through the acquisition of its competitor Accoleo. The ascent was financed by start-up investors from California and the private equity fund DST Global of Russian entrepreneur Yuri Milner. To expand, the company cooperates with Facebook and other Internet companies. Airbnb is already worth more as a public limited company than the largest hotel chains Hilton and InterConti, whose rooms are also on offer. Airbnb does not own a single private or hotel room.

Airbnb is particularly active in large cities that are also tourist centers. This has led to an increase in rents and the displacement of tenants. Because the Group does not disclose the names of the landlords with whom it places guests, Airbnb is aiding and abetting annual tax evasion of around EUR 200 million in the three German cities of Munich, Berlin and Hamburg alone.[513]

Numerous city councils have intervened here, for example in New York, Berlin, Madrid, Barcelona, Paris, with little success. But the city of Palma de Mallorca initially imposed fines on Airbnb and Homeaway because the corporations contributed to the tax evasion of landlords and rented out much more than the licensed apartments. Cheap tourism also leads to an additional shortage of drinking water. As of July 1, 2018, no rental apartments can be rented out to tourists.[514]

Job placement

Three companies are known for their digital temporary employment placement service. Amazon's Mechanical Turk (MT) brokers any kind of work, from mini jobs, for which a few cents are paid, to elaborate web design jobs. The employers set the price, usually remain anonymous, the job seekers (the

---

512   Die Welt geht auf Reisen, FAZ 28.4.2018

513   Was dem Staat an Steuern entgeht, SZ 28.1.2019

514   Palma de Mallorca stoppt Airbnb, SZ 25.4.2018

"mechanical Turks") cannot negotiate. Clients can order any digital service – including the editing of Wikipedia articles, likes to a product advertisement, entries in discussion forums.[515]

While MT classifies supplicants for jobs of any long or short duration as mechanical Turks, the job broker TaskRabbit finds a different, accurate term for the job seekers: Rabbits who race each other for the next work morsel. As a cynical compensation, the rabbits are designated as self-employed so that the employer does not have to pay them contributions to pension, unemployment and health insurance, and no sick leave or vacation days.[516]

The two temporary employment agencies oDesk and Elance were merged in 2015 to form Upwork, the world's largest employment agency. The main financiers of the merger were T Rowe Price and the venture capitalist Benchmark.[517] Based in Mountain View and San Francisco, the company has 250 regular employees. They manage 14 million jobseekers worldwide and have four million employer clients in 180 countries. The status of the self-employed rabbits is categorized in various ways: (Solo) self-employed, subcontractors, clickworkers, crowdworkers, freelancers, gig-takers. They can also be designated as day laborers or piecework employees. The countries and their employment offices know nothing about it. The German statistics authority does not know that Upwork has registered 18,000 jobseekers in Germany nor under what conditions they are placed with which employers.[518]

Arrangement of bus transport
Flixmobility GmbH, or Flixbus for short, was founded through the acquisition of small bus companies. Founder André Schwämmlein came from Boston Consulting. In early 2013, the Federal Government abolished the previous limits on long-distance bus transport by means of the amended Passenger Transport Act. Daimler Mobility Services and the Holtzbrinck publishing group bought a stake, enabling the acquisition of the smaller long-distance bus companies of Deutsche Post and Deutsche Bahn. The next acquisition of the competitor MeinFernbus was financed by the PE fund

515   Die Crowdworking-Plattformen Amazon Mechanical Turk und Upwork, https://www.bigbrotherawards.de/2015, downloaded 26.4.2018

516   Steven Hill: Die Start up-Illusion. München 2017, p. 44f.

517   Venture round Upwork, https://crunchbase.com, downloaded 26.4.2018

518   Steven Hill ibid., p. 45ff.

General Atlantic. After just a few years, Flixbus was able to control almost 90 percent of the market in Germany – and prices were promptly increased by 40 percent.[519]

With the help of the next investor Silver Lake, Flixmobility then also bought bus services in France and other EU states that had deregulated the transport sector along the lines of the German model – for example in France under Economics Minister Macron. Flixbus also only acts as a broker, does not own a single bus and has not hired a single driver. Instead, hundreds of medium-sized bus companies between Ireland and the Czech Republic are licensed and coordinated under the franchise system. The poorly paid drivers have to take on many additional tasks – customer service, check-in, cleaning – and are often on the road 13 to 15 hours a day, including breaching break times and safety defects on the buses.[520]

The centers of elitist digital populism

The founders of the largest Internet and digital corporations come primarily from two private elite universities. They have traditionally been closely associated with large private companies as well as with politicians and consultants of the two US capitalist parties: Stanford and Harvard. Studying costs between USD 60,000 and 90,000 a year. About 6 percent of the applicants are accepted at Stanford, in some cases high scholarships are awarded. The Stanford milieu includes the founders of Hewlett Packard, Sun Microsystems, Apple, Google, Yahoo, Nike, Netflix, Paypal, Instagram, Snapchat, Facebook as well as 17 NASA astronauts. Incidentally, 94 percent of the founders are male – hardly any other industry propagates diversity as loudly and performs as badly as the technology industry. Below are the numbers of the most successful platform founders and their universities of origin.[521]

---

519   Kaum noch Wettbewerb. 40 Prozent teurer! Preise für Fernbus-Fahrten in nur zwei Jahren fast verdoppelt, https://www.focus.de 17.9.2016

520   Das Risiko fährt mit, verdi publik 7/2018

521   Diversity in der IT. Noch immer weiß und männlich, HB 5.1.2018; Google CEO Sundar Pichai Has No Regret About Firing James Damore, http://fortune.com 20.1.2018

Stanford University (California, Silicon Valley)	51
Harvard University (Boston)	37
University of California	18
Indian Institute of Technology (Mumbai, Delhi)	12
Massachusetts Institute of Technology (Boston)	9
University of Pennsylvania	9
University of Oxford (England)	8
Tel Aviv University (Israel)	7
Cornell University (New York)	6
University of Southern California	6
University of Waterloo (Canada)	6

Record of the platform economy

Monopoly formation: The investors grant loans for the rapid purchase of competitors and start-ups. Competition is promoted and exploited at the lower level in order to ultimately eliminate it. Investors accept years of lean periods, but are keen to immediately exploit every opportunity for price increases.

Tax flight: Like their investors, the platform companies also have worldwide tax flight organized by professional advisors.

Precariousness: The platform companies are further pushing the practice of the *working poor*, seen in the USA since the 1960s, towards an even poorer digital precariat: The globally expanded army of millions consists of piecework receivers, pseudo self-employed freelancers, on-call workers and individualized low-wage earners. In Germany, the platform companies have about one million employees – the employment offices don't know. Social insurance organizations lose billions of euros every year.[522]

Spying: The brokers record all accessible data of their employees and customers (including keyboard entries, mouse clicks). Data processing takes place mainly in the USA.

Way of life: The business focuses on individualized services in metropolitan areas. This promotes overcrowding and contamination of the already overstretched cities.

Homelessness: The increased asociality is also reflected in the unfettered

---

522   Steven Hill: "Beschäftigte werden vom Algorithmus gefeuert", junge Welt 16.6.2017

regional housing market. California, with its Silicon Valley and San Francisco centers, has become the most asocial residential area: the highest average (!) rents of USD 4,000 a month for a small house – and the most homeless. The supermarkets also charge much higher prices.[523]

Governments as accomplices: The European Union promotes the platform model because the agencies create "flexible working arrangements and new sources of income".[524] The companies are also arming themselves against criticism. In the USA, Deliveroo, Uber and Airbnb have joined forces and are calling on the government to oppose the increased initiatives of those affected and trade unions: The labor law must be changed, adapted to the practices of the digital platform industry and a "new class of workers" legalized.[525]

Resistance: Those affected and harmed by the platform economy around the world have begun to resist.[526] Courts and municipal administrations have imposed some restrictions. But governments are blocking, left parties and trade unions are weak and ignorant.

The alternative: At the beginning of the 20th century, the 8-hour day and the 40-hour week with (at the time) adequate labor income were already possible – today, with the help of the new technologies, working time could be at least halved and evenly distributed. Labor output and incomes must and can also be distributed fairly instead of compulsively administering sick-making unemployment and stressful over- and under-employment.

9.
The civilian private army of transatlantic capital

As already mentioned, the new financial players engage a host of private consultancy firms. Their staff consists of highly paid academic professionals who come from the most prestigious private and public universities and business schools and are trained in elitism. Most consulting firms and leading media

---

523   Ein Boom, der viele arm macht, HB 11.5.2018

524   Europäische Kommission: Europäische Agenda für die kollaborative Wirtschaft, COM (2016) 356 final

525   Uber, Airbnb and Deliveroo urge labor law shake-up, http://afr.com 15.3.2018

526   Vgl. Re: Kuriere am Limit? Arte TV 14.3.2018

are represented in the LGBT network: Free sexual choice and development is more important than orientation towards universal human rights. These consultancies are at the same time actors of the largely privatized state in today's leading Western capitalist democracies.[527]

Rating agencies

Three rating agencies dominate the rating market in the Western world: the Big Three S&P, Moody's and Fitch. They were first mandated by the US government to assess the creditworthiness of companies, states and municipalities. Credit terms are based on these assessments. The agencies also appraise individual securities, which is then used by the issuing banks and other financial players to woo customers. The agencies themselves are private capitalist companies, their profit hinges on the highest possible fees paid by the rated parties. It therefore boils down to organized insider dealing.

This leads to courtesy ratings, which also degenerate into deliberately false ratings, as the US Congress established after the last financial crisis. What is more, the agencies rated all banks that were in reality insolvent, such as Lehman Brothers, and the toxic securities, as creditworthy to the end. The rating agencies were therefore partly to blame for the financial crisis.[528] At the same time, BlackRock, Vanguard, State Street, T Rowe Price, Capital Group and Bank of New York Mellon themselves were the most important owners of the two largest agencies, S&P and Moody's.[529]

In the early 2000s, the EU adopted the US rating system and also the three leading agencies – in the Basel II framework for the central bank of central banks, the BIS in Basel. The EU had its budget and the European Investment Bank (EIB) rated by the US agencies in advance. The EU, the ECB and national financial supervisors base their assessments of EU member states and their dealings with over-indebted member states such as Greece, Ireland, Cyprus, etc. on the ratings of the Big Three.

In the wake of the 2007 financial crisis, the European Parliament proposed to finally create a European agency. The European Commission thwarted the

---

527 Werner Rügemer: Die Privatisierung des Staates – Das Vorbild USA, in: Ullrich Mies u.a. (Hg.): Fassadendemokratie und tiefer Staat. Wien 2017, p. 111-124

528 Financial Crisis Inquiry Commission: The Financial Crisis Inquiry Report. New York 2011, p. 43f., 131ff., 165, 418

529 Werner Rügemer: Ratingagenturen. Einblicke in die Kapitalmacht der Gegenwart. Bielefeld 2012, p. 60

project. In Brussels the US lobby ensured that there would be no European rating agency playing in the first league.[530]

The new financial players have further expanded the agencies' business, as since the financial crisis even more financial stocks have been shifted from the traditional banks to BlackRock, Blackstone & Co. In addition, they are commissioning more and more ratings from the agencies for their increasingly numerous funds and new financial products. The stock values and profits of the Big Three also rose, most recently boosted by US President Trump.[531]

Auditors

The auditing firms PWC, KPMG, EY and Deloitte also contributed to the financial crisis. These "Big Four" from the USA, with headquarters in London and Switzerland (KPMG), are global corporations with a total of 943,000 professionals and dominate the world market. In the USA and in the EU, they have divided the audit of all large corporations among themselves, in Germany all 30 DAX corporations.

In all known major insolvencies, they covered up false balance sheets and only on rare occasions paid a piffling fine after a court settlement.[532] Until 2007, for example, they had also certified the balance sheets of banks and insurance companies such as Lehman Brothers, Goldman Sachs, Deutsche Bank, IKB (the first bank that went bankrupt in Germany), Hypo Real Estate (HRE), WestLB and American International Group (AIG) as correct to the very end – they had shifted risky loans off the books.[533] Nevertheless, these tricksters and deceivers were and are used in the EU to rescue banks and restructure public finances, and throughout Western capitalism they continue to "audit" the balance sheets of the largest companies.[534]

The auditors also have a legal mandate in the capitalist democratic states, but like the rating agencies they are private, profit-oriented companies. They audit the accounts and balance sheets of large companies in particular, but, like the rating agencies, they are selected and paid for by the audited companies themselves. In this way, the "auditors" have become insiders, self-service

530   Werner Rügemer: Ratingagenturen ibid. p. 172f.

531   Das große Geschäft mit der Unsicherheit, SZ 19.2.2017

532   Meinrad Heck: Der Flowtex-Skandal. Frankfurt/Main 2006

533   Wie sich PWC und KPMG die Bälle zuspielen, WiWo 11.6.2009

534   Sol Trumbo Vila u.a.: The Bail Out Business, TNI February 2017

operators and accomplices. In addition, they are not only paid for this statutory mandate, but they also offer companies a further, well-rewarded service: Tax advice.

The Big Four operate branches in all major financial havens such as Delaware, Luxembourg, the Cayman Islands, Bermuda and the Channel Islands and help global corporations and investors such as BlackRock with tax "structuring". In 2003, KPMG's Luxembourg office wooed corporate clients with a multilingual brochure.[535] PWC also operates particularly large branches in the most important financial havens of the EU, such as Luxembourg with 2,000 employees and 1,600 in Cyprus.[536]

While the Big Four help companies to defraud the EU states of at least EUR 50 billion a year, the European Commission pays the Big Four about EUR 50 million a year for advice on tax issues.[537] PWC in particular became a permanent advisor to the European Commission, for example on the privatization of water and municipal infrastructure. PWC also advises the Commission on free trade agreements and on EU-promoted privatizations in third countries. PWC bosses are also active in lobby organizations such as the Transatlantic Business Dialogue (TABD) and the American Chamber of Commerce to the European Union (AmCham EU).[538] The European Commission sends Deloitte, EY, PWC and KPMG to governments of EU member states, e.g. in Eastern Europe, to help with the codification of the tax system and social security systems.[539] On behalf of the German government, PWC is doing the ground work for BlackRock&Co, for example on the privatization of school operations.[540]

Commercial law firms

The new financial players turn mainly to major London and US law firms for the legal side of their transactions. They have had a global presence for decades, know the legal systems of the most important countries, explore loop-

---

535 KPMG Tax Advisers: International Tax Planning Made in Luxemburg 2003, Luxembourg 2003

536 PWC: A beginner's guide to privatisations, may 2013, www.pwc.com.cy

537 Corporate Europe Observatory: Accounting for Influence, Brussels July 2018, p. 6 and 10

538 Corporate Europe Observatory: Accounting for Influence ibid., p. 13

539 Einfach umverteilen, junge Welt 15.8.2008

540 https://www.bmwi.de/Redaktion/DEDownloads/Studien/pwc-gutachten-lang.pdf, downloaded 10.5.2018

holes and orient themselves to the standards of Anglo-American commercial law. With the new financial players, they have also increasingly taken on the legal advice of countries, for example on privatization. The most important, each with several thousand lawyers, are Freshfields, Shearman & Sterling, Allen & Overy, Clifford Chance, Sullivan & Cromwell, Linklaters, White & Case, DLA Piper and Hogan Lovells. They have offices in all major EU countries.

The law firms advise PE investors on the purchase and sale of companies and the large capital organizers on M&A. Among the 10 largest law firms operating this business in Germany, there was only one German law firm in 2011: Hengeler Müller. The other nine are US law firms, in this order of turnover: Freshfields, Sullivan & Cromwell, Shearman & Sterling, Clifford Chance, Skadden/Arps/Slate, Linklaters, Allen & Overy, Davies Ward and Lovells.[541]

In the EU, these law firms legally secured the sale and leaseback of municipal and state infrastructure – sewage systems, exhibition halls, trams, metros, aviation safety – from the mid-1990s onwards in order to provide US investors with tax advantages. This went under the name cross-border leasing. Freshfields and Allen & Overy, for example, constructed the fictitious simultaneous ownership of two contracting parties, public and private, in 1000-page secret contracts.[542]

The law firms also advised EU governments on other forms of privatization of state property and on the outsourcing of state functions to private investors, such as public-private partnerships (PPPs). Freshfields, Clifford Chance and Linklaters worked with PWC to push through PPP legislation in Germany and the UK and drafted contracts between the state and investors. Once the pattern was established in these two countries, it was also adopted by the EU.[543]

Freshfields was also commissioned by the German government to draft the two laws to save the beleaguered banks.[544] In 2002 Freshfields drafted the 17,000 page contract for Germany's largest PPP project, Toll Collect (collection of the truck toll on motorways). The investors Daimler, Deutsche Telekom and Cofiroute (Vinci) only fulfilled their contractual obligations two years later. The German government sued the investors for damages, today

541   Die Herren der Welt. Top-Anwälte mehren ihren Einfluss auf Wirtschaft und Poilitik, Focus 11/2011, p. 57

542   Werner Rügemer: Cross Border Leasing. Münster 2005

543   Werner Rügemer: Public Private Partnership. Anatomie eines globalen Finanzinstruments. Bielefeld 2012

544   Die Einflüsterer, SZ 7.3.2006; Die Gesetze der Kanzleien. SZ 14.8.2009

with compound interest a sum of EUR 9.5 billion. The federal government again commissioned Freshfields to represent them. The case was settled out of court in 2018 after 14 years, but the federal government paid Freshfields&Co EUR 244.6 million for their unsuccessful long-term advice – and the investors get off lightly.[545]

Private arbitration courts in the hands of US law firms

Against the threat of nationalization of Western property in ex-colonial states after World War II, the USA coordinated the establishment of private arbitration tribunals. In 1958, the Convention on the Recognition and Enforcement of Foreign Arbitral Awards was adopted in New York. Since then, it has been the basis for private, international arbitration. Since 1966, the International Center for the Settlement of Investment Disputes (ICSID) has been operating in the World Bank in Washington. The EU states acceded to the agreement.

Today the five international arbitration tribunals – besides Washington, the smaller ones in Paris, London, The Hague and Stockholm – are essentially in the hands of a dozen US commercial law firms. Freshfields, Shearman & Sterling, White & Case, King & Spalding, etc. in particular provide the personnel for the highly paid functions of judge, prosecutor and defense counsel. These lawyers are "experts on everything but human rights", concludes British lawyer Sebastian Perry.[546]

Management consultants

The new financial players engage management consultants for their transactions. "More profit with less staff" is the motto of the first management consultancy McKinsey, founded in Chicago in 1926. The majority of employees in the advised companies are kept on as tight a rein as possible in financial, legal and number terms, management is trained to lead and, depending on individual performance, is rewarded on a hierarchical basis for the cruelties.

McKinsey experienced its breakthrough in the 1930s when US President Franklin Roosevelt promoted social reforms with the New Deal. McKinsey was used by US corporations to defend themselves against the perennial enemies welfare state and trade unions that have been attacked to this day. With

---

545 Antwort der Bundesregierung auf die Auskunftsbitte des Abgeordneten Victor Perli/Die Linke: Stand des Verfahrens mit Toll Collect, 7.3.2018; HB 9.5.2018

546 Werner Rügemer: Das jüngste Weltgericht. Hintergrund 1/2015, p. 60ff.

the Marshall Plan, McKinsey also came to Western Europe, led the industry here for five decades and shaped the internal organization of the large stock corporations in the EU. Since the Treuhand-Anstalt in Germany – privatization of GDR companies from 1990 to 1994 – and especially with the privatization of state-owned companies in the EU, McKinsey along with PWC and Freshfields also became permanent government consultants.[547]

Thousands more business consultants have long since established themselves, but McKinsey and others from the USA are still the largest in the EU. With a global perspective, McKinsey and Boston Consulting Group (BCG) explore the exploitation of human labor, for instance through digitalization and expanded temporary work.[548] McKinsey was a member of the Hartz Commission in Germany at the end of the 1990s, which initiated the four Hartz laws for deregulating employment relationships. McKinsey and Accenture were and are the main consultants in Germany for the restructuring of the Federal Employment Agency and the job centers – contracts since the beginning of 2004 amounted to EUR 255.2 million up to 2017. McKinsey advises the German government on the most cost-effective way to deport refugees. McKinsey and its Health Institute advise governments and private equity investors on the purchase and restructuring of hospitals, rehabilitation clinics and nursing homes.

The privatization of the state and politics also comes in other forms. In Germany, McKinsey and Accenture provide state secretaries and high-ranking staff, for example in the Ministry of Defense and Development Aid. The governing CDU party under Merkel brought in the head of McKinsey Germany, Jürgen Kluge, to formulate the new party manifesto "New Social Market Economy".[549] The other governing party, the SPD, also hired McKinsey managers to get advice on the election campaigns of its chancellor candidates Frank-Walter Steinmeier and then Peer Steinbrück.[550] Catholic archbishoprics also sought advice on how they could better "sell" their "Christian" message.[551]

547   Werner Rügemer: Die Berater. Ihr Wirken in Staat und Gesellschaft. Bielefeld 2004, p. 78ff.

548   McKinsey Global Institute: What the future of work will mean for jobs, skills and wages, November 2017; Boston Consulting Group/ciett: Adaptation to Change, Bruxelles 2012

549   Die Berater-Republik, Die Zeit 7/2004

550   Steinmeier holt McKinsey-Mann als Berater, FT Deutschland 26.11.2008; Steinmeier, Steinbrück, Gabriel – Tristesse bei der SPD-Troika, RP online 27.7.2012

551   Jochen Bülow: McKinsey beim Erzbischof, in: Werner Rügemer: Die Berater ibid., p. 133ff.

Who owns the largest management consultancies?
The top ten list of management consultants in Germany looks like this, in order of turnover (as of 2016): Accenture, McKinsey, Boston Consulting Group (BCG), Mercer, Aon Hewitt, Towers Watson, Capgemini, Bain, Oliver Wyman, A.T.Kearney. Only two are not headquartered in the USA: Towers Watson (London) and Capgemini (Paris).

Let's briefly take a closer look at two of these corporations. First, the "French" Capgemini group: 4.5 percent of the shares belong to its own management, but the next largest co-owners are Vanguard, Fidelity, Norges, JP-Morgan, Invesco, BlackRock, Amundi...

Then Accenture: This consulting firm with 420,000 employees worldwide has overtaken McKinsey. The legal domicile was moved from Bermuda to the other financial haven Dublin/Ireland. And who owns the largest consulting group? It won't come as a surprise. In order of their shareholdings: Vanguard, BlackRock, Massachusetts Financial, Capital Global, State Street, Wellington, Morgan Stanley, JP Morgan, Bank of New York Mellon, Northern Trust, Geode Capital, Wells Fargo, United Bank of Switzerland, Bank of America...

Leading media

The *New York Times* (NYT) is a leading medium of the Western community of values, at least as far as print and the diffuse layer of intellectuals who see themselves as liberal are concerned. The Süddeutsche Zeitung, Le Monde, El Pais, La Repubblica and the Daily Telegraph include the NYT International Weekly as a supplement. Things are by all means sometimes critical, for example in the columns by the Nobel-award winning economist Paul Krugman. Well-researched reports revealed particularly disgusting actions by the US army in the Vietnam and Iraq wars. After the financial crisis, the fraudulent machinations of hedge funds and banks were documented. The exploitation of Walmart and Amazon workers is denounced, as is the impoverishment of the middle class. Obama and the Clinton milieu were considered exemplary American, while Donald Trump is considered sexist, racist and uneducated. But that the "free world" must be led by the world No.1 power – that remains undisputed.

Vanguard, BlackRock, Mexican multi-billionaire...
Grandchildren of the founding or heir family Ochs-Sulzberger are allowed to play a public role in the NYT, for example as publishers. But the power lies with

others. After the IPO in 1967, the then leading Wall Street bank Morgan Stanley was the main shareholder. When the newspaper belatedly and cautiously distanced itself from the US warfare in Iraq under President George W. Bush, the bank departed, and the Sulzberger family sold its Morgan Stanley shares. Inbetween, the Mexican multi-billionaire Carlos Slim, who also has a host of other stakes in the USA, saved the company and today he is still the largest individual co-owner. But institutional investors have the upper hand with 71 percent: Darsana Capital Partners, Vanguard, BlackRock, Fairpointe Capital, Wellington and so on. Darsana also has stakes in Google/Alphabet, Facebook and Netflix, and above all in Spirit Aerosystems, the world's largest supplier to the aircraft and defense industries, including Boeing and Raytheon. It is not wrong to assume that Vanguard and BlackRock are Spirit Aerosystems' main shareholders.[552]

US press agencies, Open Society Foundation
Keeping the academically educated milieu of Western capitalism, which is semi-critical on all sides, onside is (to date) not a loss-making business. To balance this, Amazon boss Bezos bought the print medium attributed to the Republicans, the *Washington Post*.

Google set up the USD 150 million *Digital News Initiative* (DNI) in 2015. Other tone-setters for Western leading media alongside the US press agencies *Associated Press, Dow Jones News, ThomsonReuters, Bloomberg and United Press International* also include US foundations. Let's pick out one: *The Open Society Foundation*. It was founded by the hedge fund manager Soros. It developed media campaigns for the "colorful revolutions" in various Eastern European countries, which were followed by the leading Western European media. The "open society" means opening up to Western financial players and NATO. This is associated with various mutations of anti-democratic politics. It is no coincidence that a Christian right-wing populist like the Hungarian Prime Minister Viktor Orban was a recipient of a Soros Foundation scholarship. This is also compatible with "Christian" tinted politics – Orban's Fidesz party is a member of the European People's Party (EPP), which is dominated by Merkel's CDU. Orban himself is Vice-President of the Christian Democratic International and the EPP.

---

552   Aktienanteile für NYT und Darsana: https://www.nasdaq.com, downloaded 11.5.2018

Macron, his Prime Minister and French journalists
The media elite from the EU is also traditionally guided by US-led foundations when it comes to military, foreign and economic policy. In France, for example, the then US ambassador James Lowenstein and members of the CFR founded the *French American Foundation* in the 1970s. Several politicians emerged from the Young Leaders Program: From the USA William and Hillary Clinton, from France Francois Hollande and the top staff of the current Macron government: Macron himself as well as his Prime Minister Edouard Philippe and ministers, deputies and speechwriters; but also employees of US companies such as Boeing, McKinsey, Lazard, Goldman Sachs, Bridgewater and A.T. Kearney; French companies such as Airbus, AXA, Areva and Vinci; employees of NATO and the US secret service NSA and the secretary of Amnesty International. This also includes journalists on both sides of the Atlantic who have learned from the Young Leaders Program which milieu they (may) belong to: journalists for NYT and Los Angeles Times in the USA, in France for Le Monde, L'Express, Les Echos, L'Eco, Le Petit Quotidien, France2/TV5Monde, Europe1 and RTL.[553]

Alpha-journalists in Germany
The network appears to be the most dense in Germany: American Institute for Contemporary German Studies (Washington), German Marshall Fund, Aspen Institute, Trilateral Commission, American Academy (Berlin), American Council on Germany. Journalists from leading public and private media are invited to the conferences – with military personnel, politicians, CEOs – on both sides of the Atlantic: ZDF, ARD, Die Zeit, FAZ, Die Welt, Süddeutsche, Spiegel, Focus.

Indoctrination is not on the menu, but journalists – who are deemed to have a certain inclination – are eased gently and step by step into an exclusive and powerful network.[554] The starting point in Germany was the *Atlantikbrücke* (Atlantic Bridge), which was launched by US High Commissioner John McCloy and German-American investment banker Erich Warburg. This was where CEOs, politicians, the military and the most important journalists from the leading West German media licensed by the US military administration, such as Die Zeit, Spiegel, Welt and Süddeutsche Zeitung, met and meet until now.[555]

553 https://frenchamerican.org/young-leaders/earlier-classes, downloaded 11.5.2018

554 Uwe Krüger: Meinungsmacht. Eine kritische Netzwerkanalyse, Köln 2013

555 Hermann Ploppa: Die Macher hinter den Kulissen. Frankfurt/Main 2014, p. 80ff.

Springer publishing house

The Springer publishing house addresses the academically educated middle class elite with the daily newspaper Die Welt – department "conservative / Christian / higher earners" – and at the same time, with the gutter rag BILD, simulates the media advocate of the small working man and the small naked woman. Following the US model, the publishing house is a member of the LGBT network and defends the "existence of the State of Israel", even if the current state lacks features of international law, e.g. defined state borders.

The Axel Springer Award for outstanding media innovations was first presented by the publishing house to Facebook boss Zuckerberg and then to Amazon boss Bezos, owner of the Washington Post. The editorial statute of the publishing house for all its media makes "solidarity in the free community of values with the United States of America" an obligation.[556] What other media do in practice is what Germany's largest print media group does explicitly: US propaganda instead of independent journalism.

Philanthro-capitalists

Via philanthropic foundations, large US corporations have traditionally helped shape domestic, cultural, health, scientific as well as global politics. They were and are linked to the US government and secret services. The best known from the founder period before World War I are the Carnegie, Ford and Rockefeller Foundations

Currently, the world's largest capital foundation of Melinda and William Gates promotes programs against child and female poverty, for environmental conservation, for genetically renewed agriculture, for inclusion, for the fight against cancer and AIDS. Among other things, Google subsidizes pro-American print media worldwide. Facebook finances research institutes at elite universities around the globe in its own areas of interest such as artificial intelligence. The wife and heiress of Steve Jobs/Apple and her foundation aim to modernize high schools in the USA (The Super School Project). The hedge fund architect and currency speculator George Soros, who presents himself as a liberal, takes on politically subversive campaigns with the Open Society Foundation and the Renaissance Foundation (Ukraine), in consultation with the State Department and NATO, such as supporting dissidents in Serbia dur-

---

556 Nachhaltigkeit.axelspringer.de/de/grundsaetze/unternehmensgrundsaetze.html, downloaded 12.5.2018

ing the NATO attacks. Soros also finances worldwide journalism, according to *Reporters Without Borders*.

With the billions in taxes that they withhold from governments, the philanthro-capitalists are increasingly taking on public tasks that belong in the hands of democratic institutions. State schools, museums, hospitals, but also international institutions such as UNO, WHO, UNCTAD are weakened, infiltrated.[557] The more anti-social the domination, the friendlier the language of the human happiness purveyors.

---

557 Jens Martens / Karolin Seitz: Philanthropic Power. Global Policy Forum 2015

II.
The relationship
USA – European Union

The transatlantic region USA – EU is the oldest and most closely interwoven capitalist region in the world. The new financial players and their civilian private army have accelerated the already long-developed dominance of the US as a capital location over Western Europe. Recently, after decades of publicly displayed harmony, a number of conflicts have broken out – in free trade, tax flight, relations with Russia, Iran and China, as well as in intelligence surveillance and arms buildup. But EU leaders have to date been neither willing nor able to assert the "greater independence" they have avowed.

1.
Reversal of the balance of power since the First World War

Until World War I, US industry and the US state were indebted to European banks. With and after World War I, the picture was reversed. Since then, US dominance has gradually grown. After World War I, the credit plans of Dawes and Young (1924 and 1929) promoted US investment in Europe, the UK, Italy and especially in Germany, which was not interrupted by the Hitler government in 1933.[1]

After the Second World War, the victorious Western power stepped up its investment in Western Europe even more. While US investment tripled between

---

1   Mira Wilkins: The Maturing of Multinational Enterprises. American Business Abroad from 1914 to 1970, Cambridge/Massachusetts 1994; Jacques Pauwels: Big Business avec Hitler. Bruxelles 2013; Edwin Black: IBM and the Holocaust, New York 2001

1950 and 1970 in Latin America, increased fivefold in Asia (including Japan) and sixfold in the traditional neighborhood market of Canada, it climbed fourteenfold in Western Europe, also supported by the Marshall Plan (1947-1952).[2]

From the 1980s Western European companies simultaneously stepped up investment in the much-admired USA. In the wake of the 2007 financial crisis, they accelerated their US investments further. Above all enterprises from the UK led the way, followed by France, Germany and Switzerland. Pharmaceutical companies like Novartis, Bayer and BASF, car companies like BMW, VW and Daimler, the technology companies Siemens and ThyssenKrupp, Continental and Deutsche Telekom and meanwhile 3,500 German SMEs in some cases record higher sales and earnings in the USA than in Germany itself.

The European capitalist states are also interlinked among themselves. Some 2,500 German companies have branches in the UK, in France around 1,000 – and vice versa. But the links with the USA are incomparably more intensive, and the defining force of BlackRock&Co is incomparably stronger than that of European investors.

USA: Economy shrinking, but capital location growing

BlackRock alone is co-owner of more than 17,000 companies around the globe, the same is true, with a lower volume, for the other major capital organizers such as Vanguard, State Street etc. The absolute focus is in the USA, followed by the EU, Asia/Pacific and in fourth place Canada. A similar picture applies to the other groups of financial players: private equity investors, hedge funds, venture capitalists, investment banks and traditional banks – US players dominate everywhere in terms of numbers, managed capital and influence.

Of the 100 most valuable companies of Western capitalism, 52 are from the USA (end-2017). At the top are GAMFA. Six companies each come from the UK and Germany, the largest European company Royal Dutch Shell is in 17th place, and the most valuable German company, SAP Group, ranks 62nd[3] – although the most important owners of these "European" companies are also based in the USA.

According to official statistics, the total stock of investment of German companies and Western European financial players in the USA amounted to

---

2   Wilkins ibid., p. 330

3   Das sind die wertvollsten Unternehmen der Welt, http://www.faznet/aktuell/wirtschaft/diginomics 29.12.2017

USD 3 trillion in 2016, the total stock of US investment in Western Europe amounted to USD 5 trillion.[4] However, this blurs the true picture as these figures do not include the holdings of the new financial players.

In reality it is approximately like this (as of 2014): The capitalist property of US owners abroad amounted to USD 25 trillion, while the capitalist property of all foreign owners in the US was worth USD 30 trillion. Europeans accounted for around half of this, i.e. around USD 15 trillion.[5]

While the share of the US in global output and world trade has been declining for decades, its importance as a capitalist location within Western capitalism is increasing further.

Among the new financial players, PE investors such as Blackstone and investment banks such as Rothschild have been driving this development forward since the 1980s. In the wake of the financial crisis of 2007, BlackRock&Co and hedge funds increasingly acquired property in the EU and restructured it, along with the national budgets and welfare systems of the EU crisis states. The European Commission and the governments of the EU member states acted as accomplices. The International Monetary Fund coordinated. In addition, Europe's major banks have repressed their symbiotic, albeit subordinate, role in the financial crisis caused by Wall Street, the new financial players and US rating agencies and have been bought up by BlackRock&Co. At the same time, with the help of the European Central Bank, the euro also remained firmly integrated within the dollar-dominated system.[6]

The world's largest financial haven: USA

At the same time the USA became the largest financial haven. Under US president Obama the state doctrine of America First also manifested itself in the *Foreign Account Tax Compliance Act* (Fatca). This act from 2010 was designed to grant the state a hitherto impossible, unique degree of transparency about the foreign incomes and earnings of US citizens. Since then hundreds of thousands of wealthy US managers, dentists, bankers, SME owners have been shifting their financial assets, which they had hidden for example in UBS accounts on the Cayman Islands, back to the USA.

---

4   Der neue Handelskrieg, HB 23.2.2018

5   Stanley Fisher: The Federal Reserve and the Global Economy, 2014 Annual Meetings of IMF and World Bank Group, Washington 11.10.2014

6   Cf. Adam Tooze: Crashed. Wie zehn Jahre Finanzkrise die Welt verändert haben. Berlin 2018

Due to this act, more than 80,000 banks, insurance companies and asset managers have registered with the supreme US tax authority, the Internal Revenue Service (IRS). These are primarily financial service providers from around the world, also from the EU, including some 2,600 from Germany.[7]

In light of Fatca, the OECD agreed on the *Common Reporting Standard*. EU member states obediently incorporated this into their own laws, Germany with the Financial Accounts Information Exchange Act (*Finanzkonten-Informations-Austausch-Gesetz, FKAustG*). More than 100 countries participate, even traditional financial havens such as Switzerland and Panama, whose banks might otherwise lose their license in the USA. Implementation is not cheap: German financial service providers alone have so far spent EUR 400m to this end.

However, there is one country that does not participate in the initiative, although it pushed the operation through: the USA. The US authorities do not notify other countries as to the beneficiaries behind the shell companies in the US financial havens used by financial players around the globe: Delaware, Nevada, South Dakota and Wyoming.

Whereas US border authorities scrutinize every new arrival, in some cases for hours on end, in Delaware an anonymous mailbox company for share packages of European companies can be set up with a licensed trustee in just a few minutes and without a passport, for example by means of an e-mail message from an office of BlackRock or Blackstone.

Switzerland's banking secrecy has only fallen as a result of pressure from the USA – at least vis-à-vis the USA, not vis-à-vis the EU states. "Now the US is developing into the world's largest tax haven and shadow financial center, because in no other country in the world do foreigners hold as much money in accounts as in the US. The tax reform passed by Donald Trump at the end of 2017 will further promote this development."[8]

The complicit subservience of EU leaders is also evident here: Their "black list of tax havens" published in 2017 after lengthy discussions does not contain the largest European tax havens. Because: Of the officially reported total US investments of USD 5 trillion in Europe, 847 billion are legally located in the Netherlands, 682 billion in the UK (i.e. in the almost one dozen financial ha-

---

7   Mariam Rostamzada: Be aware of Delaware. Die einseitigen US-Bemühungen um Steueroasen, https://www.private-banking-magazin.de 26.3.2018

8   Rostamzada ibid.

vens belonging to the financial center City of London), 608 billion in the small Grand Duchy of Luxembourg and 387 billion in the small state of Ireland – far ahead of Germany where, however, BlackRock, Blackstone, Apple&Co do most of their business.[9]

The Americanization of jobs

In the 1980s, the new financial players first accelerated the de-industrialization and impoverishment of dependent employees and large groups of the middle class in the USA, as well as the enrichment of the capitalist elites and their professional auxiliary troops. Since the beginning of the 2000s, the new financial players have also been stepping up this process in the EU.

The USA is streets ahead in the non-ratification of labor rights issued by the International Labor Organization (ILO). Of the 207 labor rights, only 12 have been recognized.[10] The USA does not recognize any of the social and labor rights of the UN's Universal Human Rights.[11] US corporations and US investors also try to enforce the associated practice abroad.

The pioneers of the brutalized accumulation after the Second World War in the USA were major corporations such as Walmart, McDonald's and United Parcel Service (UPS). Since the 1970s, they have been globalizing their business, initially in the states defeated or weakened in World War II, in Europe in particular in the UK, Germany and the Netherlands. McDonald's founded the new Federal Association of System Catering (BdS) in Germany and continues to lead the industry.[12]

The pattern – union hostility, dissolution of the 8-hour day and the 40-hour week, no compulsory social insurance, no protection against dismissal, no collective agreements, job perception – is also being pursued by US investors in Europe. To this end, the legal and media practice of "union busting" was adopted in Europe on the US model. In the early 2000s, the German government commissioned US management consultants McKinsey and Accenture to revamp the employment offices and job centers.[13] US law firms such as Allen

---

9   Der neue Handelskrieg, HB 23.2.2018

10   www.ilo.org/dyn/normlex/en

11   United Nations, Human Rights Council: Report ibid., p. 5

12   Werner Rügemer/ Elmar Wigand: Union Busting in Deutschland. Frankfurt/Main 2014, p. 38f.

13   Werner Rügemer: Die Amerikanisierung ibid., p. 9ff.

& Overy, DLA Piper, Clifford Chance and Hogan Lovells, who hold numerous mandates for the new financial players, take action in Germany against trade union strikes and works councils.[14]

High unemployment was and is statistically sugarcoated, the unemployed are disciplined, financially and morally degraded and penalized. In the case of dependent employees, some are involuntarily overburdened and others involuntarily underchallenged. Every day, entrepreneurs can violate the applicable laws – minimum wage, part-time and fixed-term work, working hours, overtime pay, social security contributions, works constitution (rights of employee representatives, if any) – millions of times without penalty.[15]

The European Commission is adopting this dismantling of trade union and labor rights, most recently through the "European Pillar of Social Rights". The most important EU states – alongside Germany – the UK, France, Italy, Belgium, the Netherlands, Ireland, Sweden and also crisis states such as Greece and Spain have followed suit with similar practices as in Germany after the financial crisis.[16]

2.
The Internet under US supervision

The Internet is a child of the US government: after the Sputnik shock in 1957, the US Department of Defense founded the Advanced Research Project Agency (ARPA). This neutrally named agency was supposed to restore the superiority of technical sciences in the USA over the Soviet Union, argued the government under ex-World War II General Dwight Eisenhower.

Essentially it was about supremacy in the military Cold War, especially in the possible nuclear war. The Air Force, in particular, needed to obtain data from the other side as swiftly as possible in order to evaluate its counter- and initial response. It was about command of the airspace. This affected

---

14   Marion Lühring: Das ist doch alles krank, verdi publik 3/2018

15   Werner Rügemer: Unternehmer als ungestrafte Rechtsbrecher, in: Klaus-Jürgen Bruder u.a. (Hg.): Gesellschaftliche Spaltungen, Gießen 2018, p. 207ff.

16   Werner Rügemer: EU – Grenzenlose Arbeits-Flexibilität, nochmal heftiger? www.nachdenkseiten.de 21.11.2017

both variants of the US military strategy from "massive retaliation" to "flexible response".[17]

Silicon Valley: Arms industry since World War II
The technical sciences in the USA were not inferior at all, apart from a narrow section of space research. But the US government and the US military, together with the arms industry, closely linked in the Military Industrial Complex (MIC), sought every reason to revive the arms business, which had collapsed after the Second World War, and to expand their superiority over the Soviet Union.[18]

In California in particular, the technological basis was already in place. At the beginning of the Second World War, a large part of the new arms industry was relocated to what was later to be known as Silicon Valley. The area was climatically more favorable than the often cold and rainy east coast, and the little agriculturally used land could be built on quickly – and there were no trade unions.[19]

It was also the site of Stanford Elite University, founded by railway king Leland Stanford. It was politically extremely "conservative" and at the same time technologically innovative with a focus on industrially exploitable sciences. In 1939, Hewlett Packard, for a long time the largest computer group in Silicon Valley, was founded in Palo Alto, the university's location. In 1956, the Lockheed armaments group settled here in the university's industrial park to push ahead with the construction of the new intercontinental missiles, which could be equipped with atomic bombs. New generations of fighter jets and bombers were produced. This required an enormous amount and speed of data processing. IBM's large computers also needed ever more powerful chips. The semiconductor manufacturers of Silicon Valley, National Semiconductor, Advanced Micro Devices, Fairchild and Intel quickly became large corporations.

Hewlett Packard boss as Defense Minister
Most of the research coordinated by the Pentagon agency ARPA was awarded to private think tanks, including the RAND Corporation, founded in Santa Monica, California in 1948 by the Ford Foundation and Douglas Aircraft.

---

17   Martin Schmitt: Internet im Kalten Krieg. Eine Vorgeschichte des globalen Kommunikationsnetzes. Bielefeld 2016, p. 69

18   Seymour Melman: Pentagon Capitalism. The Political Economy of War. New York 1970

19   Werner Rügemer: Neue Technik – alte Gesellschaft. Silicon Valley. Köln 1985, p. 105ff.

RAND coordinated research at elite universities such as Stanford and MIT in Boston. The combination of computer industry and military was self-evident.[20] No one considered it odd that David Packard, co-founder and co-owner of Hewlett Packard, became U.S. Deputy Secretary of Defense under President Nixon during the Vietnam War.

In 1968, the Air Force and the Pentagon founded the ARPANET with ARPA. The aim was to establish secure data communication between the universities commissioned by the Pentagon under the direction of MIT. The operating system Unix and the programming language C were developed for this purpose. The Secretary of Defense who promoted ARPANET was Robert McNamara. He was previously president of the Ford Group, which produced more military vehicles than civilian vehicles in World War II, not only for the US Army, but also for Hitler's Germany.

ARPANET was to network the entire military system of the USA and NATO in terms of data: Aircraft, aircraft carriers, air defense, intercontinental missiles, atomic silos, the individual military formations on land, at sea and in the air – including satellites – and the several hundred military bases distributed around the world, software and hardware. Counter-insurgency methods were developed to meet the needs of US military intervention worldwide. Changing combat situations were simulated constantly. ARPANET also financed research into behavioral psychology for this purpose.

ARPANET as military precursor of the Internet
Well into the 1980s, the military, the Ford and General Motors automobile groups, which were also active in armaments production, the Pentagon contractors IBM and General Electric, along with the ITT and AT&T telephone groups were the driving forces behind digital data processing. President Ronald Reagan's Strategic Defense Initiative Organization (SDIO) project involved hundreds of subcontractors. The same applies to the Global Positioning System (GPS), which was coordinated at Johns Hopkins University. Venture capital financiers and Wall Street banks provided the capital for a steady stream of start-ups. In the mid-1980s, 1,950 companies belonged to Silicon Valley's high-tech industry.

More and more civilian companies such as Xerox, a manufacturer of pho-

---

20   Alex Abella: Soldiers of Reason. The RAND Corporation and the Rise of the American Empire. New York 2008

tocopiers that developed the graphical user interface for the military at Stanford University, were part of the expanded MIC (Apple benefited from this, see p. 112). Telephone companies such as Bell and AT&T further developed their technologies and networked them with ARPANET.

The first software company was called System Development Corporation (SDC). It was founded in 1955 by RAND and worked for ARPA. ARPA was later renamed DARPA (D = Defense). ARPANET was founded for data transmission. In the 1980s SDC was commercialized. "The Internet developed out of ARPANET."[21]

Release for civil and commercial purposes
DARPA is still run by the Pentagon and, together with the NSA secret service, is constantly searching the free hacker scene for employees.[22] ARPANET was officially terminated with the collapse of socialism – the enemy was dead. But the communication system called Internet, which continued to exist between the companies and the universities, was released for private commercial use in 1990.

This opportunity was seized initially by US corporations and then by European corporations, such as privatized telecommunications companies, which were expanding worldwide and investing in mobile telephony. This required more computers, more memory, more software, more international submarine cables, more line infrastructure. More than 50,000 small and large companies found their specialized business areas.[23]

Thousands of university ARPANET scientists founded private companies and consultancies. These scientists flocked to Wall Street banks and computerized securities trading over the Internet.[24] For instance, David Shaw developed one of the first e-mail systems, Juno, which was used on the Internet. Shaw founded the hedge fund D.E.Shaw, which was joined by Jeff Bezos, who later founded Amazon (see p. 121). Google founder Eric Schmidt also comes from D.E. Shaw.

---

21   Schmitt ebd., p. 227

22   Schmidt/ Cohen: Die Vernetzung der Welt ibid., p. 245

23   Brent Goldfarb i.a.: Searching for Ghosts. Business Survival, Unmeasured Entrepreneurial Activity and Private Equity Investment in the Dot-Com-Era, Social Science Research Network, Working Paper RHS 6-27, Rochester 2005

24   Michelle Celarier: How a Misfit Group of Computer Geeks and English Majors Transformed Wall Street, New York Magazin 1/2018

In 2003, McKinsey predicted that thanks to the Internet, a third of all industrial and service jobs could be relocated from the US to cheaper jobs in India, China, Vietnam, Puerto Rico, the Philippines, etc.[25] Since then, both traditional industry and the traditional infrastructure in the US have been decaying.[26]

US government monitors the Internet

In 1998, under President Clinton, the US government founded the *Internet Corporation for Assigned Names and Numbers* (ICANN). This civilian, non-profit organization was supposed to coordinate the rapidly growing system, define the usage rules and, for example, assign (or delete) the IP addresses. The supervision remained with the Department of Commerce, the contract initially ran until 2009.

Early on, the People's Republic of China, Russia and other states demanded that the Internet be placed under the wing of the UN! The EU attempted to reach a compromise: to subordinate the Internet to an international council of selected governments! But the US governments rejected all proposals. After the terrorist attack in New York on 11 September 2001, the US government ended the discussion and removed the previous right of user representatives to have a say in ICANN.[27]

The UNO under Secretary-General Kofi Annan made a fresh attempt in 2005. ICANN should be replaced by WICANN: World Internet Cooperation for Assigned Names and Numbers. WICANN was to become part of the UN organization International Telecommunications Union (ITU). However, for reasons of "national security", the USA also wanted to retain control over the root server system. With the UK, Canada and Australia – these states had concluded the secret service alliance "Five Eyes" with the appendage New Zealand in World War II – the USA prevented the internationalization of the Internet.[28]

Obama's "Open Internet"

Then Obama promised an "open Internet" in the 2008 election campaign. But his government extended the ICANN oversight treaty, which expired in 2009,

25   McKinsey Global Institute (MGI): Offshoring. Is It a Win-Win Game? San Francisco 2003

26   Nick Srnicek: Plattform-Kapitalismus. Hamburg 2018, p. 26

27   ICANN, WICANN, Zeit online 5.1.2015

28   For Western Allies, a Long History of Swapping Intelligence, NYT 9.7.2013

until 2016.[29] Because of the US secret service documents published by Edward Snowden, the US government waived the extension of formal oversight: it did not want to reinforce the impression that the US would continue to monitor the Internet.

ICANN paid several million dollars to former US Secretaries of State Rice and Albright to help nudge the US government towards a favorable transition to "independence".[30] ICANN President is now the US-Egyptian investment banker Cherine Chalaby, who spent the bulk of his professional career with the US government consultant Accenture. Vice President is Chris Disspain from the consultancy WGP; he was an advisor to the Australian government when it rejected the WICANN solution together with the US government at the UN.[31] ICANN continues to be based in Los Angeles and has been subject to the Patriot Act since 2001.

3.
The capitalist-digital-military complex

As is well known, Eisenhower warned against the "catastrophic rise of the in-appropriate power of the military-industrial complex", to which he also added the secret services CIA and NSA and their numerous subsidiaries, during his farewell speech on 17.1.1961 in the Oval Office.[32] At that time the USA was still pursuing the French colonial war in Vietnam for years with new force – also with the help of fake news – and simultaneously bombed Laos and Cambodia in a "secret war".[33] Silicon Valley products and techniques played an impor-tant role in this. No US government has attempted to change this relationship. With the new financial players, the complex lives on and is being expanded.

---

29 Weltgipfel der Internetnutzer, Telepolis 2.2.2009, https://www.heise.de, downloaded 21.3.2018

30 Condi Rice, ICANN, and millions paid to lobby the US govt for total internet control, https://www.theregister.co.uk 5.11.2015

31 https://www.icann.org/profiles, downloaded 10.5.2018

32 Donald Bartlett / James Steele: Washington's USD 8 Billion Shadow, Vanity Fair March 2007

33 Armin Wertz: Die Weltbeherrscher. Frankfurt/Main 2015, p. 134f. and 140f.

The GAMFA-Pentagon-NSA Complex

As a simple matter of course, Steve Jobs, William Gates, Jeff Bezos transferred the technologies developed in ARPANET to the civilian sector. For instance, Google's successful map programs Google Earth and Google Maps with Street View are also based on the software Earth Viewer: It was developed after the CIA's venture capitalist company, In-Q-Tel, bought the Silicon Valley start-up Keyhole in 2001. Earth Viewer was used for overland espionage in the Iraq war to detect details and enemy movements on the ground from great heights. The CIA had nothing against Google buying the program in 2004 and developing it further into Google Earth.[34]

Search engine for algorithmic warfare

In 2017, the US Defense Department engaged Google to further develop the recognition software TensorFlow for war conditions in the "Project Maven". TensorFlow is part of Google's Artificial Intelligence division. For the Pentagon's Algorithmic Warfare team, Google, through its Northern Virginia-based subsidiary ECS Federal, provides not only its specialized engineers, but also its huge search engine data set. In the first year the ministry coughed up USD 70 million for this.[35]

With the adapted software, the autonomous combat drones of the future will be able to wipe out extrajudicially defined enemies around the globe better than before. The project was to be kept absolutely hush-hush: "Avoid any mention at all costs," was the message in an internal Google circular. But when 3,100 Google employees demanded withdrawal in an open letter to boss Pinchai, he had it reinterpreted in Silicon Valley speech: The project was supposed to help "save lives".[36]

Globally integrated military cloud

Jedi is the name of another Pentagon project: Joint Enterprise Defense Infrastructure. It was put out to public tender at the end of 2017. The military wants to establish a secret cloud structure to network all military formations and

---

34   Lenna Garfield: The CIA's Earth Viewer was basically the original Google Earth, www.businessinsider.com 30.12.2015

35   Lee Fang: Google is quietly providing AI technology for drone strike targeting project, The Intercept 6.3.2018

36   Ben Chapman: Google staff protest company's involvement with Pentagon drones program, Independent 5.4.2018

activities with the worldwide military bases and their logistics and with the secret services and civilian facilities such as the coast guard. The GAMFAs submitted their applications, as did IBM and Oracle. The setup is to run for 10 years, the budget is put at USD 10 billion.[37] Amazon is already developing a USD 600 million cloud service for the US secret services with its Web Services AWS, as the Washington Post, the newspaper of Amazon boss Bezos, itself announced.[38] In 2016, Microsoft sold four million Windows 10 licenses to Obama's Secretary of Defense Carter.[39]

Microsoft is doing the same in the EU: with the French arms company Thales, in consultation with the Macron government, Microsoft is developing a cloud system for the armed forces that is "suitable for the command centers as well as for the battlefield". US intelligence services have no objections.[40]

The venture capital subsidiary of the Pentagon DIUx, based in Mountain View/Silicon Valley, has the traditional ARPA task of promoting new start-ups. "We are a fast-acting government unit that provides companies with non-dilutive capital to solve national security problems," the company says.[41] The CIA alone runs 137 AI projects for which it cooperates with several Silicon Valley companies. This includes the extraction and evaluation of mass data from the "social media".[42]

Portrait: Eric Schmidt
The Google-Instagram-LinkedIn-Pentagon-Complex

The former head of Google, Eric Schmidt, embodies the close integration of civilian private companies with the military and secret services. His professional career began like that of many other founders and gurus of the digital

---

37   DoD to Award Joint Enterprise Defense Infrastructure Cloud Contract in Fall 2018, https://incyberdefense.com 23.5.2018; Pentagon updates its JEDI cloud solicitation, https://federaltimes.com 16.4.2018

38   Amazon launches new cloud storage service for U.S. spy agencies, Washington Post 20.11.2017

39   Carter's Innovation Push Hits Seattle With Cloud Focus, www.defensenews.com 3.3.2016

40   Tödliche Algorithmen. Künstliche Intelligenz in der Rüstung, HB 13.6.2018

41   https:/diux.mil, downloaded 12.4.2018

42   How the CIA is Using Artificial Intelligence to Collect Social Media Data, https://futurism.com 9.9.2017

economy at Stanford. From Xerox on the Stanford grounds, he moved to the Stanford spin-off Sun Microsystems in 1983. In 2001, he joined Google, which had previously been founded at Stanford by Larry Page and Sergey Brin. He held management positions at Google until 2015, then at the new holding company Alphabet. The multi-billionaire is Google's major sharehold-er, along with Vanguard, BlackRock, Fidelity, T Rowe Price, State Street, JP MorganChase. From 2006 to 2009, he also served on Apple's Board of Direc-tors. Since 2007, he has participated annually in Bilderberg Group conferenc-es, is a member of the Trilateral Commission and several supervisory boards, including Princeton University, Carnegie Mellon University, the 21st Century Council of the Berggruen Institute and The Economist magazine. In 2008 he was Obama's campaign consultant, in 2009 he became the president's tech-nology consultant. With his venture capital fund *Innovation Endeavors*, he financed the PR firms Timshel and The Groundwork for presidential candidate Hillary Clinton, as well as the taxi service Uber.[43] Schmidt dreams of the old Silicon Valley conditions of the 1960s, when Lockheed drove technological development forward with nuclear intercontinental missiles: "What Lockheed Martin was in the 20th century, technology and cyber security companies will be in the 21st century."

He argues for automated warfare: robots "do not get tired, they are not afraid, do not feel emotions, have superhuman powers and carry out every command. In other words, they are excellent for the military dirty work".[44] Since 2016, Schmidt has been chairman of the Pentagon's Defense Innova-tion Board, which was founded under Obama: he selects the members in consultation with the defense minister. He is supposed to ensure that the military is able to skim off the best startups early. Board members selected by Schmidt include Reid Hoffmann, president of LinkedIn; Marne Levine, head of Instagram; Michael McQuade, United Technologies; Richard Murray, Cali-fornian Institute of Technology; Milo Medin, Google; Cass Sunstein, former White House chief of information under Obama; Eric Lander of MIT; Walter Isaacson, president of the Aspen Institute; and Adam Grant, motivation con-sultant for Facebook, Google, Goldman Sachs, Merck, the NBA and the US Army, and the US Navy.[45]

---

43 Wikipedia (englisch): Eric Schmidt

44 Schmidt/ Cohen: Die Vernetzung der Welt ibid., p. 143

45 innovation.defense.gov, downloaded 10.4.2018

Surveillance of the European Union

US players control most of the infrastructure of the Internet: Transoceanic submarine cables, production of chips and software, servers and storage capacities (clouds); 80 percent of Western Internet traffic passes through the USA.[46] BlackRock's Aladdin plays the lead role in data management for Western companies, banks, stock exchanges and the ECB; Paypal and GAMFA dominate payment traffic in the EU, Google and Facebook advertising. The public administration in the EU, whether ministries, military, police and municipalities, is not only a "Microsoft colony" when it comes to software,[47] but the states and companies of the EU have also deeply integrated the services of Alphabet, IBM and Amazon into the infrastructure of hospitals, waterworks, transport systems and universities.[48] The "German" software group SAP, already owned by BlackRock&Co and focused on the US business and top-paying US intelligence services, plays a completely subordinate role.

Parliamentarians in Brussels, mayors of cities like Munich persistently wanted to become independent from Microsoft; Commission President Juncker and Chancellor Merkel declared that the EU must become "digitally independent" – but the practice is the opposite. Linux is the cheaper and safer option, but this genuine independence option stands no chance with vassals.

Individual EU states are quietly letting GAMFA in without any legal stipulations. The French Microsoft chief lobbyist was a parliamentary employee of President Macron: he wants to stick with Microsoft.[49] Facebook has set up its third data center after Ireland and Sweden in Denmark, after Apple had already set up a server farm there in Viborg. The Danish government regards GAMFA as a "sovereign state", is represented by a "digital ambassador" and is hoping for further investments.[50]

EU "helpless" against GAMFA

The EU Data Protection Directive has been in force since 1995. It only allows the data of EU citizens to be transferred to other EU countries if the data is adequately protected there. Since the data storage facilities of Microsoft and

---

46   Mit offenen Karten. Seekabel – der unsichtbare Krieg, arte TV 14.4.2018

47   Harald Schumann: Das Microsoft-Dilemma, ARD 19.2.2018

48   Evgeny Morozov: Europa im Tiefschlaf, SZ 16.8.2018

49   Schumann: Das Microsoft-Dilemma ibid.

50   Thomas Wagner: Dänemark hofiert das Silicon Valley, junge Welt 8.2.2017

Apple are located in the USA, for example, the EU declared the USA to be a "safe harbor" in the Safe Harbor Agreement; US companies have had to sign a number of commitments with the US Federal Trade Commission (FTC) since then, but compliance is monitored neither by the FTC nor by the EU.

That is why the ECJ abolished the Safe Harbor Agreement in 2015. The Austrian lawyer Max Schrems had sued. Upon request, he had received the data stored about him from the Facebook headquarters in Dublin/Ireland – on 1,222 pages, including data that he had already deleted. The court does not consider the USA to be a secure data harbor because of possible access by the secret services. But Facebook considers the ruling to be wrong and does not adhere to it.[51]

Safe Harbor was followed by the Privacy Shield agreement and the planned new ePrivacy Directive in 2018. Although new trawling tools such as WhatsApp and Facebook Messenger are to be included, users should also be able to refuse the use of cookies and tracking (monitoring the user on the Internet). But GAMFA's business partners are up in arms: For example, publishers of the leading media such as BILD, Welt, FAZ, Süddeutsche Zeitung and HB in Germany fear losses if they no longer appear so often and so prominently on Google&Co and can no longer buy so much user data from them.[52]

The tens of thousands of EU companies that have branches and customers in the US, as well as the US companies that have branches and customers in the EU, are in any case subject to the America First rules of the Patriot Act of 2001. The EU's new data protection directive of 2018 does not address this issue.

Monitoring programs that are (initially) developed for civilian purposes are also not covered by EU rules. This applies, for example, to the Amazon software Recognition since 2016. This allows faces in large crowds – on squares, airports, at concerts, football matches, demonstrations – to be identified quickly – no one is asked beforehand whether he/she declines or agrees. Data processing takes place at Amazon Web Services (AWS). Police forces in the USA use the program. The guests at the royal wedding in London in 2018 were also checked in this manner – nobody could signal consent or rejection beforehand.[53]

---

51   Was die Entscheidung des EuGH bedeutet, SZ 6.10.2015

52   Ein Albtraum für die Branche, HB 11.4.2018

53   Polizei nutzt Gesichtserkennung von Amazon, FAZ 24.5.2018

The EU secret service taboo

The EU ignores the secret service issue. The Patriot Act allows the FBI, CIA and NSA to siphon off all means of communication and accounts of anybody suspected in any way of terrorism or terrorist support, even without judicial permission; this affects US citizens as well as foreigners.

When it was revealed in 2013 that the NSA had been spying on the German Chancellor's mobile phone since 2002, it also became known: from the US embassies of 19 EU states such as France, Italy and Spain, both NSA and CIA monitored the respective government personnel. US President Obama told the Chancellor that he knew nothing about it.[54] That was probably the truth, because the smooth talkers in political office are not saddled with dirty practices. That could impair their ability to function.

EU and Germany: Transatlantic accomplices

The NSA accesses the landing sites of the transatlantic submarine cables, whether on the British west coast in Bude/Cornwall or in Marseille. This is not an issue in any EU regulations either.

The largest "German" software group SAP also serves the NSA. SAP bought the security companies Inxight and Sybase in the US and provides NSA with their personal targeting systems for remote killings – the high ethical standards of SAP co-owners BlackRock and Norges are not a hindrance. SAP representatives meet at the Intelligence and National Security Alliance in Washington with representatives of the US intelligence agencies and defense companies such as Northrop and Lockheed to agree on orders.[55]

The publishing house *Springer-Verlag* appointed Alexander Karp to the Supervisory Board in 2018. Karp is head of the NSA and FBI service provider Palantir. The company was founded by the CIA and is currently checking Muslims entering the US on the instructions of the Trump government. Groups such as Deutsche Bank, BP, Merck and Airbus are also customers. The Hessian police have been trained by Palantir employees and buy the software, whereby the actual price in the budget of the state of Hesse is given as EUR 0.01 "for security reasons".[56]

This illegal secret service subservience has a long tradition. The CIA and

---

54   Merkels Handy steht seit 2002 auf US-Abhörliste, Der Spiegel 26.10.1013

55   SAP arbeitet für die NSA, Zeit online 10.3.2015

56   Schön billig, Der Spiegel 15/2018, p. 41

the organization Gehlen, founded by it or its predecessor OSS after 1945 – from 1955 renamed as the Federal German Intelligence Service BND (Bundesnachrichtendienst) – has monitored millions of telephones, letters and parcels in the Federal Republic of Germany and the GDR in violation of the Basic Law since 1949.[57] The most important and loyal US ally, "Europe's number one economic power", is still the most closely monitored and to this end has broken its own laws since it was founded.[58]

The best-occupied best ally
Since 1955 not only an important member of the NATO military alliance founded by the USA, the Federal Republic of Germany also has an unlimited US military presence. The USA maintains about 30 military bases, also newly founded ones like AFRICOM (surveillance of Africa and the Middle East, drone guidance) as well as the significantly expanded military airport, the drone communication node and the largest US military hospital outside the USA in Ramstein/Pfalz. In addition, the US armed forces store about 200 atomic bombs in Germany – without the official knowledge of the German government and contrary to the Nuclear Non-Proliferation Treaty. The Research Service of the German Bundestag had to concede that the exact number of US bases in Germany could not be determined: "The total number of locations of the US armed forces is ... not precisely determinable, but is likely to be in the higher two-digit range."[59]

In the city triangle of Frankfurt/Main, Wiesbaden and Darmstadt, not only the civilian US secret services CIA and NSA operate their European headquarters, but also military secret services and the US Homeland Security Agency. In addition, there are US bases and US-led NATO command centers in Germany and, to a lesser extent, in other EU states – above all in the UK, Italy, Belgium and in Kosovo (military base Bondsteel). In 2018, the newest NATO command center was built in Ulm for the land march against Russia.[60] Germany is the state most intensively occupied and monitored by the USA by far.[61]

---

57   Josef Foschepoth: Überwachtes Deutschland, Göttingen 2014

58   Der Freund liest mit, Der Spiegel 2013, p. 16 and 20

59   Deutscher Bundestag: Umfang und Standorte der in Deutschland stationierten US-Streitkräfte, 18.1.2017

60   Wilhelmsburg-Kaserne in Ulm – Neues NATO-Kommando in Deutschland, https://www.zdf.de

61   B Rudolph Bauer (Hrg.): Kriege im 21. Jahrhundert. Neue Herausforderungen der Friedensbewegung. Annweiler 2015, p. 126

The world's largest Internet hub in Frankfurt/Main

Frankfurt/Main is also home to the world's largest civilian Internet hub. 1,200 cables between China, Europe and the USA converge here. The hub consists of 19 data centers distributed throughout the city, which consume more electricity than Frankfurt Airport. The Association of the Internet Economy Eco has been operating the hub since 1995 via its subsidiary De-Cix GmbH (De-Cix = Deutsche Commercial Internet Exchange). Facebook and Microsoft are also members of the association.

After the NSA's tapping activities were revealed, De-Cix brought an action against the BND, which could assist the NSA by tapping the hub; however, De-Cix no longer wanted to be an involuntary accomplice, the control by the Federal Ministry of the Interior did not work, the access of the secret services had to be stopped. The Federal Administrative Court dismissed the complaint: De-Cix was obliged to participate in the strategic monitoring; an appeal against the ruling is not permitted.[62]

4.
Free trade: The EU in conflict with the USA

The new financial players and their civilian private army have further differentiated and strengthened the dominance of US capital within Western capitalism, especially in the core states of the EU. Some conflicts with the superpower are becoming fiercer. Can the EU gain "more independence" from the US, as EU leaders have proclaimed? The biggest public conflict is free trade. Let us first outline its development since the Second World War.

Power-based harmony

Since the globalization of capitalism, "free trade" has been the demand of expanding states such as the UK and the USA to open up new markets for their companies' products in less developed capitalist countries.

The first free trade agreement, which not only covered a large number of countries but was to be based on the principle of equality, was the International Trade Organization (ITO). It was to be an institution of the newly founded

---

62   BND darf am Internetknoten weiter Daten abzapfen, SPON 31.5.2018

UNO. Universal human rights – including social and labor rights – as well as international law, i.e. the equality of peoples and non-interference in the internal affairs of another state, were to apply.

GATT: Without social and labor rights, without international law
But the US government prevented the ITO and in 1947 organized an alternative free trade institution: the General Agreement on Tariffs and Trade (GATT).[63] The USA thus excluded not only its systemic rival the Soviet Union and other socialist states, but also states that were in the process of liberating themselves from colonial dependence after the Second World War.

The GATT was launched with 23 states. Members were the USA, the European colonial states the UK, France, Belgium and the Netherlands, the Commonwealth countries Australia, Ceylon, Canada, India, Pakistan and New Zealand, other small apartheid and dependent states such as Southern Rhodesia, South Africa, Syria, Cuba, Lebanon, Burma, the pre-socialist Czechoslovakia, the small monarchies Luxembourg and Norway, the South American states Chile and Brazil as well as China, which was still dependent on the West.

In 1947, the USA had also included Cuba, which was ruled by the US Mafia and US corporations with the help of a local dictator, as a founding member of the GATT. Following the overthrow of the dictatorship in 1961 by a popular movement under Fidel Castro, the USA imposed a trade embargo that is still in force today. At the same time, they tried to topple Cuba's democratic government militarily. The secret service CIA tried several times to murder the head of government. The USA still retains the Guantanamo naval base in Cuba, which is used as a prison and torture camp, regardless of the fact that the lease has expired.

This shows that, from the outset, free trade in the US version tends not to be compatible with democracy, human rights and international law, but is associated with various forms of "America First", with exclusion, the instalment of dictators and, if necessary, military intervention.

Free trade area with Marshall Plan and NATO
In addition to the GATT, the USA established its own free trade zones, for example with Japan and South Korea. Likewise, the Marshall Plan, which the

---

63   Leo Panitch/Sam Gindin: The Making of Global Capitalism. London/New York 2013, p. 93f.

USA launched for the Western European states after World War II, aimed at a geopolitically oriented free trade and influence zone. US loans financed an investment and economic stimulus program for US companies. The USA demanded from the recipient states the dismantling of customs duties, a payment union and a uniform, transnational market. This was to become compatible with US rules.[64] The shape of the EU was also predetermined in this way.

Aid was not granted to the Soviet Union and the new socialist states, and only under certain conditions to the capitalist states: These included the anti-Communist cleansing of trade unions, administrations and governments, e.g. in the Federal Republic of Germany, Italy, the Netherlands, France, etc. Greece, for example, received aid only after the US military had defeated the anti-fascist popular movement.[65]

The Marshall Plan and NATO had the same goal: to expand and secure US-dominated capitalism. In World War II, General George Marshall was Army Chief of Staff. As foreign minister he announced the Marshall Plan in 1947 and at the same time prepared the foundation of NATO. In 1950 he became Secretary of Defense and was in charge of NATO headquarters, which was initially based in Washington.[66] Paragraph 2 of the NATO Treaty states that the members should promote "economic cooperation". NATO has its own Economic Committee for this purpose. The transatlantic economy, the EU and NATO still form a unit, as can be seen from the joint advance of the EU and NATO in Eastern Europe and in the case of Ukraine. The current NATO Secretary General Jens Stoltenberg declared: "What the EU does must be complementary to NATO."[67]

However much the US government has maneuvered the EU into a "trade war" since 2017: NATO and its leadership by the USA remain undisputed. In addition, the EU is complying with the demand already made under President Obama and repeated by his successor Trump that the European NATO states increase their defense budget to two percent of their gross national product, combined with the intensified military buildup against Russia.[68]

---

64   Siehe Michael Hogan: The Marshall Plan. America, Britain and the Reconstruction of Western Europe 1947 – 1952. New York 1986

65   Heinz Richter: Griechenland 1940 – 1950. Die Zeit der Bürgerkriege. Mainz 2012

66   Werner Rügemer: NATO – Die Gründungslüge, www.nachdenkseiten.de 4.4.2018

67   Komplementäre Verteidigungsstrategien, FAZ 2.4.2015

68   Die NATO-Militärausgaben sind nicht durchdacht, Die Zeit 9.9.2014

Privileges and embargoes

In addition to the GATT, the USA also implemented special regulations with the geostrategic important states, including Japan, South Korea and the Philippines. Thus the Federal Republic of Germany, which was particularly favored, was largely relieved of sovereign debts that had been incurred decades ago, or deferred on a long-term basis and at low interest rates; in addition, the Federal Republic was exempted from the war reparations customary under international law until today (London Debt Agreement 1953, 2 + 4 Treaty 1991).

By contrast, the socialist states have been cold-shouldered to this day. Neither the Soviet Union nor the People's Republic of China ever received even observer status in the GATT. In addition, the socialist states were boycotted.

From 1948 the USA, together with all subsequent NATO states and Japan, operated the Coordinating Committee on Multilateral Export Control (CoCom) vis-à-vis the Soviet Union, its allied states and China.[69] "Neutral" states such as Switzerland, Sweden and Austria also participated. The Committee existed until 1994 and, on a constantly updated list, defined the technical goods that could not be supplied to socialist states. CoCom was an informal club, which was not based on international law or any usual international rules of law and functioned only under extra-legal pressure from the USA.[70]

In 1962, on US initiative, the NATO Council decided that German companies were not allowed to supply the GDR with large pipes for the planned natural gas and oil pipelines from the Soviet Union. The German government and companies such as Mannesmann and Hoesch deferred.[71]

Stifled conflicts

Notwithstanding all the economic quarrels between the USA and the EU, NATO has so far remained completely undisputed. Even under US President Trump, who has otherwise been much criticized, nothing has changed. EU leaders are enthusiastically fulfilling the demand made by his predecessor Obama to increase their military spending.

---

69 Kailai Huang: American Business and the China Trade Embargo in the 1950s, The Economic & Business History Society 19/2001, p. 33ff.

70 Gunnar Adler-Karlsson: Western Economic Warfare 1947 – 1967. Stockholm 1967

71 Rainer Karlsch/Ramond Stokes: Faktor Öl, München 2003, Kapitel 10

At the economic level, the situation was somewhat different. Given its kind of globalization, the USA sparked conflicts, but the EU did not tough them out: It adapted.

North American Free Trade Agreement (NAFTA)
In the 1990s, the US created a new type of free trade agreement outside the multilateral GATT. This is exemplified by NAFTA. In 1994 it was concluded with just the two selected neighboring states, Mexico and Canada. The focus was on conditions for outsourcing, for example of the US automobile industry, and about special protection for US investors in the two countries, in Canada also for oil fracking.[72] US companies gained a competitive advantage primarily thanks to the vast low-wage sector in the Mexican supplier companies. But car and pharmaceutical companies from the EU and Japan followed suit and also set up suppliers in Mexico and Canada.

Systemic use of financial havens
Long before this, the USA had gone it alone alongside GATT. In 1971 the US Congress passed the Foreign Sales Corporation Act (FSCA). Since then, US companies have been able to operate mailbox companies in financial havens for the tax promotion of exports.

For years, the EU complained in GATT and then before the World Trade Organization (WTO) against this export subsidy, which distorted competition. Finally, the WTO ruled in 2002: This is inadmissible, the USA must pay the EU a fine of USD 4.043 billion.[73] However, the EU never demanded the fine, but adapted to US practice, allowed its own companies to do the same and opened up its own financial havens like Luxembourg, the Netherlands and Ireland to US companies.

This is why the EU's measures against tax evasion by US corporations are so feeble. Individual companies such as Apple and Microsoft briefly have their wrists slapped. Instead of, for instance, closing PWC's huge "tax structuring" office in Luxembourg and taxing profits locally and in the state where they were generated, the European Commission is proposing a defensive cop-out: A three-percent digital tax, which would only affect the

---

72   Panitch/ Gindin: The Making of Global Capitalism ibid., p. 226ff.

73   WTO Panel Sets Amount of Foreign Sales Corporation (FSC) Sanctions, https://2001-2009.state.gov/e/eeb/rls/othr/13210.htm, downloaded 10.5.2018

few well-known digital companies and, moreover, will never be introduced anyway.[74]

Exterritorial fines due to Iran embargo
European banks such as Deutsche Bank, BNP Paribas, Barclays and UBS were frequently drastically punished in the USA, for example for misleading clients there. But even under Presidents Bush and Obama, the US began to impose extraterritorial fines on European companies, even if the acts were not committed in the US. This is a breach of international law.

The French bank BNP was fined nearly USD 9 billion in 2015 for violating US sanctions rules. The investigations dated back to 2002. The bank had carried out transactions for clients from Cuba, Iran and Sudan, some of which in dollars via accounts in New York. This was based on unilateral embargoes imposed by the USA outside the GATT and WTO. The French government criticized this severely, without consequences.[75]

On the bidding of the USA, Commerzbank laid off four employees in Germany in 2015. They had spent a decade processing payments for the state-owned Iranian shipping company. This was legal under German and EU law. After four years of investigation, the bank had admitted to violations of the law. It undertook to dismiss its employees for "criminal conduct", to pay the US authorities a fine of USD 1.45 billion and, thirdly, to have itself monitored in Germany until 2018. The head of the department concerned filed a lawsuit against his dismissal and, in the second instance at the Hesse State Labor Court, was ruled to be in the right: There was no misconduct under labor law, the employment relationship still existed. (Ref. 18 Sa 1498/15). Commerzbank then argued before the Federal Labor Court that the pressure from the USA had been so "exceptional" and "enormous" that it was pointless to defend oneself. The US authorities had demanded "effective deterrence through personal punishment". The bank's lawyer therefore demanded that the Federal Labor Court recognize a breach of law: "It does not matter whether there is a reason for termination and whether the termination is compatible with German law."[76] Ultimately, in 2017, the Bank negotiated a secret termination agreement with the unemployed head of department.

---

74   EU-Digitalsteuer derzeit ohne Chance auf Realisierung, Der Standard 29.4.2018

75   Großbank BNP Paribas stimmt Rekordstrafe zu, SPON 30.6.2014

76   Stefan Buchen: Kündigung wegen US-Drucks ist rechtswidrig, NDR.de 5.8.2017

Up until 2018 Alix Partners, a consulting firm commissioned by the USA, has access to all documents requested by it from all Commerzbank branches worldwide and reports to the USA whether the bank complies with all US First Embargo rules. The costs of the surveillance are borne by the Commerzbank itself.[77]

The subservience of the German side is also reflected in the fact that Commerzbank was represented by US law firms in both countries: In Germany by Allen&Overy, in the USA by Cleary Gottlieb Steen&Hamilton. The German government also kowtows and backs the breach of law: The German state is by far the largest owner of the bank. Co-owner BlackRock also keeps quiet.

Free trade without intelligence services?
German Economics Minister Sigmar Gabriel had declared in 2013: We will not continue to negotiate the TTIP free trade agreement as long as the NSA violates German law.[78] Nevertheless, the EU continued to negotiate.

Daimler was charged in the USA with corruption in Croatia, China, Russia, Hungary, Iraq, etc. on the basis of the Foreign Corrupt Practices Act (FCPA). Daimler had not bribed anyone in the USA, but the company had used Delaware mailbox companies and US bank accounts for the bribes. It agreed to a settlement in 2010: USD 93.6 million fine, USD 91.4 million profit transfer, and the monitoring of all employees for terrorism.[79] For three years, ex-FBI director Louis Free was paid by Daimler to oversee the implementation. For example, the master data of 280,000 employees worldwide continues to be compared quarterly with terror lists delivered from the US to the EU. If the suspicion is confirmed, the contract can be terminated for "personal reasons".[80]

As with Commerzbank and BNP, Daimler is dependent on the goodwill of the USA. The company is subject to US stock exchange supervision, as its shares are listed in New York. It operates ten branches in the USA with 17,000

---

77 Werner Rügemer: Wieviel Geheimdienst steckt in europäischen Unternehmen? www. arbeitsunrecht.de 9.2.2015

78 Top-Ökonom kritisiert Anti-USA-Kurs Gabriels, HB 25.10.2013

79 United States of America, District of Columbia vs. Daimler AG, Notice of Filing of Deferred Prosecution Agreement, 24.3.2010

80 Angst vor Terrorismus. Daimler will Mitarbeiter durchleuchten – alle drei Monate. SPON 4.1.2015

employees. It benefits from US financial havens, government subsidies and tax breaks that go further than in Germany and elsewhere in the EU. In addition, it benefits from the particularly low US labor law standards, especially in the right-to-work states: there are almost no trade unions there, wages are lower than elsewhere in the USA and much lower than in Germany.[81] Sales in the USA are higher than in Germany. Since Regulation 2580/2001 of the European Council, less elaborate monitoring of this kind has applied to all companies in the EU.

Since 2007 at the latest, US intelligence services have been systematically accessing software and data flows from industrial companies and civil infrastructure facilities in other countries. This applies, for example, to hospitals, power stations and energy grids. This became known, for example, at the Belgian power company Belgacom (important, among other things, because of Brussels as the location of NATO, SWIFT, the European Commission and the European Parliament) and at the Austrian power grid.[82]

Transatlantic cashless payment transactions have been handled via SWIFT (Society for Worldwide Interbank Financial Telecommunication) in La Hulpe near Brussels, Belgium, since 1973. Since 2001, the USA has been siphoning off data here on the additional grounds that terrorists have to be tracked down. There was no agreement on this, but the competent Belgian central bank concurred. In 2010, the USA and the EU concluded an agreement on SWIFT, but this also allows data access when there is no direct terrorist connection. The EU Parliament called on the European Commission to suspend the agreement. But it did not do so.[83]

Simmering conflicts: Ukraine, Iran

Alongside the stifled conflicts, more severe conflicts have also arisen. The EU gave and continues to give way in these conflicts, too, without eliminating the potential for conflict.

---

81   Werner Rügemer / Elmar Wigand: Union Busting in Deutschland ibid., p. 15-19. "right to work": this misleading term in reality means the right defined by management to employ people who are not members of a union.

82   Svea Eckert / Alexandra Ringling / James Bamford: Schlachtfeld Internet. NDR/ARD 12.1.2015, 23.30 – 00.15h

83   Sebastian Range: Nichts dazugelernt. EU-Bankdaten gehen weiter ungehindert in die USA, Hintergrund 1/2014, p. 60

Ukraine: Caught in the pincers of EU and NATO

With the accession of former socialist states, the EU pushed ahead quickly with eastward enlargement. For almost two decades, Western investors, including BlackRock&Co, have exploited the usual opportunities. Coca Cola, McDonald's, Microsoft and Citibank have also spread from the USA to Ukraine. The Philipp Morris cigarette group bought a cigarette factory in the Ukraine from its headquarters in Switzerland and became the market leader. It also produces here with the help of the extremely low cigarette tax and complicit oligarchic governments, primarily for export and international smuggling.[84] The agricultural multinationals Monsanto, Cargill and Dupont have leased land on a large scale for 49 years.[85] Large corporations and medium-sized companies from the EU have also taken advantage of the low wages of the workforce, which was still comparatively well trained under socialism, for outsourced IT and software services, for example. Around 400 companies from Germany set up branches here, including Siemens, Puma, Linde, Bayer, BASF, SAP, Carl Zeiss, the automotive supplier Leoni, and many engineering companies such as Demag Cranes, Vaillant, Viessmann and Claas.[86]

At the same time, Russia remained Ukraine's traditionally largest investment and trading partner. This conflicted with the geostrategy of the US that dictated that only the superpower that dominates the Eurasian area with its resources between Lisbon and Vladivostok can remain the sole superpower in the long run, including vis-à-vis China. That is why Zbginiew Brzezinski, the long-standing chief strategist, had declared publicly back in 1996 that in order to weaken Russia it had to be separated from Ukraine. "The Ukraine, a new and important space on the Eurasian chessboard, is a geopolitical hub... Without Ukraine, Russia is no longer a Eurasian empire."[87] Hence, a regime change had to be organized in Ukraine, as a preliminary stage for the regime change in Russia itself. This was not about overthrowing a socialist regime, but a pro-capitalist one.

---

84   Werner Rügemer: Bis diese Freiheit die Welt erleuchtet. Köln 2017, p. 154ff.

85   Wettlauf um die ukrainische Schwarzerde, ZEIT online16.3.2015

86   https://forum-ukraine-nachrichten.de, downloaded 20.5.2018

87   Zbginiew Brzezinski: Die einzige Supermacht. Amerikas Strategie der Vorherrschaft. Weinheim/Berlin 1996, p. 74

Regime Change

Here, too, the USA showed that it does not advocate the spread of the capitalist system as such, but only a capitalism dominated by itself. The USA not only interferes superficially in elections in other countries, but uses corporations, military exercises and foundations as levers and organizes the overthrow of governments – not only in distant regions, but also in Europe.

The Open Ukraine Foundation, chaired by banker Arseni Jazenjuk – affectionately called "Jaz" by US strategists – was sponsored by NATO, the Renaissance Foundation of George Soros, oligarch Viktor Pinchuk, the Polish government, the PE fund Horizon Capital and Swedbank, one of the largest Swedish banks in Northern Europe and the Baltic states. The foundation of the US citizen Soros had already prepared the "orange revolution" of the oligarch Julja Timoshenko in Ukraine. The US government's foundation National Endowment for Democracy (NED) also contributed to Ukraine's development, for example with scholarships and media development. Philipp Morris contributed to the transformation of civil society through student and social programs.[88]

The boxing world champion Klitschko, set up by the Adenauer Foundation and the leading German media as the future Ukrainian head of government, was good for mobilizing even right-wing extremist foot soldiers on the Maidan, but had no chance in the power cartel. The US State Department took over the enthronement of Yatsenyuk with the help of various nationalist and right-wing radical forces, drastically and clearly commented by Victoria Nuland, responsible for Europe in the State Department: Fuck the EU![89] Such contempt is also accepted by EU leaders.

EU Eastward Enlargement and NATO

Military cooperation between the German Bundeswehr and other EU armed forces and the Ukrainian army has existed since 1993. NATO and the EU have advanced together.

Ultimately, the EU did not want a normal free trade agreement with Ukraine. Rather, Ukraine was supposed to terminate its previous agreements with Russia. The hesitant government at the time, which wanted to maintain its ties with Russia, was swept aside in a putsch. In 2014, the coup

---

88   Werner Rügemer: Jazenjuk made in the USA, Ossietzky 9/2014

89   "Fuck the EU"-Fauxpas, www.faz.net 7.2.2014

government signed the association agreement with the EU. Ukraine adopted all legal and economic regulations of the EU. Immediately afterwards,
Obama signed the Ukraine Freedom Support Act. The US provides military
advisers, supplies weapons and organizes military exercises along the Russian border.

Already at the beginning of the US boycott measures against Russia, German business had made a "dramatic appeal" to the EU to mediate with Russia.[90] Wolfgang Büchele, Chairman of the Committee on Eastern European
Economic Relations, calculated two years later: The sanctions against Russia
had damaged Europe to the tune of hundreds of billions. For Germany this
means a production loss of EUR 13.5 billion, which corresponds to a loss of
60,000 jobs. At the same time, states close to Russia are being damaged, especially the already impoverished Baltic states due to their EU membership.
Economic recovery in the Ukraine of all countries, which is supposed to be
being helped by EU integration, is being hampered by the sanctions. Büchele
demanded: "In the meantime the time is ripe to question this".[91]

However, at the end of the day not only the political leadership in Germany
and the EU bowed to US pressure. German entrepreneurs also acquiesced,
accepting the damage running into billions. They are expanding their investments in the USA. President Trump's tax cuts are helping. Ukraine, ruled by
the oligarch Poroshenko, is degenerating economically, poverty is spreading,
two million Ukrainians are hiring themselves out as the lowest wage earners in
the low-wage country of Poland[92] – "free trade" along US lines.

Iran

The democratically elected government of Prime Minister Mohammad Mossadegh nationalized the Anglo Iranian Oil Company in 1952 and began land
reform. The USA, assisted by the UK, organized a coup in 1953, Mossadegh
was overthrown (Operation Ajax), with Shah Reza Pahlevi a cruel, monarchi-
cally supplemented dictatorship was installed. The oil licenses were distributed to British Petroleum, Shell and smaller French and US companies. Siemens
began building a nuclear power plant in 1974. The Western players were not

90   Deutsche Wirtschaft richtet Hilfsappell an die EU, HB 23.1.2014

91   Zeit für Alternativen, HB 21.11.2016

92   Die nützlichen Migranten. Zwei Millionen Ukrainer in Polen, Deutschlandfunk
      27.2.2018

interested in the development of the national economy and improving the nation's prosperity[93] – "free trade" along Western lines.

After the Muslim popular movement overthrew the dictatorship in 1979, the USA not only imposed economic boycotts on Iran, but also supported the war of Saddam Hussein's Iraqi neighboring regime to overthrow Iran's government. Millions of Iranians were killed. Later, the US went to war with its unsuccessful and also rebellious vassal Hussein himself, overthrew him and organized the Iran boycott further – one breach of international law after the other. The development of Iranian nuclear power increasingly served as the justification.

After protracted negotiations, under President Obama, together with Russia, China, France, the UK and Germany, the USA achieved the nuclear agreement with Iran in 2014. Nevertheless, the USA upheld most of the boycott measures – the punishment of Commerzbank and BNP are examples of this. Neither the German government nor the European Commission opposed this.

Following the agreement, Western companies, especially from France and Germany, expanded trade relations and investment in Iran again. The termination of the nuclear deal by Obama's successor Trump is once again hurting Western European investors, as in Ukraine. In 2018, the EU Commission reinstated the 1996 Blocking Regulation. According to this, companies in the EU were forbidden under penalty of fines to comply with US sanctions against Cuba, Libya and Iran that breached international and trade law.[94]

But the self-subjugation of the European "friends" is preordained. Even the Blocking Regulation did not work, the EU never imposed fines. Despite all the criticism, "in the end the big European companies are likely to bow to US pressure and leave Iran", according to Western diplomats and entrepreneurs in Tehran.[95] Thus the biggest investor in Iran, the oil company Total (based in Paris), is withdrawing from Iran: it is not a "French" company at all and does not listen to the French government under Macron. Rather, Total is in the hands of Anglo-American capital: the largest shareholder is BlackRock, other shareholders are Vanguard, Wellington, Capital, T Rowe Price, Bank of

---

93 Cf. Stephen Kinzer: Im Dienste des Schah. CIA, MI6 und die Wurzeln des Terrors im Nahen Osten. Weinheim 2009

94 Council Regulation 2271/96 protecting against the effects of the extra-territorial application of legislation adopted by a third country, and actions based thereon or resulting therefrom.

95 Druck aus Washington, HB 23.5.2018

America and Norges, most of the loans come from US banks. Total's US holdings are worth USD 11 billion. Total's investment to date of USD 40 million in the Iranian South Pars 11 gas field has been forfeited without much regret.[96] Daimler, BASF, Siemens and PSA have also reoriented themselves in this way.

Even before Trump's termination of the Iran Agreement, this was the routine European declaration of submission: governments, corporate and bank bosses in the EU have "learned the lesson that no bank with global ambitions can afford to lose the world's largest capital market".[97] This is Western capitalist democracy: capital rules over democracy and law.

New investment El Dorado: USA

This has been the case for decades. All major European banks had expanded their presence in the USA since the 1980s. There they had repeatedly paid high fines. Swiss banks had accepted this, just as French and German banks had. But despite the critical political theatre from Merkel, Macron & Co against Trump, the USA is a more sought-after investment location than ever before.

"German" companies such as Bayer, BASF, Deutsche Bank, Siemens, Allianz, Fresenius, Heidelberg Cement as well as Sanofi (chemicals group in France), United Bank of Switzerland and BAE Systems (armaments group in the UK) donated more to Trump's 2016 election campaign than to the candidate Clinton.[98] After the election, they, like BlackRock and GAMFA, are placing even more emphasis on the USA as an investment location, after Trump slashed corporate and wealth taxes. The head of Deutsche Telekom praises the innovative power of Google and Facebook, which feeds into telecommunications, and that the US market is "not as restricted in regulatory terms as it is in Europe".[99]

Deutsche Telekom – the main owners are the German state and BlackRock – goes further still. It hired Corey Lewandowski as media consultant for its US businesses. Lewandowski had worked for the Americans for Prosperity lobby organization of oligarchs Charles and David Koch since 2008, before becoming Trump's campaign chief in 2015. While working for US Vice President Mike Pence in 2018, he is supposed to promote the merger of Deutsche Tele-

---

96   Druck aus Washington ibid.

97   Ralph Bollmann / Winand von Petersdorff: Supermacht ohne Skrupel, FAS 13.5.2018

98   www.opensecrets.com/2016

99   "Wir sind stark auf beiden Seiten des Atlantiks", HB 2.5.2018

kom's US subsidiary T-Mobile with the US company Sprint – co-owner among others: BlackRock and Vanguard.[100]

The US current account deficit with the EU

US presidents, along with their government and fake news apparatus, claim the US has a trade deficit with China and the EU. In 2017, it amounted to USD 153 billion with the EU. And they then demand that the guilty Chinese and Europeans must reduce the unfair trade deficit.

The statistical criteria date back to a century ago, when we were primarily talking about trade in industrial and agricultural products between states. This is why the term "free trade agreement", which is still used today, is also a fake. On a large scale, such agreements have been increasingly concerned with cross-border investment and services for three decades. Therefore, if we look at relations in macroeconomic terms, the balance is different.

Services, profits
If we include services, we arrive at a surplus for US companies in 2017: they sold USD 51 billion more in the EU than EU companies in the US. Mutually transferred profits result in a surplus for the USA of USD 106 billion. If we add to this the personal financial transfers from managers, diplomats, secret service agents and tourists – USD 10 billion surplus for the US side – we arrive at a total US surplus of USD 14.2 billion. It also becomes clear that the profit transfers go through the most important financial havens of the EU – the Netherlands, Luxembourg, Ireland and the UK; because of this complicity, EU leaders remain silent.[101]

The transnational capitalist class could burst into collective laughter at the dispute over trade and current account deficits if it had the time and inclination.

---

100 Ein Cowboy für T-Mobile USA, HB 28.5.2018

101 USA erwirtschaften Überschuss gegenüber EU, https://www.cesifo-group.de 30.4.2018; Werner Rügemer: Fake – Es gibt kein US-Handelsdefizit gegenüber der EU, www.nach-denkseiten.de 18.6.2018

III.
China –
Communist-led capitalism

The last crisis of Western capitalism has strengthened the new financial actors and further intensified the brutality of capital exploitation. The resulting further impoverishment and over-indebtedness of Western states, companies, banks and employees has also made it possible for Chinese investors to penetrate. This was and is also facilitated by the fact that China's investments are not driven by short-term capital exploitation and that China is increasingly using credit instruments independent of the IMF, has its own currency with the yuan and as a result can gradually liberate itself from "dollar imperialism".

1.
USA against Chinese self-liberation

In the process the different character of the communist-led capitalism of the People's Republic of China is becoming more apparent. If one can use a nice and non-academic term to describe US-led Western capital as "impatient", one can certainly describe China's capital as "patient".[1]

China's loans and investments both in its own territory and in other countries, often coordinated by the state, are long-term. Interest rates are usually low at 1.5 percent. Thanks to government coordination, risks can be spread, profits and loan repayments can be suspended or deferred. Loans from Chinese banks are not subject to the conditions of the World Bank, which as the

---

[1] Stephen Kaplan: China is investing seriously in Latin America, Washington Post 24.1.2018

representative of Western banks unremittingly insists on punctual and full repayment, on wage and pension cuts and on the sale of public property, even if entire states and the bulk of the population such as currently in Greece and Ukraine in particular are plunged into poverty.

At home the practice of Chinese companies also differs. Instead of concentrating on short-term profits, it is first and foremost about expanding production and secondly also about products "for the smaller wallet ". Chinese companies can therefore export more to developing or emerging countries such as India and Brazil and even to the EU – e.g. smartphones – and implement new environmental technologies on a massive scale much more quickly.[2]

Western capitalism, which has become even more fragile since the financial crisis and continues to shrink in economic terms, is thus increasingly confronted with an outsider, a powerful different logic, a center of strength that is pursuing a more sustainable and coherent development logic.

US governments, since Obama and reinforced by Trump, have claimed that China has "stolen" millions of jobs from the USA and are demanding that China buy more in the USA so that the unfair trade imbalance for the USA is eliminated. The EU demands that China grant European companies the same open access as the EU does to Chinese companies. In reality, however, the imbalances are very different. We need to go back in history for a moment.

Overcoming colonialism: Against the USA
After more than two decades of illegal activity with great sacrifices, after the Long March of the Red Army in 1934, after the struggle against the Japanese occupying power, the Mao Tse Tung's People's Liberation Army finally defeated the feudal capitalist regime under Chiang Kai Shek and his Kuomintang Party in 1949. Chiang had converted to Christianity, was allied with the old rich family clans, received support from the Western colonial and capital powers. The USA also showered him personally with gifts, such as country estates and a private plane. He had received massive support from the USA and against Mao and the People's Liberation Army, especially in the final stages of the Second World War.[3] US President Roosevelt demanded in vain that the

---

2   Der Angreifer aus China, HB 2.8.2018

3   Cf. Publications of the US journalist Agnes Smedley: China's Red Army Marches (1934), China fights back (1938) und The Great Road. The Life and Times of Chu Teh (1956)

aloof and corrupt regime of Chiang be reformed – but its anti-communism was ultimately more important to the USA.[4]

The USA, which together with the European colonial powers, had attacked and exploited China in the 19th century in the name of "free trade",[5] treated the People's Republic even more severely as an enemy, excluded it from the UN and its sub-organizations, as well as from GATT and the OECD, imposed an embargo and recognized as China's representative only Chiang Kai Shek and his party, who had fled to the island of Taiwan (Formosa). It was not until 1971 that the People's Republic was able to become a member of the UN. Taiwan is hardly recognized as a state, not even by the USA, but is heavily subsidized by the USA, especially militarily.[6]

In 1972 US President Richard Nixon made a sensational official visit to Beijing. China was to be supported in order to weaken the USA's main enemy, the Soviet Union. Moreover, the USA was not only morally, but also financially and politically beleaguered by its criminal colonial war in Vietnam. It was seeking a face-saving way out of defeat. After the amicably staged visit in 1979, the US recognized the People's Republic of China diplomatically.

2.
The dialectic of the import of capitalism

The inner-communist ideological battles with the Soviet Union also took place and, after the turmoil of the "Cultural Revolution", from 1978 the reformers around Deng Xiaoping also resorted to Lenin's New Economic Politics in addition to the misguided US teachings of the "Chicago Boys": Socialism in a country that has been kept underdeveloped for a long time has to adopt capitalist elements, otherwise it would not survive. Western companies need to come into the country, they need to be granted licenses and build modern factories, and the country must learn from capitalist methods of financing and management.[7]

---

4   Theodore White / Annalee Jacoby: Donner aus China. Stuttgart Hamburg Baden-Baden 1949, p. 250ff. (Erstausgabe New York 1946: Thunder out of China)

5   Wolfgang Reinhard: Die Unterwerfung der Welt. Globalgeschichte der europäischen Expansion 1415-2015, München 2016, p. 825ff.

6   Dirk Eckert: Amerikas treuester Verbündeter, telepolis 11.8.2018

7   Theodor Bergmann: Der chinesische Weg. Hamburg 2017, p. 27ff.

During the 1920s Ford had built a car factory in the Soviet Union, General Electric had supplied equipment for electrification and Radio Corporation of America (RCA) for radios, Standard Oil had built a kerosene plant in the Baku oil field and Morgan's Guaranty Trust had helped establish the first international bank, Raskombank. The other leading Wall Street bank, Kuhn Loeb, had provided loans for the first five-year plan. Some 2,000 US engineers had helped build levees, dams and factories – all without diplomatic relations. Transnational trade between the Soviet Union and the US, but also with Britain and Germany, was expanded.[8]

Corporations do not have to follow governments
This shows that completely different plays can be performed on the economic and political-ideological stage. Powerful, globally active corporations can do something completely different than their respective governments.

After 1933 it was the same, but the other way round: The US government under President Franklin Roosevelt recognized the Soviet Union diplomatically in 1933. But the US and other Western corporations on both sides of the Atlantic had to contend with the fear of growing socialism. Economic relations with the Soviet Union were curbed. And anyway, from 1934, the orders of the Hitler Wehrmacht and the putschists around General Francisco Franco in Spain for Ford, General Motors, Standard Oil, IBM, General Electric, ITT etc. were the much larger and ideologically more apposite business.[9]

After the founding of the People's Republic in 1949, the USA included China in the CoCom embargo (technical goods). They tightened the embargo in the 1950s – as many as 450 product groups were not allowed to be delivered to "Red China", compared with the 250 product groups that were withheld from the Soviet Union and other socialist states. However, this was then relaxed below official regulations. And, unlike the Soviet Union, China was regarded as a poor developing country and harmless in terms of power politics.

New economic policy
British companies had been in China since the 1950s – the China-Britain Business Council was founded in 1954. But the New Economic Policy only

---

8   Soviet Union Information Bureau: The Soviet Union – Facts, Descriptions, Statistics, Washington D.C. 1929; Joan Wilson: Ideology and Economics. U.S. Relations with the Sowjet Union 1918- 1933, Columbia/Mass. 1974

9   Pauwels: Big Business avec Hitler a.a.O., p. 176ff.

took hold through investment in more modern industries. The American Motors Company (AMC) and Chrysler sold (not many) cars to China in the early 1980s, but quickly discovered that they had to take advantage of the much lower wages and manufacture in the country itself.

The joint venture called Beijing Jeep Corporation founded in 1983 by AMC with a Chinese company was the first car factory of this kind. Chrysler followed in 1984. Volkswagen and Citroen followed in 1985. From the 1990s, Ford, General Motors, DaimlerChrysler and, from the beginning of the 2000s, Honda, Toyota, Nissan and Mazda from Japan, politically an arch-enemy, also founded their joint venture factories with Chinese partners.

Example electric cars

The state's requirements were clear: the foreign companies had to form a 50 to 50 joint venture with a Chinese partner, had to transfer technology, had to admit locals to higher management. The production of low-priced cars for low-income families was promoted. While initially the existing models of the foreign companies were produced, the Chinese authorities imposed ever more precise requirements in order to adapt the cars to Chinese needs.

In 2001 China enforced the acceptance of the People's Republic of China into the World Trade Organization (WTO) with the help of the automobile and other industries and European states that produced or traded in China, against the resistance of US Republicans and the American Enterprise Institute (AEI).[10] As a result, several tariffs tumbled. Foreign companies are now allowed to operate 100 percent subsidiaries in China under certain conditions. VW's leading global market position can only be maintained through production and sales in China. The country became the largest automobile market, the largest production location – and the most important driver of innovation.

Different from Mexico and Eastern Europe

During the 1990s, the same western car makers had set up production facilities in numerous other developing and emerging countries: With NAFTA in Mexico and then in the ex-socialist states of Eastern Europe such as Hungary and Poland. In Mexico and the now EU states, the governments submitted to

---

10   Dong Wang: U.S. – China Trade 1971 – 2012: Insights into the U.S.-China Relationship, in: The Asia-Pacific Journal 24/2013

the specifications of VW, Daimler, Nissan, and General Motors for continued traditional production. Innovation here was confined to the establishment of low wages and automated production.

Only China managed the qualitative turnaround, through state leadership: First, the wages of ordinary workers were raised. Second, local technicians, scientists and managers qualified. Third, China is now the leader in digitally controlled production of innovative cars and electric batteries. Fourth, vehicle construction is being greatly simplified and made cheaper; the highly complex system of a gasoline-powered car is being replaced by a simple engine system. Fifth, leaded petrol was banned completely as early as the 1990s. Sixth, in 2018, the production of 553 car models that consume particularly large amounts of gasoline was banned, including models from Chinese and European car manufacturers such as VW and Daimler.[11] Seventh, the state is setting targets not only for the complete switch to electric cars, but also for an integrated mobility concept.

This illustrates a different level of state competence than in the West, where car companies also have close ties with the state, but have the opposite effect: They rake in high profits, cheat with impunity across the board, pollute the air and drag their heels on the necessary innovations.

Electric vehicles, new registrations 2017

Country	New registrations
China	579,000
USA	195,140
Norway	62,320
Japan	56,000
Germany	54,490
UK	47,260
France	41,720
Sweden	20,310
Canada	18,390

---

11   China: Produktion von 553 Autos verboten, Die Welt 3.1.2018

It needs to be borne in mind here that electric cars were not produced in China until 2013, while more than 100,000 had already been produced in the USA and production had already begun earlier in other western countries. The potential and dynamics in China are higher.[12] Incidentally: the electric cars in Sweden come from Volvo – the loss-making company was bought up by the Chinese car maker Geely, supplied with loans and modernized.[13]

Electric buses and integrated mobility concept
Looking at electric buses, the momentum is even more impressive. 99 percent of all 385,000 electric buses worldwide operate in China. The city of Shenzen, for example, has scrapped all its diesel buses and expanded its route network with 16,300 electric buses, also on the basis of suggestions from the population. Of the 12,550 taxis in Shenzen, 7,530 have now been converted to electric engines. By contrast, German cities, where the air is still being polluted, are planning to purchase a mere 162 electric buses in 2018, on the taxi front nothing is happening.[14]

The integrated mobility concept also includes the manufacture of batteries and research. The state-owned Beijing Automotive Industry Corporation (BAIC) and the private-sector group Build Your Dreams (BYD) are the world's most successful manufacturers of electric cars. But BYD is also the most innovative manufacturer of batteries: In 1995 still a start-up, BYD now has a joint venture with Daimler in the Shenzhen special economic zone, develops and manufactures batteries, builds solar farms, and now has 10,000 scientists, including chemists and electrical engineers, researching new environmental technologies. This also allows BYD to reverse the trend in other respects: BYD has production facilities not only in China, but also in the USA, India, Hungary and Romania, and also sells battery-powered buses to municipalities in Spain and Portugal as well as to the UK capital London.[15]

The first plant for car batteries in Germany is being built by the Chinese company Contemporary Amperex Technology (CATL). This most significant industrial investment for a decade in Thuringia is expected to create 600 new

---

12   Elektroautos weltweit, HB 25.5.2018

13   Volvo&Geely: The Unlikely Marriage of Swedish Tech and Chinese Manufacturing Might that Earned Record Profits, Forbes 2.1.2018

14   Eine Stadt unter Strom, Wiwo 27.7.2018

15   www.bydeurope.com

jobs and attract suppliers. China is not only buying companies in Germany, but is also building new ones. Research is also being established. BMW has already awarded a major contract.[16] The Chinese are obviously not afraid of technology theft.

The integrated concept also includes shared mobility: not everyone has to own a car. This also incorporates networked, autonomous driving, i.e. communication between the vehicle and traffic lights, traffic guidance, weather reports and other services: To this end, Western carmakers have to cooperate with the Chinese technology groups Alibaba, Tencent and Baidu. This also includes the construction of an electric filling station network and the expansion of a high-speed rail system. The mobility concept already includes over 200 million electric bicycles and the 385,000 electric buses.

Because the Western car manufacturers (have to) accept these requirements, the Chinese leadership has partially lifted the previous requirement for joint ventures in this sector. Instead, the focus is on strategic cooperation. Carsten Breitfeld, ex-BMW manager, who heads the start-up company Byton, which is backed by state venture capital, explains the difference: "German carmakers are relying on models that have been successful so far and are only exchanging the combustion engine for an electric engine." That had no future.[17]

Admittedly, this is only a snapshot of where we stand now. The scarcity of the rare earths needed for batteries, the overstretching of individual transport inherited from old capitalist practices, the growing population and the growing urban conurbations require a further, higher level of development of transport mobility. The same applies to other areas.

Leadership in renewable energies

Because the old technologies were scarcely available and not part of daily life, the new technologies could also grow rapidly in other areas and be adapted at the same time. Because there was no credit card system, the payment services Alipay and Wechat quickly had hundreds of millions of users for paying at the cinema, restaurant, supermarket, taxi and on the Internet. 800 million of the 1.4 billion inhabitants use the Internet. The platform economy companies founded in China on the US model are growing faster than in the USA and the rest of the West: Alibaba's Internet business, the Baidu search engine, the

---

16   Battery maker to set up unit in Germany, en.silkroad.news 11.7.2018
17   "Die Zukunft der Automobilbranche wird in China geformt", HB 24.4.2018

Didi Kuaidi taxi service. The taxi service Uber, a model from the USA, was thwarted in China: Here it was not allowed to continue its ruthless handling of the drivers and abandoned the business.

China has overtaken the West for a decade in terms of investment in renewable energies. While Chinese companies invested USD 126 billion here in 2017, the figure was only USD 40 billion each in the USA and the EU. The number of jobs in China is correspondingly higher.

The dynamics also differ considerably: while the share of renewable energies in Germany rose from 3.7 to 5.2 percent between 2008 and 2017 and actually fell in the rich West, namely from 22.2 to 18.3 percent in the EU, from 11 to 10.5 percent in the USA and from 8.6 to 5.4 percent in Canada, China increased its share from 16.5 to 28.4 percent.[18] The West is suffocating in the state-sponsored BlackRock – General Motors – RWE strategy.

The ambivalence of capitalism

But China also uses the techniques of Western financial actors for its own purposes. PE investors from the USA and the EU such as KKR, Bridgepoint, Apax and EQT are proving useful in helping companies from the Middle Kingdom to identify suitable buy-ups in the EU. The Chinese buyers are pursuing different goals, but use the expertise.

PE investors such as Carlyle and the venture capitalist Sequoia from Silicon Valley have been involved in financing the start-up Ant Financial (financial technology, Alibaba subsidiary) since 2018. Since the international opening-up of the stock market, BlackRock has praised China as "one of the largest stock markets in the world, surpassed only by the US ... China is also home to more than 2,000 listed liquid companies, second only to the US".[19] In 2016, BlackRock, Fidelity, UBS and Schroder were licensed as private fund managers based in Shanghai without having to involve a local company.[20] At the same time, however, BlackRock warns against the threat of Chinese financial service providers such as Ant Financial, a globally expanding subsidiary of Alibaba, dominating the market.[21]

---

18   Der Westen lässt nach. Die Nachzügler übernehmen die Führung, HB 29.6.2018

19   BlackRock: Chinese equities. The ever-growing opportunity, February 2018

20   https://www.asiaasset.com/news/Blackrock_Schroders_CNPE2912.aspx, downloaded 28.5.2018

21   BlackRock warnt vor chinesischen Fintech-Attacken, HB 16.4.2018

Private capitalist entrepreneurs and investors are blatantly opportunistic. They could and can work with any political regime, preferably right-wing or fascist; but if it promised and promises profits, then also with socialist ones: With a social market economy, with a New Deal – or even in a contemporary way against it. With human rights – or even against them. In order to be present in the huge Chinese market, Apple deleted more than 600 VPN programs with which Internet censorship there could be circumvented. "China is crucial for Apple. That's why the company doesn't risk any trouble with Beijing."[22] God save humanity should such unscrupulous opportunists get their way. It depends on who is or becomes the stronger.

Thus, China's current capitalism by no means represents an "ideal" final state and certainly not textbook socialism. Further transformation also depends on international relations, and not only on those at state and government level. The leader of the Communist Party said in 2018 on the occasion of the 40th anniversary of the opening up of China to Western capitalism: "We are also prepared for hitherto unimaginable dangers and risks".[23]

Chinese rating agency downgrades USA

The rating is also informative for changes in western procedures. In 1994, the Chinese central bank founded its own rating agency, Dagong ("Great Work"). It is the alternative to the Big Three US rating agencies. Dagong is a private company under the supervision of the central bank.

After its foundation, Dagong initially worked with Moody's for three years to refine its own rating method and now has a global claim. This is also reflected in the name: Dagong Global Credit Rating Group. The agency has branches in Hong Kong, the USA and Europe and cooperates with agencies throughout Asia. It rates domestic and foreign companies and public entities (cities, regional governments) as well as the countries with which China maintains economic relations.

According to its boss Guan Jiazhong, a member of the Communist Party, the US agencies have lost the right to "rate the world" for good because of their complicity in the last financial crisis in 2007: they do not really pay attention to the ability to repay loans, but only to new borrowing. Unlike the Big Three,

---

22   Der Weg des Erfolgs, Apple ist als erstes Unternehmen mehr als eine Billion Dollar wert, SZ 4.8.2018

23   40 years of reform and opening up, South China Morning Post 19.12.2018

Dagong also uses economic criteria and was the first to downgrade the credit rating of the heavily indebted USA.[24]

In January 2018, after US President Trump had drastically lowered corporate taxes, Dagong lowered the US government's rating even further to "BBB+ with negative outlook". Reason: "The growing dependence of debt-driven economic development will further exacerbate the US government's inability to repay. This could become the detonator of the next financial crisis."[25]

Contract production in special economic zones

Contract production in special economic zones played an important role in China's development. The most important of these is Shenzhen. The southern Chinese city had 30,000 inhabitants at the beginning of 1980. Even before foreign companies set up production facilities in China, the Chinese leadership attracted contract production from abroad.

The reservoir of China's feudal-imperialist, impoverished, largely underemployed and unemployed rural population was several hundred million people.[26] Should and did they want to remain in this hopeless situation? It could have been said according to the principle of Western capitalism: Any work is better than no work at all. But here too the question was: if working poor is the first station out of absolute poverty, will it remain in this state like in other developing countries?

Excessive use of low-wage jobs

The upswing of the special zones accelerated after China's entry into the WTO in 2001. US technology groups such as IBM in particular had already begun in 1960 to commission low-wage suppliers in "friendly" Asian territories and states, in US-occupied Taiwan, Japan, South Korea and Thailand. Other standards, concerning the environment for instance, were also low or non-existent. In Taiwan in particular, this developed into a separate industry.

Out of this emerged the world's largest electronics supplier, the Taiwanese group Foxconn. In Shenzhen and then in two dozen smaller special zones in China, it organized large-volume contract production for Western electronics groups. In 2012, Foxconn had 1.4 million employees under contract in the

---

24   Werner Rügemer: Ratingagenturen a.a.O., p. 175ff.

25   en.dagongcredit.com/Rating Reports/America 16.1.2018

26   Wolfgang Reinhard: Die Unterwerfung der Welt a.a.O., p. 859ff.

People's Republic, mainly young female migrant workers. Hewlett Packard, Intel, Dell, Microsoft, Lucent, Nortel, Alcatel, Ericsson, Nike, Apple and others took advantage of these low-wage jobs and awarded long-term major contracts.[27]

Silicon Valley and WalMart

The targeted use of low-wage workers and sweatshops has a tradition in the USA and also in the high-tech sector of Silicon Valley that began with Vietnamese boat people and illegal Mexican women in the 1970s, long before the outsourcing to China had begun.[28]

As a very young hippie company, Apple for instance had its Apple II personal computer assembled in Shenzhen as early as 1981: Wages were much lower than in Mountain View. In the period that followed, Apple led the way in outsourcing as much as possible of component production. Initially, however, the parts had to be manufactured mostly in the USA and exported to China.

This changed even more quickly after China's WTO accession. Apple had its own engineers supervise the work in Shenzhen. The final assembly and product testing costs for the iPhone 7, which was sold in the USA for USD 549, were USD 5.[29]

The hippie-like Silicon Valley gurus Gates and Jobs and their co-owners like Founders Fund and BlackRock became stinking rich, de-industrializing the US and spreading labor poverty there. The super-rich owners of the largest US company, the retail chain WalMart, also did the same: they had 80 percent of their goods manufactured by suppliers in China.

The Chinese leadership thus promoted the expansion of jobs and continuous employment, albeit to a large extent initially at heavy human cost. Barracking, 12-hour working days, early wear and tear of the workforce were accepted: This situation was better than the poverty the prevailed beforehand.

Initially, the state tried to establish socialist wage equality: Cleaning lady, unskilled worker and engineer were to be paid equally. But from 1983 VW also enforced with immediate effect a capitalist wage spread in the first factory,

---

27   Mark Selden u.a.: The politics of global production: Apple, Foxconn and China's new working class, in: The Asian-Pacific Journal 32/2013

28   Rügemer: Neue Technik – alte Gesellschaft a.a.O., p. 28ff.

29   https://de.statista.com/onfografik/9272/herstellungsko9sten-iphone-7, 8.5.2017

which went well beyond that in Germany and Europe. The German managers were paid 200 times more than their Chinese colleagues.[30]

But it didn't stop there, the process continued. The latent potential of communist-led capitalism unfolded, slowly. Since the 1990s, permanent employees and migrant workers in thousands of companies have protested and gone on strike. A People's Republic proved to be a more favorable place, even though the state leadership and even trade unions did not support the strikes and actually opposed them.

The transposal of the working poor

In 2006, the National People's Congress presented the draft Labor Contract Act. It had been drafted with the help of Western European labor lawyers such as Wolfgang Däubler from Germany and was moderately geared to a number of ILO standards: Every worker was to receive a written employment contract – this was not usual in the western dominated companies until now. Dismissals were to be made more difficult. Temporary workers were to be given a regular job after one year. Qualified workers should also be able to change companies freely. Trade unions and company employee representatives should be able to negotiate collectively with the employer not only about remuneration, but also about working conditions, working hours, breaks, holidays, work safety, hygiene, social insurance and additional benefits. Companies should be able to be penalized for infringements. The law was supposed to bring improvements for migrant workers in particular.

Microsoft, Nike, Siemens, VW&Co defend labor poverty

The American Chamber of Commerce in China, in particular, was up in arms against these elementary, moderate labor rights. On 19 April 2006, on behalf of its 900 member companies, it sent its clichéd criticism to the National People's Congress: if the draft became law, China's competitiveness would be threatened. The companies threatened to withdraw from China and to cancel work orders. Leading chamber members were Intel, Microsoft, Google, Dell, AT&T, Nike, Ford, General Electric, UPS and Goodyear.[31]

The European Chamber of Commerce in China with 860 members, in-

---

30   Herr Xu und sein Auto, SZ 22.12.2018

31   Lawprofessors.typepad.com/china_law_prof_blog/files/AmChamChinaLaborLaw-Comments.pdf

cluding Siemens, VW, Bayer, BASF, Nokia, Veolia and KPMG, also joined in, albeit less aggressively. Incidentally: At the same time, the same Western companies also campaigned at home for the reduction of labor rights and for new low-wage jobs, in Germany with the four Hartz laws.

The People's Congress put the bill up for public discussion. In addition to the two statements of the Western Chambers of Commerce, 191,847 comments were received, mainly from workers and activists demanding more far-reaching rights.[32]

But the threats of the Western corporations were effective. The People's Congress weakened the law in several places. Recruitment without a written contract was possible, the contract only had to be concluded later. For temporary employment contracts, the duration was increased to two years, the subsequent regular employment was not made binding. Mass dismissals did not have to be approved by the trade union or employee representatives, but only "sufficiently explained". There was also still no right to strike – it had been removed from the constitution in 1982.[33]

China: The most strike-intensive country

The watered-down law, which came into force in 2008, was formally accepted by Western as well as Chinese companies, but often undermined. But for the workers it was an encouragement. Tens of thousands went to court. President Hu Jintao called for "the legitimate rights and interests of workers" to be protected.[34]

The People's Republic became the most strike-intensive country, although or because the official trade unions did not participate at all. They see themselves as co-managers and as part of the state apparatus. But for over a decade there have been hundreds of thousands of spontaneous strikes, organized by activists and increasingly supported by Communist Party factory groups. From 2010, demonstrative suicides began to accumulate in Shenzhen. "Although officially there is no right to strike, nowhere else in the world are there more industrial disputes."[35]

The state also continued to take action. The fairly autonomous provinces

---

32   www.globallabourrights.org/alerts/new-chines-labor-contract-law, September 2007

33   Vgl. Rolf Geffken / Can Cui: Das chinesische Arbeitsvertragsgesetz, mit Kommentar, 5. Auflage, Cadenberge 2016

34   Beverly Silver / Lu Zhang: China als neuer Mittelpunkt der globalen Arbeiterunruhe, in: PROKLA 161/2010, p. 607

35   Ana Radic: Zehn Tage im Riesenreich, Hintergrund 3/2016, p. 52

set minimum wages. The five-year plan for 2011-2015 set a 13 percent annual increase in minimum wages. In 2011, the Social Security Act came into force, which includes basic old-age provision for rural residents. The social security institutions were given direct access to the companies' bank accounts in order to be able to collect missed contributions by force – with the contribution tripling in the event of default. Incidentally, employers' contributions are considerably higher than in Germany, for example, and amount to more than two thirds of social security contributions.[36]

Sustained wage increases and social security
Unauthorized but tolerated strikes, state leadership and the activity of communist party members were more important than the weak law and more effective than a Western model of collective bargaining autonomy: This favors the private owners in the real-existing Western capital democracy, but does not improve the power of the majority and also makes the secretly supportive state appear innocent, as Däubler establishes by way of comparison.[37]

The average hourly wages of Chinese workers were tripled from 2005 to 2016 after adjustment for inflation – from USD 1.20 to 3.60. The People's Republic has thus overtaken the classic emerging markets of Brazil (USD 2.70), Thailand (USD 2.20) and Mexico (USD 2.10), while wages in India have been stagnating at USD 0.70 for a decade.[38] The millions of migrant workers are also benefiting from this development: Unlike before, when they were starving in poor rural areas, they now have a paid job.

China thus also exceeds the minimum wages in the EU states Bulgaria, Lithuania, Romania, Latvia, Hungary, Croatia, Slovakia, the Czech Republic and Poland.[39] This applies even more to the southern regions of Italy and Spain – Calabria, Sicily, Almeria – where illegal refugees are deliberately blackmailed, exploited, impoverished and their health damaged in the huge vegetable and fruit plantations. The EU subsidizes entrepreneurs there, even if they are linked to criminal milieus such as the mafia. EU Agriculture Commissioner Phil Hogan, who is a member of the Christian EPP, expressly supports this.[40]

---

36   Wolfgang Däubler: Arbeitsrecht in China, p. 23ff., www.nachdenkseiten.de 29.11.2012

37   Däubler, Arbeitsrecht in China ibid. p. 26

38   Wie lange bleibt China noch die Werkbank der Welt? Der Spiegel 12/2017, p. 57

39   Mindestlöhne in der EU: https://de.statista.com, downloaded 2.5.2018

40   Europas dreckige Ernte. ARD die story 9.7.2018

In this way, the EU also promotes and subsidizes particularly severe violations of human rights and the European Social Charter in its own member
states – but China is the one charged with violating human rights.

In 2014, the Chinese government launched the program to expand social
insurance, and by 2020 all Chinese should be covered by social insurance. 1.3
billion people, i.e. almost the entire population of 1.4 billion, already have
health insurance and 870 million are covered by pension insurance. Traditional and fresh differences between rural and urban areas and between state-
owned and private companies have been reduced. In 2016, China received an
award for this at the International Social Security Conference.[41]

While in China the incomes and living standards of all classes and strata
have been rising sustainably for three decades – farmers, migrant workers,
temporary workers, permanent employees, soldiers, managers, entrepreneurs,
millionaires, billionaires – income and living standards in the USA have stagnated or fallen for the majority and especially for those who are already poor.
Only about 5 percent of the US population saw a significant rise in income and
living standards.[42]

Reduction of working time
Under these conditions, China is testing the reduction in working hours possible today. The State Council approved a plan in 2015. Some high-tech companies are experimenting with the four-day week: More leisure time should lead
to more satisfaction, relaxation and more enjoyment at work. Some municipalities, such as the largest city in Chongqing with 30 million inhabitants, have
introduced the four-and-a-half-day week. Employees can spend more active
leisure time, e.g. on domestic Chinese tourism, thus reducing the savings rate
and stimulating the local economy.[43] To this end, the state is also channeling
investment into new ski and bathing resorts.

The People's Republic is thus the only nation on earth where the income,
standard of living, quality of life and security of the majority of the population,
including the poorest, have grown sustainably over decades and in which the
preconditions have been met for this to continue. By contrast, all the poverty

---

41   Regierung für Sozialversicherung ausgezeichnet, german.cri.cn/info/cri.htm 14.12.2016

42   The American Middle Class Is No Longer the World's Richest, NYT 22.4.2014

43   Emma Luxton: Is China heading towards a 4.5 day working week? https://www.wefo-
      rum.org/agenda 12/2015

reduction programs that have been repeatedly announced for decades under Western dominance have failed. The UN's success stories on poverty reduction stem above all from China's successes – without this being pointed out. And with the new financial actors, the number of working poor continues to grow, especially in the "developed" countries, the USA and the EU.

Shenzhen: From poorhouse to high-tech center
Western companies and large low-wage companies such as Foxconn are now relocating production to other western-dominated countries such as Thailand, Myanmar and Vietnam, and, exuberantly welcomed by President Trump, also to the United States. Foxconn, showered with billions in subsidies, is relocating to sparsely populated Wisconsin.[44]

In 1996 the Shenzhen High Tech Industrial Park was established. Leading technology groups such as Huawei, Tencent and ZTE, which now compete with Western groups and operate worldwide, were set up here and have their headquarters here. Tencent now manufactures more and cheaper smartphones here than Apple. Global corporations such as Siemens, Daimler, Bosch, Bayer, Airbus, Lufthansa and 200 other companies from Germany alone want, indeed have to benefit from the synergy effects that are only available here.

The city now has 13 million inhabitants. China's status as the extended workbench of Western capitalism has in many respects come to an end.

Portrait: Jack Ma / Alibaba: "Inclusive globalization"

In 1999, the 35-year-old English teacher Jack Ma, his wife Ying and 18 partners founded the private company Alibaba in his hometown of Hangzhou. In a decade it became the largest online retailer in the world, larger than Amazon and Ebay together. It provides goods and services worldwide, especially to small and medium-sized companies and traders. 25,000 employees and customers operate in 17 languages. Alibaba Holding now includes the payment service Alipay, the financial services provider Ant Financial, a majority stake in the Asian online retailer Lazada, parcel logistics, data centers in Malaysia, Dubai, Sydney, Tokyo and Frankfurt/Main, a music and a sports group as well as the newspaper South China Morning Post.

---

44   Foxconn vows to build Wisconsin plant after talk with Trump, Reuters 1.2.2019

The IPO in New York in 2014 was the largest in the USA; Ma refrained from the ritual of the CEO ringing the bell in the Wall Street trading room, but rather brought in eight unassuming customers, including a US cherry picker and a Chinese watch seller. With USD 22 billion in assets, the second richest Chinese person is in 33rd place among the richest people on earth. Ma took the name Alibaba from 1001 Nights, because it is known everywhere across all cultures; the Alibaba of the legend is a poor lumberjack who wants to help poor people. The Alibaba Foundation for Poverty Relief is also fed by company profits and finances boarding schools with bus services in poor, often very mountainous areas of China: there are small villages far apart and children often have to get by without their emigrated parents.[45] The company cannot do without international investors for its global expansion: the Japanese technology group Softbank, Yahoo from the USA and T Rowe Price are co-owners. But together with the state, Ma himself, his deputy Joseph Tsai along with other executives have control.

Against the USA: "Inclusive globalization!" Ma is not a member of the Communist Party. "I love the party like my mother. But I don't go to bed with my mother." But Ma supports the development logic organized by the CP. He agrees that Alibaba, like the other digital companies, has to finance the construction of the digital infrastructure, e.g. electric filling stations for recharging mobile phones and cars, on the instructions of the state. At the World Economic Forum in Davos, Ma read the riot act to US President Trump, who was in attendance,: "In the past 30 years, America has waged 13 wars that have cost USD 14.2 trillion." After 2008, the US had also funneled a lot of money into the bankrupt Wall Street banks, whereas the money would have been better used for infrastructure and would have benefited workers. Ma also touched on Trump's account of the US trade deficit with China: "Other countries have not stolen American jobs – no, it was your strategy. In the past 30 years, companies like IBM, Cisco and Microsoft have made a lot of money with this kind of globalization." Ma called for "inclusive globalization" and offered the US to look for sales markets in China and Asia for their small businesses and thus create jobs in the US.[46]

---

45   Alibaba sets up poverty relief fund, www.xinhuanet.com 1.12.2017; South China Morning Post 21.8.2018

46   Jack Ma: America has wasted its wealth, https://www.weforum.org 18.1.2017

3.
State, Communist Party, Socialism

Communist-coordinated capitalist practices have turned the People's Republic of China from a colonially impoverished developing country into the world's second-largest economy in just four decades.

The state has gradually replaced the centrally planned economy with a mixed but regulated economy. In 1998, the State Council abolished 15 ministries which were responsible for individual economic sectors. In some cases, the ministries were replaced by private holding companies owned by the state in areas such as energy and finance.[47]

As far as purely Chinese companies are concerned, there is a mix between state-owned and private companies. As in Western capitalism, the latter are either public limited companies, whose shares are often traded on the Shenzhen, Shanghai and Hong Kong stock exchanges, while the majority are smaller companies in the form of a limited liability company. The shares of large corporations such as Alibaba are also traded on the New York Stock Exchange, US investors such as BlackRock are co-owners.

To level the playing field, Chinese corporations also use dark practices that belong systemically to Western capitalism. For instance, a fair number of foreign investments are channeled through the financial havens of the Netherlands, Luxembourg, Ireland and the Cayman Islands. China has adopted other Western instruments in form: Venture capital financing, private equity funds and public-private partnerships. However, as illustrated by the example of the rating agency, these instruments are redesigned and integrated into a different development logic.

Political parties
This outcome was and is only possible through the state, which is controlled by the Communist Party – currently with about 89 million members.[48] The eight other parties, including the Kuomintang Party and a Taiwanese party in China, have mostly existed since the founding of the state in 1949 and have between 100,000 and 200,000 members, two have only a few thousand members. Unlike the CP, they describe themselves as democratic, represent smaller

---

47   Dong Wang: U.S. – China Trade, The Asia-Pacific Journal 24/2013

48   Cf. german.china.org.cn/de-zengzhi/2.htm

interest groups and not in principle the entire population, and do not want to participate in a communist government.[49]

Some critics in the West, who also see themselves as Marxists, complain that they "imagine socialism differently". But the Communist-led capitalism is not even presented as socialism by the Communist Party. It is, also in contrast to the founding period with Mao Tse Tung, only a goal for the medium-term future. And would a "socialist" China with 300 million poor people have been worthy of this name in the 1960s? What is more important: the name "socialism" or overcoming poverty and securing peace?

Extensive fight against corruption

Capitalism produces formation-specific criminal practices. Western capitalist democracy has made various attempts to combat such practices, but it has failed. Auditors, commercial law firms, rating agencies became accomplices in insider dealing, tax evasion, modern forms of bribery, evasion of the law. The judiciary, which is understaffed for the prosecution of corporate crime, and politically dependent in this area, tends to focus on petty criminals, preferably foreigners from poor states.[50]

The Chinese leadership has increasingly recognized that the systemic release of capitalist crime and individual, selfish and corporate greed has to be severely curbed: This goes far beyond the "ethical self-commitments" of company boards in the Western way. The judiciary has been expanded for this purpose. Between 2012 and 2016, around one million managers, also from foreign companies, and party officials were unseated, arrested and brought to justice for corruption, bribery, malpractice and nepotism.[51]

In dozens of cases this has affected the very highest ranks. Zhou Youkang, former head of security of the CP and head of the oil company CNPC, was sentenced to life imprisonment, as were the top politicians Bo Xilai and Sun Zhengcai, head of the CP in Chongqing. They had accepted millions in bribes, secretly awarded contracts to friends and handed out jobs. Such functionaries often use the connections of clan members with Canadian or US citizen-

---

49   Wikipedia: Political parties in the People's Republic

50   See Hans See: Wirtschaft zwischen Demokratie und Verbrechen. Grundzüge einer Kritik der kriminellen Ökonomie. Frankfurt/Main 2014

51   Antikorruptionskampagne. Chinas Reinigung von innen, HB 28.11.2016

ship for their money flows.[52] In Western capitalist democracies, the judiciary, which also has no political support for such cases, does not dare to take on comparable criminals.

Protectionism

The current CP Chairman Xi Jinping also presented this success story to the 2017 World Economic Forum with considerable resonance – this would have been unthinkable just a few years ago.[53]

This success includes protectionist measures against the interests of foreign investors. The joint venture rule was one of these from the outset. The Labor Contract Act is another example: workers had and have to be protected against the greed of Microsoft, Apple, VW & Co and local entrepreneurs. Certain areas have been and are being kept completely free of foreign investment or are being opened up only gradually. Renewable energies, much vaunted in the West but not realized, are enjoying an upswing only in China, thanks to state protection.

For a long time, China imported and somehow recycled about half of the plastic waste, vanadium slag and textile production residues from the USA and the EU. Since 2013, the state has gradually restricted this and banned it completely from 2018.[54]

A thorny chapter in the Internet age is the control of data flows. "On Chinese territory, the Internet is subject to Chinese law. China's Internet sovereignty must be respected and protected" – this is how the ex-Google boss and current digital advisor of the Pentagon conveys the Chinese stance. This is correct, and one could say that this is also the self-evident view of the US government and the European Commission, which are known to protect their territories through relevant laws and practices. But, in the case of China, Schmidt denounces this as "blatant censorship" and a characteristic of "authoritarian states".[55]

---

52   Chinas Sicherheitschef zu lebenslanger Haft verurteilt, SPON 11.6.2015; Ex-Politbüro-Mitglied wegen Korruption verurteilt, SPON 8.5.2018

53   Xi Jinping's keynote speech at the World Economic Forum, https://www.cina.org.cn 6.4.2018

54   China: Zentraler Recyclinghof des Planeten ist geschlossen, Telepolis 10.1.2018

55   Schmidt / Cohen: Die Vernetzung der Welt ibid., p. 132

Prohibition of Facebook&Co

Western companies have so far insisted on practicing their international communication in and from China without any control – as if such a thing were possible in the West or even in the USA!

Facebook, for example, wanted to expand its platform, open to any perversion, unhindered in China as well. The cooperation of US digital corporations with the Pentagon, CIA and NSA and the increased military encirclement of China pose a threat to the sovereignty of the state. China protects itself here with protectionist measures. If China protects its territory, it is called censorship in the West. If the West protects itself – and what is more the superpower spies on the vassals at the same time – then this is tamely repressed.[56]

In 2017, after unsuccessful calls to change their practices, China blocked Facebook, Google with all its offshoots (WhatsApp, Instagram), Twitter and Snapchat Google (The Great Chinese Firewall).

Social credit system

Since 2014, the state has been building a social credit system against socially harmful practices and against the systemic destruction of trust in unleashed, digitally accelerated capitalism. It covers both companies and individual citizens.

In the case of companies, both public and private, domestic and foreign, loan repayment, tax and advertising honesty and compliance with all relevant laws are determined. Non-repayment of loans, corruption, tax evasion, fraud, violation of copyright and labor laws, false product information etc. all collect minus points. There are currently 6,000 companies on a blacklist.[57] However, the more law-abiding the companies are, the easier it is for them to access cheap loans and orders.

Citizens are registered according to an individual system. Here, too, repayment or non-repayment of loans is the top priority – among the young generation the sometimes reckless borrowing, aided by credit cards, is a major problem.[58] The government has taken a look at the Schufa system in Germany: It has been changed twice. Not only credit behavior is recorded, but also social behavior: Anyone who cheats online, evades taxes, spreads rumors of terrorist

---

56   China geht gegen abhörsichere Internetkanäle vor, FAZ 19.1.2018

57   China improves credit blacklisting mechanism to avoid undue punishment, http://www. xinhuanet.com 6.3.2018

58   China's young consumers drive sharp rise in borrowing, FT 6.8.2018

attacks in the social media, smokes on planes, sells counterfeit tickets, bribes and violates any law whatsoever gets minus points. Sanctions include the exclusion from domestic Chinese flights, train journeys, hotel bookings, credit card use and land lease. On the other hand, donations, e.g. also blood donations and services for the common good are rewarded, for instance when it comes to credit or job allocation.[59] The second change: in contrast to Schufa and the uncontrolled growth of commercial secret service spying and exploitation with CIA/Facebook, the Chinese know about the registration and can view their records.

Leadership towards socialism

The sovereignty of the state could only be secured because, unlike in the West, it was not directly associated or subjected to private capital in many indirect and hidden forms, even concealed ones.[60]

Sovereignty over private capital means that, despite all pragmatism, the state does not sell one square meter of land to either foreign or domestic companies or speculators. Urban and industrial areas, forests, lakes and even deserts were not subject to capitalist private ownership. The state grants only temporary rights of use.

Over the past decade it was possible to partially correct, according to economic criteria, the capitalist rampage of the many individual companies with the resulting inequalities and damage, as already partially described: For example, in wages, through targets for environmentally friendly mobility, in the reduction of energy consumption, in the shift away from coal, in the targeted development of large and complex urban structures (new multi-center cities), in the reduction of industrial overcapacity, in the obligation for IT companies to invest in rural areas, in an innovative and socially balanced digital economy, in financial supervision and in international investments.

In China they are aware: We live to a large extent capitalistically, we are not yet a fully-fledged socialist society. At its 2017 Congress, the CP decided: "Material growth must be rooted in a multidimensional system of "better living," including human "happiness," and embedded on the road to a modern *socialist* country.[61]

---

59   China intensifies punishment for credit defaulters, http://www.xinhuanet.com 16.3.2018

60   Cf. Werner Rügemer: Die Privatisierung des Staates ibid.

61   Full text of Xi Jinping's report at 19th CPC National Congress, www.chinadaily.com.cn 4.11.2017

Updating Marxism

At the same time, the focus on Marxism will be intensified. The Marx project was launched in 2005. Hundreds of positions were created for academics at several institutes: School of Marxism, Center for Socialist Political Economy. To date, university economists have been dominated by those who orient themselves more or less towards the "Chicago Boys" of Milton Friedman.

On the other hand, Marxism is to be updated, but also historically deepened: The works of Marx and Engels will be translated afresh. 92 Marxist publications from the circles of the Communist Party of China in the 1920s will be reissued by 2021 – the 100th anniversary of the founding of the party. This also includes Lenin's writings.[62] Here, too, China is not in a final state, but in the midst of a struggle for a new political-economic science. In 2006, Chinese scholars initiated the founding of the World Association of Political Economy (WAPE), which meets in a different country once a year.

4.
USA: Weaken China economically, threaten it militarily

US President Clinton promoted China's entry into the WTO as a win-win situation. This would also create new jobs in the USA and new export opportunities for US industry.[63] The opposite happened. The financial actors broke free, boosted their profits globally and further weakened the US economy.

USA: Profitable reduction

Up until the 1990s, the USA became the largest investor in China: first the US car manufacturers and retailers, then R.J. Reynolds Tobacco, Coca Cola, Pepsi Cola, Gillette, Eastman Kodak, General Foods, H.J.Heinz, AT&T etc. established branches in China. This created jobs there and not in the USA. Then in the 1990s and 2000s: Above all, the new technology and digital groups

---

62   http://german.china.org.cn 4.5.2018

63   Will Kimball / Robert Scott: China Trade, Outsourcing and Jobs. Economic Policy Institute, Washington 11.12.2014, p. 3

outsourced production to the Chinese special zones without investing themselves.

As a result, job losses were highest in the US states where the industry had been concentrated, such as California and Texas. The US companies, however, not only shifted production to China, but also to Taiwan, Puerto Rico, Ireland and later opened up new countries for this purpose, for example with NAFTA also Mexico. Between 2001 and 2013 alone, some 3.2 million technology jobs were lost in the USA, especially in the computer and electronics industry.[64] At the same time, labor incomes in the USA were gradually reduced. The low legal minimum wage of USD 7.25 was not increased even during the two Democratic terms of office with President Obama – despite his election promise.

The self-organized current account deficit

65 percent of exports from China to the USA in 2003 came from US companies and US-China joint ventures that produced in China, as Stephen Roach, Morgan Stanley's chief economist, calculated.[65] So it's not as US President Trump later claimed that China had "stolen jobs" from the US: rather, the companies that received the most support from the new financial players had slashed jobs in the US and outsourced production and assembly worldwide and to China.

And because the USA continued to shrink its industrial production, it was also able to manufacture fewer and fewer products and sell them abroad. US citizens and companies *had to* buy more and more abroad.

As a result, the US trade deficit with China increased. This began in the mid-1980s and then grew faster and faster in the 1990s. From 2001 to 2013, the value of imports from China to the USA quadrupled from USD 102 billion to 438 billion. The computers, mobile phones and iPhones that were assembled for US companies came into the USA as imports.[66] This constellation continues to exist. The Apple 7 Series iPhones alone accounted for USD 15.7 billion, i.e. 4.4 percent, based on the year 2017.[67]

---

64   Kimball/Scott: China Trade ibid. p. 4

65   Stephen Roach: How Global Labor Arbitrage Will Shape the World Economy, http://www.globalagendamagazine.com/2004/stephenroach.asp

66   Kimball / Scott: China Trade ibid.

67   Designed in California, made in China, Reuters 21.3.2018

Sales bans

In addition, the USA prohibits the purchase of technological goods and companies by China for reasons of "national security". In 1975, the USA established the Committee on Foreign Investment in the United States (CFIUS). The reason for this was the defense against looming takeovers of US companies by Japanese companies: Fujitsu had made an offer to the chip manufacturer Fairchild Semiconductor. Recently, CFIUS, which reports to the Minister of Finance, banned several sales to Chinese companies, including the sale of Money-Gram to the Chinese pay service Ant Financial/Alibaba and the sale of chip manufacturer Lattice to Canyon Bridge.[68] Sany, the largest Chinese engineering group, has been banned from buying four small wind farms because they are too close to a US military base.[69] In 2018, the purchase of Qualcomm by Broadcom (Shenzhen) was banned.

The US trade deficit with China is thus based on decisions taken by US corporations and US governments, as is the case with the EU. They have miscalculated: Communist-led China, unlike other developing and supplier countries, did not remain in a status of Western exploitation and dependence, but was able to reverse the logic of development.

Profit-driven self-blindness and aggression

The unelected and elected US elites are becoming more and more afraid of the rise of China, which they themselves have promoted. They did not want or foresee this rise: This is another indication of the profit-driven self-blindness of US-led capitalism.

This self-blindness leads to military aggressiveness. In 2011, the Obama administration responded with a primarily military concept, following attempts already made under President George W. Bush. 60 percent of the strategic armed forces were relocated to the Pacific region, another part against Russia.[70] On top of this come digital upgrading, customs duties and embargoes, also against China's cooperation partners.

---

68   CFIUS: The powerful and unseen US gatekeeper on multi-billion-dollar deals, The Strait Times 13.3.2018

69   David Dollar: United States-China Two-way Direct Investment, Brookings Institution, Washington Januar 2015, p. 15

70   Hillary Clinton: America's Pacific Century, Foreign Policy November 2011; U.S. Department of Defense: Sustaining U.S. Global Leadership. Priorities for the 21st Century Defense, Washington January 2012

Strategic pivot to "Asia"

Since then, the USA has been encircling China militarily, arming other states and setting up US military bases there. US military bases have now been installed directly on China's western border in Kyrgyzstan, Turkmenistan, Tajikistan, Afghanistan and Pakistan. To the south of China are bases in Thailand, Singapore and Diego Garcia. On the eastern border, existing bases in Japan have been expanded, a little further away also on the Midway, Wake and Marshall Islands, on Guam, Hawai, the Johnson and Kwajalein Atolls and in American Samoa. In Port Darwin at the northern tip of Australia, the USA has expanded a second fleet base.

After the Marcos dictatorship, the USA had abandoned its traditional military bases in the Philippines, now new ones are being built. Japan and South Korea, each with two dozen US military bases, which the USA has been stuffing with military power for decades, are being encouraged to revive old quarrels with China. In South Korea, an additional nuclear-weapon capable missile base was installed. Immediately after the announcement of Obama's pivot doctrine, the Air Force simulated nuclear bomb attacks on North Korea, an ally of China.[71]

Obama negotiated five new bilateral military alliances with Japan, South Korea, Thailand, Australia and the Philippines. In Japan's constitution, the peace imperative that had existed since the Second World War – enforced by the USA itself – was deleted. Regional, joint military maneuvers under US leadership are on the increase. The US armed forces of all genres under US Pacific Command (PACOM) now comprise 320,000 military personnel.

Economic exclusion, securing raw materials

It is clear to the US players: Asia with China is by far the most dynamic economic growth region. Almost two thirds of the world's population already live here. All countries, including those friendly to the West, are economically intertwined with China. And China's incipient integration with Russia's land and resources is a great danger for the "sole superpower" – whereas growth in the US-dominated regions of old capitalism has slackened at a high level and the active approval of their impoverished and demoralized population majorities has dwindled.

---

71   Joseph Gerson: Obamas "Pivot". Neuausrichtung der USA auf Asien und den Pazifik, Wissenschaft & Frieden 4/2013, p. 7

Obama had deliberately announced the new doctrine during a visit to Australia. Previously, the US government had concluded eight new bilateral free trade agreements in the Pacific region. They are limited to the closest allies, however small they may be: the Sultanate of Brunei, Chile, Peru, Singapore, Malaysia, Vietnam, Australia and New Zealand. The economically most important states were excluded because they are considered unreliable, e.g. India and China. Matching his successor Trump's idiocy, Obama justified the exclusion of China with the argument that the People's Republic was to blame for the US trade deficit. The 2016 Transpacific Free Trade Agreement (TPP), later terminated by Trump, included additional, larger states such as Japan, Mexico and Canada and was also intended to curb China's influence.

At the same time, it is about the oil and raw material reserves in the South China Sea. China should be prevented from extracting them. This sea is also an important transport route for oil from the Middle East.[72]

Despite all the military and political hostility, US companies do not want to lose their access to the huge Chinese market and production location. In addition, the new financial players such as BlackRock, Blackstone and venture capitalists – politically extremely right-wing and anti-communist – have become active. They organize ownership stakes, advisory mandates and securities trading with and in China – regardless of whether the US government is demanding and can enforce China's dismantling of customs duties and more purchases in the USA.

Military build-up and boycott against Russia
The US military has also largely subordinated Russia to PACOM, although it is actually part of the US Regional Command for Europe EUCOM. Only the state that dominates Eurasian territory and its resources between Lisbon and Vladivostok can remain the "sole superpower" in the long run – as already quoted above, this is how the geostrategic advisor of several US presidents, Brzezinski, updated the US doctrine after the collapse of socialism. "The most dangerous scenario would possibly be a grand coalition between China, Russia and Iran."[73]

However, this "grand coalition" is already taking shape, not least driven by the conditions created by the USA. More than ever, the EU is "America's indis-

---

72   Gerson: Obamas "Pivot" ibid. p. 10

73   Brzezinski: Die einzige Weltmacht a.a.O., p. 87

pensable bridgehead on the Eurasian continent" for all US governments. And within this EU, Germany has the leading role: Germany is "Europe's model pupil and America's strongest supporter in Europe".[74]

Thus, the obedient model-pupil elite, accepting economic and moral damage, followed and follows the US-Ukraine policy, the Russia boycotts and the military build-up against Russia – and Germany and the EU now also restrict Chinese investments in order to protect their "strategic interests".[75]

Admittedly, in view of the escalation staged by the US President, the question is how the oh so powerful, oh so weak EU can hold its own – caught between the all-powerful, weakened and highly armed old superpower and the powerful, modern, economically aspiring developing country China, on which European, above all German companies depend not only as a market and production location, but also as a location for innovation.

Digital and nuclear upgrading

The US military doctrine is aimed at reducing the number of boots on the ground, but to strengthen digitally controlled remote action, especially from the air and sea (Air Force; 3rd and 5th US fleets). This is why unmanned, transnationally deployed killer drones and new missiles with modernized atomic bombs play an important role.

As already mentioned, the Obama administration increasingly involved Internet companies such as Microsoft and Google in the technological upgrading of the military. Google's long-time CEO Schmidt acts as Chairman of the Defense Innovation Board.

USA: Globalization with military support

China's only military base outside the immediate vicinity is in the East African state of Djibouti. One of the most important sea trade routes runs there. The purpose is protection of the port of Doraleh, which is operated by a Chinese company. Since 2017 some 300 soldiers have been stationed there.

China, however, is the last country to have a military presence in Djibouti. France, Italy and Japan have been operating larger military bases here for some time, the USA since 2007. While the Chinese military protects a civilian facil-

---

74   Brzezinski ibid. p. 91 and 95

75   European Commission: State of the Union 2017. Foreign Direct Investment – An EU
       Screening Framework, Brussels 14.9.2017

ity, the US camp Lemonnier with 4,000 soldiers was and is integrated into the US-Africa command AFRICOM (headquarters in Stuttgart) and thus into military operations such as regime change in Libya (overthrow of Ghaddafi), in Somalia and currently in Yemen.

So China's only military base abroad, which is also not the launchpad for military operations, is matched by around 1,000 US military bases, which are spread around the world over some 60 countries and US-owned territories and islands and integrated into global military operations. China established new military bases in the South China Sea when the US began military encirclement in neighboring states, including the US nuclear-capable missiles in South Korea installed under Obama.

The USA does not spend its military budget on self-defense, but on global presence and intervention. In addition, the United States maintains its largest military bases in major allies such as Germany, Italy, Greece, Japan, South Korea, the United Kingdom and Kosovo.

The military budget of the USA in 2017 was USD 686 billion, of the NATO states a total of USD 921 billion. If we add the military spending of the most important other allies of the USA – Saudi Arabia, Japan, South Korea and Australia – we arrive at USD 1.1 trillion. China's military budget, on the other hand, was USD 228 billion. The territory that China must protect is much larger than that of the USA, and it is much more vulnerable because of the incomparably longer land borders. In addition, Russia, which counts as an ally of China, reduced its military spending in 2017 and spent USD 66 billion – whereas NATO, which is rearming against Russia, is increasing its spending, led by the USA.[76]

"Human rights"

Criticism of China is often justified with the violation of human rights. But the USA is the pioneer in demanding human rights that it persistently violates itself. For example, the US Declaration of Independence of 1776 referred to human rights and in particular to the right to individual happiness. At the same time, the right to slavery and exploitation of dependent labor was maintained. This was later merely modernized.[77] The struggle of the US and other West-

---

76   Militärausgaben der NATO-Staaten im Verlgleich, https://de.statista.com 12.7.2018; https://www.sipri.org/yearbook/2017

77   Rainer Roth: Sklaverei als Menschenrecht. Frankfurt/Main 2017

ern corporations in 2006 against the Chinese Labor Contract Act and for the maintenance of labor poverty in China illustrates this. And there is probably no illegitimate state in which US and Western corporations have not used and continue to use slave-like and labor relations in breach of ILO-conventions, whether directly or in the ever longer and professionally nested supply chains.

The representatives of Western capitalist democracy select the rights of minorities from the general human rights: Private entrepreneurs (the very big ones again, with more rights), sexual minorities (lesbians, gays, bisexuals, transgender/LGBT, on Facebook there are about 40), women in leadership positions. The rights of ethnic, religious and racial minorities are also emphasized – but only selectively feudal and anticommunist-oriented, such as the Tibetans represented by the Dalai Lama, while the indigenous US people and blacks etc. in the US, and Arabs, Druze etc. in Israel may be discriminated against – not to mention the prevailing anti-Islamism.

In 2006 the UNO founded the Human Rights Council: The USA was alone in voting against, together with its curious vassal mini-club comprising Israel, the Marshall Islands and Palau. In the Human Rights Council, the narrow US selection of human rights – freedom of opinion, free choice of gender, free occupation rights for Israel – was not enforceable. That is why the USA withdrew in 2018: The Council was a "cesspit", it too often spoke out against the Israeli government, and China, together with other countries, too often questioned human rights in the USA.[78]

For Western opinion makers, however, it still suffices: Whoever is "against the government" in China is a human rights activist. In 2010 Liu Xiaobo received the Nobel Peace Prize. Together with the artist Ai Weiwei, he had promoted Charter 08. In it, he praised the "advent of European culture" in 19th century China as the beginning of modernization – in reality, this "culture" consisted of brutal colonial politics. Although the Charter generally invoked universal human rights, it specifically named the Western selection of individual rights to freedom, religion, opinion and assembly. Since the 1990s, Xiaobo has received a regular salary from the CIA offshoot, National Endowment for Democracy (NED), for the publication of a magazine, even when he was in prison.[79]

---

78   USA treten aus UN-Menschenrechtsrat aus, Die Zeit 19.6.2018

79   Liu Xiaobo erhält den Friedensnobelpreis, chinesische und deutsche Fassung des Charta-Textes: http://www.oai.de; who is Liu Xiaobo? www.chinadaily.com.cn 27.10.2010

Just imagine: For instance, Mumia Abu Jamal of the Black Panthers and Leonard Peltier of the American Indian Movement, who have been imprisoned in US prisons for over three decades – these political prisoners were to be financed by the Chinese secret service, would have a manifesto circulated and would be awarded the Nobel Peace Prize for their advocacy of freedom of religion, opinion etc!

Wars as an independent business field
Since the Vietnam War at the latest, for the military-economic complex the wars of the USA no longer necessarily have to be won. The most lucrative thing is the global maintenance of tensions and unresolved conflicts: Following regime change, as in Iraq, Afghanistan and Libya, leave behind a failed state and continue to occupy the country; support "rebels" in Syria, fight the Islamic State a little, but let it continue to fight against the Syrian government; sell arms from BlackRock armament factories to confused and frustrated US citizens as well as to regional war states like Saudi Arabia; steer political movements with GAMFA technologies; maintain war capability at the highest level worldwide; constantly develop and sell new killing instruments – even without ordering death, it will come. Highly professional, alert sleepers promote shooting sprees and wars constantly and everywhere.

Hence, the USA no longer acts at even the lowest level of international law: they wage wars without formally declaring them. The USA acts in a permanent state of war with worldwide military operations of all kinds, whether openly or secretly and through third parties.

5.
China: Economic and peaceful globalization

In his opening speech at the 2017 World Economic Forum, Communist Party Chairman Xi Jinping criticized the current wars of the West and "the excessive pursuit of profit by financial capital... the growing inequality between poor and rich and between North and South... The richest one percent of the world's population has more wealth than the rest of the 99 percent... For many families, a warm home, enough to eat and a safe job is still a distant dream". The turnaround can only be achieved through equitable and peaceful globalization.[80] China has practiced and continues to practice such globalization.

Gradual advance into the capitalist center

Two decades after Western companies had invested in China, Chinese companies began investing abroad. The Going Global strategy has been in place since 2000. The investments initially concentrated on Asian countries, including Australia and New Zealand, then on Africa and on the raw materials necessary for expanded production: China is, apart from coal and rare earths, a country poor in raw materials, similar to the USA and the EU.

Since and after the Western financial and economic crisis of 2007, China has increasingly been buying companies and stakes in the central capitalist states, in the USA and in the EU – in the EU first in the traditionally connected UK, then in Germany, France, Italy and also in Switzerland. This began at the same time as the BlackRock&Co acquisitions. However, the volume of Chinese investments in the center of Western capital is still much lower to this day, amounting to 0.3 percent of all foreign investments in Germany,[81] but causes a thousand times more public uproar.

In 2015, Chinese investment abroad exceeded foreign investment in China for the first time.[82] While in 2000 China was still in 32nd place in international comparison in terms of the volume of foreign investment, in 2015 it ranked third behind the USA and Great Britain.[83] More than 20,000 Chinese companies are (co-)owners of companies abroad, spread across 140 countries.

Unlike in the case of US financial investors, the acquisitions are not aimed at exploiting existing assets and generating fast and high profits. Rather, the Chinese economy and Chinese companies are to be modernized and completed. The "Made in China 2025" strategy is intended to further improve production in China itself – development of domestic production and the domestic market. That is why the state is now publicly reprimanding "irrational" and debt-financed investments by private Chinese corporations abroad and is calling for correction.[84]

---

80   Xi Jinping's keynote speech ebd. p. 2, 4, 10f.

81   BertelsmannStiftung: Chance und Herausforderung. Chinesische Direktinvestitionen in Deutschland, Gütersloh 2016, p. 25

82   www.mofcom.gov.cn 20.1.2016

83   BertelsmannStiftung: Chance und Herausforderung ibid., p. 17

84   Unterstützung von ganz oben, HB 25.6.2018

As a result, and in conjunction with the Trump government's punitive tariffs and the dutiful restrictions imposed by EU states such as Germany, Chinese investment in the West has been declining slightly since 2017.[85]

State and private corporations on a global shopping spree
Large state-owned enterprises are just as active in acquisitions as private enterprises. The state-owned corporations include the four largest banks, which have also become the largest banks in the world, then for instance the telecommunications group China Mobil, the power grid operator SGCC, the railway manufacturer CNR and the oil company CNP. Among the globally active private groups are the Internet platform Alibaba, the technology group Huawei, the smartphone manufacturer Xiaomi and the food group Yili.

Purchases abroad have changed. In Europe, the focus was initially on mechanical engineering, energy and automotive suppliers, followed by high tech/IT, pharmaceuticals and financial services. They are currently being supplemented by biotechnology, medical and environmental technology, the textile and logistics industries, as well as tourism and the hotel industry. In each country the best and most suitable is sought, in France for example also wineries, which do not continue as family businesses.

In addition to investments in the EU, Russia has become an increasingly important location. Since the start of the New Silk Road in 2013, China has increasingly invested in Southern and Eastern European EU states, Portugal, Italy, Greece and Cyprus, but also in the impoverished EU states of the Balkans.

Example Germany
Since the beginning, the largest destination for Chinese investments in Europe was the UK. However, the most important industrial technology for China is now in the hands of highly qualified, specialized German medium-sized companies. Germany as a business location, combined with its economic and political position in the EU, is the most important "gateway to Europe".[86]

Chinese companies have increased their investment stock in Germany fortyfold from EUR 129 million in 2004 to EUR 5.9 billion in 2014.[87] At the end

---

85   Chinesische Investoren verlieren das Interesse, FAZ 27.12.2018

86   BertelsmannStiftung ibid., p. 32

87   BertelsmannStiftung ibid. p. 29

of 2016, the German investment stock in China is estimated at EUR 60 billion and the Chinese investment stock in Germany at EUR 7.55 billion. There were 8,000 German companies in China and a good 2,000 Chinese companies in Germany – out of a total of 16,000 foreign companies. The US investment stock in Germany is more than one hundred times higher.[88] But according to prevailing US and EU thinking, it is already becoming dangerous.

In purely economic terms, it is also clear in capital-friendly circles: investment from China helps growth in the EU, brings innovation, creates new jobs and opens up China's emerging market.[89]

China's company purchases in Germany (selection)

Year	Purchased company	Chinese buyer
2005	AWP Aluminum	Cathay Merchant Group
2011	Medion/electronic consumer goods	Lenovo
	Preh/Car supplier	Ningbo Joyson Automotive
2012	Putzmeister/Concrete pumps	Sany
	Kion/Forklift and storage technlogy	Weichai Power
	ThyssenKrupp/Sheet metal divi.	Wuhan Iron& Steel
2013	ZF Friedrichshafen/Rubber+Plastic	Zhuzhou TMT
	Thielert Aircraft	AVIC (Flugzeugzulieferer)
	KHD Wedag/Engineering	AVIC
2014	Boge Elastmetall	Zhuzhou TMT
	SAG Solarstrom	Shunfeng Photovoltaic
	Sunways AG/Solar inverters	Shunfeng Photovoltaic
	Kokinetics/Car seats+locks.	AVIC
	Hilite/Gear valves+camshafts	AVIC
	Cybex/Retail.	Goodbaby International
	Columbus/Consumer goods	Goodbaby International
	Tom Tailor/Textiles	Fosun International
2015	Hazemag&EPR/Engineering	Sinoma Engineering
	WEGU/Car supplier	Zhongding Sealing Parts

---

88   "Kein Ausverkauf Deutschlands", HB 25.11.2016

89   Mercator Institute for China Studies/Rhodium Group: Chinese FDI in Europe and Germany, June 2015, p. 6

2015	Waldaschaff Automobil/Car suppl.	North Lingyun Industrial
	Jobspotting/E-commerce	Horizons Ventures
	Nordic Hotels	Jin Jing International
	LuraTechImaging/IT	Foxit Software
	Lyomark Pharma/Biotechnology	Hainan Pharma
	Bendales/Biotechnology	Hainan Pharma
	Lloyd Werft/Transport logistics	Genting Hongkong
	High Tech Gründerfonds	Donghai Securities
	Triumpf/Textiles	Hup Lon
2016	EEW/Energy prod. from waste	Beijing Enterprises
	KraussMaffei/Engineering	ChemChina
	Kuka/Robots	Midea
	Bochumer Ver./Railway wheelsets	Full Hill Enterprises
	Bilfinger/Water technology	Chengdu Techcent
	Schimmel/Pianos	Pearl River
	Smaato/Information technology	Spearhead
	Cideon/Engineering technology	China Railway Construction
2017	Bosch SG/Starters+Generators	ZMJ/CRCI
	Ista/Meter reading service	Cheung Kong Infrastructure
2018	Cotesa/Aircraft supplier	Advanced Technology
	Grammer/Car-aircraft supplier	Ningbo Jifeng

Most of the purchases (7) were made by the automotive supplier Ningbo Joyson Holding, followed by the sewing machine manufacturer Shanggong Group (5), the automotive supplier Ningbo Huaxing Electronic (5), the aircraft supplier AVIC (4) and the conglomerate Zhongding Group (4). Several thousand patents were taken over, about 700 at Kuka.[90] The acquisitions involve the complete takeover or a controlling stake; minority shareholdings with other motivations, for example at Deutsche Bank and Daimler, are not taken into account here.

In addition, globally operating companies from China have opened branches in Germany, such as Huawei (telecommunications), COSCO (container shipping) and the Industrial and Commercial Bank of China (ICBC), the largest bank in the world.

---

90 Chinas Shoppingtour in Deutschland, HB 3.11.2017; Mercator Institute ibid. p. 17

Prospects for employees and new markets

In 2016, the Chinese company Midea had bought the largest German robot manufacturer Kuka. Management, shareholders, the works council and the IG Metall trade union voted in favor of the sale. 12,000 jobs in Germany were at stake. Only China, the largest market for the production and use of robots, offers a future.[91]

In contrast to Blackstone&Co, the Chinese buyers do not offload the purchase loans onto the purchased medium-sized companies. The Chinese keep the local management in office, give long-term guarantees for the jobs and open up a large market in China. For example, the German company Kiekert was first bought by Permira in 2000, plunged into excessive debt and shrunk and then resold to new Western PE investors: Kiekert did not emerge from the crisis until 2012, when the company was taken over by Lingyun. Hundreds of new jobs were created. As a result, "managers, employees and even trade unions have become accustomed to preferring Chinese investors over private equity funds."[92]

Even the China-critical Bertelsmann Foundation attests the Chinese investors: "They bring fresh capital into the country, create and maintain jobs... (They mean) long-term commitment to the location, employment guarantees and improved access to the Chinese market."[93]

State economy?

In line with the German government and the business lobby, the "Bertelsmen" criticize the fact that state subsidies and state-owned enterprises distort competition in China. But government control is necessary if the economy as a whole and individual technologies are to be advanced.

The very Western states which rage against China's state economy, above all the USA, systematically subsidize the private sector – not to mention the social relief provided by tax waivers. In 2015 alone, US states and local governments subsidized the establishment of private companies with USD 45 billion.[94] New York alone is subsidizing a new Amazon headquarters with USD 4 billion, the

---

91   Werner Rügemer: Wenn Peking Schätze hebt, der Freitag 30.1.2017

92   Private Equity Helps Chines MNEs Beat A Path to Europe, Forbes Asia 25.3.2016

93   BertelsmannStiftung ibid. p. 5

94   Timothy Bartnik: A New Panel on Business Incentives offered by State and Local Governments in the U.S., W.E. Upjohn Institute for Employment Research, February 2017, p. 10

state of Wisconsin is subsidizing the arrival of the low-cost producer Foxconn with USD 3 billion.[95] Silicon Valley's much-admired high tech also owes its rise to state protection.

China's company purchases in the EU (excl. Germany, selection)[96]

In other EU states, too, Chinese investors purchase company stakes which enable strategic influence, allocate capital to the firm and open up the Chinese market.

Firm/Product	Country	Chinese buyer
Elkem/Special materials	Norway	China National Chemical
Syngenta/Chemicals	Switzerland	China National Chemical
Pirelli/Rubber/Chemicals	Italy	China National Chemical
GDF Suez/Exploration	France	China Investment Corp.
Energias de Portugal/Energy	Portugal	China Three Gorges
Nidera/Trade	Netherlands	Cofco Corp.
CDP Reti/Electricity grid	Italy	State Grid of China
Terna+Snam/Gas-electricity grid	Italy	State Grid of China
Ansaldo Energia/Power stati. supp.	Italy	Shanghai Electric
Avolon Holdings/Aircraft leasing	Ireland	HNA (airports)
Gategroup/Catering	Switzerland	HNA
Swissport/Airport operation	Switzerland	HNA
Supercell/Games	Finland	Tencent (Technology)
Bio Products Laboratory	England	Create Group
Punch Power Train/Car supplier	Belgium	YinYin Group
Club Méditerranée/Tourism	France	Fosun
Thomas Cook/Tourism	England	Fosun
Airport Toulouse-Blagnac	France	Symbiose
SMPC/Mode (Sandro, Maje, Pierlot)	France	Alibaba
Opera Software/Browser maker	Norway	Golden Brick Silk Road

---

95   Mitten im Westen, SZ 8.2.2019

96   Forbes Asia 25.3.2016 ibid.

Ernst&Young also confirmed that investors from the People's Republic of China are more popular and successful than US investors in the EU because the Chinese "score points in takeover battles with US companies who want to break up companies and cut jobs on a grand scale".[97]

USA and EU against China

The sale of Kuka to Midea was preceded by fierce criticism from the German government and the European Commission. They warned: German technology would be "siphoned off" to China. They hectically searched for another buyer in Europe – in vain. But the "Kuka case" prompted the European Commission to examine Chinese investments for the violation of "strategic interests".

In doing so, the EU follows the USA. In 2016, the German Minister of Economics had already granted permission for Fujian Grand Chip (FGC) to buy the German technology company Aixtron. The Aixtron shareholders had agreed, as had the management, supervisory board and works council. But US secret services intervened: The national security of the USA was endangered because of the Aixtron branch with 100 employees in California. Minister of Economics Sigmar Gabriel withdrew the already granted approval. US President Obama finally banned the sale in December 2016: The basis is the Defense Production Act of 1950, which was supposed to safeguard civil and military production for the Korean War.[98]

The media-political elite of the West criticizes US President Trump for his uncouth "unpredictability". But it nonetheless complies with his main instructions. The Chinese company Huawei leads the world in 5G technology (complex and fast mobile communication). The US government banned its use for "security reasons", the ban was instantly followed by the remaining members of the Five Eyes war coalition from World War II – the UK, Canada, Australia, New Zealand. Canada immediately arrested the Huawei Chief Financial Officer at the request of the US judiciary. The EU governments also hesitantly but obediently follow the ban, even though they cannot identify any security-relevant back doors in Huawei technology.[99]

---

97   Kaufrausch süß-sauer, HB 1.4.2016

98   Die Chinesen sollen lieber draußen bleiben, WiWo 2.1.2017

99   Hört, hört, SZ 14.12.2018

NATO impedes the development of Greenland

Greenland, located in the Arctic North Atlantic near Canada, has an area six times larger than Germany, but only 56,000 inhabitants. They live almost exclusively from fishing (halibut, cod, crabs), which accounts for 90 percent of exports.

ut Greenland is rich in natural resources: Ore, zinc, lead, uranium, oil, precious stones, rare earths. Due to its geographical and climatic location, development has so far been impossible. Individual attempts by British and Norwegian companies have not progressed. But in 2014 the Chinese mining company General Nice Group (GNG) bought the insolvent British company London Mining and its licenses in Greenland. GNG, with 12,000 employees and branches in 80 countries, is an important supplier to the global steel industry. The Greenland government pins great hopes on it.[100]

In order to extract the mineral resources and improve the infrastructure for the inhabitants, who live in 17 distant cities, the government has invited tenders for the construction and operation of three airports – at present there is only one. It is also intended to promote tourism, and roads are to be built at a later date. Eleven companies from Denmark, Canada, Iceland, the Faroe Islands and the Netherlands – and China – registered for the new airports. Greenland's Prime Minister Kim Kielsen had visited Beijing, and the Chinese applicants had the best prospects thanks to their integrated approach and favorable price.

Suddenly NATO pops up

But now the Danish and US governments are intervening. In 1941 the USA had established a military base in the Greenland colony of the Kingdom of Denmark. In 1951 Greenland was declared a NATO defense area – the US military base Thule Air Base has been steadily expanded to this day and, with several substations, monitors the Arctic region, especially Russia.

For a decade now, Greenland has no longer been a colony, but a subordinate independent state, but continues to be subject to NATO member Denmark for foreign and security policy purposes. In 2016, the Danish government wanted to sell an abandoned naval base in Greenland. When a Chinese company became interested, the Danes quickly withdrew the offer – out of consideration for the USA.

---

100 Andreas Uldum, Minister for Finance and Mineral Resources, The Government of Greenland: New strong force behind London Mining Greenland A/S, http://naalakkersuisut.gl/en 8.1.2015

The US has also raised "security" concerns because of the Chinese offers for the new airports. The USA wants to operate its military base in Greenland in peace and quiet. They also fear the expansion of the "Arctic Silk Road", a Chinese plan: Development of a port system to shorten sea routes. Behind the scenes, Danish government officials confess that the "interests of our closest ally, the USA," must be considered.[101]

Denmark as a multi-use US vassal
Throughout the whole of the 20th century the USA was keen to prevent the economic connection between the European central state Germany and Soviet Union/Russia, under whatever political constellation. At present, this is directed, among other things, against Russia's natural gas supplies to the EU.

The USA is interfering in the disputes over the Nord Stream 2 gas pipeline. Eastern European countries such as Ukraine fear the loss of transit fees if the new pipeline does not pass through their territory. The USA is pushing for a stop in Poland and Germany. They want to sell their own – more expensive – fracking gas to the EU. They are exerting pressure not only on the German companies Wintershall and Uniper, but also on Shell (British-Dutch), Engie (France) and OMV (Austria).

For example, under pressure from across the pond, little Denmark has also banned the initially approved laying of pipes along the Danish coasts. At the same time, the USA and Denmark have intensified their energy trade. And Facebook has installed its new European data center in Denmark with special privileges.[102]

Following a meeting at the end of May 2018 with US Defense Secretary Jim Mattis, the Danish Defense Minister declared: The Pentagon does not want Chinese investments in Greenland – that threatened "security". For the public it remained unclear which or whose security was at stake.[103] The Partii Naleraq, which insists on independence, left the governing coalition. Ultimately, the Danish government stepped in and is investing in Greenland's airports to keep China out.[104]

---

101 Denmark "deeply concerned" over Chinese bids to build Greenland Airports, http://www.globalconstructionreview.com 26.3.2018

102 Auf die harte Tour. Welthandel, Der Spiegel 24/2018, p. 64f.

103 Greenland's plans to build new airports gather momentum, arctictoday.com 29.5.2018

104 Werner Rügemer: Grönland – US-Militär gegen chinesischen Ausbau der Infrastruktur, www.nachdenkseiten.de 16.10.2018

Cooperative globalization: The New Silk Road

China has been investing in almost all other countries for two decades. China has become the largest trading partner for over 90 countries, including the most powerful such as the USA, Japan, Germany, Brazil and Russia.

Unlike Western countries, China does not make its investment and trade relations dependent on friend-or-foe criteria. The People's Republic is developing relations with Iran and Saudi Arabia, Israel and Palestine, Ukraine and Russia. Peaceful and inclusive globalization is the motto. While the USA is moving further and further away from the UN, China is orienting itself in principle towards UN international law: equal rights for states (e.g. also in the WTO and IMF), participation in UN peace missions, a multipolar world system, development of cooperation, no political interference.

West wins system competition (for the time being) through interventions

In a sense, China is reviving the broad movement of the "non-aligned". In 1955, states that had freed themselves from colonial dependence and fascist occupation had joined forces: The leaders were China with Zhou Enlai, Yugoslavia with Josip Tito, Indonesia with Sukarno, Egypt with Abdel Nasser, Ghana with Kwane Nkrumah and India with Jawarhal Nehru. Numerous post-colonial "developing countries" from Africa and Latin America joined up. But the US-led West removed progressive governments (Mossadegh/Persia, Sukarno, Allende/Chile, Bolivia) via a putsch, secret services murdered politicians (Lumumba/Congo, Sankara/Burkina Faso, Bishop/Grenada, Ben Barka/Morocco), dictatorships were rearmed (Haiti, Guatemala, Venezuela, Apartheid/South Africa), Argentina, Uruguay), puppet governments were established (Japan, South Vietnam, South Korea, Taiwan, Honduras, Colombia, Panama, Caribbean), reactionary government clans were bribed for favorable investments and military cooperation (Shah Reza Pahlevi/Iran, Marcos/Philippines, Suharto/Indonesia).[105] The US-led West would never have won the peaceful system competition.

In 1973, socialist and developing countries formed the G77. With their majority, the UN adopted the New International Economic Order: equitable economic relations, disarmament and recognition of the UN Charter. But the

---

105 Jason Hickel: Die Tyrannei des Wachstums. München 2018, Kapitel "Das Zeitalter der Staatsstreiche", p. 153-207

US-led West destroyed this development. In 1975, the USA, the UK, France, Japan, Italy, Canada and West Germany formed the counter-revolution with the G7; the IMF and the World Bank, together with the precursors of the new financial actors, organized the over-indebtedness of states and strong-armed privatizations and regime changes (Mexico, Brazil, Venezuela, Argentina, Egypt, Morocco, Yugoslavia, South Korea...).[106]

China's current construction of global infrastructure, the development of various regional alliances, coupled with China's economic strength and credit potential, can give a new, sustained, strategic impetus to this quashed but now reviving aspiration in many dozens of states and regions.

In addition to the development of infrastructure neglected by the West, Chinese products also offer an unbeatable advantage: technologically, they are at least as good as Western products, but simpler and, above all, much cheaper. This applies to mobile phones, for example. In the mass markets of large emerging countries such as India, Brazil and Indonesia, Huawei, Xiaomi and One Plus devices are now more popular than Apple and Samsung, and even in the USA they are about to break through.[107]

Regional and continental cooperation

With continued international investment and trade relations, China has initiated several regional and continental cooperation projects. They are adapted to the respective situation.

Shanghai Cooperation Organization (SCO)

The Shanghai Cooperation Organization (SCO) was founded in 2001 on China's initiative. As a Eurasian Union, it includes Russia, India, Pakistan, Kyrgyzstan, Tajikistan, Uzbekistan and Kazakhstan in addition to the People's Republic. About 40 percent of mankind live in these states. Mongolia, Afghanistan, Belarus and Iran were added as observer states. A further 10 states have dialogue and guest status. The founding objective was to combat terrorism and separatism, hence smaller military maneuvers are also organized.[108] In the period that followed, economic cooperation projects were added. The IMF, which has made itself unpopular, is gradually being replaced by Chinese

---

106   Ernst Wolf: Weltmacht IWF. Chronik eines Raubzugs. Marburg 2014, p. 43ff.

107   Angriff aus China, HB 2.1.2018

108   See eng.sectsco.org

lenders. While the West is burying itself militarily in Afghanistan, the SCO is developing infrastructure projects even there.[109]

BRICS

The affiliation of China with the emerging countries Brazil, India, Russia and South Africa (BRICS) is based on other common and by no means uniform interests. They represent almost half of the world's population. Since 2009, governments have been meeting in turn in the respective capitals to agree on cooperation. China has invited Egypt, Mexico, Thailand, Tajikistan and Guinea to participate.

In response to the Pacific Free Trade Agreement (TPP) initiated by Obama – now blocked by Trump anyway – China is pushing ahead with an Asia-Pacific Free Trade Area (FTAAP). The sanctions imposed by the US government under Trump not only against China but also against US allies such as the EU and Canada led to a joint protest at the 2018 BRICS meeting in South Africa: The multilateral institutions UNO and WTO and the rule of law must be strengthened.[110] In addition, government delegations from 18 African states as well as Argentina and Turkey took part in the consultations.[111]

Forum on China-Africa Cooperation (FOCAC)

Within a decade, China also became the largest trading partner for countries on the African continent. In the Forum on China-Africa Cooperation (FOCAC), founded in 2000, all countries on the continent became members, with the exception of Swaziland – the only country to maintain diplomatic relations with Taiwan. China promotes the establishment of small businesses, small textile factories and decentralized solar and biogas projects, as well as the extraction of oil and the cultivation of cotton. This is linked to the development of infrastructure. In Tanzania, for example, Chinese companies are building the rail link between the port of Dar es Salaam and neighboring Zambia. Factories are being built along the route as Sino-Tanzanian joint ventures. The 725-kilometer rail link between Addis Ababa and Djibouti is the first fully electrified line in Africa.[112]

---

109 David Noack: West- oder Ostanbindung? junge Welt 16.12.2016

110 BRICS Nations Stand Against the 'New Wave of Protectionism', https://thewire.in 5.6.2018

111 Meeting of BRICS leaders with delegation heads from invited states, en.kremlin.ru 27.7.2018

112 See www.focac.org/eng/

McKinsey feels obliged to note: The approximately 10,000 Chinese, mostly private, companies on the continent contribute to reducing the price of products and to the targeted training of managers and workers. China's investments are "extremely positive for Africa's economies, for governments and workers".[113]

Many African states are economically and politically dependent on Western states. But China shows what the way out of underdevelopment can look like. For instance, African companies can invest much more easily in China. Of late, cooperation in defense, security, counter-terrorism and arms supplies is also being intensified with 49 African states.[114]

China-CELAC Forum

On the time scale, South America is the last continent China is tapping. For important states such as Brazil, Peru, Chile and Venezuela, the People's Republic quickly became the largest trading partner.

The delay has to do with the fact that, for over a century, South America has been, and in many cases still is or is supposed to become again, the "backyard" of the USA, dominated by the military, secret services and indigenous oligarchs. The USA is once again promoting corrupt elites and right-wing radical politicians. Impoverishment and emigration, also in the direction of the USA, are the result.[115] The 33 states of South America themselves did not join forces until 2011 to form the Comunidad de Estados Latinoamericanos y Caribenos (CELAC). This is to replace the Organization of American States (OAS, based in Washington), which was founded and dominated by the USA after World War II. All states of the continent and the Caribbean are members of CELAC – with the exception of the remaining colonial territories of the Netherlands (Antilles), France (Guyana), the UK (Falklands, Cayman and Virgin Islands, Bermuda) and the USA (Bahamas), which continue to depend on their former masters and queens in foreign, trade and tax policy terms.

In 2013, US Secretary of State John Kerry announced that the era of the Monroe Doctrine was over. This only rhetorically abandoned the "backyard" status of South and Central America. The US had been criticized in several states on the continent as an obstacle to development, for example by the

---

113   The closest look yet at Chinas economic engagement in Africa, https://www.mckinsey. com, June 2017

114   Chinese defense minister meets with African guests, eng.chinamail.cn 11.7.2018

115   Kontinent der Verlierer, SZ 29.12.2018

Venezuelan government under Hugo Chavez. As early as 1997, the USA had moved its Southern Command from Panama to Miami. In 2000, after a century, Panama assumed control of the Panama Canal from the USA.

In 2014 China initiated the China-CELAC Forum. The cooperation plan adopted in 2015, which runs until 2019, regulates the various forms and forums of cooperation at the level of governments, companies and experts. A 19,000 km long high-performance submarine cable is to be laid between Chile and China. China has also invited the CELAC states to join the Asian Investment and Infrastructure Bank (AIIB).[116] However, it is not only about infrastructure, technology and finance, but also about culture, education, environmental protection and tourism.[117]

Global electricity grid
Since 2013 China's overarching international concept has been the New Silk Road. One sub-project, which had already been launched previously, is the Global Electricity Network.

The state-owned grid operator State Grid Corporation of China (SGCC) coordinates the participation in electricity grids in other countries, such as Laos, Brazil, Chile, Portugal, Italy, Spain, Greece, Mozambique, South Africa and the Philippines. SGCC is the world's second largest Fortune 500 company after Walmart.

Chinese companies have further developed the ultra-high voltage (UHV) cables produced by Siemens and Asea Brown Boveri (ABB). They are the fastest and most efficient in the world with the lowest transport loss. SGCC has already laid 37,000 kilometers in China. The cables are also installed in foreign power grids. The aim is an intercontinental power grid, in which around 100 countries participate by 2050.

At the same time, electricity production from renewable energies is being promoted. This is intended to reduce costs and environmental pollution, also by making it easier to compensate for overloading and underloading. One of the scenarios is: electricity produced in Congo by hydroelectric power will be transported to Europe by UHV.[118]

---

116 Antonio Hsiang: As America Withdraws from Latin America, China Steps in, https://thediplomat.com 4.1.2018

117 See www.chinacelacforum.org/eng

118 China's plan to connect the world, FT 8.6.2018

National and global lending

China has already invested USD 452 billion in the network from 2013 to early 2018. For the New Silk Road, which will ultimately encompass all continents, considerably more loans are needed. In addition to electrical engineering groups such as SGCC, China has a wide range of lenders. Four Chinese banks are the world's largest banks in terms of turnover.

Four Chinese banks among the world's 10 largest banks[119]

Bank	Turnover 2017 (USD trillion)
Industrial and Commercial Bank of China	4.0
China Construction Bank	3.4
Agricultural Bank of China	3.2
Bank of China	3.0
Mitsubishi UFJ Financial (Japan)	2.8
JP MorganChase (USA)	2.5
HSBC (UK)	2.5
BNP Paribas (France)	2.4
Bank of America (USA)	2.3
Crédit Agricole (France)	2.1

There is a systemic difference: Western banks have lower turnover, but a higher share value. The Chinese banks promote the real economy, including rising wages, while the Western banks deplete the real economy – especially manpower and irreplaceable resources – and use this to boost their own value.

In addition, the China Development Bank and numerous special funds finance climate, energy and agricultural projects. On China's initiative, the Asia Infrastructure Investment Bank (AIIB) was founded in 2015, China holds the blocking minority, and five dozen Asian and EU countries are involved. With the BRICS states, China founded the New Development Bank (NDB) in 2014 to liberate itself even further from the World Bank and IMF; in contrast to

---

119 These are the biggest Banks in the World, https://www.businessinsider.de, downloaded 5.6.2018

the World Bank, where the voting rights depend on the amount of the capital contribution of the states and the USA dominates, in the NDB all states have an equal vote.[120]

The Belt and Road Initiative

The New Silk Road, Belt and Road Initiative (BRI), ties in with the old Silk Road: This was a network of trade routes that have transported goods between China and the Mediterranean since ancient times. At that time, it took caravans up to two years – if they could get through at all – to cover at least 6,400 kilometers. In 2008 freight trains needed more than a month, soon they will need only 10 days between Suzhu/East China and Duisburg. Electronics produced by Hewlett-Packard and Asus in Chongqing are already being transported to Duisburg, and on the way back the container trains transport BMW parts from Leipzig to China.[121]

BRI is currently the largest economic cooperation project mankind has seen to date. It can also be viewed as a tangible alternative to the failed Western free trade concepts such as GATT and WTO.

The New Silk Road consists of two main routes, the economic belt by land and by sea. Both routes are connected by interlinking corridors, secondary routes, industrial settlements and infrastructure projects.

The overland route consists of three major freight train connections: 1. China-Mongolia-Russia, 2. New Eurasian land bridge, 3. China – Central Asia – West Asia. Other secondary lines are to branch off from them. The sea route includes the route connecting China's east coast ports with the new and modernized major port of Piraeus/Greece and with the major port of Rotterdam/Netherlands.

So far, 68 countries are involved, 23 from Europe and Eurasia, 16 from the Middle East and Africa, 13 from East and Southeast Asia, 13 from Central and South Asia – more may be added. So far, China has invested, agreed or planned about USD 1 trillion. At the same time, participating states and companies are also investing.

---

120 See https://www-ndb.in/
121 Vom Duisburger Hafenkai in die Volksrepublik, HB 30.12.2016

Silk Road projects
(selection, investment volume in USD billion)[122]

Country	Project	Invest. vol.
Pakistan	Deep sea port Gwadar+railway	54.0
Russia	Gas liquifying plant Jamal	28.2
	Petrochemical complex Wostotschny	25.2
	Eurasia high-speed train	22.6
	Gas processing plant Amur	21.8
	Gas pipeline Sila Sibiri	18.9
Kenya	Mombasa: Port+industry+transport	15.3
Malaysia	Railroad East Coast	13.1
	Deep sea port Melaka Gateway	10.2
Tanzania	Deep sea port+industry+airport+city	10.0
Egypt	Special economic zone on Golf of Suez	10.0
Myanmar	Special economic zone Kyaukphyu	10.0
Tansania	Port Bagamoyo	10.0
Ethiopia	Natural gas plant and pipeline	4.3
Saudi-Arab.	Polyester Manufacturing Complex	3.8
Portugal	Sines, Lissabon, Leixoes: Container ports	2.5
Maledives	Airport+bridge to main island	1.2

With these investments, new industries and services are also to emerge and mutual trade is to continue to grow. From the outset, the exports of the participating states to China grew faster than China's exports to these states. To date, some 200,000 new jobs have already been created in the BRI projects.[123]

Traditional Chinese medicine is also a part of this
Traditional Chinese medicine, for example, is also integrated into the Silk Road. It is increasingly being promoted in China. Two dozen centers for research and practice have already been established abroad. Comparable methods in other cultures are being experimented with, for example in connection with acupuncture and modern medical technology.

---

122   Chinas gigantisches Handelsprojekt, HB 1.6.2018

123   BRI offers new path to common prosperity, www.xinhuanet.com/english/2018-05-17

In Africa, for example, local doctors work together with Chinese "barefoot doctors" to develop the connection with African medicinal herb treatment. They cooperate with the international organization "Doctors without Borders". At the Center for Traditional Chinese Medicine at the University of Guangzhou, research is being conducted into how the immune system can be strengthened in the case of AIDS. The development has also gained attention in the established public after the pharmacologist Tu Youyou was awarded the Nobel Prize for Medicine in 2015 – she is researching the treatment of malaria using old methods.[124]

Eastern and Southern Europe
In the 1990s, after the break-up of Yugoslavia and the collapse of the other socialist states, the EU launched various plans for economic reconstruction in Eastern and Southern Europe. At their 1994 conference, which was deliberately held in Crete, the EU transport ministers defined "priority corridors" for modernized railway connections with the accompanying extension of roads and waterways.

But these plans came to almost nothing. The austerity policy imposed by the Troika contributed to this, as did the lack of interest on the part of the new financial players: something new had to be built up before it could be exploited according to the BlackRock, Blackstone & Co method. Individual "lighthouses" were placed in the landscape, such as the pay highways built by the US Bechtel group in Croatia, but they contribute to Croatia's permanent over-indebtedness. Across the country, infrastructure is decaying. Millions of migrant workers are fleeing the neglected EU periphery. Apart from providing low-wage workers, it is only good for accommodating new Amazon and NATO bases. The special economic zones promoted by the EU are pressed into permanent underdevelopment, politically supported primarily by nationalist-right-wing radical parties, which the EU itself describes as corrupt, but promotes in order to sweep away socialism.[125]

A particularly striking case is Ukraine after the "colorful revolution" promoted by the USA, NATO and the EU: "IMF, World Bank and EU are supporting the corrupt system in Ukraine with billions in loans".[126]

---

124 China strengthens TCM cooperation with Belt and Road countries, www.xinhuanet. com/english/2017-12-23

125 Stiefkinder des Kontinents, Der Spiegel 26/2017; Jaroslav Fiala: The rule of the market in East-Central Europe is absolute, http://political critique.org 28.7.2016

126 Neuer Sündenfall in Kiew, SZ 21.12.2018

Greece

Greece is one of the countries killed by EU and Western financial actor auster-ity. The EU has indeed forced Greece to privatize the major port of Piraeus in order to repay credit and interest to Western banks. But the EU and Western financial actors were not interested in modernizing and expanding the port. That is why China is the only one to come to the rescue so far. The Chinese shipping group COSCO is alone in investing in the port (which it has leased for 35 years).

Although it was the largest European passenger port, it was decrepit and had no railway connection. COSCO has been modernizing it since 2008, re-newing its logistics and incorporating it into international trade and the new Silk Road through two new container terminals. Since then, the number of containers handled annually has risen from 880,000 to four million, and by 2022 it is expected to be 7.2 million.[127]

The products manufactured in China by foreign and Chinese compa-nies – Hewlett Packard, Sony, Huawei, ZTE – are now distributed to Europe via the port. Hewlett Packard has set up a new European distribution center here. COSCO has also put three new dry docks into operation where ships are maintained and repaired. New jobs are being created.[128]

Global port network

In Greece, the expansion of the ports of Thessaloniki, Kavala and Alexan-dropoli is part of the Silk Road project. They will be connected to the Bulgar-ian Black Sea ports of Varna and Burgas and the inland port of Ruse on the Danube. The Silk Road also includes two existing inland canals, which are to be connected and thus extended: The Danube-Oder-Elbe Canal and the Dan-ube-Aegean Canal (with Serbia and Macedonia). The planned Eurasia Canal will connect the Caspian Sea with the Black Sea.

The International Association of Ports and Harbors, founded in 1955 in the USA, now based in Japan and with 180 ports in 90 countries, praised the Silk Road at its last conference in Baku, Azerbaijan. The next conference will take place in 2019 in Guangzhou/China.[129]

---

127   Neue Ära im Containerterminal Cosco Piräus, Österreichische Verkehrszeitung 12.2.2018

128   Neue Seidenstraße: China baut seinen Einfluss in Europa aus, Deutsche Wirtschaftsnach-richten 4.3.2018

129   IAPH Conference in Baku, the pearl of Caspian, makes a new record, https://www.iaph-worldreports 17.5.2018

Greece in the European electricity grid

SGCC acquired a 24 percent stake in the Greek network operator ADMIE. For a decade, SGCC has been procuring loans worth billions to connect the numerous Greek islands to electricity production on the mainland via submarine cables. At the same time, ADMIE is already connected to the electricity grids of neighboring countries Albania, North Macedonia, Bulgaria, Turkey and Italy. Networking with Cyprus, Israel and North Africa is planned. ADMIE thus acts as a hub in Europe for the Global Electricity Network.[130] The state-owned Shenhua Group has acquired a 75 percent stake in four Greek wind farms and plans to expand them further.[131]

The Silk Road projects also include bringing together well-trained Greek technicians and engineers in the Lefkippos and Patras science parks and several technology parks such as those in Thessaloniki and Crete.

EU/NATO: Greece as geopolitical outpost

For the alliance between the EU, the USA and NATO, reaffirmed as "for eternity" by Commission President Juncker,[132] the military integration of Greece has priority. In 2018 Greek President Prokopis Pavlopoulos, for example, was delighted with "the geopolitical upgrading" of his impoverished country: "Greece is much stronger at NATO level in terms of fulfilling its mission than it was just a few years ago".[133]

Balkans: Excitement in the EU

Although the EU had already planned the construction of the new railway line between Budapest and Belgrade, nothing came of it either. The Chinese Export-Import Bank is now granting Hungary a two billion loan. This high-speed line will also be connected to the port of Piraeus. Chinese companies are also financing and building an east-west tangent in North Macedonia, the public transport network in the capital Skopje and a power station in Serbia.

---

130 State Grid Purchases a Stake at ADMIE, www.sgcc.com.cn 21.6.2017

131 Chryssa Liaggou: Shenhua joins power market through deal with PPC, Copelouzos, ekatherimi.com 2.11.2017

132 Interview zum Treffen mit US-Präsident Trump in ARD 27.7.2018, Protokoll in www.nachdenkseiten.de 30.7.2018

133 Griechische Botschaft Berlin: Griechenland ist ein ausgestreckter Außenposten des Westens und der EU im Osten, Pressemitteilung 1.7.2018

Since 2012, China has been gathering Central and Eastern European countries annually for an investment conference with the 16+1 platform. It takes place in turn in one of the capitals. The five still non-EU states Albania, Montenegro, Serbia, Bosnia-Herzegovina and Macedonia as well as the 11 EU member states Poland, the Czech Republic, Slovakia, Bulgaria, Romania, Hungary, Croatia, Slovenia and the three Baltic states attend the meetings. Several hundred entrepreneurs and experts from both sides take part. In addition to infrastructure projects, tourism and cultural projects are agreed. China is increasingly purchasing agricultural products here.[134]

EU leaders could by rights be content that their impoverished member states are being lifted out of underdevelopment. But since 2017, the EU has suddenly become extremely worried. "Beijing is using the internal weakness of the EU to exercise power in eastern Europe," write German alpha journalists.[135] They ignore the fact that the EU itself is responsible for underdevelopment in Eastern Europe – Serbia was bombed and conquered by NATO, socialism and its remains were destroyed: mission accomplished. In early 2018, EU Commissioner Juncker hastily travelled to these countries to keep China out with financial promises.

Peaceful, equitable and cooperative globalization

The Chinese leadership is sticking to the concept of "globalization". The affiliations initiated by China – SCO, FOCA, China-CELAC Forum, 16+1 – confirm that a multipolar world order is possible and beneficial for all participants.

Multipolar world order or America First

This is at odds with the USA's approach: it practices the claim of the "sole superpower". It also manifests itself in key concepts such as America First, national interest and God's own country. It is constitutionally anchored in the fact that the country is the only major country that does not have a foreign ministry, but a State Department.

This ministry was and is the state-organized center for the integration of foreign territories and states first into the US state (conquering expansion of the founding state in North America – except Canada, which remained in the British sphere of influence) and then for different forms of penetration

---

134   See www.china-ceec./org/eng/

135   China macht sich Osteuropa gefügig, SZ 28.11.2017

or inclusion into US territory. This claim was enforced by genocide, investments, treaties, alliances, wars, first on North American territory, then with
wars and regime changes in Central America and the Caribbean, then in the
Pacific (Philippines, various islands). The claim was first formalized as official
government policy by the Monroe Doctrine in 1823: in the overall area, which
was called "America", foreign powers – at that time aimed at Europe – are not
allowed to intervene, here only the state of the USA prevails. Hitler's crown
lawyer, Carl Schmitt, had formulated this with the formula "prohibition of
intervention for foreign powers" in the same sense. After the Second World
War, the claim was ultimately extended to the whole world.

As described above, the claim also manifests itself at present in the name
of "national interest" when military bases are operated around the globe,
when the UN is neutralized or lied to in the event of military intervention,
and when extraterritorial punishments are carried out against foreign companies, states and individuals. According to the UN Charter, however, "national interest" consists precisely in respecting the national interests of other
nations as equal.

China: Rise and globalization without military accompaniment

Since its existence as a state, China has behaved in the opposite way. For two
millennia, China had no foreign ministry, not to mention a state department.
China did not conquer foreign territories. Only after the European colonial
powers and the USA, which invaded China in the 19th century and opened up
China as a market for opium, textiles, railway investments, mineral exploitation and Christian missionaries with unilateral free trade agreements (Open
Door Policy) and the military and in 1901 established an "overriding government" with their ambassadors in Beijing, did the Chinese government set up
an equivalent authority.[136]

Only when the USA under President Obama rearmed against China with
its strategic pivot of its military engagement to "Asia" did the People's Republic
follow suit, but limited to its immediate neighborhood and in the sense of
defending its territory. While US warships patrol in Asia and near China, not
a single Chinese warship patrols near the US. While the USA has established
more and more military bases in China's immediate neighborhood, China
does not operate a single military base in the vicinity of the US.

---

136 Reinhard: Die Unterwerfung der Welt loc.cit., p. 866ff.

Incidentally: It is not only today that China renounces military operations and coups abroad. China's economic rise – both before and after the socialist revolution – was also possible without wars, military interventions and coups in other states – in contrast to US-led Western capitalism, which was only able to expand further with the help of wars, coups, regime change, media and secret service interference. And intends to do so in the future as well.

IV.
Present and Future of Earthly Society

Between the two great political-economic antipodes USA and China, each respectively entwined in their own international relations and alliances, the dominant dynamic of today's earthly society has developed.

The two antipodes embody the opposing developmental logics: On the one hand, Western capitalist democracy led by the USA, whose economically meaningful performance continues to shrink and which is mercilessly using and destroying more and more human labor and nature; violating international law and most human rights; which at the same time is already armed to the teeth globally and continues to arm itself lucratively as well as dishonestly, and, apart from the smaller wars, is preparing for possible military conflict with China and, above all, Russia. On the other hand, China's communist-led capitalism, aspiring for economic and social sustainability, which acts in accordance with international law, is catching up on human rights, sustainably creates mass incomes, promotes environmentally-friendly products and technologies, is rearming only in a militarily defensive sense and is endeavoring to help shape a multipolar world order.

The EU will play an important role in how this major conflict unfolds: Will it gradually be able to loosen its even deeper dependence on the US as a result of the new financial players? Does it wish to establish itself between the two antipodes as a new second-tier imperial power?

The course and outcome of the system conflict, which plays out in many very different venues and processes, will also be shaped by how the emerging countries and practically every state on earth behave – as well as the diverse terrestrial civil society, whose importance and responsibility is growing.

The aggressive decline of US capitalist democracy
The new US-dominated financial players and their civilian private army have intensified transatlantic capital integration. They are exploiting and squander-

ing the economic substance created so far, siphoning off short-term profits and hiding them in the parallel society of financial havens. Full employment, over-all economic development, the welfare state, nature conservation, democracy, human rights, responsibility and transparency are at best demagogic rhetoric. The anti-democratic transformation of the "western community of values" to-wards an even more aggressive imperialism – internally and externally – is being promoted unintentionally and intentionally, partly consciously, partly in systemic self-blindness.

The current US President Trump, in the most prominent position that Western capitalism has to offer, embodies the human behavior explicitly and above all implicitly promoted by the new financial players as well as by the got-rich-quick billionaires of the second and third generations: Autocratic ful-filment of the capitalist entrepreneur's life, combined optionally with racism, sexism, nationalism, also avowed Christianity, i.e. all forms of populism, as well as with the targeted violation of international law, for example with the threat of the use of the atomic bomb, with worldwide drone executions and with the bombardment of Yemen by Saudi Arabia, the accomplice armed by the West; be it in the permanent oppression of the Palestinian people by the nationalist, racist, fundamental-religious and terrorist state of Israel, in fla-grant breach of international law and human rights.[1]

Systemic human rights violations

Prompted by the Trump presidency, the Human Rights Council of the UN summarized in 2018 the current situation of human rights in the USA: The Trump milieu operates entirely within the previous form of government. Pre-vious US administrations also doggedly refused to recognize social and eco-nomic human rights, including the rights to education, health care and social protection. The US is also the only state that has not ratified the UN Conven-tion on the Rights of the Child.[2]

The USA has produced by far the highest income inequality of all OECD countries. The wealthy are the most socially irresponsible by international standards. Five decades of poverty reduction programs have not reduced pov-erty, on the contrary: the USA has the highest poverty rate among the "de-

---

1   Werner Rügemer: Lumpenproletariat der High Society, in: Melodie & Rhythmus 2/2017

2   United Nations, General Assembly. Human Rights Council loc.cit., p. 5f. The report does not explicitly address the non-ratification by US governments of 195 of the 207 ILO labor rights.

veloped" countries, millions of US citizens actually live in "absolute poverty under Third World conditions". Poor women are particularly often deprived of health services. The indigenous minorities are even more severely affected by poverty, unemployment and early death than the much-discriminated blacks and Latinos. "Infant mortality rate, at 5.8 deaths per 1,000 births, is much higher than in the other OECD countries" – and at the same time: "Punishing and imprisoning the poor is the typical American answer to poverty in the 21st century".[3]

In the USA, for example, there is the highest youth unemployment and the highest infant mortality rate among all OECD states (also in comparison to demonized Cuba). The majority of US citizens live shorter and sicker lives, the proportion of obese is the highest, as is the proportion of prison inmates. Military expenditure is increased, but important aid is denied to veterans who have returned home.

The poor and non-whites (including the homeless and former prisoners) are prevented from voting far more than in other countries. In 2016, only 64 percent of eligible voters were registered; residents of Puerto Rico, which belongs to the United States, are only allowed to vote fictitiously. Thus, this extreme social inequality and contempt for the poor also leads to the "capture of state power by a small group of economic elites".[4]

These elites of the superpower they themselves have weakened economically and morally at the same time keep other states and regions underdeveloped and increasingly seek the way out in military aggressions in breach of international law. On the border with Mexico, refugees from all over South and Central America are discriminated against, detained, imprisoned or actually allowed in and then humiliated anew in the USA as illegally held, blackmailed low-wage earners.

Human rights and international law in the EU

In some respects, things still look better in the EU than in the US. But EU leaders never dare to point a finger at the real situation in their leading power. And with the advance of the new financial players and their civilian private army into the EU as an economic and political location, with the welfare state and labor law "reforms" and with the intensified investment of Western European

---

3   United Nations ibid, p. 18

4   ibid., p. 19

corporations in the USA, the EU has become even more integrated into the dumping mechanism of downward alignment than before.

The political, legal and moral plight in the EU part of the "western community of values" also consists in the fact that, although there is superficial grumbling about some of Trumpkins' personal characteristics, the new financial actors and their civilian private army are not regulated; they are promoted by the European Commission, played down and pampered by governments and leading media. Some well-known US companies such as Apple receive a small rap on the knuckles for tax evasion, some like Google are sometimes hit with a cartel fine – but, all told, the Silicon Valley hype is enthusiastically adopted.

In the "trade war", unleashed by Trump first against China and then against the EU, the nationalists on both sides of the Atlantic are at loggerheads. The transatlantic capital links and the complex internationalization of supply chains show that the haggling is largely a populist theatrical thunder for the respective electoral donkeys. Thus, in July 2018, the President of the EU Commission and the US President agreed on declarations of intent essentially in favor of the USA (increased purchase of fracking gas and soybeans) and on a common front against China. The Western European vassal leader celebrated this as a victory, because the humiliation was carried out in very friendly fashion and crowned with a brotherly kiss. At the same time, the first-order vassals – the EU, Canada and Japan – are moving closer together.[5]

As much as EU officials criticize Trump's planned defensive wall against refugees from Mexico (occasionally, outside Washington), the wall that is being erected around the EU fortress is far more lethal. Thousands of refugees are mercilessly allowed to drown in the Mediterranean Sea and brutally imprisoned in failed states like Libya, which have been reduced to such with the aid of the USA itself. The humanitarian achievement that people must be rescued from distress at sea without regard for their person is being ruthlessly thrown overboard.

Despite all the superficial, sometimes hefty criticism of US governments by EU leaders, the superiority of the superpower's military and secret services remains untouched. International law, agreed in the UN Charter (prohibition of violence, non-interference), is systematically violated by the USA and US-led "coalitions of the willing". The EU concurs with the fake enemy image "Russia/ Putin" as well as the US-led deployment in Eastern Europe. The USA's targets

---

5   EU and Japan sign landmark political and trade agreements, eeas.europa.eu, 17.7.2018

for an increase in the "defense" budget are also fulfilled, both inside as well as outside NATO.[6]

The founding lie of NATO is being perpetuated: The Soviet Union neither wanted nor was able to occupy Western Europe, nor does Russia want to or can do so. Moreover, Western Europe is not only an integral part of US-led NATO, but is also peppered with additional US military bases, and new ones are constantly being added – first and foremost in Germany with its dozen main US military bases and their numerous outposts, which are also integrated in the US global strategy. In 2017, the Academic Service of the German Bundestag had to admit that it only has "incomplete data" on this and that it receives no response to inquiries submitted to the US Department of Defense and the US armed forces.[7]

Aggression in decline

The attackers disguise themselves as those being attacked. The message from the expansion of NATO after the collapse of socialism after 1990: The West is not concerned with the establishment of democracy in Russia, but with the domination of Eurasia from Lisbon to Vladivostok: this is what the security advisor of several US presidents, Brzezinski, declared publicly as early as 1996. At that time, he had already described Ukraine as the decisive intermediate step, and the European NATO members were naturally regarded as "American vassals". With gushing approval, the German Foreign Minister Hans-Dietrich Genscher had written the foreword to the German edition of Brzezinski's book.[8]

Leading political figures in the EU publicly hush up and in practice promote the transatlantic integration of capital and the transnational capitalist class organized by the new financial players, including low-wage labor and the systemic transfer of property rights to financial havens, the resulting impoverishment of population majorities and the promotion of extremely anti-democratic policies. The tolerated and promoted advance of BlackRock & Co, Blackstone & Co, Amazon & Co, McKinsey & Co in the EU has led to the moral discrediting of the hitherto self-proclaimed "people's" parties – whether

---

6   Daniele Ganser: Illegale Kriege. Wie die NATO-Länder die UNO sabotieren. Zürich 2016

7   Deutscher Bundestag, Wissenschaftlicher Dienst: Die Entwicklung der Personalstärke der US-Streitkräfte in Deutschland, WD2-3000-009/17, p. 12

8   Werner Rügemer: NATO – Die Gründungslüge. www.nachdenkseiten.de 4.4.2018; Zbigniew Brzezinski: Die einzige Weltmacht. Weinheim/Berlin 1996, p. 58 and 81 (Ukraine)

Christian, conservative, bourgeois or social democratic – and the capitalist democracy they represent.

Following the integration of Ukraine into the Western system of NATO and EU, the aggression continues. Russia is now enemy number one. To the public, Emmanuel Macron, Angela Merkel, Jean-Claude Juncker, and other EU governments, including those of the peripheral states in Eastern Europe and the Balkans, reproduce their respective variants of "America first". They also populistically simulate the respective "national interest". German politicians and opinion makers in particular also cultivate EU nationalism: "Our national German interest has a name: Europe", said the German Foreign Minister.[9] The result is rearmament within NATO and additionally within the EU.

Economic contraction. Self-enrichment of the rich and at the same time impoverishment and job and life insecurity for the majority of the population, more money for arms and international military action: In this way, the primary populists of the disintegrating "people's" parties, who have ruled up to now, are also promoting the new nationalist secondary populism and, together with it, discriminating against those who work for international understanding and unwavering democracy.

The peaceful rise of the People's Republic of China

The USA initially demonized and fought against the People's Republic of China after its foundation. Then, under President Richard Nixon and his security advisor Henry Kissinger, the USA tried to exploit China as a counterweight to the even more demonized Soviet Union, which at the time was economically and militarily stronger. Then the communist reformers adopted capitalism. US corporations, then other Western companies, used China's low wages and its huge market to maximize profits.

The representatives of Western capitalism attempted to set China's underdevelopment in stone – through the CoCom embargo, by excluding the country from trade agreements and, until 2001, from the WTO, and then, for example, through resistance to the new Chinese labor law. But after the self-blindness fueled by profit and power, the West now has to admit with astonishment: The People's Republic has acquired its own development logic from Western capitalist practices and, with approval on all continents, is expanding it further around the globe.

---

9   "Trump darf uns nicht spalten", https://www.auswaertiges-amt.de 19.7.2018

China has thus achieved something that no other developing and emerging country has achieved. All these countries have been overrun with outsourced cheap production and raw material extraction by Western capitalist corporations, but all these countries remain, to varying degrees, underdeveloped (measured by their potential) and dependent. Here the lowest wages are stagnating, in China labor income is rising exponentially.

The People's Republic of China can thus act as a natural ally and essential co-organizer for the aspirations of these countries for independence and economic development. This applies not only to the post-colonial dependent states of Africa and to some extent also to the Latin American states of the traditional US backyard, but even to the impoverished regions of the EU periphery, in Greece, Portugal, Eastern Europe and the Balkans.

In contrast to the West, this type of globalization is not accompanied by military interventions of a direct and indirect nature, nor by the establishment of military bases.

State capitalism – but how?

The People's Republic of China is criticized by the West as "state capitalism". This criticism also applies, in a moderate form, to the states of India, Russia, South Africa and Brazil as soon as they stand up for state sovereignty, workers' rights and regulation of foreign investors. The US secret services assume this: Today's system conflict no longer takes place between capitalism and socialism, but between two forms of capitalism: the superior "liberal capitalism" of the West and the "state capitalism" of China and the BRICS states. This is what the 2008 report "Global Trends 2025" of the combined US secret services says. It contained the guidelines for the newly elected US President Barack Obama.[10]

This position has also been endorsed by "critics of globalization", "human rights activists" and "leftists" in the West. But this overlooks key factors:

1. Western capitalism itself embodies excessive state capitalism. The state organizes the degrading low-wage labor, lets private companies violate labor laws millions of times over, tolerates and promotes tax evasion by wealthy individuals and companies, tolerates and promotes the poisoning of its own

---

10   National Intelligence Council (NIC): Global Trends 2025, Washington November 2008, www.dni.gov/nic/NIC_2025_project.html

population through the burning of lignite and diesel in favor of the respective private corporations, maintains secret services and the military from taxpayers' money for international interventions and to secure private investment and raw materials. Western states organize binational and multinational trade agreements with unilateral protection for private investors.

The US State Department, the Treasury Department and the US Embassies are primarily staffed by entrepreneurs, their representatives and consultants in executive positions and act worldwide as representatives of US corporations. High technology à la Silicon Valley owes its rise not least to the state, the military and the secret services.

Since its inception the European Commission's extensive, highly paid, tax and legally privileged bureaucracy has safeguarded the interests of private companies in the EU and worldwide, but not those of dependent employees and consumers. And the EU states launch programs worth billions to promote business, for example in digitalization and artificial intelligence. Central EU states such as Luxembourg and the Netherlands organize tax flight for wealthy individuals and corporations.

Thus, a form of state capitalism prevails in the West, in which the state, its administrative apparatus, as well as its governmental and political operations are characterized by private capitalist interests.[11]

2. The criticism of China as "state capitalism" suppresses the fact that the state has a different quality. It is not based on capitalist interests, but on a socialist revolution. The state is not led by capitalists and capitalist-financed, promoted parties and politicians, but by a communist party. China's capitalism is communist-led, in the interests of the majority of the population. Logically, this includes the fundamental interest in maintaining world peace.

This does not mean that this state always has to be absolutely right. Other states, governments and movements do not have to imitate this if they can achieve their goals differently. And in China no final state has been reached anyway, class struggle is underway here as well. Even after a socialist revolution, a just and peaceful society does not fall from the sky or as a gift from the casket of grace of Western imperialism.

---

11   Werner Rügemer: Die Privatisierung des Staates. Das Vorbild USA und sein Einfluss in
      der EU, in: Ullrich Mies / Jens Wernicke: Fassaden-Demokratie und tiefer Staat. Wien
      2017, p. 111-124

Joint development

The US-led West would have long since lost the race of systems if it had not for a century, through coups, wars and the support of anti-democratic regimes and movements on all continents, obtained short-term and brutal advantages and historical breathing space. But the zenith of this imperialism, which for three decades has been further enhanced by neoliberalism, has passed.

Humanity must free itself from this development logic, which still prevails on a large area of the earth. This might seem impossible. But we, the majority of states, populations and people, must declare that this claim is reasonable and self-evident. Otherwise we will not survive.

As a consequence of the Second World War, the states capable of international action at that time founded the United Nations (UN) and laid down the principles of action in the UN Charter and the Declaration of Universal Human Rights – including labor and social rights. Peacekeeping, economic development, humanitarian aid, for example for refugees – the system was further expanded with numerous sub-organizations, for example for business and culture. As the only universally recognized body of international law, it is mankind's greatest political achievement to date. Today, all 193 states of the world are members.

However, from the start this system was and is weakened and undermined by the USA as required and, since 2000, has been instrumentalized through the Global Compact of Western corporations, in which the new financial players dominate.[12] This must be changed. It is important to return to the beginnings in the sense of the multipolar, peaceful, post-colonial, democratic world order established in the UN. The majority of UN members manifest this through resolutions, such as the prohibition of nuclear bombs in 2016.

International relations, including trade organizations and bi-national and multinational trade treaties and military alliances, must be reviewed on the basis of the UN Charter and universal human rights.[13]

To this end, many people in civil societies are organizing themselves in accordance with these values, increasingly outside established forms of organization. Thus, as described above, progress in the employment relationships of

---

12   UN Global Compact in der Kritik, https://www.global-ethic-now.de, abgerufen 15.6.2018

13   Cf. Andreas Fischer-Lescano: Globalverfassung. Die Geltungsbegründung der Menschenrechte. Weilerswist 2005; Norman Paech: Aktionsfeld Weltinnenpolitik. Völkerrechtliche Grundlagen einer global governance. Hamburg 2003

the People's Republic of China was not achieved by trade unions, but primarily through grassroots initiatives and spontaneous strikes. In the USA and on all continents, for example, employees of the large platform corporations are organizing themselves with the trade unions and, if necessary, without them. In the movements against free trade agreements, hundreds of thousands have recognized the unjust practices of globalization to date. The initiatives for alternative energies, women's rights, disarmament and the reception of refugees are uncounted and mostly still internationally uncoordinated.

Admittedly, these initiatives are currently powerless against the regimes promoted by the new financial players. That is why governments must either be forced or replaced in order to take the necessary decisions. That sounds hopeless today, but here too we must declare such claims to be reasonable and self-evident: Regulation of the new financial players, including a ban on socially harmful financial products and corporate practices; the use of new technologies to drastically reduce and fairly distribute working hours and workloads; the dissolution of the criminogenic parallel society of financial havens; the taxation of large capitalist private profits and the operation of a public infrastructure that benefits all citizens; a ban on parallel private justice and the expansion of the rule of law; a ban on products and production processes that are harmful to the environment and the climate; and, above all, the cessation of all military and secret service operations and operations that contravene international law: Disarmament, abolition of nuclear bombs, creation of collective security systems to end and prevent wars.

The conflicts of US-led Western capitalism with the People's Republic and its alliances have only just really begun, also in the USA, in Europe, on all continents. History has yet to unfold, and all of us on this earth are involved, wherever we live and wherever we flee to.

Ultimate question

"Do we have to save humanity?" The answer to this popular and wrongly posed question is: No, we don't have to save humanity. There are people we don't have to save. And who are "we"? Those who stand up for human rights, international law, democracy – we are the ones who must join forces.

List of Abbreviations

AI	Artificial Intelligence
ARPA	Advanced Research Project Agency (Pentagon agency)
ARPANET	Advanced Research Project Agency Network (Internet precursor)
AUM	Assets under Management
AWS	Amazon Web Services (cloud service)
Bafin	Bundesaufsichtsamt für Finanzdienstleistungen (German supervisory authority for financial services)
BCG	Boston Consulting Group
BRI	Belt and Road Initiative ("New Silk Road")
BRICS	Brazil Russia India China South Africa
CELAC	Comunidad de Estados Latinoamericanos y Caribenos
CEO	Chief Executive Officer
CFIUS	Commission on Foreign Investment in the US
CFR	Council on Foreign Relations
CIA	Central Intelligence Agency
DARPA	Defense Advanced Research Project Agency
DAX	Deutscher Aktienindex (German stock index)
DGAP	Deutsche Gesellschaft für ad hoc-Publizität (German Society for ad hoc publicity)
ECB	European Central Bank
ETF	Exchange Traded Fund
EU	European Union
EY	Ernst&Young
FDI	Foreign Direct Investment
FAS	Frankfurter Allgemeine Sonntagszeitung
FAZ	Frankfurter Allgemeine Zeitung
FT	Financial Times
FOCAC	Forum China Africa-Cooperation
GAMFA	Google Apple Microsoft Facebook Amazon

GATT	General Agreement on Tariffs and Trade
HB	Handelsblatt
HNWI	High-net-worth Individuals
ILO	International Labor Organization
IMF	International Monetary Fund
KfW	Kreditanstalt für Wiederaufbau (Credit Institute for Reconstruction – German state-owned bank)
M&A	Mergers and Acquisitions
NAFTA	North American Free Trade Agreement (USA-Mexico-Canada)
NSA	National Security Agency
NYT	New York Times
PAC	Political Action Committee (corporate donations for politicians)
PE	Private Equity
PPP	Public Private Partnership
PWC	PricewaterhouseCoopers
SE	Societas Europaea (plc according to EU law)
SEC	Security Exchange Commission
S&P	Standard & Poor's (Rating agency)
SCO	Shanghai Cooperation Organization
SPON	Spiegel Online
SZ	Süddeutsche Zeitung
UHNWI	Ultra High-net-worth Individuals
WiWo	Wirtschaftswoche
WTO	World Trade Organization

Bibliography

Azar, José u.a.: Anti-Competitive Effects of Common Ownership, Ross School of Business Papers Nr. 1235, July 5, 2016

Béchat, Jean-Paul / Felix Rohatyn: The Future of the Transatlantic Defense Community. Final Report of the CSIS Commission on Transatlantic Security and Industrial Cooperation in the Twenty-First Century, Washington D.C. 2003

Bergmann, Theodor: Der chinesische Weg, Hamburg 2017

Bertelsmann-Stiftung: Chance und Herausforderung. Chinesische Direktinvestitionen in Deutschland, Gütersloh 2016

Bianco, Anthony: WalMart. The Bully of Bentonville. How the High Cost of Everyday Low Prices is Hurting America, New York 2007

Bobsin, Rainer: Finanzinvestoren in der Gesundheitsversorgung in Deutschland. 20 Jahre Private Equity, Hannover 2018

Boston Consulting Group /ciett: Adaptation to Change, Bruxelles 2012

Brummer, Alex: Britain for Sale. British Companies in Foreign Hands, London 2012

Brzezinski, Zbginiew: Die einzige Supermacht. Amerikas Strategie der Vorherrschaft, Weinheim/Berlin 1996

Buchter, Heike: Blackrock. Eine heimliche Weltmacht greift nach unserem Geld, Frankfurt/Main 2015

Celarier, Michelle: How a Misfit Group of Computer Geeks and English Majors Transformed Wall Street, New York Magazin 1/2018

Corporate Europe Observatory: Accounting for Influence. How the Big Four are embedded in EU policy making on tax avoidance, Brussels July 2018

Däubler, Wolfgang: Arbeitsrecht in China, www.nachdenkseiten.de 29.11.2012

Déléan, Michel / Dan Israel: Ubérisation – une enquete judiciaire ouverte sur Deliveroo, www.mediapart.fr 7.6.2018

Deutscher Bundestag: Umfang und Standorte der in Deutschland stationierten US-Streitkräfte, WD 2-3000-005/17, 18. Januar 2017

Engdahl, William: Manifest Destiny. Democracy as Cognitive Dissonance, Wiesbaden 2018

Europäische Kommission: Europäische Agenda für die kollaborative Wirtschaft, COM (2016) 356 final

Financial Crisis Inquiry Commission: The Financial Crisis Inquiry Report, New York 2011

Fisher, Stanley: The Federal Reserve and the Global Economy, Washington 11.10.2014

Foschepoth, Josef: Überwachtes Deutschland, Göttingen 2014

Geffken, Rolf / Can Cui: Das chinesische Arbeitsvertragsgesetz, mit Kommentar, 5. Auflage Cadenberge 2016

Gospel, Howard u.a. (Hg.): Financialization, New Investment Funds and Labour, Oxford University Press 2014

Gross, James: Broken Promise. The Subversion of U.S. Labor Relations Policy 1947 – 1994, Philadelphia 2003

Hill, Steven Hill: Die Start up-Illusion, München 2017

Jakobs, Hans-Jürgen: Wem gehört die Welt? Die Machtverhältnisse im globalen Kapitalismus, München 2016

Jowett, Paul / Francoise Jowett: Private Equity. The German Experience, New York / London 2011

Jugel, Stefan (Hg.): Private Equity Investments, Wiesbaden 2003

Kimball, Will / Robert Scott: China Trade, Outsourcing and Jobs. Economic Policy Institute, Washington 11.12.2014

Kodres, Laura: What's Shadow Banking? in: Finance and Development (IMF), June 2013

KPMG Tax Advisers: International Tax Planning Made in Luxemburg 2003, Luxembourg 2003

Krüger, Uwe: Meinungsmacht. Eine kritische Netzwerkanalyse, Köln 2013

Kuczyinski, Jürgen: Gesellschaften im Untergang. Vergleichende Niedergangsgeschichte vom Römischen Reich bis zu den Vereinigten Staaten von Amerika. Köln 1984

McKinsey Global Institute (MGI): Offhsoring. Is It a Win-Win Game? San Francisco 2003

Ders.: What the future of work will mean for jobs, skills and wages, November 2017

McKinsey: Das Krankenhaus der Zukunft. Healthcare Systems and Services 2016

Murray, Georgina / John Scott: Financial Elites and Transnational Business. Who Rules the World? Cheltenham / Northampton 2012

Oppong, Marvin: Verdeckte PR in Wikipedia. Das Weltwissen im Visier von Unternehmen. Frankfurt/Main 2014

Panitch, Leo / Sam Gindin: The Making of Global Capitalism. The Political Economy of the American Empire, London / New York 2013

Pauwels, Jacques: Big Business avec Hitler, Bruxelles 2013

Pincon, Michel / Monique Pincon-Charlot: La Violence des Riches, Paris 2013

Price Waterhouse Coopers: A beginner's guide to privatization, May 2013

Rosenberg, David: Israels Technology Economy, London 2018

Rainer Roth: Sklaverei als Menschenrecht, Frankfurt/Main 2017

Rügemer, Werner: Neue Technik – alte Gesellschaft. Silicon Valley, Köln 1984

Ders.: Cross Border Leasing. Ein Lehrstück zur globalen Enteignung der Städte, Münster 2005

Ders.: Investitionen ohne Arbeitsplätze, WSI-Mitteilungen 1/2005, p. 49-54

Ders.: Der Bankier. Ungebetener Nachruf auf Alfred von Oppenheim, Frankfurt/Main 2006 (3. geschwärzte Ausgabe)

Ders.: arm und reich, Bielefeld 2009

Ders.: "Heuschrecken" im öffentlichen Raum. Public Private Partnership – Anatomie eines globalen Finanzinstruments, Bielefeld 2. Auflage 2012

Ders.: Ratingagenturen. Einblicke in die Kapitalmacht der Gegenwart, Bielefeld, 2. Auflage 2012

Ders.: Die Privatisierung des Staates – Das Vorbild USA, in: Ullrich Mies u.a. (Hg.): Fassadendemokratie und tiefer Staat, Wien 2017, p. 111-124

Ders.: Varianten des Kapitalismus – ein Vergleich des westlichen mit dem chinesischen Kapitalismus, www.nachdenkseiten.de 7.10.2017

Ders. / Elmar Wigand: Die Fertigmacher. Arbeitsunrecht und professionelle Bekämpfung der Gewerkschaften, 3. erweiterte Auflage Köln 2017

Diess.: Union Busting in Deutschland, Frankfurt/Main 2014

Scheuplein, Christoph: Private Equity Monitor 2017, Mitbestimmungsreport Nr. 40, Düsseldorf 2018

Schmidt, Eric/Jared Cohen: Die Vernetzung der Welt, Reinbek 2013

Schmitt, Martin: Internet im Kalten Krieg. Eine Vorgeschichte des globalen Kommunikationsnetzes, Bielefeld 2016

Schumann, Harald / Arpad Bondy: Das Microsoft-Dilemma. ARD 19.2.2018

See, Hans: Wirtschaft zwischen Demokratie und Verbrechen. Grundzüge einer Kritik der kriminellen Ökonomie. Frankfurt/Main 2014

Sekanina, Alexander: Finanzinvestoren und Mitbestimmung, Mitbestimmungsreport Nr. 42, Düsseldorf 2018

Srnicek, Nick: Plattform-Kapitalismus, Hamburg 2018

Turner, Fred: From Counterculture to Cyberculture, Chicago 2006

United Nations, Human Rights Council: Report of the Special Rapporteur on extreme poverty and human rights on his mission to the United States of America, New York 4.5.2018

Vila, Sol Trumbo u.a.: The Bail Out Business, TNI Februar 2017

Wang, Dong: U.S.-China Trade 1971-2012: Insights into the U.S.-China Relationship, in: The Asia-Pacific Journal 24/2013

Wilkins, Mira: The Maturing of Multinational Enterprises. American Business Abroad from 1914 to 1970, Cambridge/Mass. 1994

Printed in Great Britain
by Amazon

47861931R00187